Where **CHINA** Meets
SOUTHEAST ASIA

The **Institute of Southeast Asian Studies (ISEAS)** was established as an autonomous organization in 1968. It is a regional research centre for scholars and other specialists concerned with modern Southeast Asia, particularly the many-faceted issues and challenges of stability and security, economic development, and political and social change.

The Institute's research programmes are Regional Economic Studies (RES, including ASEAN and APEC), Regional Strategic and Political Studies (RSPS), and Regional Social and Cultural Studies (RSCS).

The Institute is governed by a twenty-two-member Board of Trustees comprising nominees from the Singapore Government, the National University of Singapore, the various Chambers of Commerce, and professional and civic organizations. An Executive Committee oversees day-to-day operations; it is chaired by the Director, the Institute's chief academic and administrative officer.

Where CHINA Meets SOUTHEAST ASIA
Social & Cultural Change in the Border Regions

edited by
Grant Evans
Christopher Hutton
Kuah Khun Eng

Palgrave Macmillan
INSTITUTE OF SOUTHEAST ASIAN STUDIES, Singapore

Published by
Institute of Southeast Asian Studies
30 Heng Mui Keng Terrace
Pasir Panjang
Singapore 119614
Internet e-mail: publish@iseas.edu.sg
World Wide Web: http://www.iseas.edu.sg/pub.html

First published in the United States of America in 2000 by
St. Martin's Press, Scholarly and Reference Division
175 Fifth Avenue, New York, N.Y. 10010

All rights reserved.
No part of this publication may be reproduced, translated,
stored in a retrieval system, or transmitted in any form or by any means,
electronic, mechanical, photocopying, recording or otherwise,
without the prior permission of the Institute of Southeast Asian Studies.

© 2000 Institute of Southeast Asian Studies, Singapore
Softcover reprint of the hardcover 1st edition 2000 978-0-312-23634-2

*The responsibility for facts and opinions in this publication rests exclusivɩ
with the author and his interpretations do not necessarily reflect
the views or the policy of the Institute or its supporters.*

Library of Congress Cataloging-in-Publication Data

Where China meets Southeast Asia : social and cultural change in the border regions
/ edited by Grant Evans, Christopher Hutton, Kuah Khun Eng.
    p. cm.
Includes bibliographical references and index.
ISBN 978-1-349-63100-1   ISBN 978-1-137-11123-4 (eBook)
DOI 10.1007/978-1-137-11123-4

    1. China--Foreign economic relations--Indochina. 2. Indochina--Foreign
economic relations--China. 3. China--Foreign economic relations--Burma.
4. Burma--Foreign economic relations--China. 5. China--Boundaries--Indochina.
6. Indochina--Boundaries--China. 7. China--Boundaries--Burma. 8. Burma--
Boundaries--China. I. Evans, Grant, 1948- II. Hutton, Christopher. III. Kuah,
Khun Eng.

HF1604.Z4I489   2000
303.4'8251059--dc21   00-035258

ISBN 978-981-230-040-9 (hardcover, ISEAS, Singapore)
ISBN 978-981-230-071-3 (softcover, ISEAS, Singapore)

For the USA and Canada, this hardcover edition is published by St. Martin's Press,
New York.

Typeset by International Typesetters Pte. Ltd.

Contents

Contributors — vii

Introduction: The Disappearing Frontier? — 1
The Editors

1. Where Nothing Is as It Seems: Between Southeast China and Mainland Southeast Asia in the "Post-Socialist" Era — 7
   Peter HINTON

2. The Southern Chinese Borders in History — 28
   Geoff WADE

3. Ecology Without Borders — 51
   SU Yongge

4. Negotiating Central, Provincial, and County Policies: Border Trading in South China — 72
   KUAH Khun Eng

5. The Hmong of the Southeast Asia Massif: Their Recent History of Migration — 98
   Jean MICHAUD and Christian CULAS

6. Regional Trade in Northwestern Laos: 122
An Initial Assessment of the Economic Quadrangle
Andrew WALKER

7. Lue across Borders: Pilgrimage and the 145
Muang Sing Reliquary in Northern Laos
Paul T. COHEN

8. Transformation of Jinghong, Xishuangbanna, PRC 162
Grant EVANS

9. The Hell of Good Intentions: Some Preliminary 183
Thoughts on Opium in the Political Ecology
of the Trade in Girls and Women
David A. FEINGOLD

10. Cross-Border Mobility and Social Networks: 204
Akha Caravan Traders
Mika TOYOTA

11. Cross-Border Links between Muslims 222
in Yunnan and Northern Thailand:
Identity and Economic Networks
Jean BERLIE

12. Trade Activities of the Hoa along 236
the Sino-Vietnamese Border
CHAU Thi Hai

13. Cross-Border Categories: Ethnic Chinese and 254
the Sino-Vietnamese Border at Mong Cai
Christopher HUTTON

14. Regional Development and Cross-Border 277
Cultural Linkage: The Case of a Vietnamese
Community in Guangxi, China
CHEUNG Siu-woo

15. Women and Social Change along the 312
Vietnam-Guangxi Border
XIE Guangmao

Index *328*

Contributors

Jean BERLIE is Fellow at the Centre of Asian Studies, University of Hong Kong, Hong Kong.

CHAU Thi Hai is Research Fellow at the Institute of Southeast Asian Studies, 27 Tran Xuan Soan, Hanoi, SR Vietnam. Fax: 84-4-8245966

CHEUNG Siu-Woo is Assistant Professor of Anthropology at the School of Humanities, University of Science and Technology, New Territories, Hong Kong. E-mail: hmcheung@uxmail.ust.hk.

Paul T. COHEN is Senior Lecturer in the Department of Anthropology, University of Macquarie, North Ryde, NSW 2109, Australia. E-mail: PCOHEN@bunyip.bhs.mq.edu.au.

Christian CULAS is Research Associate at the Institut de Recherche sur le Sud-Est Asiatique (IRSEA-CNRS), 389, av. du Club Hippique, 13034 Aix-en-Provence, Cedex 2, France. E-mail: IRSEA@romarin.univ-aix.fr.

Grant EVANS is Reader in Anthropology in the Department of Sociology, University of Hong Kong, Hong Kong. E-mail: Hrnsgre@hkucc.hku.hk.

David A. FEINGOLD is Director Ophidian Research Institute, P.O.

Box 967, Prakanong, Bangkok 10110, Thailand. heann@ibm.net.

Peter HINTON is Senior Lecturer in the Department of Anthropology, University of Sydney, Sydney, NSW, Australia. E-mail: peter.hinton@anthropology.usyd.edu.au.

Christopher HUTTON is Senior Lecturer in Linguistics in the Department of English, University of Hong Kong, Hong Kong. E-mail: Chutton@hkucc.hku.hk.

KUAH Khun Eng is Associate Professor of Anthropology in the Department of Sociology, University of Hong Kong, Hong Kong. E-mail: Kekuah@hkucc.hku.hk.

Jean MICHAUD is Lecturer in the Department of Politics and Asian Studies, University of Hull, Hull HU6 7RX, U.K. E-mail: j.michaud@pol-as.hull.ac.uk.

SU Yongge is Research Fellow at the Yunnan Institute of Botany Chinese Academy of Sciences, Kunming, Heilongtan 650204, People's Republic of China.

Mika TOYOTA is a Ph.D. candidate in the Department of Politics and Asian Studies, University of Hull, Hull HU6 7RX, U.K. E-mail: m.toyota@pol-as.hull.ac.uk.

Geoff WADE is Research Officer at the Centre of Asian Studies, University of Hong Kong, Hong Kong. E-mail: Gwade@hkucc.hku.hk.

Andrew WALKER is Research Fellow in the Department of Anthropology, RSPAS, ANU, Canberra, ACT, Australia. E-mail: ajwalker@cres.anu.edu.au.

XIE Guangmao is Curator at the Museum of Guangxi, Minzu Road, Nanning 530022, Guangxi, People's Republic of China.

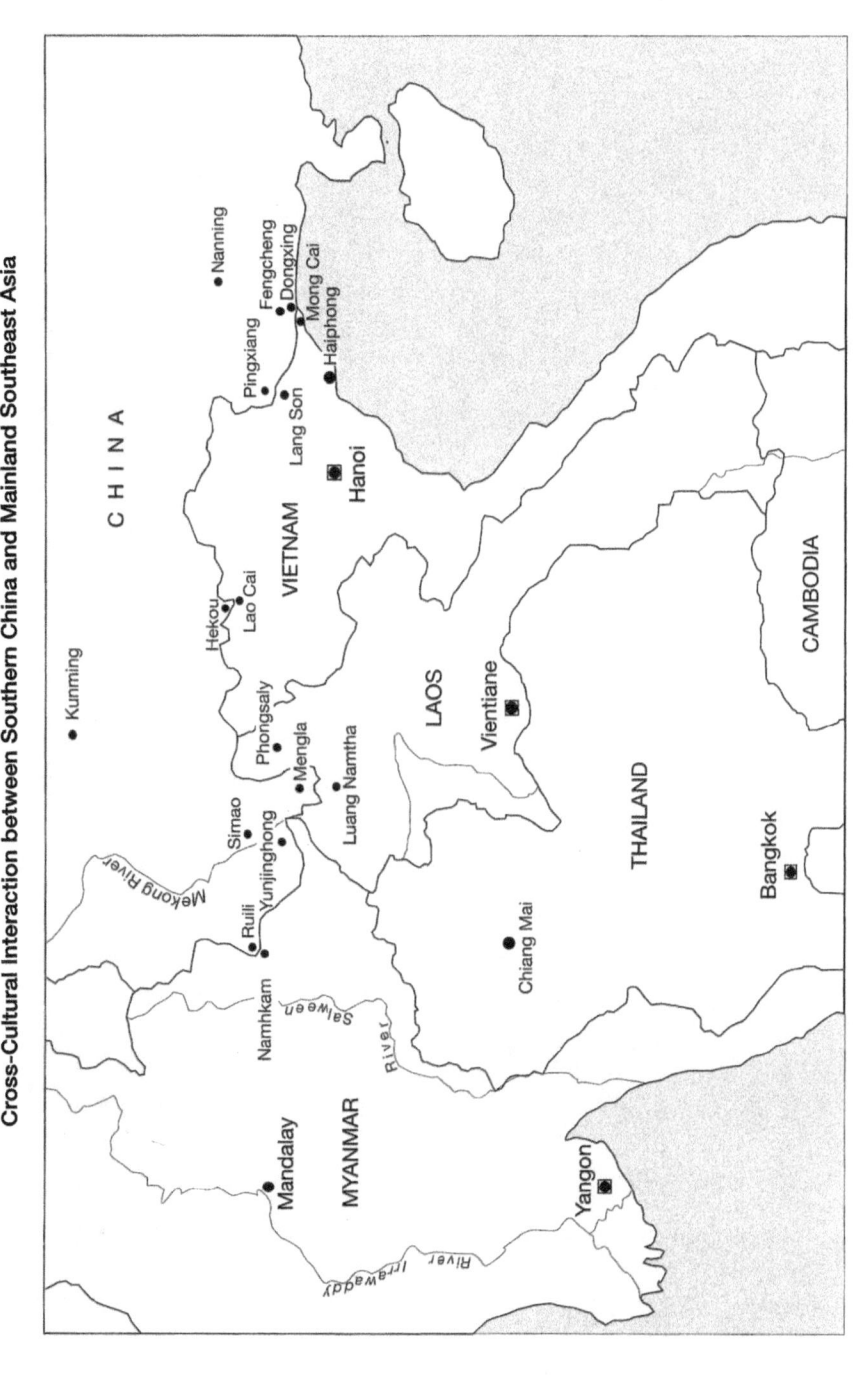

Figure 1
Cross-Cultural Interaction between Southern China and Mainland Southeast Asia

Introduction:
The Disappearing Frontier?

The Editors

The chapters for this book were all written in headier days — not too long ago — when the "Asian Economic Miracle" was still riding high. When words like "free-wheeling" and "dynamic" were bandied about freely, conveying a sense of limitless investment opportunities and a new age of growth which would soon overflow into general affluence, and further down the line, human rights and democratic freedoms.

But even then people knew that there was an underside to the Asian dream: official corruption, environmental havoc, the exploitation of marginal or vulnerable social groups (migrant workers, rural women, children, ethnic minorities), the appropriation of land, the spread of drug abuse, prostitution. This was a vision of capitalist greed backed by state controls, a nightmare world in which the worst of capitalism meets the worst of Stalinism, where workers locked in at work die in factory fires, border guards are drug smugglers and forestry officials are loggers and poachers.

The Asian economic crisis that began with the collapse of the Thai baht in mid-1997, along with the pall of haze which hung across Southeast Asia as a result of the enormously destructive forest fires in Indonesia, swung attention to the downside of the seemingly fast-fading miracle. International commentators now focus on the effects of corruption and cronyism in government across the region, and there is an embarrassed silence about the earlier upbeat assessments.

The chapters in this volume, all written during the final heydays of the "Tiger Economies", are neither enthralled by the "miracle", nor do they simply focus on its downside. Instead, they all convey a rare understanding of the complexity of the changes engulfing the region. Indeed, the chapter by Hinton, "Where Nothing Is as It Seems", is not only a careful critique of many of the conceptualizations of the changes in the region. It is also a statement about how difficult it is to conceptualize such diverse changes, and diverse capitalisms (rather than some fictitious, singular "Asian capitalism"), and he warns us about how easy it is to be smug in retrospect.

This tendency to see complexity where others see simple visions is a hallmark of social science, and most of the authors are either anthropologists, linguists, or sociologists, with a historian and ethno-botanist thrown in for good measure. They study and write about people rather than concentrating on economic statistics and aggregate figures, all of which may look wonderful from boardrooms and prime ministerial offices, but look much more problematic on the ground. Unlike political scientists who focus on political borders, or indeed economists who see these borders disappearing, the contributors in this book recognize that these political borders do not coincide with cultures — Vietnamese overlap into China and vice versa, Hmong, Akha, Yao Lue, and so on all overlap the borders of the region, just as languages flow back and forth across them (see the chapter by Hutton). At a cultural and social level the frontiers have been borderless for a long time.

The reports from the field, from the borderlands between China and mainland Southeast Asia, contained in this book provide readers with the first survey of social conditions since the opening of the borders there in the early 1990s. That is, following radical changes in the economic policies of the various states involved, in particular, China, Vietnam, and Laos.[1] Most of the chapters provide a close-up survey of a particular area and problem, but cumulatively they provide an invaluable general picture of social and cultural change in the border regions *Where China Meets Southeast Asia*.

Commentators who have focused exclusively on economics (and readers will note that economists are not represented in this collection at all) have been led to make extravagant claims like those of Kenichi Ohmae:

> Public debate may still be hostage to the outdated vocabulary of political borders, but the daily realities facing most people in the developed and developing worlds — both as citizens and as consumers — speak a vastly

different idiom. Theirs is the language of an increasingly borderless economy, true global market-place. But the references we have — the maps and guides — to this new terrain are still largely drawn in political terms.[2]

While it would be foolish to deny the tremendous power of the global market-place in the late twentieth century, the economy is always embedded in social, cultural, and political structures, as many of the chapters in this book demonstrate. But what is also clear is that economic change along the border has meant a closing of the frontier there. Unlike clearly demarcated borders, frontiers can be regions that are sparsely settled, or fall at the margins of the market economy and central regulation. The closing of the frontier entails incorporation into the mainstream of national life, into the national and international markets, and a concerted attempt by the state to turn the frontier into a clearly marked and regulated border. The increasing flow of goods, capital, people, and animals across the borders has called for closer state monitoring of these flows in the form of decisions about visas, taxation, banned substances or endangered species, and so on.

Not too long ago, for example, the border between Laos and southern Yunnan was completely closed, then only closed to foreigners. When in 1993 the government in Vientiane relaxed its rules and Grant Evans crossed from the province of Luang Namtha into Xishuangbanna in southern Yunnan, there were few other foreigners to be seen. But within a year the backpacker network and the local tourists industries were demanding that the Lao government facilitate easier travel in the region. Now, tourists along with traders flow through the region with ease, but not without regulation. Previously, border guards did not have to even think about these problems; now they do — just as governments now have to pay attention to the economic and cultural consequences of this mobility. Borders may become porous, but that does not make them borderless. They were only borderless in the past when Akha or Muslim caravaners, or other ethnic groups in the region wandered across it without paying attention to borders drawn up in far-off capitals. But those days are gone.

Three of the countries represented in the chapters in this book — China, Vietnam, and Laos — are still ruled by communist parties. Previously relatively autarkic and closed, they have all since the mid-1980s gradually opened themselves up to the world outside and carried through radical economic reforms. These communist states, whilst highly interventionist in economic planning, cultural and social policy, and restrictive of population movements, paradoxically left many regions and human and natural ecosystems relatively undisturbed. Social upheavals such as the Great Leap Forward and the Cultural Revolution in China and the periodic migrations and conflicts in the history of post-war Vietnam did have dramatic effects on human culture and the natural environment. However, in many respects these communist states lacked the resources and the will to assert full and continual control over border and mountain regions and the peoples who live there. The implementation of market reforms in post-Mao China and the collapse of the Soviet Union largely signalled the end of state monopoly control over the economy in Asian states (North Korea being the obvious exception). The opening up of these economies to market forces, the rise of a consumer culture with its demand for higher-quality domestic and imported foreign goods, the loosening of internal migration controls, the rise of tourism, and so on, have created a cycle of rising demand requiring ever-increasing supply. Development means construction (offices, roads, hotels, ports); construction requires raw materials; and raw materials transported in larger quantities require better infrastructure. Economic development demands migrant labour; it also creates a new upper middle class (made up in part of the old state élite) with money to spend and to invest.

This process creates pressures on land, not only in the core areas of development (Shanghai or Ho Chi Minh City), but also in the peripheries where timber and other raw materials are obtainable, and where possibilities for tourism exist (regional or international). The traffic in drugs and in migrant prostitutes expands with an increasingly mobile labouring population and with a rise in the circulation of commodities of all kinds. We see local cross-border trading networks co-opted and integrated into the wider economy. Long-standing relationships may be subverted or transformed; women traders may take up key positions in the micro-economy with important consequences for their social standing (see the chapter by Xie); party officials may become entrepreneurs; police and customs officials may transform their enhanced regulatory roles into profit-making ones; cross-border contacts may be renewed and remade; and ethnic loyalties reassessed and re-evaluated as trading networks are established with wider links into the regional and national economy (see the chapters by Chau, Toyota, Berlie, and Cheung).

While border regions between power centres have for obvious reasons always been sites of conflict, modern states (both colonial and postcolonial) have different notions of borders and sovereignty. For them, sovereignty is an all-or-nothing concept; the border is defined not as a sphere of influence or suzerainty, but in exact geographical detail. Economic development requires infrastructural development and "isolated" regions are thus incorporated willy-nilly into the larger national context. Migrations from lowlands to uplands accelerate. The state as it were begins to expand right up to its own borders; opening the border creates new opportunities for state intervention at the border and expands the regulatory power of official state agencies (see the chapter by Walker).

This process, however, does not imply necessarily the levelling out of all ethnic diversity and the beginnings of total assimilation (for example, of minorities into the Han Chinese or Vietnamese Kinh mainstream). Some ethnic groups see their identity strengthened as their cross-border kinship networks become powerful economic instruments; other groups are reinvented or reinvent themselves as tourist attractions and icons for the region's "culture" (ethnic food, dance, the exotic); groups with limited official representation and without a strong power base may lose their access to land or hunting terrain and find themselves in competition with a new migrant semi-urban poor; some identities become "irrelevant" or are lost by migration and assimilation. This is not a simple process to evaluate or to judge ethically. To be "ethnic" often means to be poor, and most people do not want to be poor. All ethnic groups are the products of assimilation and migration and of complex processes of identity construction. In a market economy the process of change is accelerated, and those groups who cannot barter their ethnicity in the new economy must seek other means to survive in competition with cheap migrant labour (see the chapter by Evans).

Our purpose in putting together this book was to go beyond the all too abundant clichés about the region and look in detail at social and cultural changes in this crucial border region following the demise of rigid central planning in the People's Republic of China (PRC) and its Southeast Asian confrères. Researchers with different academic backgrounds and nationalities brought their expertise and knowledge of particular regions and languages to bear on the complex developments that have been taking place along the Chinese border with mainland Southeast Asia over the last decade.[3] The chapters provide both more general perspectives on the history and recent development in the region and studies based on particular areas and problems. Wade offers a historical perspective on the southern borders of China; Michaud and Culas give an overview of recent migrations of the Hmong. Feingold looks at the links between the opium trade and trafficking in women (the subject of women and prostitution is also treated by Xie); Kuah gives an overview of official PRC policy towards border trade in the region. Other chapters concentrate in particular on two geographical areas: the first is the western end of the border region, where the links between Yunnan province in China and Laos and Myanmar are analysed (Berlie, Cohen, Evans, Toyota, Walker); the second area of particular focus is the eastern Guangxi-Vietnam border in the area around Dongxing/Mong Cai (see the chapters by Chau, Cheung, Hutton, and Xie).

Of course, the volume by its very nature cannot claim to be exhaustive. There are many more topics and many more locales that could be studied in depth, and we hope that the research represented here will stimulate further fieldwork in the border regions. But we do claim that these chapters provide information and insights that are unobtainable elsewhere, and that they also provide a healthy corrective to the avalanche of economic studies done on the region. After the deluge, we hope that economists and policy-makers will turn to these pages to gain a more complex and subtle understanding of social and cultural changes in the interstices of *Where China Meets Southeast Asia.*

NOTES

1. There has been, however, a survey of "Ethnic Minorities on the Borderlands of Southwest China", a Special Issue of *Asia Pacific Viewpoint* 38, no. 2 (1997), edited by John McKinnon.
2. Kenichi Ohmae, *The End of the Nation State: The Rise of Regional Economies* (New York: The Free Press, 1995), p. 8.
3. This volume brings together papers first presented at a conference held in the University of Hong Kong from 4 to 6 December 1996. The conference entitled "South China and Mainland Southeast Asia: Cross-Border Relations in the Post-Socialist Age" offered a forum where, for example, scholars from Laos, Vietnam, and the People's Republic of China could meet and exchange ideas. The conference was supported by a project funded by the Hong Kong Research Grants Council, awarded to Evans, Hutton, and Kuah, and was organized in co-operation with the Centre for Asian Studies at the University of Hong Kong.

Where Nothing Is as It Seems: Between Southeast China and Mainland Southeast Asia in the "Post-Socialist" Era

Peter Hinton

INTRODUCTION

This chapter concerns broad issues of understanding and interpreting patterns and trends in the region. To the layperson, this may appear to be a task beyond the scope of anthropology, which is usually perceived as being the study of the local and the traditional. But in a world that is becoming increasingly integrated, anthropologists are realizing that it is no longer possible to confine themselves to their traditional field without also bearing in mind the general and the global.

Anthropology also has an important role to play in its guise as a discipline that is sceptical of what Marcus (1998, p. 16) has recently called "naturalized categories" — those categories that we take so much for granted in our everyday lives that they become "natural" to us. These are frequently legitimized by experts in various academic and non-academic fields concerned with the world today, and which try to identify future trends. There is little doubt that the dominant "naturalised categories" in the region have been shaped by the discipline of economics, which has achieved a decisive influence on the interpretation of trends, and the formulation of policy. Some sections of this chapter suggest ways of approaching this important task of "de-naturalization".

This endeavour has been made a lot easier by the collapse of the Southeast Asian economies in 1997–98, because this "meltdown", as it is often described, has thrown the confident predictions of the economists, political scientists, and management gurus who saw only the rise and rise of the Asian "tigers" into spectacular disarray. There were many writers whose works were prominently displayed in bookshops throughout the region, and whose every word was earnestly absorbed by audiences on lecture tours which spanned the globe. It will suffice to mention two here by way of illustration: Ohmae (1995) and Naisbitt (1995). Ohmae predicted the early end of the nation-state in Asia as elsewhere in the world before the irresistible force of the global markets, while Naisbitt asserted that "mega-trends" originating from Asia would change the way in which business was done and economies were organized throughout the world. But contrary to both prophecies, over the past two or three years there has been a resurgence of nationalism in the region, and the intervention of the International Monetary Fund (IMF) in an attempt to prop up the collapsing economies of several nations. It seemed possible at one stage that the "Asian contagion" would spread throughout the world, causing global recession — but this was hardly the "mega-trend" that Naisbitt had in mind.

A new generation of pundits has offered diagnoses of the crisis, and some, with understandable caution, are beginning to sketch out medium- to long-term future trends. Perhaps quickest on their feet were Pasuk Phongpaichit and Chris Baker, who in *Thailand's Boom*, published shortly before the crisis in 1996, analysed the dynamics of country's apparent economic miracle. Then, in 1998, after the collapse, they published *Thailand's Boom and Bust*, which explained the reasons for the bust as well as the boom. But at least Pasuk and Baker, unlike the host of gung-ho official, academic, and journalist commentators, showed an acute awareness of the downside of the boom in their earlier book, and, could justly claim to have identified the seeds of disaster even at the height of the "miracle".

So it is still as important as it ever was to think beyond the "naturalized categories" given to us by many high-profile academic disciplines, government technocrats, and business boosters. This chapter is written in this spirit, and each of its headings covers areas in which I think scepticism is particularly justified.

Borders are areas where ambiguities and contradictions are particularly apparent, as many of the chapters in this collection indicate. My contribution is written on the basis of field research in the borderlands of Thailand, Laos, Myanmar, and Yunnan since 1992, and on the basis of a comprehensive reading of the literature on the region.

IS THIS REALLY A POST-SOCIALIST ERA?

It is frequently asserted that this is the "post-socialist era". But how true is it to say that socialism in Asia is a thing of the past?

There were three socialist countries in Asia: China, Vietnam, and Laos.[1] Although there have been market reforms in all three over the past fifteen years, there has been no defining moment that has brought a decisive break from socialist policies. There has been no Asian equivalent of the tearing down of the Berlin Wall, which signalled the end of Soviet communism. Leaders in the three countries have been able to keep their options open, even although there have been dramatic reforms to encourage free-market economics. In China, Mao's successors introduced the Household Responsibility System in 1979, which effectively abolished collectivized agriculture, and paved the way for rural industries by allowing the establishment of Township and Village Enterprises. "It does not matter whether the cat is black or white", said Deng, in his oft-quoted aphorism, "so long as it catches mice". In Guangdong, most restraints on trade with wealthy neighbour Hong Kong were removed, triggering an unprecedented boom.

Deng's black and white cats are, of course, representative of capitalism and socialism, and his aphorism is usually taken to mean that if the capitalist cat catches more mice, then it should be encouraged. But it could also mean that there is a role for both cats, for the two ideologies to exist side by side. The latter interpretation seems to be a truer reflection of the policies of the Chinese Communist Party since 1979 than the conventional wisdom in the Western financial press, that the "economic miracles" that have occurred in Guangdong and Shanghai will be replicated throughout China. This entirely overlooks the fact that special concessions were allowed in Guangdong that were not granted elsewhere, and that the Communist Party retains a very tight rein on the country.

My firsthand observation, admittedly limited to Yunnan, is that both cats are at work, although not always in easy partnership, and there is no linear trend to phase out the socialist moggy. A recent article in *The Economist* suggests that Chinese rural people have increasingly taken the business of improving infrastructure and establishing market enterprises into their own hands.[2] It went on to say that they have been encouraged in so doing by Beijing authorities, who are receptive to appeals against obstructive local party officials. It concludes by suggesting that while the central government is as authoritarian as ever, there is a nascent "trickle up" of democracy.

However, whatever might have happened at Pingyuan, "a dirt-poor village in the mountains outside Beijing", the case cited in *The Economist* report, does not necessarily reflect events in far-off Yunnan or Guangxi. In fact, there are forces at work that make early reform unlikely. These are primarily of a fiscal nature, where the central government is maintaining an ever-increasing proportion of the revenue coming into its hands, thus forcing the provinces to raise their own funds. The provinces have in turn tried to devolve fund-raising to their constituent prefectures, which in turn have increased levies on the counties. These exactions have tended overwhelmingly to be regressive, rather than being structured so as to encourage market enterprise which in the mid to long term might yield greater revenue.

Overall, although the extremes of the command economy have been removed, the Communist Party remains very firmly in power at all levels. And, apart from entrenched interests, both individual and institutional, the positive aspects of socialism need some recognition. In China, the communists did achieve greater equity in the distribution of food and other essential commodities, in housing, health, and education. In fact, one of the impediments to market reforms in the former Soviet Union, which will come into play in China, is the resistance of people to the reduction in what they have come to regard as their entitlements.

Socialism in Vietnam and Laos was very different from that in China. It is thus to be expected that the transition to a partially liberalized economy should be occurring along different paths. In Laos, the transition has been harmonious compared with China and Vietnam. This, Grant Evans asserts, is due to the fact that

> socialist institutions existed in Laos for a very brief period and few strong social interests became attached to them, in the way they have in China or in Vietnam. Hardly even a generation was socialised in the schools of the new regime, and many of the institutions of the old civil society in the villages, along with religion, survived intact, unlike China or northern Vietnam where the long years of Stalinist communism, often combined with bloody repression, was the destruction of many features of the old civil society. (Evans 1995, p. xxviii)

This may be so, but a continuing legacy of the socialist era is a government that is authoritarian by instinct.

I know very little about Vietnam, so will not comment on the state of "post-socialism" there, except to remark that after a period of *doi moi* — free market — there has been a conservative backlash in which the Communist Party has reasserted control, frightening off a lot of foreign capital.

1. Where Nothing Is as It Seems

Finally, it is a truism, but one that should be repeated as a further caution against easy generalization, that socialism does not always breed fraternity. After all, the division between China and the Soviet Union was arguably as deep as that between the socialist and capitalist blocs during the Cold War. In our region of interest, China invaded North Vietnam in a 1979 reprisal for Vietnam's invasion of Pol Pot's Cambodia, which China had backed. A bitterly fought war ensued, causing many casualties and great damage. And, while it is true that Vietnam and Laos have had fraternal relationships, they have always been very much on a younger brother–older brother basis.

CAPITALISM IS NOT MONOLITHIC

The nature of global capitalism has changed dramatically since the end of the Cold War, a mere ten years ago. The new capitalism, as many commentators have recognized, is radically de-centred, having moved away from national and even corporate foci. Finance capital has become vastly more mobile, its mobility being facilitated by the successful promotion of a free-trade ideology by the West, particularly the United States, as much as by the technology of instant electronic transfer.

There global developments provided a context for the rise of the Southeast and East Asian tigers — and for their subsequent bust. Before the bust, it was common for regional commentators (both Asian and non-Asian) to try to account for the success of their economies in terms of a specifically Asian way of doing business which was essentially different from conduct in Western economies. They were saying, in effect, that capitalism is not monolithic, and that the Western way is only one amongst many possibilities.

The character of Asian capitalism was the theme of a conference I attended in Chiang Mai in March 1994. The idea actively promoted by the organizers was that in Asia it is more appropriate to think in terms of "growth circles" than triangles, squares, or quadrangles. The conference was funded by the Chaiyong Limthongkhul Foundation. The theme was the strongly held view of Sondhi Limthongkhul, founder of the institution and of its chief executive officer, Chai-anan Samudavanija. Sondhi is a prominent Thai businessman who made a fortune through investment in hotels and other developments and who subsequently diversified into media interests, before losing most of his wealth in the collapse of 1997. His company published *The Manager* and *Asia Inc* magazines and in 1995, in a highly ambitious venture, launched the first regional daily newspaper, *Asia Times*. Chai-anan is a leading Thai political scientist and academic who has been adviser to several prominent politicians.

At the conference, Chai-anan and Sondhi put forward the idea that circles are more appropriate analogues than more angular geometrical figures because while the latter denote bi-partite or quadra-partite agreements between governments to promote trade and development, the circle "symbolises interdependence, networking and cross-cultural interactions which at each point could be connected without any structural domination" (Chai-anan 1994, p. 5). Chai-anan agreed with Kenichi Ohmae (whom he frequently quoted) that the nation-state is an anachronism, an artefact of nineteenth century European mercantilism which is irrelevant to the emerging "more borderless Asia". He regarded "regional experiments" like growth triangles, quadrangles, special economic zones, and so on as regressive: "We prefer to think of them as circles, a word implying both territory and businessman to businessman *guanxi*, the evocative Chinese term for 'connections'." (Ibid., p. 37.)

During question time at the conference, an American businessman suggested that while *guanxi* might be a nice idea, it was not possible to do serious business unless there was the "rule of law", enabling contractual agreements and other legally binding arrangements. In response, Sondhi said that he had been involved in many major business deals in both Asian countries, and to an extent in the United States. He had never been cheated in Asia, despite the fact that agreements were sealed with a handshake rather than a contract. However, in the United States, he had once lost millions of dollars on a deal which was covered by a supposedly impeccable contract: all it took was a smart lawyer to exploit the inevitable loopholes.

A map given to conference participants was headed "Asia's New Growth Circles: An Alphabet of Opportunities as the Millennium Nears". The circles are very large. One extends from Guiyang in the north to Cam Ranh in the south and from Hong Kong in the east to Vientiane in the west. They seem almost deliberately arbitrary, provisional and fuzzy-edged presumably to indicate "interdependence, networking and cross-cultural interactions without any structural domination and centralisation" (ibid., p. 5).

The picture of the networking, family-structured, *guanxi*-driven, flexible yet dynamic proclivities of the Overseas Chinese has become almost a trope in discussions of cross-border (the term preferred to "international" or "transnational") relations in Asia today. John Naisbitt, author of the best-selling book *Asian Megatrends* says:

> Networks are replacing nation states. As borders are erased, networks will become larger and more important. The place to start is the Chinese Overseas Network. ... The economy of the borderless Chinese Overseas is the third largest in the world. We are not used to thinking this way: counting the GDP of a network, rather than the GDP of a country. ... The Chinese Overseas Network is a lot like the Internet. If you know how the Internet works, you know how the Chinese Network operates. (Naisbitt 1996, p. 192)

It is thus that the *gemainschaft* of the traditional kinship structure becomes ludicrously associated in the imagination with the *gesellschaft* of the high-technology global computer virtual society to create an invincibly dynamic machine for capitalist expansion.

It would appear that the business gurus, finding that Economics does not explain all, have discovered Culture. Because Asian culture is different from European culture, the way they do business is different and uniquely suited to the new free-wheeling, global business environment. The Asians' far-flung family networks, enterprise, capacity for hard work, and flexibility have enabled them to succeed where conventional European corporations are doomed to failure.

This depiction of the dynamic Asian family firm is disconcertingly like the flip side of the myth of the lazy Asian which was the rationale for the exploitation of colonial populations in "the Far East".[3] It is also bad history and sociology. One need only point to the dynastic family structures so often characteristic of successful American businesses in the first part of this century to realize that this configuration is likely to be as much a stage in the development of business organizations as a manifestation of Culture. In support of this view are signs that successful and expanding Asian family firms are under increasing strain as economies develop. One problem (which was recurrent in early Western capitalism) is to secure a smooth succession between the founder and following generations. There are reports of flourishing enterprises being split asunder by such disputes.[4] Furthermore, as businesses grow, it may become necessary to raise capital on the open market, a move which almost inevitably loosens the grip of the family on the firm. This trend has also occurred in the West.[5]

In sum, there are different capitalisms present in our region, but they are by no means as clearly different as the business gurus, or the Asian advocates of "the Asian way" suggest. There are Western and transnational corporations present, but these are as different from one another as they are similar. These enter into diverse arrangements with indigenous firms. Then there are state firms, not only in the socialist countries, but in distinctly non-socialist Thailand as well. Finally, there are the hosts of small traders who merge seamlessly with the mainstream economy, and who are relegated to "the informal economy" in conventional analyses. I shall have more to say about them in a later section.

The Growth Circles conference was in 1994. It is perhaps ironic that only three years later, in 1997, Sondhi Limthongkul was one of the earliest and most spectacular victims of the meltdown. *Asia Inc*, *Manager*, and *Asia Times* are all defunct, and Sondhi is no longer in a position to bankroll his foundation. The possible irony lies in the fact that he was brought down by the very forces that he denied as having essential influence in the supposed Growth Circles of the region.

So the question remains: Is there an essentially Asian way of being capitalist? I am prepared to believe that there is, partly because of the at least partial failure of IMF nostrums for the region's economic problems, which suggests that approaches relevant in the West may not be of universal applicability. The underlying reason for this is undoubtedly the different cultural and institutional settings of the region.

In the long term, then, Sondhi and Chai-anan might turn out to be right.

THE PROBLEMATIZATION OF THE RELATION BETWEEN INFORMATION FLOWS AND POWER

Authoritarian governments have long recognized that control of information and knowledge is one of the essential tools for the maintenance of power. Their monopoly of the media and control over the arts are uncompromisingly maintained. These controls remain substantially in place in China, Vietnam, and Laos, despite the partial liberalization of the market. They are difficult to reconcile with the need for actors in a market economy to have comprehensive and reliable information on prices and products, let alone with the idea of a "free market" that is intrinsic to a more fully liberalized political order.

However, this control is always contested by those who are affected. This is very much the case in the borderlands of China and Southeast Asia where the aspirations of the people have been raised by the removal of some controls, and where knowledge of the outside world, particularly as purveyed through Thailand, is accessible as never before.

1. Where Nothing Is as It Seems

During fieldwork in rural Yunnan in 1993, we were frequently asked by the managers of township enterprises for advice as to how and where to market their produce. Along the borders there were no such problems. Strangely, borders, which may conventionally be regarded as barriers, become places of accelerated information flow. This is nowhere more so than at crossing points like Ruili and Mengla where the ready movement of people to and fro across the border constantly updated information about prices, commodities, political changes.

On moving away from the border, even relatively short distances, the flow of information seems to dry up. It is as if the border crossers proceed to distant destinations in the hinterland — particularly the booming Kunming area — along the main traffic arteries, of which there are few in rugged Yunnan, taking with them both the trade goods and the knowledge they have gleaned about the outside world. We were constantly surprised at how little even people involved in local planning and management knew of the outside world. This is partly a function of strict regulations governing travel which remain in place even in the "post-socialist" era. There is little movement of people from rural areas to the towns and cities of Yunnan. People still must have special permits to live in the towns for longer than very short periods. The authorities maintain the Maoist priority of ensuring that the masses remain on the land producing agricultural staples. There is no sign of the mass movement of people to the cities, that elsewhere in China is making places like Shanghai and Guangdong such crucibles for social change.

Partly in an effort to keep people in rural areas, the Beijing government has, for the past fifteen or so years, been promoting Township Enterprises (TE) and Village Enterprises (VE). In Yunnan these produce a wide range of goods, from value-added agricultural produce like packaged honeyed walnuts, corn crisps, and tea, to manufactures such as furniture, clothing, and paper products. Management of these enterprises had a great deal of autonomy over what to produce and how to sell it. However, their capacity to make good judgements was impeded by lack of information on markets and prices. Some had entered into joint ventures with businesspeople from the booming southern seaboard cities, but there was a general lack of confidence about these arrangements. We heard many anecdotes about enterprises that had suffered in dealings with unscrupulous operators from Shanghai or Fuzhou. Local managers, who had little knowledge of conditions outside their locale, were at a distinct disadvantage.

Official recognition of these problems led to the establishment of

Foreign Trade Corporations (FTC) in all regions of China by the Beijing Ministry of Foreign Economic Relations and Trade (MOFERT) in the 1980s. These were to be agents between Chinese enterprises and outside buyers. They were to provide information, and extend financial services. Unfortunately, bureaucratic habits died hard, and it soon became evident that the FTCs were more interested in maintaining control than they were in facilitating trade. The success of trade in Guangdong was achieved because of local initiatives, not because of bureaucratic facilitation. It remains inconceivable that the Beijing authorities would extend the liberties allowed in Guangdong to the rest of China.

The question of the informal flow of information under authoritarian polities is an intriguing one. Anyone who knows Laos will know the Nam Phu, the fountain near the centre of Vientiane. There are seats and tables arrayed around the fountain where people sit to enjoy a beer and snacks at dusk. As Vientiane is a small place, it is common to run into acquaintances by the Nam Phu. It is by the Nam Phu, as much as anywhere else in Vientiane that personal networks are maintained and extended. It is also the place where rumours are initiated and nurtured.

In Laos, as in China and Vietnam, the authorities maintain strict control over the media. The only official publications are daily broadsheets in Lao and French, which are still roneoed, and which regale readers with stories of official unveilings and other good works of government agencies. Apart from this there is an English-language weekly, the *Vientiane Times*, which is published under the strict supervision of the authorities. None of these is widely circulated outside Vientiane.

It is in this setting that word of mouth communication remains important. That is why what is said at the Nam Phu and in other places where people congregate in Laos is so important. I have heard that a Lao Aviation (which flies domestic and international routes) aircraft had crashed, killing a number of passengers, in one of the northern provinces. It was rumoured that the authorities had deliberately suppressed this story because they did not want to put people off travelling by the national carrier. I have also heard that there was to be a coup ("any day now"). This notion was evidently fuelled by the common knowledge that manœuvrings were going on in the politburo, and the observation that a curfew was being enforced by the police and the military. Both the aircraft crash and the coup stories turned out to be untrue.

Rumours lead strange lives. It is rarely immediately possible to vali-

1. Where Nothing Is as It Seems

date a rumour: false rumours as well as true ones affect the way people act. The stories I have recounted above may have led some people to cancel plans to travel by Lao Aviation, or, fearing political instability, to delay plans to invest in the country. The cumulative effects of the many rumours that are circulating at any particular point in time must be considerable. Their power is demonstrated by their influence even in supposedly open societies where, despite the availability of authorized information, they may, for instance cause rises and falls on the stock market. In authoritarian states like China, Laos, and Vietnam they run rampant.

In such polities, rumours may have subtly subversive effects. Here is an interesting comment from Russia, where, until recently, another authoritarian order prevailed:

> It is strange, but totalitarian regimes are very sensitive to social pressure, though they carefully hide this. These regimes are maintained by fear and the silent complicity of those who surround them. Each person should be absolutely powerless before the state, completely without rights and generally to blame. In this atmosphere, the *word* (even spoken from abroad) comes to have a huge strength (it is not by chance that they executed poets amongst us). At the same time, both the powers and the people understood perfectly the illegality of the regime, its *illegitimacy.* (V. Bukovskii, quoted by Humphrey 1995, p. 45)

THE MULTI-FACETED GEO-POLITICS OF THE MEKONG RIVER SYSTEM

The Mekong River might perhaps be better regarded as a lightning rod for regional conflicts than a resource to be developed in the interests of all riparians. There has been a lot of talk about development, with grand hydropower visions being formulated by the Mekong River Commission and other bodies. These organizations hold many meetings, conferences, seminars, and workshops. However, most of these have remained at a blandly technocratic level and make little effort to tackle the deep-seated political differences between the riparian nations.[6]

These differences persist, generating controversy about how the river should be developed (or left alone), where any developments should occur, and who should benefit (or be deprived). However, I believe that controversy has two different forms in our region of interest: firstly, concerning Chinese dams on the mainstream and, secondly, in regard to proposals for Lao dams on several major tributaries.

THE CHINESE DAMS

A report in the *Bangkok Post* about flooding in some of the northern provinces during the 1996 monsoon, stated that

> local authorities believed enormous amounts of water had been released into the Mekong by eight hydroelectric dams in China to siphon out water from its flood-stricken areas.[7]

While this report is inaccurate — the Chinese have so far built only one of eight projected dams on the Mekong — it was not the first time that concern had been expressed about the alleged effects of the Chinese dams on the river downstream. In 1995 the Lao could not hold their traditional annual aquatic festival at Luang Prabang during the dry season because, it was said, work on the Chinese dams had required diversion of the river. At the same time, farmers in Chiang Rai province in northern Thailand noted that the level of the river had dropped to such an extent that it became difficult for them to lift the water onto their fields. A complaint was lodged by the governor of the province with his Chinese counterpart in Yunnan. The latter, while acknowledging that it "was necessary" for Chinese engineers to temporarily curb the flow of the stream in connection with some tunnelling, was unrepentant, refusing even to agree to notify the Thai if such works were planned in the future (Hinton 1995).

These reports sit uneasily with assertions by advocates of the Chinese dams that those downstream will actually benefit from their construction. Chapman and He (1996, p. 22), for instance, suggest that the capacity of any dams built on the mainstream in Laos would be boosted by the greater volumes of water created by releases of water from the Chinese dams during routine power generation in the dry season.[8] Moreover, this factor will, they say, facilitate irrigation of the arid northeast of Thailand during the dry months. They conclude by suggesting that

> China (with its planned dams on the Lancang Jiang) may turn out to be helping, by gently offering a set of opportunities to the Lower Mekong countries. Will they be equal to the challenge? (Ibid., p. 23)

"Gently" is not an adjective commonly applied to official Chinese dealings with neighbouring countries, which could be more accurately described as "assertive". In this context, it is dubious that Chinese hydropower authorities would give much thought to the needs of countries downstream, even in the unlikely event that mainstream dams were built. After all, the Chinese, who occupy the territory through which the upper reaches of the Mekong flow, have consistently displayed little interest in joining the Mekong River Commission and its predecessor, no doubt because they felt that membership would constrain, rather than facilitate, their use of the river. In sum, while some of the specific mishaps that have been attributed to "the Chinese dams" by Lao and Thai downstream have little foundation in fact, the disquiet underlying these reactions is far from irrational. Even with the best of Chinese intentions, little is known of the effects of the dams in a lot of important respects, from fisheries, to sedimentation, to flood patterns. With an absence of good intentions, or rather, given the likelihood of determined self-interest, those downstream will be left with the residue after the Chinese have used the river.

It should be said that the Chinese are not exceptional in this regard. The stakes over the use of the river are such that none of the riparian nations have shown much regard for their downstream neighbours. The Thai, for instance, have consistently earned the ire of the Cambodians and Vietnamese, with their proposals to divert large volumes of the water of the mainstream for irrigation purposes.

THE LAO DAMS

While it is true that the Chinese dams are on the mainstream of the Mekong, the tributaries upon which the proposed Lao dams are to be built contribute a significant proportion of the volume in the mainstream. Overall, an estimated 60 per cent of water in the river comes from Lao watersheds. In contrast to the Chinese dams, there has been remarkably little concern expressed by the downstream nations — Thailand, Cambodia, and Vietnam about the Lao proposals.

This is not to say that they are not controversial: in fact, the controversy surrounding them is at least as intense as that about the Chinese dams. However, the focal issues are different. In China, geo-politics are to the fore, with fears about Chinese expansionism being the sub-plot. In Laos there are two central matters of concern: first, the economic viability of the dams, and second, their environmental impact. As I shall explain, the two are closely interwoven.

The Lao dams are a matter of world attention in business circles because they are be being almost entirely built with private funds. In the past, large infrastructural projects in the Third World were financed by grants from political allies, or by multilateral agencies. Laos' existing dam, Nam Ngum, was financed in this fashion. In other cases "soft" loans were provided by the World Bank and other multilateral lenders.

This had all changed during the 1990s, when the impulse to privatization of public institutions and utilities had become global. The Lao dams are not pioneering in any technical engineering sense, but because they are being built by consortiums of private construction companies, each of which raises its portion of the capital on the international money market. Having built the dams, the companies will operate them for a time, earning a pre-determined return on their investment. They will then hand them over to the Lao government, which would then earn regular income by selling electricity to Thailand. This arrangement is known as Build, Own, Operate, and Transfer (BOOT). It has been used frequently in recent times on small projects, but never for enterprises of the magnitude of the Lao dams. Therein lies the interest of the financial and construction industries in the dams.

The consortium which plans to build the Nam Theun 2 Dam on the Nam Theun River, which flows in a generally east-to-west direction, entering the Mekong in central Laos, is taking the highest profile. Although up to fifty dams have been proposed for Laos, many of these are paper projects only, designed, say critics, more to allow loggers free access to the forests growing on their watersheds than as serious construction projects. Nam Theun 2, on the other hand, has been deemed by the Mekong River Commission to be one of the best sites in the region. Its project development group has been quick to underline this assessment.[9]

The consummation of this project is vital to the prospects of other, less attractive projects. If it is stymied, the task of the latter to gain political support and financial backing will become much more difficult. Conversely, critics of the whole concept of large-scale dam construction in Laos have directed much of their attention at Nam Theun 2, considering it to be a vital test case. Most of this fire has come from non-governmental organizations (NGOs), which argue that the dams will have detrimental social and environmental effects. Nam Theun 2, for instance, will flood the Nakai Plateau, the habitat of threatened species of flora and fauna. By altering the flow of the river, it will affect aquatic species — including economically important fisheries — far downstream. The critics go on to say that it will not only affect the quality of life of surrounding communities — those downstream as well as those displaced by the rising waters — but it will also wipe out a whole style of

1. Where Nothing Is as It Seems

life that has been characterized by a high degree of economic and social autonomy.

It is interesting that the NGO critics, whose arguments at first reflected their admiration for the self-sufficiency of the Lao rural people, and a recognition of the uniqueness of much of the Lao environment, are now augmenting their case by using arguments against the financial and economic viability of the dams.[10] They say that BOOT arrangements of this magnitude are untried, that the Lao government is effectively shouldering the burden of financial risk, that the returns the dams will earn thirty or so years down the track, when full ownership is transferred to the Lao government, remain uncertain and that the prices negotiated with the Electricity Generating Authority of Thailand (EGAT) are unfavourable to the Lao.

The companies, which have been slow to make their case in the public forum, belatedly realizing that their critics have been making the running, have lately been attempting the tackle the NGOs on their own ground. They say that the latter fail to recognize the increased income and opening to the outside world that the dams will bring to the people. On the environmental issue, they mobilize experts to argue that environmental impacts have been exaggerated by the NGOs. They have even asserted that the dams will facilitate the protection of the environment. This, they say, is because they have an interest in having an intact environment in the watershed, as this will minimize run-off of soil which would clog the dams, and other detrimental effects. They point out that at present the destruction of flora and fauna, particularly in the Nam Theun 2 area, is being carried out primarily by Vietnamese from across the nearby border, who are logging, and carrying off many rare species of plants and animals for sale in markets. This would all be stopped once the dam construction commenced.

It is ironic that Laos, not long ago a theatre for the bitter international conflict between Left and Right ideologies, should have recently become the site of a stand-off in the new global struggle between the proponents and opponents of economic development. Now, as then, the outcome of the confrontation will have world-wide repercussions, despite the apparent remoteness and insignificance of the country.

It is in this sense that economics, environment, and geo-politics of nations merge and the significance of the Mekong dams in Yunnan and Laos become as one.

IT IS INAPPROPRIATE TO SEPARATE THE "FORMAL" FROM THE "INFORMAL" ECONOMIES

"The formal economy" is the realm of professional economists and national planners. Figures of gross domestic product (GDP), employment and unemployment, current accounts, and export/import ratios, all relate to this sphere. The activities of people operating in what is commonly called the "informal economy" are excluded from it. It also excludes activity deemed to be illegal or criminal.

This conventional way of reckoning is deficient in two respects. Firstly, in developing countries the "informal sector" may comprise a very large proportion of total productive activity: to omit it from calculations builds in significant distortions. Secondly, it is erroneous to make a sharp distinction between the two because are they are intertwined in complex ways.

In our region, much of the cross-border trade would fall into the informal sector. At major crossing points there are customs stations and transactions are monitored by the authorities. However, borders are so long, and so porous, that many transactions are neither recorded nor taxed. But the conventional informal/formal dichotomy does not stand up because the two sectors are seamlessly integrated.

This is nowhere more evident than in the narcotics trade. The scale of this trade is not always recognized, but it is enormous. In 1993, 183 metric tonnes of heroin was exported from Myanmar. Virtually all of this was produced in the area adjacent to the Chinese, Lao, and northern Thai borders — the so-called Golden Triangle. Its value at Bangkok prices (approximately US$9,000 per kg) was around US$1.65 billion. This considerable sum is best put in perspective by comparison with the export income earned by another major commodity in the region, Thai exports of rice. Thailand is one of the largest producers of rice in the world. In 1993, the value of rice exports was about US$1.32 billion. The value of heroin exported from Myanmar was thus US$33 million greater than the value of rice from Thailand in that year.[11]

This heroin was exported through Yunnan, Laos, and Vietnam and (to a lesser extent in the past) through Thailand. The organizations doing the exporting were not small. Business interests reached to the capitals, and acted with the complicity of the Burmese military government, the State Law and Order Restoration Council (SLORC). Although the SLORC is widely and justifiably condemned, its role in narcotics is not surprising. It is only the latest of a chain of institutions and movements which have benefited from the trade. The British, the Imperial Chinese, the United States during the Vietnam War are examples. It is also frequently suggested that the Maoist army was financed by the proceeds of opium during the period it spent consolidating in Yunnan. Narcotics are such a significant — even if uncounted — element in the local economy that it is difficult for even the most self-righteous of movements to avoid involvement with it. This would quite likely include the National League for Democracy (NLD) in Myanmar, were it ever to come to power.

The "black economy" involves a lot more than narcotics, and the "informal" activities of myriad small traders. It also includes smuggling of many commodities (oil, for instance, is frequently smuggled into Thailand), organization of illegal migrants, of whom prostitutes are only a proportion, and underground lotteries. In all, the *Far Eastern Economic Review* estimates that the black economy is equivalent to a staggering 57 per cent of the "official" gross national product (GNP). It is with little doubt that there is at least as high a proportion of the formal economy in Laos, North Vietnam, and southern China.

Figures of these magnitudes must call the official statistics, and the policies upon which they are based, into serious question. This is the more so when it is recognized that funds from the "black", "informal" economy flow into and underwrite the legitimate "formal" economy. Money is laundered in a variety of ingenious ways and often with unacknowledged official sanction. This occurs on such a scale that it has been said, only partly in jest, that the whole economy of northern Thailand would collapse overnight if it were magically possible to shut down the illegal activities.

CONCLUSION

A consensus at the conference was that the rapidity and complexity of change in the cross-border area between China, Laos, and Vietnam rendered analysis of the processes at work extremely difficult. "If only they would all stop for a few months so that we could catch up!" was the plaintive cry of one participant. This problem may not be altogether a bad thing because the search for understanding may generate innovative modes of analysis which constitute a movement away from the economistic framework that has exerted such a subtle and pervasive influence over studies in the region. This could diffuse outwards into reinterpretation of regional trends in East and Southeast Asia.

So pervasive are the dominant discourses of the era in which one is living that it is difficult to a see beyond them. Looking at the comparatively recent past, there is abundant literature about the extent to which colonialist sentiments influenced Western writers during the colonial era, even when they were anthropologists whose stock in trade is supposed to be scepticism of the values of their own society.[12]

It is easy, with the advantage of hindsight, to write about the misconceptions of social scientists in the past, more difficult to write critically about the conventional wisdom of our own time. One way of overcoming this is to place a little less emphasis on issues such as ethnicity and life at the grassroots, and devote greater energy to the critical analysis of the conceptions and activities of powerful actors such as technocrats, planners, NGOs, businessmen, and politicians.[13]

The insights of non-academic writers about the region should not be ignored. A recent book by Tim Page (1995), who was a correspondent during the Indochina War, is an example. Page recently revisited Vietnam. His description of life on the border between Vietnam and China, where attempts to open trade are being reflexively hindered by party cadres, where the residue of tension remaining from the bitter 1987 border war between Vietnam and China is palpable, where the efforts of people to reconstruct lives that have been torn apart by decades of conflict are at once pathetic and awe-inspiring makes powerful reading.

Some descriptions of life in very different parts of the world may be of further assistance. For instance, in a review of one of Marquez's novels on South America, Salman Rushdie writes:

> "magical realism", at least as practised by Garcia Marquez, is a development of Surrealism that expresses a genuinely "Third World" consciousness. It deals with what Naipaul has called "half made" societies, in which the impossibly old struggles with the appallingly new, in which public corruptions and private anguishes are more garish and extreme than they ever get in the so called "North", where centuries of wealth and power have formed thick layers over the surface of what's really going on. In the work of Garcia Marquez, as in the world he describes, impossible things happen constantly, and quite plausibly, out in the open under the midday sun.

The South American consciousness is made up, on the one hand, of a syncretism of Catholicism and Indian animism and, on the other, of a weary scepticism of the inflated rhetoric of would-be revolutionaries which would be comical if it did not have often lethal consequences.

Cultural and religious eclecticism is also a characteristic of Laos, north Vietnam, and the adjacent borderlands of China. The people who live there, like the Latin Americans, have also had long experience of self-righteous, authoritarian, and downright greedy overlords. Once there were princes and assorted strongmen. Now there are authoritarian cadres, the agents of trade — those whom Joseph Conrad ironically referred to as "the Pilgrims" in his classic, *Heart of Darkness* — and the technocrats, who although wearing an increasingly "privatized" face, are in the same lineage as the colonial public servants of times gone by.

In our region, the contradictory, the paradoxical, the absurd is as ever present at least as much as it is in Latin America. It has not been recognized, because the "rationalist" attempts to explain what is happening have been so compelling. As a consequence it may be that we have a lot more to learn from Marquez, Naipaul, Rushdie — and Page than we do from Naisbitt or Ohmae.

ACKNOWLEDGMENT

Research on which this chapter is based was carried out under two Large Australian Research Council Grants, 1992–94 and 1995–97.

NOTES

1. Pol Pot's monstrous regime in Cambodia cannot be properly called "socialist" but must be placed in a category of its own.
2. "China's Grassroots Democracy". *The Economist*, 2 November 1996.
3. There have been some interesting recent critiques which have drawn attention to the neo-Orientalist sub-plots in Western writing about modern East and Southeast Asian political economy. One of these is Susan Greenhalgh's 1994 paper, "De-Orientalising the Chinese Family Firm". More recent one is Mark T. Berger's 1996 paper, "Yellow Mythologies: The East Asian Miracle and Post-Cold War Capitalism". The latter examines, amongst other matters, the "fixed cultural/racial assumptions [which] often see the industrialization of East Asia as a menace to the West". However, counterpoised to these are discourses produced in East Asia itself, generated by people like Lee Kuan Yew and Mahathir Mohamad which "also rest on fixed conceptions of culture/race" (p. 120).
4. See, for example, "Fissiparous Fortunes and Family Feuds", *The Economist*, 30 November 1996.
5. There is a considerable literature on the rise and eclipse of American corporate

dynasties. One of the more interesting recent accounts, of the financial empire founded by J. Pierpont Morgan is Ron Chernow's 1990 work, *The House of Morgan*.
6. See "Is it Possible to 'Manage' a River? Reflections on the Mekong" for an analysis technocratic discourses as they apply to the Mekong (Hinton 1996).
7. "Tropical Storm Devastates the North with Flash Floods", *Bangkok Post*, 30 July 1996. The Chinese have, in fact, built only one dam, although they have plans for others.
8. The Chinese have completed one major dam, Manwan, on the mainstream. This has an installed capacity of 1,500 megawatts (MW) and has a dammed waterhead 99 metres high. They have plans for three more major dams to be completed before the year 2010, the largest being Xiaowan with a massive dammed waterhead of 248 metres and an installed capacity of 4,200 MW. Three other dams are projected post-2010. The total installed capacity of the seven-dam "cascade" is 15,400 MW (Chapman and He 1996, p. 19).
9. Interim Mekong Committee, *Perspectives for Mekong Development* (1998), pp. 57–61.
10. Several articles in the July–October 1996 edition of *Watershed*, a magazine published by Towards Ecological Recovery and Regional Alliance (TERRA), a Bangkok-based conservationist NGO, exemplify this trend.
11. The figures are from the U.S. State Department for quantities of heroin (Bertil Lintner, personal commmunication), the U.S. Drug Enforcement Agency, quoted by Booth (1996, p. 331) for prices of heroin, and the National Statistical Office, Thailand, *Key Statistics of Thailand, 1995* for rice figures. The calculations are my own.
12. For a critical analysis see, for example, the papers in Asad (1973).
13. This has long been on the anthropological agenda, less frequently followed up. See, for example, Laura Nader's often cited paper, *Up the Anthropologist: Perspectives Gained by Studying Up* (1974), and more recently, Marcus and Fisher's (1985) suggestions for analysis of the institutions and values of our own society.

REFERENCES

Asad, Talal, ed. *Anthropology and the Colonial Encounter*. New Jersey: Humanities Press, 1973.
Berger, Mark T. "Yellow Mythologies: The East Asian Miracle and Post–Cold War Capitalism". *Positions* 4 (1996): 90–125.
Booth, Martin. *Opium: A History*. London: Simon and Schuster, 1996.
Chai-anan Samudavanija. "Capturing Opportunities and Managing Constraints in the New Growth Circles". Paper presented at the Conference on Asia's New Growth Circles, Chiang Mai, 3–6 March 1994.
Chapman, E.C. and He Daming. "Downstream Implications of China's Dams on the

Lancang Jiang (Upper Mekong) and Their Potential Significance for Greater Regional Cooperation, Basin-Wide". In *Development Dilemmas in the Mekong Subregion*, edited by Bob Stensholt, pp. 16–25. Melbourne: Monash Asia Institute, 1996.

Chernow, Ron. *The House of Morgan: An American Banking Dynasty and the Rise of Modern Finance*. New York: Simon and Schuster, 1990.

Evans, Grant. *Lao Peasants under Socialism and Post-Socialism*. Chiang Mai: Silkworm Books, 1995.

Greenhalgh, Susan. "De-Orientalising the Chinese Family Firm". *American Ethnologist* 21 (1994): 746–75.

Hinton, Peter. "Growth Triangles, Quadrangles and Circles: Interpreting Some Macro-Models for Regional Trade". *Thai-Yunnan Project Newsletter*, no. 28 (1995), pp. 2–7.

─────. "Is It Possible to Manage a River? Reflections from the Mekong". In *Development Dilemmas in the Mekong Sub-Region*, edited by Bob Stensholt, pp. 49–57. Melbourne: Monash Asia Institute, Monash University, 1996.

Humphrey, Caroline. "Creating a Culture of Disillusionment: Consumption in Moscow, a Chronicle of Changing Times". In *World Apart: Modernity through the Prism of the Local*, edited by Daniel Miller, pp. 43–68. London: Routledge, 1995.

Interim Mekong Committee. *Perspectives for Mekong Development* (1988), pp. 57–61. Bangkok: Mekong Secretariat, 1988.

Marcus, George E. *Ethnography through Thick and Thin*. Princeton, New Jersey: Princeton University Press, 1998.

Marcus, George E. and M.J. Fischer. *Anthropology as Cultural Critique: An Experimental Moment in the Human Sciences*. Chicago: University of Chicago Press, 1985.

Nader, Laura. "Up the Anthropologist: Perspectives Gained from Studying Up". In *Reinventing Anthropology*, edited by Dell Hymes, pp. 284–311. New York: Vintage Books, 1974.

Naisbitt, John. *Megatrends Asia: The Eight Asian Megatrends That Are Changing the World*. Hong Kong: South China Post, 1995.

─────. "Global Forces Shape Asia". *Far Eastern Economic Review 50th Anniversary Commemorative Edition: Telling Asia's Story*, 1996, pp. 192–93.

Ohmae, Kenichi. *The End of the Nation State: The Rise of Regional Economics*. London: Harper Collins, 1995.

Page, Tim. *Derailed in Uncle Ho's Victory Garden: Return to Vietnam and Cambodia*. London: Simon and Schuster, 1995.

Pasuk Phongpaichit and Chris Baker. *Thailand's Boom*. Chiang Mai: Silkworm Books, 1996.

─────. *Thailand's Boom and Bust*. Chiang Mai: Silkworm Books, 1998.

The Southern Chinese Borders in History

Geoff Wade

During a recent talk about the ancient Vietnamese Dong-son bronze drums, a member of the audience was heard to opine that as "Vietnam belonged to China during the Han dynasty", such drums are Chinese drums.[1] A statement such as this brings into focus a number of important and perhaps intractable questions: What constitutes China? What constitutes Chinese culture? To what degree has the Chinese state, throughout the millenia, exercised control over areas which were, or are now, claimed as parts of China? How "Chinese" are these areas in cultural terms? Why are cultural areas that were previously considered to be non-Chinese included today in the Chinese state? In any exploration of questions such as these we need to determine or create boundaries or borders. The way people create and perceive borders, however, differs markedly with the culture and polities from whence they come. We can see an excellent example of this by looking at the maps of Ming China contained within the *Cambridge History of China*.[2] While the map in the original edition portrays Ming China as extending westward only to Yunnan, Sichuan, and Gansu, the map in the People's Republic of China (PRC) translation shows the Ming state extending west to the Pamir Mountains in central Asia and northwards far beyond Lake Baikal.

The aim of this chapter is to place the other contributions to this volume within a broader historical context, by examining the southern Chinese borders through history. These borders are at times defined culturally, and at other times, geographically, economically, or politically. The validity of these categories can of course be discussed almost *ad infinitum*. I will, however, attempt to show, that many of the topics discussed in this volume have historical precedents. They are not solely issues of the present and, in some cases, constitute aspects of trends and processes which extend back for millenia.

CHINESE BORDERS AND BOUNDARIES

The studies of Chinese borders and boundaries, of core and periphery, of self and other, and of liminality, have in recent years become popular fields of enquiry in history, anthropology, and cultural and literary studies. These are opening up broad new vistas of enquiry into definitions, divisions, and categories.

While researchers have continued to examine Chinese borders in a traditional way, new ideas of boundaries have been explored in works such as *Boundaries in China*, edited by John Hay. In this work, the more general and less concrete boundaries for categories such as bodies, space, time, and discourse in China are defined.[3] Hay suggests that

> the strongest impetus within this movement [the study of "borders" and "boundaries"] has perhaps been an interest in the structure and dynamics of transgression, especially where such transgressions predicate boundaries as a necessary resistance. (Hay 1994, p. 6)

This is very much an extension of ideas found in the realm of literary theory.[4]

New avenues for exploring Chinese borders/frontiers have also been produced by the annual University of Oklahoma symposia on frontier theory, established to further the studies of frontier theory initiated by Frederick Jackson Turner. Jan English-Lueck (1991) has, for example, examined the Chinese scholars studying and working in the United States as nodes on the Chinese frontier/interface with non-China.

Also, the importance of images, rhetorical and otherwise, and concepts of space in Chinese societies, and the relations of these with frontier perceptions and policies, have recently attracted increasing scholarly attention.[5]

Other scholars have, furthermore, critically examined the borders of ethnicity and regional identities in Chinese contexts and questioned the certainty with which such boundaries have been previously accepted (for example, Hershatter et al. 1996[6] and Gladney 1996).

THE CULTURAL BORDERS

The idea of a cultural border is one of the most persistent, and perhaps the most clichéd, idea of the borders which over the centuries have divided China from non-China, and civilized China from non-civilized other.

From the very earliest days of Chinese polities, the idea of a cultural difference between the Chinese and the non-Chinese has been enunciated through various theories and rhetorical devices. The *Yugong*, or "Tribute of Yu", which forms part of the fifth century BC text *Shujing*, contains a description of five concentric spheres expanding outward from the centre, which was constituted by Yu's capital. The division under the Zhou dynasty was described as being ten concentric domains.[7] These domains, including the "nine divisions" which constituted political China at that time, were both geographic and cultural, and, as the model suggested, the further each domain was from the imperial centre, the greater the degree to which the inhabitants diverged from the ideals of Chinese culture. This was the conceptual framework that informed most Chinese writing on peoples on and beyond the Chinese frontiers for the last 3,000 years. Frank Dikötter (1992, pp. 1–17) has suggested that the distinctions being made by the Chinese were physical, or distinctions of "race", but his claims are not universally accepted. While the descriptions of "those beyond culture" were often accentuated by physical difference — as shown, for example, by the perforated-chest people, the three-headed people and so on, who are detailed in the *Shanhai Jing*, or "Classic of Mountains and Seas" — such physical difference was neither a necessary nor universal characteristic of those beyond Chinese culture. The essential distinction, as reflected in Chinese texts throughout history, remained a cultural one.

In respect of this cultural distinction, which played such a major part in Chinese perception of the borders and those who lived there, Wang Gungwu has explored what he calls "the Chinese urge to civilize" and its relationship to aspects of change in Chinese society (Wang 1984, pp. 1–34). He stresses the importance of the concept *hua* in Chinese history, as it was this mechanism of *hua* (change brought about through moral authority, ritual, or education) which was depicted in Chinese texts as an essential element of the civilizing process within Chinese society. By extension, *hua* was a necessary element to be applied to border areas perceived or depicted as being non-civilized. Professor Wang, nevertheless, concludes that in practice there was no evidence of a great

2. The Southern Chinese Borders in History

"urge to civilize ... the urge to *hua*, 'to change others for the better'" (Wang 1984, p. 6). However, this ideological claim did provide a rhetorical basis and a moral authority for actions by the Chinese state in respect to those outside Chinese culture. This will be further explored later in this chapter.

The concepts by which the Chinese literati understood, or at least represented, those on and beyond its borders have been referred to by some as the "Chinese world order". Various elements of this "world order" are detailed in the essays contained in John Fairbank's book *The Chinese World Order: Traditional China's Foreign Relations*, published in 1968. While the essays in this collection refer specifically to foreign polities, there was no real distinction between frontier and foreign polities in traditional China. Foreign polities were often simply considered as frontier polities further removed geographically, and equally subject to tribute payments. If the possibility or the need arose they were incorporated into the Chinese state.

CHINESE POLITICAL BORDERS

Borders have always held an important place in Chinese political writing. As has been noted above, this was partly due to the cultural distinctions through which the Chinese élite defined themselves, but also to political and defence needs.

The early official dynastic histories all included sections that described the peoples on the borders and also biographies of civil and military officials who were appointed to posts on or near the borders of the Chinese polity (Yang 1975).[8]

The importance of the borders as defensive regions has received great attention in the writing of the Chinese literati. From the earliest concerns about the *xiongnu* (the Huns) on the northern borders 2,000 years ago, expressed in works such as the *Shiji* and the *Hanshu* (Sima Qian, *juan* 113; and Ban Gu, *juan* 94), to the detailed studies of northern and coastal border defences in the Ming and Qing dynasties, the borders were long examined in terms of the military strength or weakness both of China and of those beyond.

Relations with the non-Chinese peoples resident in the border regions remained, throughout Chinese history, a major element in Chinese writing on the borders. It was one of these peoples — the Manchus — who were to conquer China in the seventeenth century AD and establish the Qing dynasty. The attitudes of Chinese cultural superiority mentioned above remained, however, very much in circulation, despite Qing efforts to quench them. At the end of the nineteenth century and the beginning of the twentieth century, these anti-Manchu sentiments, which had been kept alive by secret societies throughout the Qing, saw a resurgence. Zou Rong's call to "annihilate the five million and more of the furry and horned Manchu race" was a somewhat overstated expression of more popular resentment (Zou 1968, p. 58). At the same time, many of the ideas of Social Darwinism, prevalent among the revolutionaries at the time, melded with these anti-Manchu sentiments in producing the idea of a strong, "racially pure" China, which excluded or, if necesssary, assimilated those non-Chinese who had been subject to the Qing state. Scholars such as Wang Jingwei held that a state comprising a single "race" was far superior to one comprising a *melange* of different peoples, and that nations coterminous with "races" were far stronger than those which were not (Duara 1995, p. 141).

The political needs of the impending republic required, however, that a theoretical construct that would include those non-Chinese peoples occupying about half of the Qing territory be established. The precise mechanisms by which this came about are still being researched. In a speech in 1912, the first year of the Republic, Sun Yat-sen noted that "The Chinese Republic unites the five great races of Han, Manchus, Mongols, Hui and Tibetans to plan together for happiness" (Deal 1971, p. 49). He used the term *tongbao* (compatriots, but literally "womb-mates") to incorporate the non-Chinese within the new structure of the Republic. The flag of the new Republic also comprised five colours representing the five major "races" of the newly emergent China. This was partly a response to burgeoning secessionist movements in Mongolia and Tibet and partly a necessity to provide the theoretical basis for incorporating areas traditionally inhabited by non-Chinese peoples within the Chinese state. While the Republic nominally accepted some degree of autonomy for these border peoples, the new *Guomindang* leaders at the same time advocated a policy of assimilation and therefore promoted Han occupation of the "border lands" (Deal 1971, pp. 142–44).

Throughout the years of the Republic of China (ROC), it was the imperative of incorporating securely the territories of the non-Chinese peoples within the Chinese state which informed studies on border regions. Border studies were thus very much a political question rather than a geographic or cultural issue. Mongolian and Tibetan affairs dominated the early Republic's border concerns, but with the Japanese occu-

2. The Southern Chinese Borders in History

pation of north China in the 1930s, studies relating to the southwestern border and the peoples thereon gained increased importance. A programme put forward in 1938 emphasized broad acculturation in this region (Deal 1971, p. 57). Contradictions between proposals for self-determination for border peoples and proposals urging assimilation continued throughout the whole republican period. The journals *Pien-cheng Kung-lun* ("Frontier affairs") and subsequently *Chung-kuo Pien-cheng* ("China's border administration") were the primary organs of the ROC government detailing thinking and policies in this sphere.

The new regime of the People's Republic of China (PRC), established in 1949, continued many of the border policies employed by the Republic. A major difference, however, was that the PRC stressed that the purpose of the liberation of the border peoples was to end class oppression within their societies. The new regime further stressed that local nationalisms no longer had any role to play, as all workers and agriculturalists within China were members of the proletariat (the most advanced class). However, the debate between proponents of autonomy and those urging assimilation of non-Chinese peoples living in the border areas continued. At a Nationalities Affairs Commission meeting in 1957, one of the members, Wang Feng, debunked the idea of cultural plurality in China:

> The gradual fusion of the various nationalities on the basis of equality is the natural law governing social development. ... Certain signs of fusion have appeared among the nationalities. ... Such fusion is desirable ... (Deal 1971, p. 138)

Not many years later, however, Wang Feng was again making statements on nationality policy, noting that regional autonomy should be more fully developed (Dreyer 1976, p. 185). Such reversals demonstrate the continuing inconsistencies and uncertantites in PRC nationality policies, partly as a result of ideological struggles within the Communist Party of China.

In recent years, border studies have assumed an increasing importance in PRC scholarship and, consequently, a journal entitled *Zhongguo Bianjiang Shidi Yanjiu* ("Studies in the geography and history of China's borders") is now being published.[9] The surge in research on Chinese borders is, in part, again due to the needs of the Chinese state to provide a theoretical validation of its current borders. A succinct summary of the overarching theory within which current PRC border studies operate is provided in a recent work by Liu Hongxuan (1995). In this work,

Liu details three "high-tides" in "the process of melding the Chinese nation" — the first during the Qin-Han period, the second during the Sui-Tang period, and the third during the Yuan-Ming-Qing period. Liu explains the border-expanding actions of the successive Chinese states as interactions between fraternal ethnic groups, who have shared a common modern history of oppression either by imperialists or the landlord classes. This explanation thus provides a basis not only for a multi-ethnic "Chinese" state, but also for including within that state the territory of any peoples who have interacted with the Chinese state at any time in the past. This national narrative, which in many ways is a continuation of the imperial histories, is an essential part of the politics of the modern state. Even if one does not agree with the need to or possibility of "rescuing history from the nation", as urged by Prasenjit Duara (1995), it is obvious that the "powerful repressive and appropriative functions of national History", which according to him need to be challenged (Duara 1995, pp. 232–33), remain dominant elements in the writing of PRC border history.

THE SOUTHERN CHINESE BORDERS

Compared with the studies of China's northern, northeastern, and northwestern borders, which have been the subjects of much research, few studies have been conducted on the southern borders. What has given rise to this neglect? One explanation is the fact that there has been no clear-cut economic/geographic distinction to the south, where most societies on both sides of the borders practise some form of agriculture. The northern borders have by contrast been more obviously marked by the traditional distinction between the mainly agricultural Chinese societies and the nomads of the steppes, which Lattimore refers to as marking the "persistent lack of integration between China and the Steppe" (Lattimore 1951, pp. 549–52).[10] Another equally important reason is that the threats and sometimes usurpation by outsiders had, until the late Qing, always originated with peoples in the north or northwest. The steppe nomads threatened the northern dynasties for centuries, the Mongols occupying China and establishing the Yuan dynasty in the thirteenth century AD, while the Manchus invaded and assumed political control of China through the Qing dynasty in the seventeenth century AD. Such threats were, of course, the reason for the successive walls to the north which culminated in the Great Wall, completed only during the Ming dynasty.

2. The Southern Chinese Borders in History

How then does the modern Chinese state — the PRC — portray its southern borders over history? The set of historical maps edited by Tan Qixiang (1982–87) provides a guide to what the PRC historians consider to be the southern Chinese borders over history. In the map depicting China during the late *chunqiu* period in the fifth century BC (Tan 1982–87, vol. 1, pp. 20–21), no southern border is formally delineated. City names extend to just south of the Yangtze, and the area beyond is shown as "Yue". The map of the Qin state *circa* 200 BC shows a formal border that approximates the modern southern border of China, including within China what is today Guangxi and Yunnan (Tan 1982–87, vol. 2, pp. 3–4). The map representing the Eastern Han dynasty (AD 25–220) shows the southern border extending south along the coast to what is Hue in Vietnam today and includes much of what is today northern Myanmar in the southwest (Tan 1982–87, vol. 2, pp. 40–41). Similar southern borders are depicted for the Western Jin (AD 265–317)[11] and Eastern Jin (AD 265–419),[12] the Southern dynasties (AD 420–581),[13] the Sui (AD 581–618),[14] and the Tang (AD 618–907).[15] It is only with the map of the Song dynasty (AD 960–1178) that areas of modern northern Vietnam are excluded from the map of China (Tan 1982–87, vol. 6, pp. 42–43). In all of these maps polities such as Xicuan, Nanzhao, and Dali are depicted in the area of modern Yunnan and are indicated to have been Chinese polities. All of the maps also include the islands of the South China Sea, and in the maps of the Song dynasty they are named (implying their incorporation into the Chinese polity).

The maps discussed above are informative of the aims of modern cartographers and their political masters in that they suggest that China's southern border, since *circa* 220 BC, has been at or beyond where it is today. Actions by the Chinese state subsequent to that time have consequently simply been "incorporation" of Chinese areas rather than "expansion" of the state. As has already been noted, much historical cartography in the PRC is informed by current political needs rather than historical texts. Therefore, the degree to which Chinese political control was exercised over the areas depicted on these maps as being "within" China remains contentious.

THE EXPANDING SOUTHERN BORDERS THROUGH HISTORY

Where then did China end in its southern extremity in various periods throughout history? This is a difficult question to answer. One problem is that in many cases the only basis for verifying claims to control is limited to what is contained within Chinese texts. Another problem is that modern maps show Chinese control historically extending over vast swathes of territory, while it was often the case that the actual Chinese presence was restricted to commanderies on important communication and trade routes, and little political control was in fact exercised over surrounding areas. Chinese states, like all other empires, expanded their territory through the threat or use of military might.[16] Here follow a few examples of the military expeditions by which Chinese political control was extended southwards.

The first major Chinese push into the region which is today southern China was a remarkable expedition in 234 BC by Qin Shi Huangdi, commonly called the "first emperor" of China, against the "Yue" people who resided in the Lingnan area ("south of the ranges"). To support further troop movements, huge canals were built, connecting southern Hunan with the West River. Chinese settlers were also sent into areas which are today Jiangxi and Hunan. The state of Chu, which had long remained outside the true borders of "China", and which had exercised some sort of political and cultural domination in areas which are today Hubei/Hunan, was also invaded and incorporated by the Qin in 223 BC. The state of Nan Yue,[17] which subsequently had been established in the region of modern Guangdong, then challenged the power of the Chinese state. Thus in 112 BC the Han court sent forces against this polity, destroying its political centre and expanding its own influence southwards into what is now northern Vietnam.

Efforts by non-Chinese to retain political power free of Chinese domination were marked by the attempts of the famous Tru'ng sisters of Jiaozhi (now Vietnam) to re-assert indigenous power in the region, in the middle of the first century AD (Taylor 1983, pp. 37–41). This resulted in one of the most famous of the "southern expeditions" which, under the command of Ma Yuan, the "Wave-Calming General", destroyed the power of the Tru'ng sisters and began to lay foundations for Chinese political power in the Red River plain. Ma Yuan subsequently became a cult figure among Chinese in many areas of southern China, representing the domination of Chinese over non-Chinese peoples. Chinese control over this region, however, was not a wide-ranging political control, but was restricted to commanderies mainly in the Red River Delta.

Over the following centuries of Chinese colonization, there was both sinicization of the Yue inhabitants of the Jiaozhi area as well as a

Yue-ization of Chinese peoples who settled there. The alternating periods of Yue/Viet political dependence on, and independence of, Chinese power over the next few centuries produced a culture greatly influenced by China but also greatly antagonistic to the Chinese state.[18] The failure of the successive Chinese invasions, aimed at incorporating Vietnam within China, manifests the intensity of this antagonism. The real political and economic incorporation of areas south of the Yangtze into the Chinese state accelerated during the eighth and ninth centuries AD. This promoted the fuller integration of the Yue and Min polities in the coastal areas south of the Yangtze in what are today Guangdong and Fujian.

On the other side of southern China, there was also expansion southwards into Sichuan, and subsequently into what are today Yunnan and Guizhou. Parts of Sichuan, and particularly the states of Shu and Ba, had links with the Chinese states along the Yellow River from at least the third century BC, at which time they were invaded and incorporated at least nominally into the state of Qin. More remote areas of Sichuan were only fully incorporated into the Chinese state during the nineteenth century AD.[19]

The beginning of the Chinese push into the Yunnan region was marked by the efforts of the Tang in the eighth century AD to incorporate the state of Nanzhao, centred at Dali, and by the subsequent Nanzhao attacks on the Tang. The Mongol Yuan dynasty (1260–1368) brought the succeeding Dali kingdom into its huge empire, but it was only with the Ming invasion of Yunnan in the 1380s that parts of Yunnan were formally incorporated within the Chinese state. Major Tai polities, however, remained powerful in the region. The Tai Mao kingdom, known to the Chinese as Luchuan, was only destroyed by three massive military expeditions involving hundreds of thousands of Ming troops in the 1430s and 1440s AD.

These formerly powerful polities have since been subsumed in the overall narrative of Chinese national historiography, and as a result, virtually no research is conducted within the PRC on the processes and mechanisms of Chinese political expansion. The perhaps belaboured point being made is that the borders of the Chinese polity were gradually expanded southwards through military conquest. The processes of these military conquests, the degree to which control was exercised in areas invaded, and the social, economic, and political methods of incorporation within the Chinese polity are topics which remain almost entirely unresearched.

METHODS OF INCORPORATION — THE TUSI

When a border polity was defeated militarily by a Chinese state, or when it required Chinese assistance in fighting another foe, the Chinese polity frequently used its dominant position to institute indirect rule of the area, utilizing indigenous rulers or members of traditional local élites to govern the areas and assigning them titles for this purpose. Thereby, the Chinese state could in effect claim "control" of the region and demand grain, silver, or labour, but did not have to expend the usual funds necessary to maintain an administration. Initially, this was referred to as keeping these areas on a "loose rein". When the Qin emperor expanded his empire in the second century BC, he "pacified Shu [in today's Sichuan], and reduced the king of Shu, changing his title to marquis" (Sima Qian 1963, vol. 7, p. 2284). The policy continued through the Han, the Three Kingdoms, and right into the Song dynasty (Gong Yin 1992, pp. 1–21). In respect of the Tai peoples in what is today Guangxi, an official named Fan Chengda noted:

> They have given their allegiance since the Tang dynasty, and the tribes have been divided. The larger have been made into subprefectures, the smaller into counties, and the smallest into minor administrations. Under the present dynasty [Song], there are over 50 subprefectures, counties and minor administrations. Their outstanding chiefs have been appointed as leaders, and the people have been enrolled as liable to military service. The people are uncivilized and ferocious, their customs are wild and strange, and they cannot be properly ruled using Chinese education and law. Thus, they are just kept on a loose rein. (Fan Chengda 1986, p. 179)

Subsequently, this policy became more refined and, after subduing or achieving the submission of a border polity, the Chinese state, through the use of threat or military force, divided it into smaller administrative units and instituted a *tusi* or "native office" administration. What this meant was that these former polities became, at least in Chinese eyes, informal[20] parts of the Chinese administration. As previously noted, the Chinese state either allowed the traditional ruler to remain in place or appointed a new indigenous ruler, under the policy of "using *yi* to rule *yi*".[21] The quid pro quo for this recognition was often cession of territory to the Chinese state, provision of annual silver and gold payments, and provision of troops or corvée labour.[22] In this way, some of the "native offices" of Yunnan, Guangxi, and Sichuan were little different from the "native states" administrations in India and Malaya under the British empire — nominally autonomous but actually subject to the military might of the colonial power.

When Chinese populations or Chinese military control increased sufficiently, these "native offices" were subjected to a policy known as *gaitu guiliu* (literally: "change the native, institute the circulating". On some pretext (death, disability, failure to meet obligations, disloyalty, and so forth), the traditional ruler was removed and replaced by a formal member of the Chinese bureaucracy; the polity was then designated as a county or prefecture, and the area was formally absorbed into the Chinese state. This was often recorded as being done at the request of the local residents or of the rulers themselves. However, the intensity of the response by these polities to these enforced changes can, for example, be seen in an incident in AD 1778 when the people of Wumeng in Yunnan killed 500 of the Qing troops who had come to enforce the new arrangements. In response, the Qing general E-er-tai annihilated over 30,000 persons in the area (Zou Qiyu et al. 1989, p. 77).[23]

The system of *tusi* remained part of the Chinese administrative structure until the first half of this century, particularly in Yunnan and Guangxi provinces.[24] The last *tusi* ruler of Xishuangbanna, in Yunnan, is still alive today, residing in Kunming, well away from his traditional power base.

CHINESE CONCEPTUAL AND RHETORICAL MECHANISMS IN RESPECT OF THE SOUTHERN BORDERS — THE TOPOI

One of the most significant aspects of the southern Chinese borders in history is the way in which Chinese actions upon those borders have been represented in Chinese historiography. Recognizing the mechanisms innate in this representation is of great relevance to understanding the Chinese past and to comprehending China's relations, historical and contemporary, with its southern neighbours.

Above, I have discussed how modern PRC scholars have depicted the changing southern borders of the Chinese state over time. On the one hand, they incorporate, often uncritically, many of the claims made in the official and non-official histories of the imperial past. On the other hand, because of the very tight links which continue to exist between Chinese historical scholarship and the Chinese state, there is a tendency to write the past in ways that accord with the political exigencies of that state.[25] Some of the rhetorical and conceptual devices which have been and continue to be employed in this respect are discussed below.

THE TOPOI OF CLASSICAL CHINESE HISTORIOGRAPHY

The classical rhetoric of imperial historiography has produced a momentum which brooks little critical examination in China even today. Here I would like to detail some of the topoi, comprising rhetoric and images, which inform traditional Chinese writing about the southern borders. These topoi have long roots, some stretching back over 3,000 years.

The idea overarching all rhetoric was that the Chinese emperor, as the Son of Heaven, bore Heaven's mandate. Thus, actions by the Chinese state were by definition divinely sanctioned and "just and correct to the minutest degree" (*Ming Yingzong Shilu*, juan 190, pp. 12b–13a). As profoundly benevolent and as the protector of life, the emperor was depicted as having a distaste for war. A Ming emperor, for example, is recorded as stating:

> I manifest Heaven's love for all living things and I am convinced that if the Imperial Army is despatched, it will be impossible to avoid harming the innocent. Also, my heart could not bear taking men away from their fathers, mothers, wives and children. (*Ming Yingzong Shilu*, juan 43, p. 2*b*)

There is a multitude of references through official Chinese historiography proclaiming or demonstrating the benevolence of the emperor and by extension the Chinese state *in toto*. Further, as fairness and justness incarnate, as the father or even the "parents" of all people, and as the maintainer of peace, the emperor could not act in ways deleterious to the interests of "the people", regardless of where they resided. These characteristics were summed up by the emperor's possession of *de*, which can be considered an intrinsic virtuous power of benevolence. In the *Shuijing Zhu*, we read a poem written in the Han dynasty, which contains the line: "The virtuous power (*de*) of the Han has no borders" (Wang Guowei 1984, p. 1150). The implication was, that through the emperor's *de*, actions could be taken anywhere "under Heaven".

The representation of Chinese culture as worthy of emulation was also a persistent characteristic of Chinese traditional historiography. In the 1420s AD, the Xuande Emperor is recorded as stating: "Using Chinese ways to change *yi* (non-Chinese) ways — there is nothing more important than this" (*Ming Xuanzong Shilu*, juan 3, pp. 12b–13a). More specifically, when efforts were being made in the fifteenth century to send the sons of indigenous rulers in Yunnan to receive a Confucian education, the imperial assessment was as follows:

> In this way, the habit of the *man* and the *mo* of struggling for succession will gradually die out and the civilizing influences of Chinese propriety and righteousness will reach to the distance. How wonderful this will be! (*Ming Xianzong Shilu*, *juan* 212, pp. 6a–6b)

The "other" in this essential dichotomy were the non-Chinese of the southern border. They were those who provided the antithesis in the defining of Chineseness. They were referred to by numerous terms, including *man*, *yi*, and *fan*, and were often depicted in almost non-human terms. In the mid-sixteenth century, the Ming emperor Jiajing opined: "The *yi* and *di*, like the birds and the beasts, are without human morality" (*Ming Shizong Shilu*, *juan* 199, pp. 6b–7b). As well as being without the essential morality necessary for a human being, they were "wily and deceitful", "barbarous, rebellious and perverse". The essential (represented) barbarity of these peoples, implicitly, and often explicitly, portrayed in the historiographical tradition validated any actions which the Chinese state took against such peoples. This relates back to the ideas of *hua* mentioned earlier in this paper.

The polities of the south were also represented within a discourse which gave the Chinese state a moral and political right to control.

> I am the Emperor and, having received Heaven's great mandate, I rule the Chinese and the *yi*. The one culture/language provides a norm for the 10,000 places, while cultural influences educate beyond the four quarters. Of all who are covered by Heaven or supported by the Earth, there is none who does not submit in heart. (*Ming Yingzong Shilu*, *juan* 337, p. 4b)

So wrote the Tianshun Emperor to Lê Hao, the ruler of Dai Viet in AD 1466, in order to explain the model relationship between China and its "tributary" states. Regardless of whether the rulers of other polities recognized any submission or tribute obligations to the Chinese state, such rhetoric was important self-validation within the Chinese tradition for any actions the Chinese state took against polities to the south. When polities were brought under the control of the Chinese state they became, in the Chinese record, *tusi* or "native offices", as mentioned above, which, in terms of providing taxation, labour, and troops, made them more subject to the controls of the Chinese state.

These topoi were utilized collectively in Chinese historiography to validate Chinese actions against non-Chinese peoples. A few representative examples relating to the southern border will suffice to demonstrate how they were used.

In the 1380s AD, military forces numbering in the hundreds of thousands were sent by Zhu Yuanzhang, the first Ming emperor, to capture areas which are today part of Yunnan. After capturing the area and instituting political control, Zhu Yuanzhang validated these actions as follows:

> The territory of Yunnan is already ours. It may appear that it was taken by force. That is not so. The Liang Prince, who was the grandson of the Yuan emperor Shizu, using his claim as a descendant of the Yuan court, gave shelter to our criminals, received our fugitives and lured away our frontier guards. Thus, there was no other way than to despatch an army to punish him. (*Ming Taizu Shilu*, juan 244, pp. 2b–4a)

A second example is the following. In AD 1406, the forces of the Emperor Yongle invaded Vietnam and occupied it for the following twenty years. Blaming the situation on the Vietnamese person Li Jili (Hô` Qúy-ly), the Emperor, in his instructions to the departing forces, noted:

> He has oppressed the people of the country and the people hate him to the marrow of their bones. The spirits of Heaven and Earth are unable to tolerate this. I have respectfully taken on the mandate of Heaven and treat the people on all sides as my children. I thus dare not fail to correct this situation. I am especially sending you to lead troops to console the people and to punish those who have been rebellious. The people of Annam are all my children. Now they are in a helpless situation as if suspended upside down. You are proceeding there to relieve them of their suffering and must not be tardy in this. (*Ming Taizong Shilu*, juan 56, pp. 1b–3a)

The third example took place during the 1440s AD. The Chinese court sent three huge military expeditions against the Tai Mao polity, known to the Chinese as Luchuan, which extended over much of what is today western Yunnan and northern Myanmar. The Tai Mao ruler Sirenfa was vilified in Chinese texts, and the following validation for the Chinese expeditions is contained in a letter sent to neighbouring polities:

> Recently, Sirenfa, the refractory bandit of Luchuan, rebelled and deviated from right. He invaded neighbouring territory and carried off people and livestock. Initially, I could not bear to send troops against him. However, despite sending him repeated Imperial orders of pacification and instruction, he has remained unrepentant. His avaricious heart is not yet satiated and he wants to swallow you all up. This is unacceptable to Heaven and Earth and the spirits, and I have already ordered the regional commander to advance the troops to eliminate him. (*Ming Yingzong Shilu*, juan 76, pp. 7b–8a)[26]

2. The Southern Chinese Borders in History

Thus, we see in respect of three essentially aggressive actions by the Chinese state towards polities on its southern border, that Chinese history records them as actions by a benevolent emperor/state acting justly, with divine endorsement, to preserve order. The rhetoric continues today, with all modern history texts noting Zhu Yuanzhang's military activities in the early Ming as being aimed at "pacifying" Yunnan (Ma Yao 1991, p. 142). The invasion of Vietnam in the early fifteenth century AD is today described as "punishment" of Annam for having transgressed the Chinese border and deceived the Ming court (Liao 1988). Much of the rhetoric echoes that of 500 years ago. The destruction of the Tai Mao polity is validated in modern Chinese texts as "military actions by which to maintain the centralized power and unity of the Ming court" (Ma Yao 1991, p. 154), and "stabilizing the Yunnan situation and safeguarding the unity of the country" (Weng 1990, p. 649).

While the successive Chinese states "punished" bandits, "pacified" areas, "soothed" polities, and "instructed" and brought to surrender recalcitrant polities, they never, and linguistically could not, "invade" others. By contrast, the military actions of all non-Chinese polities to the south are, in both classical and modern Chinese texts, almost exclusively described as "aggression" or "invasion". The actions of the Chinese state have always been, according to the continuing rhetoric, morally and even divinely valid. Even if we look at the Chinese invasion of Vietnam in 1979, we see that it was described in Chinese texts as a "punishment", with all the implications that it was valid and justified.

However, if one ignores the topoi of Chinese history — or, more precisely, regards them as self-validating rhetorical devices — the actions by the successive Chinese dynasties appear less benevolent, less necessary and less divine, and more self-serving, aggressive, and expansive.

The above topoi might be dismissed by some as irrelevant, as fairy-tales from the past. However, they are not fairy-tales and they are not irrelevant. They are the way in which Chinese historiography, both official and non-official, has represented the Chinese state's actions in respect of the polities and peoples to China's south. As such, they are the basis of modern Chinese history-writing, and thus the basis of what is taught daily in Chinese schools. There is a critical "glass ceiling" beyond which analysis almost cannot proceed.

The failure of Chinese historians to address and investigate the mechanisms by which the Chinese polities expanded from a few states on the Yellow River to where China now includes half of East Asia is in part a result of the political exigencies of the PRC. The failure is, however, equally due to the traditional rhetoric of Chinese historiography, which has covered and concealed the actions of the imperial Chinese states under the rhetoric of benevolence and righteousness.

Even today, when the issue of historical expansion is addressed, it is disguised behind the modern rhetoric of PRC historiography which includes: the "border regions" being "opened up" (for example, Lü Yiran 1991, and Ma and Ma 1990); fraternal yet sometimes fractious nationalities/ethnic groups have all contributed to the making of Chinese history; and modern China is the result of an inevitable coming together of the various parts of what might be considered "proto-China" (for example, Jiang Yingliang 1991). This is all part of the nationalist rhetoric so necessary for the maintenance of the current Chinese territory and the remolding of a national pride.

This rhetoric is of course not something unique to China. All of the major empires of the past have utilized similar justifying and rationalizing rhetoric in describing their actions. The major difference is that while the rhetoric of western imperialism has over the last few decades been subject to incisive analysis and deconstruction, the rhetoric employed by the successive Chinese states has by contrast remained virtually uncontested. As has already been noted, this is in part the result of Chinese scholarship having remained so closely tied to the state and its interests, and also because the product of Chinese sources has been, in many cases, the only texts available to us.

There is a need to recognize the purposes of the rhetoric (topoi) used in traditional Chinese histories, because only by recognizing and analysing these rhetorics will the writing of more valid historical scenarios be possible. The recognition that various Chinese states throughout history have been not only capable of, but quite inured to, the use of force against other polities will be beneficial to those who live within China and to those who live on and beyond its borders.

CONCLUSION

About 1,000 years ago, during the Song dynasties (AD 960–1278), one of the most pervasive influences on Chinese society was the emergent and subsequently thriving mercantilism. Commerce brought vast changes to Chinese society *per se* and to the areas bordering the Chinese state. Shiba Yoshinobu (1970) has pointed out the importance of this commercial revolution on social change in the Song period, and particularly that of the commercialization of agriculture. He stresses that it promoted the development of interlinked rural markets, trade associations, communications, and transport. Yoshinobu further notes that new business forms, such as partnerships, primitive joint-stock companies and trading combines, came to prominence, and that this in turn promoted a rise in urbanism, an increase in money and credit circulation, and a growth in overseas trade.

These remarkable changes in Song China had dramatic effects on the southern and southwestern borders. Von Glahn's excellent thesis (1983) reveals how this affected the area of the Upper Yangtze in Hunan and Sichuan, and how proposals by the official Wang Shao provided inspiration for frontier expansion and commercial exploitation of these areas. The economic value of the southern lands remained, Von Glahn suggests, "a central political preoccupation" of the Chinese state. He then cites the memorial of another Song official, Su Xun, which noted:

> Guangnan and Sichuan are the springs of wealth and goods, and the northern provinces depend on them for provisionment. Bringing the southern tribes under control is an urgent priority. (Von Glahn 1983, p. 452)

This resulted in the Song annexing large territories and extending claims over many non-Chinese peoples. The areas to the very south failed to provide the riches promised by the memorials, simply because the communications and technologies were insufficient to allow exploitation. However, areas along the Central and Upper Yangtze were brought under more direct Chinese governance, and were settled by large numbers of Chinese settlers who traded, planted, and maintained links, commercial and otherwise, with other areas of Chinese settlement, thereby drawing these areas into the Chinese sphere.

Over the last ten years the PRC has again seen a burgeoning mercantilism, with new forms of business organizations and practices emerging. The world of the twentieth century is certainly a very different place from that of the eleventh century. Modernity and new forms of international relations have vast influences on perceptions and actions, and new cultural complexes challenge the domination of Chinese culture in Asia. This, however, does not mean that the past is irrelevant. It would be remarkable if the mercantilism of late twentieth century China was not, like that of 1,000 years ago, to have major effects on the southern border and the polities beyond. How the commerce is affecting and will continue to affect the border regions are questions which researchers will increasingly be drawn to. In any such research, the cited characteristics of the southern Chinese borders will need to be broadly considered, as they constitute the historical backdrop to the enormous changes now taking place.

NOTES

1. This talk was held in early 1996 at Hong Kong University. The Dong-son bronze drums are found mainly in what is today northern Vietnam and in Guangxi province in southern China.
2. These maps appear in the English-language original and Chinese-language translation of the Ming volume of *The Cambridge History of China* (Chinese Academy of Social Sciences, 1992).
3. Much of this work derives from ideas enunciated in Michel Foucault's *L'archeologie du Savoir* (1969).
4. The study of transgression and the predication of borders is by no means absent from traditional studies of political and geographical boundaries.
5. A recent example was the symposium entitled "China and Her Neighbours: Borders and Visions of the Other, Sung to Ch'ing", convened at Ludwig-Maximilians-Universität, Munich in July 1996 (Dabringhaus and Ptak 1997).
6. See, for example, the essays by Lipman, Millward, Honig, Cole, and Goodman in Hershatter et al., eds. (1996).
7. For a translation of the *Shujing* text, see vol. III, "The Shoo King" (Legge 1994, pp. 128–51).
8. For a collection of relevant sections from the imperial histories, see Yang (1975).
9. The journal is published by the Chinese Borders' History and Geography Research Centre under the Chinese Academy of Social Sciences.
10. Professor F.W. Mote's recent studies of Ming borders have drawn attention to this distinction between the northern and southern borders.
11. Tan (1982–87, vol. 3, pp. 33–34).
12. Ibid., vol. 4, pp. 3–4.
13. Ibid., vol. 4, pp. 25–26.
14. Ibid., vol. 5, pp. 3–4.
15. Ibid., vol. 5, pp. 36–37.
16. The successive military expansions southward of the Chinese empires have been detailed in Wiens, *Han Chinese Expansion in South China* (1967) and C.P. Fitzgerald, *The Southern Expansion of the Chinese People* (1972).
17. Some claim that, despite its sinicized élite, the state of Nan Yue was essentially a Tai state (Wiens 1967, p. 133).

2. The Southern Chinese Borders in History   47

18. For details of this period in Vietnamese history, see Taylor (1983) and Holmgren (1980).
19. Von Glahn's thesis (1983), provides an excellent example of how areas within modern Hunan and Sichuan were brought within the formal administration of the Chinese state over the eleventh to the thirteenth centuries.
20. "Informal" here means under the Chinese state, but not under formal, local Chinese bureaucrats.
21. *Yi* means "non-Chinese".
22. For details of the *tusi* system, see Wu (1988).
23. A study of how the *tusi* system was enforced and changed during the Qing dynasty is provided in a recent article by Herman (1997).
24. For an exhaustive list of the *tusi* administrations, see Gong (1992).
25. For many examples in this respect, see Duara (1995).
26. For a recent account of the expeditions against Luchuan, see Liew (1996).

BIBLIOGRAPHY OF WESTERN WORKS CITED

Dabringhaus, Sabine and Roderich Ptak, eds. *China and Her Neighbours: Borders, Visions of the Other, Foreign Policy 10th to 19th Century*. Wiesbaden: Harrassowitz, 1997.
Deal, David Michael. "National Minority Policy in Southwest China, 1911–1965". Ph.D. dissertation, University of Washington, 1971.
Dikötter, Frank. *The Discourse of Race in Modern China*. Hong Kong: Hong Kong University Press, 1992.
Dreyer, June Teufel. *China's Forty Millions*. Cambridge, Massachusetts: Harvard University Press, 1976.
Duara, Prasenjit. *Rescuing History from the Nation: Questioning Narratives of Modern China*. Chicago, Illinois: University of Chicago Press, 1995.
English-Lueck, Jan. "A Journey to the West: Historic and Modern Chinese Frontiers and Han History". Paper presented at the Eleventh Oklohoma Symposium on Comparative Frontiers Studies, University of Oklahoma, 1991.
Fairbank, J.K. *The Chinese World Order: Traditional China's Foreign Relations*. Cambridge, Massachusetts: Harvard University Press, 1968.
Fitzgerald, C.P. *The Southern Expansion of the Chinese People: "Southern Fields and Southern Ocean"*. London: Barrie and Jenkins, 1972.
Foucault, Michel. *L'archeologie du Savoir*. Paris: Gallimard, 1969.
Gladney, Dru. "Relational Alterity: Constructing Dungan (Hui), Uygur, and Kazakh Identities across China, Central Asia, and Turkey". *History and Anthropology* 9, no. 4 (1996): 445–77.
Hay, John, ed. *Boundaries in China*. London: Reaktion Books, 1994.
Herman, John E. "Empire in the Southwest: Early Qing Reforms to the Native Chief-

tain System". *Journal of Asian Studies* 56, no. 1 (1997): 47–74.
Hershatter, Gail et al., eds. *Remapping China: Fissures in Historical Terrain*. Stanford: Stanford University Press, 1996.
Holmgren, Jennifer. *Chinese Colonisation of Northern Vietnam*. Canberra: Australian National University Press, 1980.
Lattimore, Owen. *Inner Asian Frontiers of China*. New York: American Geographical Society, 1951.
Legge, James, trans. *The Chinese Classics*. Reprint. Taipei: SMC Publishing, 1994.
Liew Foon Ming. "The Luchuan-Pingmian Campaigns (1436–1449) in the Light of Official Chinese Historiography". *Oriens Extremus* 39, no. 2 (1996): 162–203.
Shiba Yoshinobu. *Commerce and Society in Sung China*, translated by Mark Elvin. Ann Arbor, Michigan: Centre for Chinese Studies, University of Michigan, 1970.
Taylor, Keith Weller. *The Birth of Vietnam*. Berkeley: University of California Press, 1983.
Twitchett, Denis and John K. Fairbank, eds. *The Cambridge History of China*, vol. 7, part 1, "The Ming Dynasty (1368–1644), edited by Denis Twitchett and Frederick W. Mote. Cambridge: Cambridge University Press, 1978–.
Von Glahn, Richard L. "The Country of Streams and Grottoes: Geography, Settlements, and the Civilizing of China's Southwestern Frontier". Ph.D. thesis, New Haven, Connecticut: Yale University, 1983.
Wang Gungwu. "The Chinese Urge to Civilize: Reflections on Change". *Journal of Asian History* 18 (1984): 1–34.
Wiens, Herold J. *Han Chinese Expansion in South China*. Hamden, Connecticut: Shoe String Press, 1967. [Originally published as *China's March toward the Tropics*]
Zou Rong. *The Revolutionary Army*, translated by John Lust. The Hague: Mouton, 1968.

CHINESE BIBLIOGRAPHY

Ban Gu. *Hanshu, juan* 94. Beijing: Zhonghua Shuju, 1975.
Fan Chengda (annotated by Hu Qiwang and Qin Guangguang). *Guihai Yuhengzhi Jiyi Jiaozhu*. Chengdu: Sichuan Minzu Chubanshe, 1986.
Gong Yin. *Zhongguo Tusi Zhidu*. Kunming: Yunnan Minzu Chubanshe, 1992.
Jiang Yingliang. *Zhongguo Minzu Shi*. Beijing: Minzu Chubanshe, 1991.
Liao Xiaojian. "Lun 1406 nian Mingchao yu Annan Zhanzheng de Yuanyin". *Yindu Zhina*, no. 1 (1988), pp. 11–15.
Liu Hongxuan. *Zhongguo Jiangyu Shi*. Wuhan: Wuhan Chubanshe, 1995.
Lü Yiran, ed. *Zhongguo Bianjiang Shidi Lunji*. Harbin: Heilongjiang Jiaoyu Chubanshe, 1991.
Ma Ruheng and Ma Dazheng, eds. *Qingdai Bianjiang Kaifa Yanjiu*. Beijing: Xinhua Shudian Chubanshe, 1990.
Ma Yao. *Yunnan Jianshi*. Kunming: Yunnan Renmin Chubanshe, 1991.
Mou Fuli, Cui Ruide, eds. *Jianqiao Zhongguo Mingdai Shi*. Beijing: Zhongguo Shehui Kexue Chubanshe, 1992.

Sima Qian. *Shiji*. Beijing: Zhonghua Shuju, 1963.
Tan Qixiang, ed. *Zhongguo Lishi Dituji*. Beijing: Ditu Chubanshe, 1982–87.
Wang Guowei. *Shuijing Zhujiao*. Shanghai: Shanghai Renmin Chubanshe, 1984.
Weng Dujian. *Zhongguo Minzu Guanxi Shi Gangyao*. Beijing: Zhongguo Shehui Kexue Chubanshe, 1990.
Wu Yongzhang. *Zhongguo Tusi Zhidu Yuanyuan yu Fazhan Shi*. Chengdu: Sichuan Minzu Chubanshe, 1988.
Yang Jialuo, ed. *Lidai Bianzu Zhuanji Huibian*. Taipei: Dingwen Shuju, 1975.
Zou Qiyu et al. *Zhongguo Renkou: Yunnan Fence*. Beijing: Zhongguo Caizheng Jingji Chubanshe, 1989.

參考書目（按漢語拼音序）

范成大原著（胡起望，覃光廣校注），《桂海虞衡志輯佚校注》，成都，1986。
范宏貴，"我國壯族與越南岱族儂族的古今關係"，見范宏貴，顧有識（編），《壯族論稿》，南寧，1989。
樊綽，《蠻書》。
傅恆等（編），《皇清職貢圖》，遼瀋書社，瀋陽，1991。
龔蔭，《中國土司制度》，雲南民族出版社，1992。
廣西壯族自治區少數民族古籍整理出版規劃領導小組（主編），《古壯字字典》，廣西民族出版社，1989。
江應樑，《中國民族史》（上，中，下），北京，1991。
藍勇，《南方絲綢之路》，重慶，1992。
李龍華，"明代的開中法"，《香港中文大學中國文化研究所學報》第4卷第2期（1971）。
廖小健，"論1406年明朝與安南戰爭的原因"，《印度支那》1988年第1期。
呂一燃（主編），《中國邊疆史地論集》，黑龍江教育出版社，哈爾賓，1991。
呂一燃（主編），《南海諸島：地理，歷史，主權》，黑龍江教育出版社，哈爾賓，1992。
呂昭義，《英屬印度與中國西南邊疆（1774–1991年）》，中國社會科學出版社，北京，1996。
羅香林，《蒲壽庚研究》，香港中國學社，1959。
馬汝珩，馬大正（編），《清代邊疆開發研究》。
馬曜（主編），《雲南簡史》，雲南人民出版社，1983。
歐陽修，《新唐書》。
錢古訓原著（江應樑校注），《白夷傳》，雲南人民出版社。
司馬遷，《史記》。
譚其驤，《中國歷史地圖集》（8冊），北京，1992。
王國維（校），《水經注校》，上海再版，1984。
翁獨健（主編），《中國民族關係史綱要》，北京，1990。
吳永章，《中國土司制度淵源與發展史》，四川民族出版社，1988。
鄒啟宇，苗文俊（主編）《中國人口（雲南分冊）》，中國財政經濟出版社，1989。

GLOSSARY

Beijing	北京	Nong Zhigao	侬智高
Chaozhou	潮州	Pien-cheng	《边政公论》
Chung-kuo Pien-cheng	《中国边政》	Kung-lun	
		Qin	秦
Chu	楚	Qin Shi Huangdi	秦始皇帝
Dan	蜑	Qing	清
E-er-tai	鄂尔泰	Quanzhou	泉州
Fan	番	Shu	蜀
Guangdong	广东	Sichuan	四川
Guangxi	广西	Sirenfa	思任发
Hainan	海南	Song	宋
Han	汉	Su Shi	苏轼
Hubei	湖北	Su Xun	苏洵
Hunan	湖南	Tongbao	同胞
Huizhou	惠州	Tusi	土司
Jiangxi	江西	Wang Feng	汪锋
Jin	晋	Wang Jingwei	汪精卫
Kunming	昆明	Wang Shao	王韶
Li	黎	Wumeng	乌蒙
Li Jili	黎季厘	Xishuangbanna	西双版纳
Lianhua Rapids	莲花滩	Yao	瑶
Liao	僚	Yi	夷
Luchuan	麓川	Yongle	永乐
Ma Yuan	马援	Zhangzhou	漳州
Man	蛮	Zhao Tuo	赵佗
Ming	明	Zhu Yuanzhang	朱元章
Nanyue	南越	Zhuang	壮
Nong	侬	Zou Rong	邹容

3

Ecology Without Borders

Su Yongge

Ecology, as conventionally defined, is a science that deals with interactions between living organisms and their physical environment. Human beings have now achieved such a dominant role that they are an unprecedented ecological factor controlling ecosystems on the planet. A more practical way to define ecology might be to say that it concerns human beings in relation to their living environment, a relationship which has developed into a serious crisis.

All things undergo change in structure and function through time and space, and ecosystems are no exception. To define how "ecochange" works in practice is difficult, but it may be useful to express ecochange in terms of the loss of biological diversity. Biological diversity or biodiversity is the totality of genes, species, and ecosystems in a region. Human cultural diversity could also be considered part of biodiversity.

Borders are frontier areas of national states. In imagination and application, borders are political constructions which cut across the natural environment. There are of course differences in political systems, economic processes, and cultural activities between states. However, the differences on the ground are not great in the border areas between China and mainland Southeast Asia. For instance, there are eighteen transboundary ethnic minorities in these border areas (Liu Zhi 1994): the Zhuang, Dai, Bouyei, Miao (Hmong), Yao, Yi (Lolo), Hani (Akha), Jingpo (Kachin), Lisu, Lahu, Nu, Achang, Derung, Wa, Blang, Deang,

Kemu, and Mang. Each group speaks its own language, but also shares some cultural experiences in the management of the natural resources with other ethnic groups. The border to them may be either meaningless or merely artificial; the ethnic groups of southwest China are bound by geography and history to the ethnic groups of mainland Southeast Asia.

Certainly, plants and animals do not carry passports to cross such borders. Ecology has no borders, but rather has niches. The borders of states are not binding on biological aspects of ecology. In fact, the interchanges among all living forms, including human beings and their environments, follow the interflow of energy and materials.

Nonetheless, borders in some sense separate not only human beings but also divide the natural environment. This can be seen if we consider changes in ecology brought about by state policies and by differing perceptions of nature on different sides of the border. The following review of the historical aspects of ecological change around border areas from 1949 to the present confirms this. From this point of view, we can see that ecology does have borders.

ECOLOGICAL CHANGES ALONG THE BORDER BEFORE 1990

The borders between and among China, Vietnam, Laos, and Myanmar were only delineated in the late nineteenth and early twentieth centuries (Liu Zhi 1994). Since 1949, the borders have been modified only a little.

Southern Yunnan and the western part of Guangxi province, together with the northern part of mainland Southeast Asia, are in the same geographical zone. The tropical climate and abundant rainfall have created huge areas of dense forest cover, fertile land, and a richness of natural resources. As a result, these areas are not only the kingdom of plants and animals, but have also been an early place of settlement for various ethnic groups. The numerous river valleys used to be passageways for their ancestors to migrate and corridors for exchange among human cultures.

Even if a degree of deforestation resulted from shifting cultivation practised by transboundary minorities in the tropical forests of Southeast Asia, the damage to ecosystems was minimal. The reason for this was the low population density, less than fifteen people per square kilometre, and the use of only sharp sticks or hoes to cultivate (Liu Zhi 1990).

3. Ecology Without Borders

The population density of the Xishuangbanna area in southern Yunnan was 10.4 persons per square kilometre in 1949. By comparison, the density had climbed to 41.4 per square kilometre in 1990. Historically, the tropical border areas in southern Yunnan had been perceived by most Han Chinese as infested with malaria. They were afraid to go there for fear of "breathing in malaria", which would cause rapid death. Thus in 1949, the Han population of Xishuangbanna was only 5,000 (Liu Zhi 1990). In contrast, by 1990 the Han population had reached 201,540, or about 25 per cent of the total population in Xishuangbanna (Zheng 1993).

It is hard to estimate how many species there were in this border area before 1949, but we know that humans had relatively little impact on the ecology there. In 1949, Xishuangbanna was home to many wildlife species such as Asian elephants, tigers, leopards, gaurs,[1] Asiatic black bears, slow lorises,[2] monkeys such as the pigtail macaques and the Francois' leaf monkeys, Chinese pangolins,[3] green peafowls, water monitors,[4] Burmese pythons, and Asian cobras. A seventy-three-year-old Dai informant from Man Jinglan village, near the Mekong River south of Jinghong in Xishuangbanna, told me that before 1949 there was a huge dense tropical forest around their paddy fields. If fewer than three people went out to work in the fields, they were afraid of being attacked by large animals such as elephants, tigers, and black bears. Green peafowls were commonly seen near the banks of the Mekong River. Villagers used to hunt at least one wild boar per day. Pheasants were often hunted. Therefore, in terms of ecological balance in the border area, man had limited ecological impact. As the population doubled or tripled, the percentage of forest cover decreased at the same rate.

Since the establishment of the People's Republic of China (PRC), forest coverage in the whole country had decreased from 21 per cent in early 1949 to less than 9 per cent in 1990; in Yunnan the percentage fell from more than 50 per cent to approximately 12 per cent in 1988.

Land-use policy has been reformed several times since 1949, with the main changes occurring in 1950, 1958, and 1982 (Guo 1995). The land-use policy from 1950 to 1958 was that all land was taken over by the state. Land and forest ownership tentatively belonged to, and was managed by, the Farmers' Union. People in the villages, organized into family units, shared these resources uniformly and equitably. In carrying out this policy the government did not pay enough attention to local wishes, especially to traditional perspectives on nature and the environment. Primeval forest was disturbed and replaced by artificial forest. Trees for firewood and special cash trees such as rubber were planted and developed.

The period that began with the appearance of People's Communes and the Great Leap Forward in 1958–59 and ending with the nightmare of the Cultural Revolution (1966–76) created by Mao Zedong was the darkest time in China not only for its people but also for its natural environment. Land, forests, and other property were taken over by the collectives. Members of the collectives worked, reaped, and shared forest resources together. During this period, regulations on the ownership of the land for private use and for raising livestock changed several times (Guo 1995). During the ill-fated Great Leap Forward, state-planned logging was carried out on a large scale, resulting in serious damage to forests and the environment.[5] Other factors, such as collective iron and steel smelting, collective kitchens, and the releasing of "satellites" (a term for the reporting of fictitious data designed to please those higher up the bureaucratic hierarchy) also led to the destructive cutting of forest for fuel. In that period, even in forestry areas without roads, trees were cut down although there was no way to move them out. In one year, the forestry department of Yangwu, for example, left about 80,000 cubic metres of wood to rot, and the Nanpanjiang department cut 30,000 cubic metres that were also left to rot just in order to report the economic output to the government (Zhang and Yang 1994). At the time, there was no awareness of the need to protect nature, and this period was one of the biggest forestry disasters in China's history.

The Cultural Revolution led to further havoc. This movement attempted to destroy traditional Chinese culture and establish a new Chinese socialism. The forest became no one's property. The whole country was in an anarchic situation. Consequently, there was great freedom to abuse natural resources. In order to extricate themselves from the difficulties caused by the Cultural Revolution, that is from the lack of work, of schooling, of food and clothes for survival, people individually or in groups took up "a few axes" to chop down trees. In this way, Yunnan lost huge volumes of forests. In many places, the forest lost the capacity to recover on its own. This can now be seen most clearly in central Yunnan.

According to a survey made in Yunnan between 1978 and 1980, the relationship between natural growth in forest volume and consumed volume of forest was as follows. The consumed volume of forest was 26,900,000 cubic metres per year and the natural growth volume of forest was 14,700,000 cubic metres per year. Thus the net consumed volume of forest resources was 12,200,000 cubic metres annually. According to Zhang and Yang (1994), consumed forest can be divided thus:

- wood for fuel: 16,500,000 cubic metres,
- forest fire and destructive cutting of forest 2,000,000 cubic metres,
- forest for industrial use 8,400,000 cubic metres (that is, planned cutting of 2,000,000 cubic metres and unplanned cutting of 6,400,000 cubic metres)

Further deforestation followed the implementation of *liangshandaohu*, a policy that allocated land and forest for private use to individual households, and of the *linyesanding* policy in the period 1979–84 in Yunnan. *Linyeshanding* is a Chinese forestry policy term, sometimes called the "Three Objects of Forestry", meaning stabilizing forest ownership, confirming, and delimiting forest land owned by individuals and establishing the responsibility system for forestry products (Zhao 1993). Most of the collective land was allocated to households under the responsibility system. This seemed a positive development in responding to the needs of people and local communities. However, throughout the period from the land reform of the 1950s to the adoption of the "Three Objects of Forestry" in the 1980s, ownership of forest was unstable, confused, and unclear. This touched off a big debate on landholding rights. Because of the recently experienced nightmares of the "Anti-Rightist Campaign", the "Great Leap Forward", the "Same Big Pot", the "People's Communes", and the "Cultural Revolution", people were afraid that government policy would again be changed, hence they felt they should cut the forest while they could. For instance, in the Zhuoxi village of the Akha in Mojiang county in Yunnan, in a single day nearly four hectares of state-owned natural forest was cut for shifting cultivation (Guo 1995). In the Jiangbian forest, hundreds of people went into a logging frenzy and cut down trees for no clear purpose, heedless of the consequences. The forest was disappearing at a shocking rate. The local government had to use force to control the situation (Zhang and Yang 1994).

Tropical southern Yunnan, especially the area of Xishuangbanna, has suffered additional damage from the transformation of tropical forest to rubber tree plantations and other cash crops. The Xishuangbanna Dai Autonomous Prefecture, whose head of government has to be a member of the Dai nationality, is located in the northern fringes of the tropics in south Yunnan and has an area of 19,112.5 square kilometres. Of this, more than 60 per cent was covered with forest in the 1950s.

Xishuangbanna used to be regarded as a beautiful, mysterious, and remote place, inhabited by more than thirteen ethnic groups. In 1949 the Dai made up 53 per cent of the population as compared with 2.5 per cent of Han Chinese.

By the end of 1989, forest area covered by rubber plantations had already reached 886.67 square kilometres or about 7 per cent of the total land area. However, in pursuing big profits to be made from the rubber business, twice the area of the rubber plantations had to be cleared for houses, roads, and other purposes. Therefore, about 14 per cent of the total land of Xishuangbanna had been transferred to rubber plantations or to land related to them by the year 1990. The area covered by primary forests was reduced by about 20 per cent, because the plantations occupied mostly low hills situated at the edges of valleys, *bazhi* at an elevation below 900 metres above sea level. These hills were the "Sacred Hills" of the Dai ethnic groups (Zhu 1993; Liu, Xu, and Tao 1993) and used to be covered by tropical rainforests. During the Cultural Revolution, the veneration of the "Sacred Hills" was considered superstitious, and most of these hills were destroyed and turned into rubber plantations. While the move to plant rubber started out in the context of a political agenda, it continued under subsequent economic planning. The rubber industry in Yunnan was by no means the optimal way to achieve the goals of the ideology of the "three main benefits", namely, the social, economic, and ecological benefits.

Since 1958, the provincial government of Yunnan has set up twenty-four nature reserves. Due to human interference, fourteen were seriously damaged and none of them survived entirely intact. The result was the loss of biological resources as well as a decline, especially in the 1980s, in the value and significance attached to the issue of conservation. For example, the Damenglong Nature Reserve[6] in Xishuangbanna is now totally covered with rubber trees; originally the reserve was 400 square kilometres in area. The area of the Mengyan Nature Reserve is now less than 300 square kilometres. The Menglun Nature Reserve was 70 square kilometres, but has now been reduced to nothing. The Mengla Nature Reserve was also made smaller by rubber plantations and the introduction of cash crops such as Flower Amomum (*Amomum villosum*, a fruit for medicinal use), Tsaoko Cardamom (*A. tsao-ko*, a fruit used as a medicine and a spice), and sugar-cane.

These ecological changes within China, with Yunnan as an example, are mainly a result of the land-use policy changes and political movements. The above events are the main reasons for the decline of the forest coverage in Yunnan, from more than 50 per cent in the early 1950s to less than 12 per cent in 1990. This has caused many precious species there to move to the edge of extinction.

OPENING OF THE BORDER AND ITS ECOLOGICAL IMPACT

One of the policy options open to a state that seeks economic development is frontier trade. Since 1985, the land borders between China and the states in mainland Southeast Asia have opened one after the another, following the normalization of diplomatic relations. Many new industrial centres and special economic zones have been established along the borders, such as Dongxing, Pingxiang, Hekou, Jingshuihe, Canyuan, Jinghong, Wanding, and Ruili in China; Mong Cai, Lang Son, and Lao Cai in Vietnam; Phongsaly, Oudomxay, Luang Namtha, and Muang Sing in Laos; and Menlar, Bangsa, Nemkan, and Muse in Myanmar.

Between 1985 and 1995 frontier trade between Yunnan province and its neighbouring countries (Vietnam, Laos, and Myanmar) gave rise to an unprecedented level of prosperity. At the same time, the availability of natural resources from these countries stimulated market demand for wildlife to be used in Chinese traditional medicines and food. This cross-border trade involves more than 190 vertebrate species (Li et al. 1996), as well as commercial timber, which is either destined for the Chinese market or is re-exported from China to international markets such as Taiwan, Hong Kong, Japan, and Europe.

CHINA

The Yunnan provincial government has, since the mid-1980s, promoted a strategy of "Onward toward mainland Southeast Asia". Since 1988 the central government has developed several guiding principles, such as "the East connecting with the coasts, the West towards Southeast Asia"; the "Opening up to the outside world, mainly Southeast Asia" in 1990; and the "Opening up of the southern gate of China, onward to Asia and the Pacific" in 1991 (Song 1993).

In talking about local forest resources, Xu (1993) has written:

> The richest forest resources are to be found near China's borders. Sixty square kilometres of teak trees and 133 square kilometres of various species of hardwood were discovered recently just outside of Yinjiang County ... As for the exploitation of forest resources from northern Myanmar for

export to China, transportation is much easier, costs are low and it is convenient to bring Chinese labourers into Myanmar to cut trees. ... Myanmar has made several requests to us for the exploitation of its forest resources jointly with China. ... Importing timber from Myanmar has many advantages. Firstly, there are many species of trees, in good quality, obtainable at a cheap price; secondly using timber from this source can support the increasing demands from China's domestic markets and reduce the amount of the forest cut in Southwest China, thus protecting our environment ... Thirdly, we can develop our timber processing industries (cutting of teak, producing wood fibre, paper mills, furniture manufacturing), and assist local economic development ... Myanmar is the only country in which we do not have to pay foreign currency (we can pay directly in Chinese yuan, renminbi) for imported timber.

In fact, Myanmar is playing the leading role in compensating for the shortfall in the consumed volume of forest in Yunnan.

Ecosystem level

The establishment of the Tongbiguan nature reserve, located in the counties of Yingjiang, Longchuan, and Ruili in Yunnan on the northern Myanmar border, was approved in 1986. In fact, local people and the government had since 1949 been regarding it as a protected area. The nature reserve covers an area of 341.58 square kilometres, of which 90 per cent is southern sub-tropical seasonal rainforests, with rare flora and fauna. Precious trees found there include *Cinnamomum tamala, Depterocarpus turbinatus, Phoebe lanceolata,* and *Shorea assamica*; animals found there include white-handed gibbons, tigers, gaurs, and deer. From 1991 to 1993, a modern road was built through the core areas of the nature reserve, dividing it into two parts. Interestingly, the purpose of the road was to allow the easy transportation of timber and other natural resources from Myanmar. Consequently, people could now easily exploit the resources of the nature reserve as well as poach wildlife.

The same development is true for the town of Guanlu, in Mengla county in Xishuangbanna, in an area covered by huge tropical rainforests. A small ferry used to ply across the Mekong River. There were no roads, and humans had little impact. However, in 1994, the centuries-long isolation was broken by the construction of 28 kilometres of highway connecting Guanlu to Mamushu and further to the capital of Mengla county. Guanlu became a huge cargo port in 1995, due to the demands of frontier trade with Houei Sai, Pak Beng, Luang Prabang, and Vientiane in Laos and Nong Khai in Thailand. Like other frontier ports, Guanlu was quickly full of uniform Chinese-style buildings and "land" diggers

3. Ecology Without Borders

in the real-estate business. (Guo and He 1993).

An old Dai gentleman whom I met for the first time in 1996 was standing, bamboo walking stick in hand, overlooking Manzhang Dai village in Dalou. He was contemplating the construction of buildings on the paddy fields where he had spent almost his entire life. The village is covered with concrete roads and buildings for the new Dalou port, in the Dalou Economic Zone. He said he could not understand this, and that no one in the village wanted to be a "city citizen" of the economic zone. When they were classified as city dwellers they lost their right to use their farmland. After that, the local government was able to get the land from the farmers for a very modest commpensation or even as a "donation to the construction of the Motherland". The government was then free to sell the land to enterprises, making a big profit.

What kind of feelings did the old man have towards the frontier trade going on in his hometown? He told me: "We are indigenous people who have been changed into outsiders." What a strange game! Let the developers lose their rights to develop!

Species level

If one simply asks people involved in selling wildlife in local markets and restaurants along the border whether their trade is illegal, the answer will probably be:

> Yes, this is illegal trade, but these animals and plants are from abroad. This is 'foreign wildlife', so it is not a serious problem at all; at least we do not hunt and sell the wildlife of the motherland.

The unceasing lust for wildlife, due to frontier trade, has made Hekou, a Chinese border town with a population of less than twenty-five thousand, a well-known place in Yunnan for legal shopping and the eating of wild animals. This is the only tourist attraction of the town. Nearby, between Hekou county and Pingbian county, is the Daweishan Nature Reserve covering an area of 153.65 square kilometres. It is inhabited by rich fauna and flora, with more than twenty nationally protected animals.[7] Ironically, in the town of Hekou situated less than 80 kilometres from the reserve, many of these species can be found caged and offered for sale from stalls specializing in the wild animal trade. In Hekou, this trafficking in "foreign animals" has existed since 1988. The animal trade reached its peak in the period between 1990 and 1994; in that period almost all the restaurants served dishes of wild animals to attract customers.

Recently, although business has not been as frenzied as before, at least ten stalls were dealing in this evil and "legal" business. I was once witness to a confusing scene involving the "illegal" and "legal" trafficking of wild animals in Hekou. A man selling slow loris and some snakes was fined by an official of the county's forestry department because he had not paid the business and management tax to the department — about 300 yuan per month (about US$37). This made his activity illegal. Five metres away was another wild animal stall. This one was legal, because the tax had been paid. This phenomenon leaves no doubt that ecology does have its "artificial border".

Another time I observed a local bus driver who was carrying a big snake in a plastic bag. He sold it to one of the stalls in Hekou. He told me that occasionally, on his regular bus duty, he took wildlife from local people and sold it to animal stalls in Hekou. A wild animal seller in Hekou admitted that he had purchased many local animals and sold them for the same price as those from Vietnam. (Some of these animals are actually from the Daweishan Nature Reserve.) In such cases, no one knows where the animal comes from; animals have no passports or indentity cards to show. From this point of view, there is no such thing as a "foreign animal". Borders, foreign countries, foreign peoples, and foreign traditions have nothing to do with the conservation of ecology. These factors only result in the exploitation of natural resources for short-term economic gain.

Human beings have also created another artificial border. The same rare animal or plant is regarded differently depending on where it lives. If it lives in China it is protected by Chinese laws, but if it is from elsewhere, its consumption is permitted inside China. Many rare species in the border areas are also exempted from tax on the Chinese side, so it is easy to understand why trade in wildlife has become so rampant since the opening of the borders for frontier trade. Ecology, as a result of man-made borders, consequently has its "borders", because wild animals and plants are categorized differently in the "domestic" and "foreign" systems.

Objectively, this attitude to wildlife, with one eye open and the other shut, provides a clear opportunity as well as stimulation for trafficking in wildlife. This follows the common custom expressed in phrases such as *Ye sheng wu zhu, Shui lie shui you,* "wildlife has no owner; whoever hunts it, owns it". It offers many opportunities for local people along borders to improve their living standard by poaching, smuggling, trafficking, and exploiting wildlife. One day, for example, I was on the

3. Ecology Without Borders

way to Mohan port to do my morning market surveying. I saw a guy in the distance catch a rat-like animal. Later I recognized that it was a Chinese bamboo rat (*Rhizomys sinesis*), which is an endangered species. The terrified animal was tied around its neck and it could hardly breathe. It was left on display in the market for only 5 minutes and was then sold for 25 yuan (about US$3) to three Han Chinese men. I interviewed both the seller and buyers. The seller said he saw it first, so it belonged to him; the buyers said they had bought it from the market — there was nothing wrong with that, and they were not guilty of anything. Imperceptibly, this created a circumstance in which wildlife could be consumed in public without any of the guilt normally associated with illegal activities. Markets represent the attitude of government. If you can sell something in a market, I can buy it without problem. This is the logic behind this different sense of "legal" and "illegal". Now that many people are involved in trafficking wildlife, prices have fallen to a level that most Chinese can afford. This rise in demand further stimulates supply, and the cycle turns even faster.

Misfortunes never come singly. The drinking water supply for the 140,000 people of Pingbian county comes from the Daweishan Nature Reserve, which apparently was full of tsaoko cardamom plantations. Tsaoko cardamom was in short supply in the Hekou market, and demand exceeded the supply from Vietnam. Therefore, both local government administrations and individual farmers swarmed into the forests of the nature reserve and quickly cleared the ground for plantations even deep inside the forest. Again, the local forestry department taxed the plantation owners twenty to thirty Chinese yuan per *mu* (about 1/15 hectare) to compensate for the loss of natural resources. This then became legal too.

Bounded by Pingbian and Hekou counties, Jinping county (on the border with Lai Chau in Vietnam) once had a nature reserve called Fenshuiling. This was in an even worse situation than the Daweishan Nature Reserve, not only because of the planting of cardamom and amomum, but also because of the destructive cutting of primary forest. The primary forest has been totally replaced by secondary forest. Late in autumn, many species of migratory birds fly to tropical Yunnan to live through their winter in this so-called kingdom of animals. However, one cannot be optimistic about the fate of these birds. What awaits them are hunters, the market-stall, and the cooking pot. Recently this bird hunting has been especially popular in Jinping county as a seasonal fashion. According to the statistics of the forestry department of Jinping county, about 17,400 wild animals and 15,800 "harmful birds" were hunted in 1957. From 1957 to 1990, the total number of wild animal skins purchased by local commercial departments was 165,800, that is, an average of 5,024 per year. From 1972 to 1984, 26,400 kilogrammes of wild animal bones were sold. This resulted in many wild animals (such as tigers, leopards, black bears, gaurs, muntjacs,[8] and monkeys) disappearing from the region. I was told by local Yao people living there that they had not heard of any large mammals being seen for many years. This may be why eating migratory birds has become popular — because there is nothing else to hunt. For years now, birds such as sparrows, for example, have disappeared from most places in Yunnan. Also the local people in Xishuangbanna have observed this change. They told me that they can hardly bear the silence all year round, and that they miss the songs of birds, that of the sparrow in particular.

Although China has laws to protect plants (China Environmental Conservation Agency 1991) and animals (Ministry of Forestry 1994), in practice the laws seem to be weak and seem to have no power, especially in the border areas.[9] This doctrine of "economy first" has been applied everywhere along the border areas. Objectively, there is nothing wrong with human economic development in the region. However, treating nature as a static and unfeeling background awaiting human change, and viewing with hostility local forms of natural resource management, favours the interests of state and private enterprises over local interests. This violates the principle of sustainable development. Once in a discussion with an Xishuangbanna official concerning the relationship between economic development and conservation of natural environments, I was clearly told that we cannot have both. Man will always triumph over nature.

MYANMAR AND TIMBER TRADE

The timber trade is one of the most significant causes of forest degradation and loss world-wide. The forests of northern Myanmar bordering China are under pressure from timber exploitation as well as from the encroachment resulting from logging roads and camps.

Since 1988, China has accelerated the speed of its timber imports from Myanmar. Most of the timber is excellent hardwood, including teak. There are about 12,000 recorded species of trees in this area, of which less than eighty have been classified as having the potential for industrial use (Myanmar Delegation 1994). However, it is hard to say which species are under threat from logging, because the area covered by forest is so huge. People in Myanmar see forests as an inexhaustible resource, because they are renewable. Thus the clearing of primary forests along the main roads extending for about 40 kilometres into Myanmar makes perfect sense. Large numbers of businessmen from places such as Taiwan, Hong Kong, Japan, and China have arrived to exploit the link between timber, forests, and border trade. Timber has simply become the number one business on the China-Myanmar border. There is not a single firm, company, or businessman here that does not deal with timber. There are now several Chinese ports specializing in timber imports; in Pianma, Tengchong, Yingjiang, Zhangfeng, Ruili, and Wanding one can see mountains of timber. Trucks carry timber in a seemingly endless convoy into China. Many sawmills have been built along the border area on the Chinese side. In 1988 there were, for example, only thirteen small factories manufacturing wood in Dehong Prefecture, each with an annual output of about 10,000 Chinese yuan. In 1996, there were seventy-four sawmills in the area with an average annual output of over 100,000 yuan each, out of a total amount of about 80 million yuan (about US$10 million). What a business!

Logging is often carried out under contracts made between Chinese firms and the local authorities, who are often the same as the anti-government armed forces. The procedure is as follows. A down-payment (usually about US$2,500) is given in order to obtain a permit from the local authorities. This enables the company to assume temporary possession of the forest. Then the Chinese company is allowed to bring Chinese labourers into Myanmar to build roads and cut trees. At the Burmese check-point before entering China, each firm has to pay 130 yuan per cubic metre of logs. The problem for most firms is that the mountain roads are not good and that each year the rainy season is five months or longer. If they only could, they would cut every tree and transport every log into China. The rain, however, slows down the progress of logging as well as the transporting of it. For example, during the dry season, the Houqiao port has 150 timber trucks arriving daily; in peak season this number will reach 200. In fact, most crossing-points between China and Myanmar are always busy with timber transportation.

As the by-product of the timber trade, the trade in wildlife has, of course, never before been so prosperous as it is today. In Ruili, wild animal parts such as Asian elephant skins, gall bladders of the brown bear (*Ursus arctos*), and bones and skin of the Indochinese tiger (*Panthera tigris*) are for sale in the markets,[10] and game is also served in some restaurants. During a wildlife conservation campaign in Ruili city on 20 September 1996, more than 3,100 wild animals were found captive.[11] These were freed from their cages of the damned and returned to nature. The threat to natural forests is directly related to the timber trade, a trade that not only causes the loss of species and genetic material, but also soil erosion and a decreased ability to function as effective watershed catchments.

After the forests are gone, what will the local people do for a living in the huge waste lands that they will be left with?

VIETNAM AND TRADE IN WILD ANIMALS

From my own fieldwork, and based on what I have read, it is clear that the greater part of the trafficking in wild animals in China is related to the opening of the border with Vietnam. Although there is inadequate baseline data regarding the flora and fauna in the forests along the border areas in Vietnam, it is evident from what one can observe and what one hears repeatedly about the wild animals traded either in local markets or even in Kunming, Guangzhou, Nanning, Chengdu, Wuhan, Nanjing, Shanghai, and Beijing, that these forests possess great biological richness. These wild animals are served in local and city restaurants, and are also used in traditional medicinal manufacture. People consciously or unconsciously exploit the power of the "Chinese tradition" to make disproportionate profits from wild animals.

According to the surveys (Li et al. 1996) conducted in Guangdong and Guangxi provinces between 1990 and 1995, more than 190 vertebrate species were found in the trade from Vietnam. Among them were twenty-one species which according to the Convention on International Trade in Endangered Species (CITES) of Wild Fauna and Flora are classified as Class I (fully protected) and seventy-three species as Class II (trade requires permits). The purpose of CITES is to protect engangered species world-wide. China became a member of CITES in 1981, and this should have resulted in the protection of many of the species traded in the border region, but unfortunately has not.

Of the hundreds of thousands of freshwater turtles and tortoises traded in Vietnam each year, the vast majority are taken from the wild. Although some of this trade occurs within the country, the trade is dominated by the demand for reptiles in China, where they are used for food and in the preparation of tonics and medicines (Duc and Broad 1995).

The saddest thing I saw in Hekou was the trade in various species of monkeys, especially the slow loris.[12] Based on my own investigation, I estimate that at least one slow loris per day disappears from the planet in these ugly cages and stalls. This, in one year is 365 and in ten years is 3,650. The mortality of wild animals in illegal trade is supposed to be about 80 per cent, that is, if two reach the market successfully, eight have already died on the way from a forest to a market. This works out to 18,250 slow loris being destroyed over a period of ten years in Hekou. Unfortunately, because so little is known about the actual conditions in which these wild animals are living, it is impossible at present to quantify the effects of the frontier trade. With a borderline of about 5,000 kilometres and around 150 official land ports and passages between China, Vietnam, Laos, and Myanmar, one can only imagine what goes on. It is truly a pity that some species that even trained biologists find hard to identify in the field have become part of traditional food and medicine.

The Vietnamese are the largest suppliers of wildlife, the Chinese are the biggest consumers of wildlife and, by all accounts, Yunnan seems to be the best place for a slaughterhouse of wild animals. This is because in Chinese the name Yunnan means the "kingdom of animals" and consequently attracts wild animal eaters. For example, Magouhe, situated half way between the cities of Kunming and Qujing, was once a small village town with fewer than 100 households. Here drivers and passengers would take a rest and have a meal in one of the few restaurants. Not long ago, the number of restaurants increased rapidly and the town became well known because of the real wild animal dishes that were openly served there. Magouhe now has more than 120 restaurants and is not only a place where wild animal dishes are served, but is also a centre for gathering and distributing wild animals. Nobody knows exactly how many wild animals have been destroyed here, where these animals come from, or how they got here. The provincial department of forestry security took sudden action and carried out an inspection of restaurants in Magouhe from the 10 May to 20 June 1996. Within forty days, 1,715 wild animals were found.[13] And this is from only one single operation carried out by a local forestry official within a six-year period. How many such forty-day periods are there in six years?

LAOS AND WILDLIFE

The cross-border trade in wildlife in northern Laos is not as overt as in

Vietnam, although it has been going on since the opening up of the land borders with China in 1985. The rapid growth of the Chinese population in the area provides a link between market demand and wildlife. In 1995, there were about 20,000 Chinese people living and working in northern Laos, mainly working for Chinese companies building roads, bridges, houses, and hydro-electric power stations.

Two Chinese families from Sichuan live in Oudomxay in Laos, and have a big business trading in wild and endangered animals, especially young ones. People call their house a "mini zoo". In their small rented rooms (the rent is around US$12 per month), there were several crudely constructed animal cages. Here I saw a three-kilogram baby Asiatic Black Bear (*Ursus thibetanus*). I was told that this animal was often sold to an animal bile pharmaceutical factory in China for making gall bladder tonic. In the first three months of 1995, nine baby Black Bears had already been sold. I also saw many softshell turtles,[14] some shells of Chinese pangolins (*Manis pentadactyla*) that are used for medicinal purposes, several species of monkeys, including slow loris (*Nycticebus coucang*, called "Lazy Monkey" in Chinese), and a Rhesus Macaques Monkey (*Macaca mulatta*) who was trying to get out of the cage. I was amazed that there was a living baby spotted leopard (*Panthera pardus*) in a bamboo cage. They kept telling me that if I was really interested in buying a baby tiger (*Panthera tigris*), they would bring it to me immediately from a nearby house.

No one seems to know that wild animals are not supposed to be hunted and traded. The two Chinese families were proud of their business because in three years they did not had any losses (for example, being caught by the police). I was told that the best business is selling turtles and shells of pangolins. They also explained that it would not be a problem to send the animal directly to Mengla in China if I would buy one, because they have their methods of smuggling animals across the borders. One method is to hide them in a Chinese company car, jeep, or truck which usually is checked carelessly by Laotian custom agents, because these vehicles are identified as belonging to "Chinese experts" or, in other words, to Chinese aid projects in Laos. Another method is to smuggle the animals along a certain path through the tropical rainforest at a certain time by a certain group of people. Not many people know about these paths, especially not the government people on both sides.

There is another option open for local people who wish to participate in the cross-border trade in wildlife. Mrs Ila (not her real name) is a Dai woman, a mother of two children living in a village near the China-Laos border on the Chinese side. She is doing business in the wild animal and rare plant trade. Once every two weeks she travels back and forth from Mengla to Oudomxay and Pak Beng. There she gathers the shells of pangolins, the hides of wild animals (black bear, tiger, leopard, wild cat, and so forth) and some medicinal plants such as the one which is commercially called *Jinxianchao* (*Anoectochilus roxhurghii*), belonging to the orchid family and intensely desired by Taiwanese businessmen.[15] It is very expensive in the Chinese market, fetching around US$10 per kilogram when fresh. The problem is that the source of the plant species in tropical Yunnan has been exhausted for several years now, as a result of illegal trafficking. Mrs Ila has no language problems in dealing with Lao and Chinese traders, and also knows Laotian customs. She has had more success than other Chinese-speaking traders. She carries the "goods" from Laos directly to her home, where Chinese businessmen know they can buy the "goods" at a certain price. Some things are clearly out of the government's control, especially the black market for wild and rare animals and plants.

This has been the story of what has been happening to natural resources since the opening of the border, a story that is written in blood.

CONCLUSION

Ecology has no borders. Like other parts of the world, the tropical forests and other fragile ecosystems of mainland Southeast Asia are disappearing as a result of the open border policy. Many species, both plants and animals, are threatened with extinction.

Borders are political constructions which cut across the natural environment. By opening up the borders for frontier trade, the ecology around the border areas has been dramatically affected, because of the political, economic, and cultural differences between the neighbouring countries. The impact is more profound than at any other time in history. A peaceful co-operation between the countries on the issue of nature conservation is required in order to maintain a good environment and sustainable development in the border areas.

The rapid growth of China's economy has led to demands for natural resources such as timber, minerals, and raw materials for pharmaceuticals. The traditional health and food habits of the Chinese lead to a demand for rare animals and plants. This has created great pressure on the ecology of mainland Southeast Asian states. For some people, the aim is to extend the politics, economy, and culture of China across the borders, while for others, the aim is merely to exploit the natural resources for economic gain. In this regard, Vietnam, Laos, and Myanmar are in fact part of China's ecosystem.

By studying the consequences of ecological, cultural, and political changes in the area since the opening up of the borders, I have attempted to show the interrelation between ecology and the borders. Borders are the outcome of narrow nationalism. There is only one earth. Any behavior that damages nature, either on the part of individuals (poaching, smuggling, and trafficking in wildlife) or governments (using the pretext of economic development to transfer their own problems and pressures across the border) should be prohibited. In felling trees, we strike at the basis of human existence.

The border areas between China and mainland Southeast Asian states are dominated by transboundary ethnic groups and are relatively rich in natural resources. The economic, agricultural, and health conditions of the people are dependent on these resources. Local peoples have traditionally and historically been stewards of most of the natural resources. An inextricable link exists between culture and biodiversity. When natural resources are exploited and when the economy in particular areas is developed, the indigenous cultures, the life-styles, and the knowledge about the traditional resources should be respected and taken into consideration. Representatives of the native ethnic groups should form part of the management of natural resources in order to avoid the impoverishment of these marginal ethnic groups.

The land border between China and mainland Southeast Asian states serves not only as a demarcation between countries, but also as an invisible factor leading to profound ecological change. The contrasting ecological changes that we can see in the various regions arise from different rates of economic expansion, population growth, and demands on natural resources. When the destruction of forests by humans has reached a certain point, the social-economic development will be restricted. Once the balance of mutual benefits between humans and nature is destroyed, the economy will decline. Eventually, a new economic cycle may start again. It seems like a never-ending game which humans like to play: ecology without borders and borders without ecology.

ACKNOWLEDGMENT

I am especially grateful to Dr Grant Evans who directed this study. Without his help

3. Ecology Without Borders

this study could not have been accomplished. Thanks also due to Miss Janet C. Sturgeon, Dr Ken Marr, Dr Geoff Wade, Dr Christopher Hutton, Dr Zhang Rong, Professor Long Chunlin, Mr Bai Xingui, and Khamngern, for their constant assistance and interest.

NOTES

1. Gaur is the name for wild "Indian" cattle, or wild oxen.
2. The slow loris is a monkey-like animal.
3. The Chinese pangolin is a scaly ant-eater.
4. Monitors are large tropical lizards of genus *Varanus*, and they emit warning signals on the approach of crocodiles.
5. For instance, the small forestry department of Jiangbian in Yunnan cut down 500,000 cubic metres of timber during the year 1958. This was done only so that they could report to the higher authorities that they had successfully fulfilled the state plan.
6. The Biogeographical Community Research Station of Tropical Forests is situated in this nature reserve. The station was established in the 1950s by the state.
7. Examples of nationally protected animals found in Daweishan are black gibbons, the slow loris, tigers, leopards, bears, *Eurypholios major* (a poisonous snake), oriental long-tailed lizards, Chinese pangolins, Rusa unicolors (a kind of deer that lives in forests), large Indian civets, tokays (a lizard), *Gallus gallus* (wild chicken), pythons, cobras, silver pheasants, green peafowls, and owls.
8. Muntjac is a small deer, originally from Southeast Asia, of genus *Muntiacus*, the male of which has tusks and small antlers.
9. Most of the species discussed in the present chapter are found in the list of Carey (1996), which includes more than 240 endangered animals and more than 170 endangered plant species.
10. Other wild animal parts traded in Ruili are bones and skin of the leopard (*Panthera pardus*), horn of rhinoceros (*Didernocerus sumatrensis*), and gaur (*Bos gaurus*).
11. Among the wild animals found captive were the green peafowl (*Pavo muticus*), sun bear (*Helarctos malayanus*), the monkey Assam macaque (*Macaca assamensis*), Burmese python (*Python molurus*), and wild chicken (*Gallus gallus*).
12. In Hekou, freshwater turtles and tortoises are the most commonly traded animals. Other animals observed in the market and reported by informants were the lesser slow loris (*Nycticebus pygmaeus*), pileate gibbon (*Hylobates pileatus*), flying squirrel (*Hylopetes alboniger*), *Agkistrodon acutus, Eurypholis majoy, Ocadia sinensis, Cyclemys trifasciata*, red child salamander (an amphibian, *Tylototriton verrucosus*), and birds such as the barn owl (*Tyto albo*), the cat face owl (*Tyto capensis*), the great barbet (*Megalatima virens*), the crested myna (*Acridotheres crista*), and the grey-headed parakeet (*Clamator coromandus*).

13. Wild animals and animal parts found included twenty-four water monitors (*Varanus salvator*), nine slow lorises (*Nycticebus coucang*), two Indian pythons (*Python molurus*), one piece (about 1 kilogram) of Asiatic elephant skin (*Elephas maximus*), seventy Chinese pangolins (scaly anteater: *Manis pentadactyla*) and its shells (about 150 kilograms), seven Chinese tragopans (a bird: *Tragopan temminckii*), 188 snakes, one horsefield's tortoise (*Testudo horsfieldii*), a whole leopard skeleton (*Panthera pardus*), and two pieces of leopard skins.
14. The softshell turtles that I saw were the Asian giant softshell turtle (*Pelochelys bibroni*), the Chinese softshell turtle (*Trionyx sinensis*), and the Wattle-necked softshell turtle (*Trionyx steidachneri*).
15. The purchase of plants of the orchid family is prohibited in accordance with the Convention on International Trade in Endangered Species (CITES) of Wild Fauna and Flora.

REFERENCES

Carey, Geoft, ed. *A Biodiversity Review of China*. Hong Kong: World Wide Fund for Nature, 1996.

China Environmental Conservation Agency, Division of Natural Conservation and Department of Management for Nature Reserve and Species. *Rare and Endangered Plant Conservation and Study*. A collection of laws, regulations and documents related to plant conservation. Beijing: China Environmental Science Press, 1991.

Duc Le Dien and Steven Broad. "Investigations into Tortoise and Freshwater Turtle Trade in Vietnam". *TRAFFIC Bulletin* 15, no. 2 (1995): 34.

Guo Huijun. "The Impacts of Land Use Policy on Forest Resource and Biodiversity in Yunnan, China". In *Proceedings of the Regional Dialogue on Biodiversity and Natural Resources Management in Mainland Southeast Asian Economies*, edited by Mingsarn Kaosa-ard and Guo Huijub [The conference was held in Kunming, China, 21–24 February 1995]. Bangkok: Thailand Development and Research Institute, 1995.

Guo Laixu and He Daming. *Opening Up of Passages between China, Laos and Thailand, and the Port Construction of Mengla*. Beijing: China Science and Technology Press, 1993.

Li Wenjun, Todd K. Fuller, and Wang Sung. "A Survey of Wildlife Trade in Guangxi and Guangdong, China". *TRAFFIC Bulletin* 16, no. 1 (1996).

Liu Hongmao, Xu Zaifu, and Tao Guoda. "The Changing Tendency of Plant Species Diversity in Different Status of Xishuangbanna Holy Hills". *Collected Research Papers on Tropical Botany*, no. 2, pp. 32–37. Kunming: Yunnan University Press, 1993.

Liu Zhi. *Enlightenment and Choice: The National Problems of Neighbouring States and a Study of Yunnan Opening Up to the Outside World*. Kunming: Yunnan People's Press, 1994.

Ministry of Forestry, Division of Wildlife and Forest Plant Protection. *A Collection of Laws, Regulations and Documents Related to Wildlife Conservation* (in Chinese). Beijing: China Forestry Publishing House, 1994.

Myanmar Delegation. "The Country Status Report on the Forestry Sector of Myanmar: General Forestry Situation". In *Proceedings for the Workshop on Trans-Boundary Biodiversity Conservation in the Eastern Himalayas*, edited by Ji Weizhi and Alan Rabinowitz, pp. 72–78. Kunming: Conservation Biology Centre at Kunming Institute of Zoology, 1994.

Song Linqing et al. *Towards Southeast Asia: A Study of the Export-Oriented Economy and Port Development in Yunnan.* Kunming: Yunnan People's Publishing House, 1993.

Xu Chenwen. *The Choice beyond Cross-Border Trade.* Kunming: Yunnan People's Publishing House, 1993.

Zhang Maoqin and Yang Huiqiong. "The Contradiction Analysis and the Right Way of Exploitation and Conservation of Ecological Environment of Forest in Yunnan". In *The Study of Co-ordinated Growth of Economic Exploitation and Ecological Environment of Yunnan*, edited by Yao Naizhe and Zhou Yonghua. Kunming: Yunnan People's Press, 1994.

Zhao Junchen. *Social Forestry in Yunnan.* Kunming: Yunnan Science and Technology Press, 1993.

Zheng Peng. *Brief Introduction to Xishuangbanna.* Kunming: Yunnan National Press, 1993.

Zhu Hua et al. "A Survey of the Vegetation on Holy Hills of the Dai Nationality in Xishuangbanna". *Collected Research Papers on Tropical Botany*, no. 2, pp. 14–31. Kunming: Yunnan University Press, 1993.

Negotiating Central, Provincial, and County Policies: Border Trading in South China

Kuah Khun Eng

China has a long border, which it shares with numerous neighbours. In the northeast are the Jilin and Liaoning provinces, both sharing a border with North Korea; in the northwestern region Xinjiang shares a border with Russia; Mongolia is its northern neighbour; Heilongjiang has Russia as its northern neighbour; the west has Kashmir, Nepal, Sikkim, and Bhutan as its neighbours; the southeast has India; and the southwest provinces of Yunnan and Guangxi share a border with Myanmar, Laos, and Vietnam.

Traditionally, mountain ranges have formed natural barriers on long stretches of China's border. These mountains have obstructed communication and social interaction among the many neighbours that live in proximity to one another. Increasingly, however, it is the political boundary that serves to artificially segregate the people living along the border, irrespective of their cultural background. Thus, some scholars argue for the need to explore and study cultural areas instead of political areas. Despite the tight control over border regions, those living along the borders have continued to communicate, interact, and trade with one another, albeit on a small and restricted scale.

Since the communist victory in the civil war in China in 1949, the border regions have been closely guarded and tightly sealed to prevent outside influences from entering China. Apart from political considerations, there were fears that cultural and other forms of social pollution would enter China and thereby upset the morals of the Chinese people. The

4. Negotiating Policies: Border Trading in South China

border regions remained closed until the 1980s. After the death of Mao Zedong in 1976, China under Deng Xiaoping embarked on a new direction of economic liberalization and modernization. This was the 1978 Reform Era, which has become a new watershed for China's economic development. The 1978 Reform has provided the border regions with a legitimate excuse to reopen their borders for trade with neighbouring countries.

The 1980s and 1990s are important decades in the development of the economy of the border regions. During this period, the central, provincial, and county governments devised regulatory frameworks to facilitate the opening of border trade and to ensure that they would be able to have effective control over it. The hope was that these measures would help the region to develop faster.

This chapter examines various policies related to the opening up and management of border trade, the roles of the central, provincial, and county governments in managing this trade and the extent to which politics intrude into border trading. This study is based primarily on official documents, secondary Chinese sources, and some fieldwork.

ECONOMIC REFORM AND BORDER TRADING

For centuries, the border people of the Yunnan and Guangxi provinces have traded with their counterparts across the border.[1] The development of border trade can be divided into three major periods: the first is 1949–78, the second, 1979–91; and the third, from 1992 until the present. During these three periods, different policies governed the development of border trade.

From 1949 until 1978, the trade conducted was small in scale and carried out by farmers on both sides of the border. During this period, border trade was governed by the "Border Trade Policy" administered by the State Council of the central government. Under this policy, there was restriction on the amount of goods one could sell or purchase. Chinese farmers were allowed to purchase up to 30 renminbi worth of goods across the border at each transaction. The exchange boundary was confined to a 10-kilometre stretch from the border to allow those living along the border to buy and sell and to exchange goods — primarily to make up for shortages and to sell the surplus of agricultural produce. This was a closed market situation where the primary aim of trading was to resolve problems of deficiency or surplus pertaining to local production and to cater to the daily needs of the border residents. The border trading permitted then was never intended for conducting trade with foreign neighbours.

This restriction ruled out large-scale trading and also excluded the participation of those living beyond the 10-kilometre zone in the border trade. Despite the restrictions, trade among the residents on both sides of the border continued because of the lack of political will, ineffective border patrol, corrupt officials who were susceptible to bribes, and the resourcefulness of border traders who often smuggled goods across the border. The Chinese side imported raw materials while the Vietnamese and Burmese wanted Chinese manufactured goods that were in constant short supply, and this made the border trading a very lucrative business.

The second phase started with the 1978 Reform and gained momentum during the 1980s. Deng Xiaoping's often-quoted "It does not matter whether it is a black or white cat; it is a good cat as long as it catches mice" (不管是黑猫还是白猫，能捉住老鼠的就是好猫) ushered in a new phase in economic development and modernization in China. The 1978 Reform was a watershed that introduced market socialism and socialist capitalism. The creation of special economic zones and the designation of some coastal cities as important growth nodes were aimed at pushing China into rapid economic development and modernization. These special economic zones and coastal cities were attempts at integrating the Chinese economy into the global economy. In these special regions, joint partnerships with multinationals and transnationals were seen as essential for infrastructure development, technological transfer, and capital and foreign reserve accumulation. They were meant to catapult China into a new phase of development in the twenty-first century.

In creating a liberal developmental environment, the other regions of China were also being brought into the developmental cycle and obliquely, into the global economy, albeit on a restricted scale and at a slower pace. Provincial and local governments also sought greater autonomy in their quest for faster development within their provinces. Those provinces that share political borders with other countries also utilized cross-border trading as a development strategy. It is possible to argue that the new policies pertaining to market economy and international openness had benefited the coastal, interior, and border provinces in different degrees. The slower pace and restricted nature of trading in the interior could be attributed to the fact that the central government had continued to adopt a cautious approach to market socialism.

The second phase culminated in the expansion of the "Border Trade Policy" and the introduction of a formal set of policies formulated by all levels of government, to facilitate the further expansion of trade.[2] This was the famous "Eighth Five-Year Period" (八五期间) of 1985, hence the "1985 Period".

The third phase was brought about specifically after a speech made by Deng Xiaoping in 1989, which placed greater emphasis on border trade as a key factor in the development of the interior and border provinces. This phase started in the early 1990s with the introduction of another set of policies in 1992.

The border regions are treated differently from the interior provinces. The fact that the border provinces share a common boundary with neighbouring countries is seen as an advantage for trade development as it provides an impetus for rapid economic development in these landlocked provinces where the geographical isolation has often been regarded as an economic liability. These border provinces are now seen as strategically located to tap into the potential vast market of the border countries and to expand beyond these border countries.[3] However, at the national level, the central government continues to see the opening of the border as one great security risk. On the social front, there is a fear of the flow of undesirable influences such as cultural pollution and drug abuse, into China via its back doors.

In the border regions, trading has increased significantly and become a part of life among the border residents. It is not uncommon to see 50 to 80 per cent of the border residents engaged in some kind of petty trading in the region. Likewise, border trading has become an important source of revenue for local and provincial governments. In Yunnan and Guangxi, border trading and related activities contributed over 50 per cent of their provincial and county revenue.

The neighbouring border countries — Myanmar (previously known as Burma), Laos, and Vietnam — have become important trading partners with these southwestern Chinese provinces. Border trade has renewed economic as well as social relationship between the people living at the border. From the 1980s onwards, kin relations and minorities from both sides of the border have begun to interact with one another, re-integrating, and revitalizing minority cultures along the border region. For the first time it is possible to speak of an integrated cultural area instead of one separated by a political boundary. By 1992, there were fifty-six border towns opened to border trading and social interaction in Yunnan and Guangxi.

Although the border trading that is carried out is small in scale, attempts have been made to regionalize, if not globalize, trading activities in the border region. Provincial and local governments have, since economic liberalization in the 1980s, argued for the expansion of border trade and the integration of the border provinces into the wider global and international economy.

THE ROLE OF THE CENTRAL GOVERNMENT

Economic liberalization has brought about institutional and structural changes as well as policy changes. One of the key characteristics of the 1978 Reform is the decentralization of the decision-making process, which gives provincial and local governments more autonomy to implement economic policies and changes (Chung 1992).

Since the 1980s, the central, provincial, and county governments have adopted policies aimed at creating a more liberal economic environment to encourage development in the border regions. Most of these policies are aimed at providing traders and investors with guidelines concerning the operation and management of their enterprises. However, the decentralization of decision-making was not given to the border provinces until the mid-1980s. The central government continues to exert a strong influence on the border provinces through various policies, and the provincial governments of the border region are required to adhere to the policies drawn up for them.

The "1985 Period" provided a watershed for provincial and county governments to take greater control of their border regions. At the provincial level, one main policy was to improve relationships with their border neighbours although the boundary continued to be under the administration of the central government.

In 1985, two sets of regulatory frameworks were established by the State Council of the central government as policy guidelines for conducting border trade and investments. The first set of regulations was "The Import and Export Custom Tax Guidelines of the People's Republic of China" (中华人民共和国进出口关税条例), which was announced on 7 March 1985. The second set of regulations formulated was the "Rules and Regulations Pertaining to Outside Investment by the State Council" (国务院关于鼓励外商投资的规定), which came into effect on 11 October 1986 (Liu and Lia 1993, pp. 380–83). Since then, these guidelines have undergone two revisions aimed at encouraging more trade and investments in the border region. The first revision was completed and announced on 12 September 1987 under the document "State Council Revised Import and Export Custom Tax Guidelines of the People's Republic of China" (国务院关于修改中华人民共和国进出口关税条例) and came into immediate effect. Further amendments followed, and a comprehensive revision was done and put into effect on 1 April 1992 (ibid., pp. 383–90).

During the "1985 Period", the central government issued a document on "Temporary Policy for Small-Scale Trading along the Border Region". One of its aims was to encourage economic participation by minority groups that resided along the borders. Under this policy, the border people were encouraged "to search for their own market sources, to do their own negotiation, and to be responsible for their own dealings". The document encouraged the provincial officials to "adopt more liberal thinking, be more daring, widen the steps of reform and open widely the border door for border trade". The stipulated policy also granted permission for co-operation between internal and foreign investors in trading and technological transfer in the border region.

It was only by 1992 that the central government handed over to the provincial governments the rights to implement regulations and control, including the management and policing of border trade (ibid., p. 154). This step was taken fifteen years after the first move towards economic liberalization. It also reflected the cautious attitude of the central government towards the border provinces where the border is still considered a politically sensitive region and where the central government continues to impose stricter restrictions in comparison with the coastal provinces.

In 1992, the State Council revised its trading policies. Two sets of policy guidelines pertaining to bilateral trade with neighbouring countries and the opening up of border towns were formulated. The first set of policies governs trading activities with Myanmar. This is spelt out in the document "Custom Inspection and Preferential Tax Privileges Pertaining to Trading along the Sino-Myanmar Border of the People's Republic of China" (中华人民共和国海关对中缅边境民间贸易的监管和收税优代). This set of policies was simultaneously adopted and announced in Beijing and Kunming on 25 January 1992 (ibid., pp. 391–96). One document, "A Notice for Further Liberalizing the Border Towns and Counties of Nanning, Kunming City, Pingxiang Town, Ruili, and Hekou County by the State Council" (国务院关于

进一步开放南宁，昆明市，凭祥市，瑞丽，河口县等五个边境城镇的通知) (ibid., pp. 396–98), led to the opening of these five state-level cities and towns as growth nodes for the development of border trade and investment.

Another policy pertains to tax reforms. The central government outlined measures for low taxation, which was subsequently adopted by the provincial governments. This low-tax policy takes into account all types of enterprises, trading methods, the small scale and volume of trade, as well as the scattered nature of trading activities. For example, in July 1993, the central government listed five policies regarding preferential treatment and tax concessions for border trading in the Guangxi province. They include the abolition of permits for all import and export items except three varieties of grains — barley, beans, and sesame seeds; the granting of permission for various trading companies to set up import and export services in the region; tax concessions for all imports except Chinese-produced electrical appliances, motor-cycles, women's cosmetics, alcoholic drinks, cigarettes, soft drinks, and small vans. These Chinese products were sold at cheaper prices in the neighbouring countries and traders found it to their advantage to buy them across the border and resell them at a profit along the Chinese border. To prevent cash outflow, these products incurred a 100 per cent tax. To encourage local traders venturing beyond the border, no profit tax was levied for the first five years on business operating across the non-Chinese border of neighbouring countries. A 20 per cent tax would be levied on the profits of these firms after five years of operation.

Although the central government has implemented strict regulations on trading and investment in the border region, it nevertheless lacks the power to fully monitor the implementation of such policies. The centre is simply too far away from the provinces to be able to exert any effective monitoring of its policies. At the same time, by giving provincial and local governments in the border region the power to exercise autonomy in trade and investment, the central government's control on these provinces is further reduced.

In a move to regain its control over these provinces, the central government, once again, tightened its grip on trading in the border provinces in 1995. It introduced a tax policy that reinstated taxation on 162 types of goods that previously were given tax exemption. It also introduced tighter goods inspection and customs control along the border region.

PROVINCIAL GOVERNMENT STRATEGIES AND POLICIES

Given greater autonomy in economic policies by the central government, the provincial governments have successfully restructured and introduced rapid economic reforms into the border region. Through a series of policies formulated at the provincial level, they have greatly transformed the economic landscape of the border provinces.

The provincial and county governments introduced the following policies to facilitate border trading and investments. There are policies that encourage the expansion of internal and external markets, and the re-allocation of the provincial budget for infrastructure development in the border region, especially for the development of roads and port facilities including cargo terminals. There are also policies on customs inspection, close supervision on market competition and co-operation, and policies for a freer market. Other policies are aimed directly at attracting food and agricultural industries, raw material–processing industries, and small and medium-sized manufacturing industries to the border towns. Finally, there are policies to encourage the use of the renminbi as the medium of exchange in the region. This is done by standardizing the exchange rate of the renminbi and creating a small-scale financial trading and money market.

An example of the regional autonomy exercised by provincial governments in the border region is that of the Yunnan provincial government. When the central government handed over greater autonomy to the provinces, the Yunnan provincial government acted fast and promulgated its first trade policy, "Temporary Regulations Governing Border Trade in Yunnan" (云南省关于边境贸易的暂行规定), on 27 March 1985 (ibid., pp. 497–500).

During the "1985 Period", the Yunnan provincial government adopted an interventionist approach to trading and investment. It emphasized "self-reliance in the search for market sources and markets, in conducting negotiations, in venturing, and eradicating obstacles". The main concern of the Yunnan provincial government was to improve conditions for investment in Yunnan through fiscal and institutional changes. There were major tax concessions and exemptions. At the institutional level, there were massive reforms to cut down bureaucratic red tape. The Yunnan provincial government also conducted nation-wide publicity of the border region, drawing attention to the opportunities and the products, and emphasizing the quality and uniqueness of the region. In 1989 the Yunnan provincial government organized the first "border trade fair" in Kunming City.

In 1991, the Yunnan provincial government established another set of supplementary policies to further improve border trading. "The Yunnan People's Government Supplementary Policies Pertaining to the Promotion of Border Trading" (云南省人民政府关于发展边境贸易的若干补充规定) and "The Yunnan People's Government Policies Concerning the Encouragement of Outside Investments" (云南省人民政府关于鼓励外商投资的规定) (ibid., pp. 492–97) are two examples of policies implemented (ibid., pp. 501–4).

The Yunnan government also established a Foreign Investment Management Centre to provide assistance to foreign investors. Its members helped with the application for business licences, and guaranteed licence approval within twenty working days. Foreign firms also received legal protection from the provincial government. Investors who chose to invest in designated towns would be given additional incentives by the Yunnan government.

Through such policies, the Yunnan provincial government has elevated the status of Kunming and other border towns. It has also made Yunnan an important centre for border activity. Although the provincial government has been a given certain level of autonomy in decision-making and policy implementation, the central government continues to have overarching control. But in ordinary times, the central and provincial governments work side by side and both sets of policies are seen as complementing each other.

In 1992, the Beijing government also gave Yunnan certain preferential policies to bolster its border trade. One of the policies designated Ruili, Wanding, and Hekou as state-level border towns. The central government also approved, within these three towns, the creation of an economic co-operation district in collaboration with Myanmar, Laos, and Vietnam, respectively.

Another area for development is border tourism, which is seen as important in bringing in foreign currency. To encourage both trading and tourism, the Yunnan provincial government has simplified visa and customs procedure for those who want to make visits across the border, permitting multiple re-entries on a daily basis. The issuing of these permits now lies in the hands of the Tourism Department of the Yunnan provincial government. In so doing, the local people can now travel daily across the border. Cars and buses can also ply across the border several times a day, and it is now common for busloads of organized tourist-traders to travel across the border. Tour companies have recently emerged to cater to such demands.

The fast response and initiative of the Yunnan provincial government has enabled Yunnan and its border towns to seize the opportunities and establish themselves as important border trading towns within a decade. Despite the fluctuating trade, these towns continue to be important trading centres.

The situation in Yunnan is in contrast with that in Guangxi, where the cross-border trade was impeded by the outbreak of the Sino-Vietnamese War in 1979. It was only after the normalization of Sino-Vietnamese relationship that cross-border trading was encouraged by both the Chinese and Vietnamese governments (Hood 1992; Guo et al. 1986).

Economic liberalization only reached Guangxi in the 1980s. As late as 1983, only limited border trading was officially permitted in Guangxi. It was not until the 1985 Period that the Guangxi provincial government was allowed to take the initiative to implement policies to actively encourage border trading. By the end of 1988, such trading had become the main activity in the province. Most of the trading involved local produce of the border region. One initiative taken by the Guangxi provincial government was to encourage Chinese traders from other regions to trade in the newly opened border towns of the province. During this period, a sizeable number of out-of-town Chinese traders could be seen trading in the region.

The Guangxi government had also taken other initiatives and successfully concluded a series of bilateral agreements with the Vietnamese government. In November 1988, an agreement was reached between the two governments which permitted border residents to cross the border on social visits to see relatives and for individuals to purchase their daily needs. By June 1989, small-scale businesses were permitted in the border region.

Greater autonomy was handed over from the central government to the Guangxi provincial government in the beginning of the 1990s. This enabled the Guangxi provincial government to issue three set of policies in 1991 aimed at further promoting trade and investment in the border towns. The first was the "Guangxi Zhuang Minorities Autonomous Region Preferential Tax Policies Pertaining to the Encouragement of Outside Investment" (广西壮族自治区关于鼓励外商投资的税收优代政策) (Liu and Lia 1993, pp. 519–28). The second set of policies concerned the leasing and management of land for industrial and commercial purposes. This was the "Guangxi Zhuang Minorities Autonomous Region

Temporary Law for the Leasing and Management of Land for Development Purposes by Outside Investments" (广西壮族自治区关于外商投资开放政策) (ibid., pp. 528–32). The third set of policies was aimed at attracting Chinese overseas to invest in the region. This was the "Guangxi Zhuang Minorities Autonomous Region Regulations Pertaining to the Encouragement of Investment of the Taiwanese" (广西壮族自治区鼓励台湾同胞投资若干规定) (ibid., pp. 532–35). With the Guangxi provincial government taking charge of development and trade in the border region, it is clear that greater emphasis is placed on encouraging ethnic minorities to participate in the trading activities of the region. These policies targeted at specific ethnic groups differ greatly from those issued by the central government. How successful these policies are in encouraging the participation of the ethnic groups remains to be seen.

ECONOMIC CO-OPERATION DISTRICTS AS A DEVELOPMENT STRATEGY

By the 1990s, provincial governments had been given a high level of autonomy to operate their regional economy and to implement policies to hasten the development of their provinces. Since then, in Yunnan and Guangxi the provincial governments have been given authority to manage the five centrally approved state-level border towns of Pingxiang, Dongxing, Wanding, Ruili, and Hekou with minimal central intervention. The provincial governments are now given the responsibility of issuing contracts as well as controlling and overseeing the operation of processing and manufacturing factories in the border towns. They also implement policies aimed at encouraging export-oriented and value-added enterprises to operate in their official border towns. In the agricultural sector, encouragement is given to cash-cropping for export purposes. To facilitate these activities, the import of seeds, seedlings, animals, and animal feeds, as well as industrial equipment for operating factories are given preferential privileges and exemption from import duties.

Provincial governments are also given a free hand to encourage investments from within China and overseas. Since 1985 they have been given the power to encourage the relevant types of enterprises into the border towns. Processing and manufacturing industries that use locally produced raw materials and agricultural products are highly encouraged. These industries are given a 24 per cent tax reduction on profits.

Manufacturing industries that use local products are also given a 50 per cent reduction in production and sales taxes. However, goods produced in a region that enjoys tax and preferential treatment can only be sold within the region, a policy that continues under central government directive.

Apart from using fiscal policies to encourage investment in the border region, the provincial governments also seek to create economic co-operation districts within these border towns, which again have the blessings of the central government. They see these economic zones as an important development strategy that would encourage more active cross-border trade. The economic zones would also serve as a nuclei for the conglomeration of various types of industries that would take advantage of economies of scale of production. Furthermore, within the zones, the provincial governments would have been able to develop basic infrastructure with the help of these industries. Manufacturing, processing, and service industries are encouraged to operate in the region.

Within these economic co-operation zones, machinery and other basic industrial needs required for production could be imported with no import tax. Likewise, a 24 per cent reduction in export tax is given to enterprises with neighbouring countries as foreign joint owners for products that are sold to these neighbouring countries.

The provincial governments also have the right to approve investments of less than US$1 million in their respective provinces, bypassing the central government. The issuing of licences to operate within the towns and districts, however, remains in the hands of the Special Economic Zones Division of the State Council in Beijing.

In agreeing to the creation of special economic districts, the central government has provided subsidies in the five state-level border towns and also helped to arrange for low-interest loans to the provincial governments especially for infrastructure projects. The 1985 Period witnessed the People's Bank of China arranging cheap loans to these towns under the instruction of the central government. Wanding and Ruili, for example, received a 10 million renminbi loan each, while Pingxiang, Dongxing, and Hekou received a 20 million renminbi loan each. These loans were made out for infrastructure projects and investment purposes only. Additionally, the provincial governments were permitted to levy a charge of 0.6 renminbi per ton of trade that was conducted within these towns. The levy collected could only be used to fund infrastructure development. However, the loans were deemed as grossly insufficient given the extent to which the Yunnan and Guangxi provinces needed to develop their transportation system, particularly roads and railways, and power stations.

The central government has also permitted a restricted number of vehicles for industrial purposes to be imported tax-free into the region. However, such vehicles can only be used within these districts and not sold or used outside the stipulated areas.

While the provincial government is given autonomy to decide on the types of industries and the functioning of the economic zones, the central government has the final say in stipulating the extent to which the boundary of these economic co-operation zones lies on the Chinese side of the border. This is determined by the Office for Special Economic Zones within the State Council in Beijing. Despite the trade and economic liberalization, the central government continues to monitor its political boundary with great vigilance. Anything that hurts national security would not be permitted. The border region in Yunnan and Guangxi continues to be regarded as important to China's national security. So, even as trade liberalization proceeds and more regions are accorded the status of "economic zones", the border region continues to be closely monitored.

The creation of the joint economic districts that straddle across borders requires the co-operation of the local governments on both sides of the border and of the two central governments. Fortunately, the warming of political relationship on both sides has encouraged such zones to be established. Since the mid-1980s, the bilateral agreements signed by the Chinese government with neighbouring countries have ensured a high level of support for such projects. This has culminated in a call for regional co-operation where, at the macro level, there is the creation of the Golden Quadrangle Economic Bloc (金四角) and the Mekong River Economic Sub-Basin (湄公河经济区).

At the micro level, there is the cross-border economic co-operation districts and sister towns (姉妹城) along the borders of Yunnan-Myanmar and Guangxi-Vietnam. Examples of these include the Sino-Burmese Street (中缅街) and Pingxiang–Lang Son economic co-operation district (凭祥谅山经济合作区) along the Yunnan-Myanmar border; and the Dongxing–Mong Cai free trade zone (东兴－芒街自由贸易区) and Hekou–Lao Cai economic co-operation district (河口－老街经济合作区) along the Guangxi-Vietnam border.

To the provincial and local governments, the economic co-operation zones are seen as growth nodes that will bring about concentrated growth within these districts. Such growth is seen to have a spillover effect and will stimulate growth outside the zones.

The liberal attitude adopted by the provincial and local governments in treating foreign investors in these interior cities has important repercussions. For the first time, foreigners and foreign investors could venture into the interior and border provinces which have hitherto been closed regions. This opening up has allowed the flow of commerce, technology, and more importantly — information into the region. It has also allowed the external world to communicate with the people living in these regions.

THE ROLE OF THE LOCAL GOVERNMENTS: DEHONG COUNTY AS AN EXAMPLE

Apart from provincial governments, the local governments at county level also play an active role in the border trade. Many local governments have seized the opportunities arisen as a result of the open-door policy. They have also negotiated with their provincial government for greater autonomy to implement economic policies and devise strategies to achieve economic growth in the county under their rule.

With the generally conducive economic environment, policies are also issued at the county level. The Wenshan county government of Guangxi province has also embarked on rapid economic development. It encourages trading and capital investment in its border towns. The state-level town Pingxiang has been designated as the "Open Trading District" of the county. The county government in Pingxiang has been issued the "Policies Pertaining to the Guangxi-Pingxiang Border Trading Open District" (广西凭祥边境贸易开放区) (Liu and Lia 1993, pp. 536–39), which is aimed at transforming the district into an economic zone.

In Yunnan, the local government of the border counties has also laid out guidelines and policies to lure both foreign and internal investors to invest and trade in their stipulated border regions. For example, in January 1991 the Xishuangbanna Tai Minority Autonomous County government promulgated the "Xishuangbanna Tai Minority Autonomous County Government Encouragement of Outside Investment Guidelines" (西双版纳傣族自治州人民政府鼓励外地投资的若干规定) (ibid., pp. 510–14) to encourage potential investments into the district.

Individual county governments and city administrators are also scrambling to come up with their own preferential policies and treatments to encourage investors to invest in their localities. Thus, the government of Kunming city has implemented the following set of policies in the hope of encouraging investments in its city. It issued the "Kunming City Encouraging Outside Investment Policies" (昆明市关于鼓励外商投资的规定) (ibid., pp. 505–9) on 19 August 1992.

This is also the case for the Dehong county government in Yunnan, which has established the Jiegao trading district in the state-level town of Ruili. To streamline economic policies pertaining to economic activities and investment opportunities in this district, the Dehong county government promulgated on 1 February 1992 the policy document "Regulations and Policies Governing Yunnan Jiegao Border Trading District" (云南姐告边境贸易经济区若干政策的规定) (ibid., pp. 514–18).

Dehong county, with Ruili as its most active trading town, has become one of the most important border counties in terms of border trading and border development (He 1992; Dehong Tai Minority Autonomous County People's Government Reports 1985). Since 1991 there has been an increase in the varieties of goods traded in the region. A large volume of Chinese-produced machinery has made its way into Myanmar. In 1991 trade accounted for 100 million renminbi and made up 50 per cent of the revenue of Dehong county. In 1993 the volume of trade totalled 200 million renminbi (Xi 1995, pp. 65–68). There has also been a move away from trading to joint ventures of industrial production plants and technological co-operation in the county.

The rapid development of Dehong county has been attributed to the actions of the local government and its official cadres. An important area of attention has been to create a climate conducive to investors. The government, for example, has set up an information centre to provide investors and enterprises with information about policies required for county border trading. At the same time, the local government has also made adjustments and changes to various policies pertaining to customs inspection, taxation, customs duties, border control, external relations, industrial development, banking, tax department, and Overseas Chinese department. One major aim has also been to strengthen and build the infrastructure, including transportation and cargo terminals for the towns (ibid., p. 20).

A second area in which the county government has a say is the elimination of inefficient and profit-losing county-owned companies. It has embarked on industrial restructuring, and in 1989–90 the county government closed down fifty-one county-operated firms and re-allocated cash flows to other profitable enterprises (ibid., p. 20). This industrial restructuring, together with its encouragement of joint ventures, has brought about a new economic climate.

4. Negotiating Policies: Border Trading in South China

Furthermore, in 1990 the Dehong county government instituted price controls for certain agricultural commodities to stabilize the trading environment that was often affected by price fluctuations. The products included sesame seeds, bean products, cotton, and frozen fish (ibid., p. 20).

Publicity campaigns are also used to lure investors into the county. For instance, publicity materials produced for potential investors include a list of enterprises that have achieved success. This is to boost confidence in investing in the region.

Tourist trade is also promoted, especially one-day tours to the Myanmar border towns of Muse and Namhkam. Now about 200 Chinese from Ruili and Wanding go to the Myanmar towns daily. During peak periods, especially in the months of January/February and November/December, as many as 1,000 Chinese cross the border daily (ibid., p. 19).

Recently, the Dehong county government has come to focus on the following strategies which it calls "two breakthroughs" (俩个突破) and "two linkages" (俩个接连 (ibid., p. 21). They are breakthroughs first, to Myanmar and second, from Myanmar to other Southeast Asian countries. The county government hopes that by focusing on these two breakthroughs, it would be able to increase the volume of exports and to lure foreign investors into joint-venture projects with it. The first breakthrough is the "entry from West and exit to the East"(西进东出) (ibid., p. 21). Its aim is to bring the region closer to the coastal region by way of a continuous link between the interior western region and the eastern coastal seaports. The second breakthough is to use border enterprises as a springboard to encourage joint ventures and to turn the county into specialized production and service zones by encouraging the grouping of enterprises that provide similar goods and services. Here, the focus is on the formation of trading groups (团体化) (ibid., p. 21). These strategies represent the orientation of the Dehong county government towards Sino-Myanmar trade development.

As there is relatively little competition, the county government has been able to establish a trading niche for itself and export Chinese goods to the Myanmar markets, thereby improving its foreign currency reserves. Through this, it has been able to encourage the growth of a multiple currency market.

However, the Dehong county government is also facing some problems. Transportation including roads is inadequate and cannot handle the demands of the growing trade. There is also poor management in the bureaucratic sectors which hinders the import and export of goods. Control over counterfeiting is also insufficient and there is thus a rise in the export of low-quality counterfeit goods into neighbouring countries (ibid., pp. 21–22).

PROBLEMS AND SOLUTIONS TO BORDER TRADING

At the three levels of governance, the central, provincial, and county governments have been able to come up with policies aimed at creating a more relaxed and liberal economic environment to encourage development in the border regions. The initial encouragement of border trade has been replaced by a move to promote industrialization in these regions. Trade and commerce are important activities that will open the border area to the outside world. But these two activities are also regarded as being too volatile to create a stable economic environment. So, the second stage of development is industrialization and the production of value-added and manufactured goods to cater to both the local and the foreign market.

Most of these policies are aimed at providing traders and investors with guidelines concerning the operation and management of their enterprises. It also sets out preferential treatment given to traders and investors with regard to customs inspection and taxation as well as attempts to reduce massive bureaucratic red tape and loosen entrenched bureaucratic rigidity.

Although border trade is part of the process of marketization and trading, government bureaucracies, like those elsewhere in China, have also become increasingly involved in trading, particularly joint-venture activities. Provincial and local governments have become increasingly involved in joint ventures with private and foreign enterprises. Such governmental involvement has resulted in three scenarios. First, there is rapid economic growth and economic returns for these joint ventures. Second, with the government assuming the status of an "economic person", those officials who have authority over licensing and the rights to production tend to favour their own enterprises and joint operations for quick profit-making. Other officials are also susceptible to corrupt practices and bribery. Much of the official funds have been siphoned off into personal accounts. The result is irregularities in income and lost of profit for a large number of central and state-level enterprises. Third, with more government departments seeking joint ventures and setting up their own companies, competition for licences to operate has become very intense. Those with connections, *guanxi*, with the relevant officials would be favoured over others, resulting in the failure of some state enterprises to obtain the relevant licences to operate in the border region. The result is a less-than-harmonious relationship among the officials.

There is also a lack of proper administrative and management skills to cope with this sudden explosion of trading activities along the border towns, leading to much confusion. Unlike the coastal cities which in the past had experience in dealing with trade and industries, regions in the interior, especially the border regions, can boast of none of such background. There is also inadequate knowledge of the market and experience in investment, and many state corporations end up with severe losses. This is especially so as most of the state enterprises are relatively large in scale compared with the demands of the market. With competition, many of the less efficient and competitive state enterprises have been forced to wind down after several years of operation. Only those with market niches have survived.

A major reason for the failure of these enterprises can be attributed to the limited scope and scattered nature of border trade. There has been a general recognition by provincial and county governments that trading alone could not sustain the rapid economic development and modernization of the region as it is subjected to a volatile supply and demand market, on the one hand, and the political vacillations of governments, on the other. A more permanent form of economic activities lies with industrial manufacturing activities. Thus, from the 1985 Period and especially after 1992, the provincial and local governments have embarked on a policy of encouraging investments to create "special economic districts" (经济特区) for various types of economic activities (Zhou Jianming 1994). Within such districts, there would be enterprises specializing in trading, commerce, finance, and manufacturing. Both foreign and internal investors from within China have been encouraged to invest in these districts. The numerous preferential privileges and tax incentives as outlined in the various documents were meant to encourage these foreign and internal investors to invest and set up factories in the region. The provincial and local governments hoped that the special economic districts would eventually become part of the wider regional economy.

The broad categories of policies implemented by the provincial and county governments to facilitate economic functioning are aimed at the following issues. First, there are policies that encourage the expansion of internal and external markets. Secondly, there are policies for the reallocation of the provincial budget for the development of infrastructure in the border, particularly the development of roads and port facilities, including cargo terminals. Thirdly, there are policies pertaining to closer supervision and customs inspection, closer supervision on market competition, and co-operation and for a freer market. Fourthly, some policies are aimed directly at attracting food and agriculture and raw material–processing industries to locate at the border towns. Other policies aim to attract small and medium-sized industries to these economic districts. Fifthly, there are policies aimed at the use of the renminbi as the medium of exchange in the region, standardizing the exchange rate of the renminbi and creating a small-scale financial trading and money market.

Another problem facing traders and consumers in the region is the transaction of inferior and imitation products. Counterfeiting has become a trade unto itself. Both the central and provincial governments have looked on counterfeiting and imitation as serious problems as they destroy the reliability and the name of locally produced Chinese products and of Chinese products in general. To counteract the problems, the following measures have been taken. The central government has instructed that administrative and management regulations regarding border trading be streamlined. In this regard, the provincial government and its various administrative and management teams have been instructed to investigate and stop the work of counterfeiting at the source. They should aim at eradicating such practices at the earliest possible time.

Related to this is the problem of smuggling. Restrictions are imposed on various types and quantities of manufacturing goods that can be traded in the border region, as well as certain endangered wildlife and plants. Nevertheless, manufactured goods, wildlife, and drugs continue to be smuggled into China via the border, and this rampant smuggling has been exacerbated by corruption and weak policing along the border regions.

There have been calls to implement favourable policies at the central, provincial, and local levels to support foreign firms and their operations in the border region. The provincial and local governments are encouraged to import and export genuine products and boycott counterfeit ones. Furthermore , stricter inspection is imposed on food products and only those that have passed stringent tests and obtained official approval from the the public hygiene authority could be sold on the market.

4. Negotiating Policies: Border Trading in South China

Increased supervision and inspection of production is also considered necessary. Those producing and selling pirated goods are subjected to harsh punishment according to rules laid down by the State Council and other relevant authorities. Serious offences are handled by the Central People's Committee. Those whose offences concern production and sale of animal products are punishable under the "Regulation Concerning Criminal Offences Regarding the Hybridization and Sale of Improper Goods". Conversely, those who reported on such offences are rewarded.

There are also calls for the Customs and Inspection Departments to take prompt and legal actions towards such violations. The two departments are to co-ordinate their activities with those of the Production and Inspection Units. The latter two units are expected to strengthen and tighten their management control as well as exercise close inspection over the quality of products in the border towns. Furthermore, there are strict directives from the central government for the establishment of customs check-points in all border towns. There is also a tightening in the control of goods passing through the border, including personal effects carried by tourist-traders. At present, such matters are outside the control of provincial and local governments; instead they come under the purview of the central government or the international convention that governs the flow of goods across international borders. Customs officers are instructed to examine all goods leaving and entering the border. Goods carried by foreigners are subjected to central-level policies while those borne by local nationals are subjected to local policies. Violations against customs regulations is punishable by the law.[4]

Furthermore, the central government has also issued several directives to control border trade. In the 1995 tax policy, tax exemption was withdrawn from 162 types of goods that previously enjoyed such exemption. Border tax was also subjected to tighter inspection and customs control, the argument being that it had become impossible to institute a proper system of tax rebates given the poor banking facilities in the border region. Some local enterprises that previously acted for foreign corporations were no longer able to act as sole dealers or distributors. So, to treat everyone equally, permission is denied across the board, so that "all wear one cap" (一頂帽子大家戴) (Law Department 1993, p. 2).

In 1996 the State Council of Beijing announced its dissatisfaction over what it perceived as perennial problems pertaining to border trade. It issued a statement "Announcement of Several Problems Pertaining to Border Trade", stating that the border region suffered from bad management, poor business acumen, and corruption, resulting in badly managed state, provincial, and county enterprises. Of the 2,130 state-owned enterprises, one-third were straddled with debt accumulation (Lin 1996). It blamed bad management practices for the unproductive competition that led to depressed export prices; excessive demand for imported goods was also blamed for the inflated prices of imports. At the next level, provincial and county governments were chastised for failure to follow regulations, which led to market instability and a rise in smuggling. Furthermore, it bemoaned the lack of strict control over product quality and the rise in counterfeiting, and highlighted the failure of provincial and county governments to encourage industrialization and technology development in the border region.

To tackle these shortcomings, the central government re-issued policy directives in the following areas. First, "border region" is defined as strictly confined to the region within 20-kilometres from the border. Within this border region, there are only twenty-six officially recognized market districts and towns. The central government has specified that provincial and county governments cannot practise "border trade without boundary" (边贸无边) (ibid., p. 1). It has also specified that only two types of border trading are permitted. The first type is the small-scale buying and selling engaged by border residents. The maximum amount of such trading that qualify for tax exemption is 1,000 renminbi, and taxes will be levied on transactions exceeding the 1,000 renminbi limit. The second type of border trading concerns border enterprises, and the types of enterprises that are allowed to function along the border region are to be determined by the External Trade Division of the State Council.

SOCIAL IMPACT OF THE OPENING OF THE BORDER

In Guangxi, border trading has impacted greatly on the life-style and standard of living of residents living in the region. There has been a general rise in the standard of living. For example, at the provincial level, a survey of the old Shuikou Street (老水口街) shows that the 199 households living in the street had been enjoying a rise in income. In 1988 the average income was 150 renminbi a month, but it rose to 350 renminbi in 1989 (Zhou Zhongjian 1995). Likewise, at the provincial level, the 285 households of Ningming Aidan Street (宁明爱店街) also experienced a rise in income, from 120 renminbi in 1988 to 400 renminbi in 1989 (ibid., 1995). And at the state level, some residents of the town of Pingxiang registered a monthly income of 3,000 renminbi during the period 1988–92 (ibid., 1995).

These border towns have also grown relatively prosperous. The combined revenue of the twelve Chinese border towns increased from 25 million renminbi in 1989 to 244 million renminbi in 1992.

THE POLITICAL IMPACT

Another characteristic of border trade is the politicized nature of the region. Here economic development is often secondary in importance. This has been the case throughout Chinese history, where the border regions have been tightly shut to foreign intrusion. But even after doors have been opened for trading, the question of a regulatory framework for policing the border region remains the utmost concern at all levels of government, especially the central government. If the political climate is friendly, the doors would be more open, otherwise, the doors would remain shut. So in recent years Beijing has come to adopt an active role so as to facilitate economic co-operation with China's neighbours. The Chinese leaders have visited Myanmar, Laos, and Vietnam and have thereby smoothed the political relationship with these countries. This is seen as a move to facilitate border trading. Southeast Asian leaders have in turn visited China. Likewise, provincial governments in the border regions have met with their counterparts in Myanmar, Laos, and Vietnam to sign bilateral agreements for border trade as well as for joint ventures.

However, in the recent past, when political tensions between the Chinese government and its neighbours surfaced, the border region became politically sensitive and would be closed to all activities including cross-border trading and businesses. This was the case during the Sino-Vietnamese War in 1979, when all border relations were suspended and patrol tightened on both sides of the border. Another incident was when tensions arose over the Spratly Islands, and also because of Vietnam's trade protection policy in 1993. Again, trading was badly affected: during that period the combined revenue of border trade between China and Vietnam dropped to 176 million renminbi. The Vietnamese government stopped the entry of seventeen types of Chinese-produced goods and imposed heavy import taxes for certain categories of Chinese goods to protect its own industry. For example, Chinese-made alcohol and beer were subjected to a 80–150 per cent import tax. Despite these hiccups, revenues continued to surge in these towns (Zhang 1993).

At another level, the success of border trade is also dependent on the level of trust each government accords to others. For example, Guangxi province's border trade has been very much affected by Vietnam's policies, and there is a general dissatisfaction over the frequent policy changes instituted by the Vietnamese government as a result of the low level of trust between governments across the borders. Such attitude continues to impede the rapid growth of border trade between the two countries.

THE ETHNIC IMPACT

Another feature of border trade is the ethnic factor. A large majority of those living along both sides of the border belong to the same ethnic minority groups. The border region of Yunnan is, for example, inhabited by the Tai, while the Guangxi province is inhabited by the Zhuang minority. Each minority group, regardless of which side of the border it lives on, shares ethnic and linguistic traits, and is therefore able to negotiate and communicate at ease with one another. In fact, the minority groups on both sides of the border have all along been trading with one another — long before economic liberalization had become an official policy.

One key feature that the provincial and county governments decided to tap into is the ethnicity factor of the minorities. This is the so-called "human affinity" (人缘) factor. Thus, one set of policies have been implemented by the Yunnan and Guangxi provincial governments in order to encourage the border residents to "straddle over border and ethnic boundary" (跨国民族). Specific policies favouring the ethnic population are promulgated to encourage the ethnic minorities to engage in trading and businesses and to induce them to become actively involved in economic development at the borders. For example, the Yunnan provincial government advised the Dehong Tai minority to act according to the slogan "Trade first, regard agriculture as the foundation, industry as the dependable backbone, and engage in reforms and liberalism". The strategy would be one of "overall development for trading, agriculture and industry, and for trading to supplement agriculture and industry".

Towns on both sides of the border have consequently emerged to cater to the needs of the growing markets. The towns continue to prosper with the new open-door policy. Both the Yunnan and the Guangxi provincial governments have thus encouraged their ethnic minorities to become actively involved in border trading.

Border trading encourages both economic and social interaction, and this is imperative for the revival of a cross-border common ethnic identity. It will facilitate the creation of an ethno-cultural area within the border region where with the border trade and the flow of human traffic across the border, minorities of the same ethnicity can now rekindle their lost kinship ties and re-establish as well as enlarge their social networks. In this sense, border trading has become an important idiom for resurrecting not only the economic life but also the social life of the border region.

CONCLUSION

In conclusion, the opening up of the border region has brought about economic as well as social changes to the region. However, such changes can only be effected through an intricate compromise of the governments at the central, provincial, and local levels. The most effective method is through policy changes and implementation.

However, the border region continues to be regarded as a politically sensitive area. As a result of its geographical location, the central government continues to have close supervision of the region. In times of peace, the provincial and local governments are able to effect policies that facilitate cross-border trading and investment. But in times of political tension, as demonstrated by the various wars, trading and economic activities with cross-border neighbours would be suspended. Thus, in negotiating policies pertaining to border trading in South China, the central government continues to be the ultimate decision-maker while provincial and local governments are merely secondary players that function within an established framework laid down by the central government.

ACKNOWLEDGEMENT

The author wishes to acknowledge the following: the University Grants Council of Hong Kong for a grant which made possible the project "The Pioneering Frontier: Border Trade and Cultural Transmission in Yunnan, Guangxi-Vietnam, Laos-Axis"; the Department of Sociology, University of Hong Kong, for infrastructure support and assistance given by Qian Jiang; and other Chinese colleagues for help with data collection. The sources cited in the References are all in Chinese, unless otherwise specified.

NOTES

1. For background information on the border trade, see Shi (1996).
2. For a discussion of the expansion of border trade in the 1980s and 1990s, see Shang (1995).
3. For a discussion of cross-border economic co-operation, see Wang Silu (1995); see also Xian (1992).
4. For a discussion of the policies implemented, see Law Department (1993).

REFERENCES

Chung Jae Ho. "Studies of Central-Provincial Relations in the People's Republic of China: A Mid-Term Appraisal". *China Quarterly* 142 (1992): 487–508.
Dehong Tai Minority Autonomous County People's Government Reports Concerning the Decisions on the Liberalisation of Border Trading. Monthly reports. Dehong County, Yunnan: Dehong County Government, 1985.
Guo Min, Luo Fangmin, and Li Baiying. *Contemporary Sino-Vietnamese Relationship*, vols. 1–3 (in Chinese). Beijing: Modern Publishing House, 1986.
He Ping. "A View of Sino-Burmese Border Trade from the Perspective of Dehong County Border Trading" (in Chinese). *Yunnan Academy of Social Sciences, Centre of Southeast Asia Studies: Yunnan and Southeast Asia Studies* 3 (1992): 19–22.
Hood, S.J. *Dragons Entangled: Indochina and the China-Vietnam War*. Armonk: M.E. Sharpe, 1992.
Law Department, People's Republic of China. "State Council's Report on Policies Pertaining to Regulating of Border Trade and Control of Counterfeit Goods" (in Chinese). Beijing: Law Department of the State Council, 23 September 1993.
Lin Ming. "Present and Future Trends of Yunnan Border Trade" (in Chinese). *Southeast Asia Economic Report*, July 1996, pp. 1–3.
Liu Baorong and Lia Jiasheng, eds. *The Liberalisation of Border Region and the Markets of the Neighbouring Countries* (in Chinese). Beijing: Legal Publishing House, 1993.
Shang Nan. "The New Trend of Border Trading" (in Chinese). *Henan Zhengzhou University Journal* 2 (1995): 1–6.
Shi Liming. "The Development of Guangxi-Vietnam Border Trade 1885–1949" (in Chinese). *Guangxi Academy of Social Sciences, Centre of Southeast Asian Studies, Southeast Asia Journal* 2 (1996): 4–9.
Wang Silu. "Thoughts on the Developing Economic Co-operation between Southwest China and Northern Burma, Laos, Thailand and Vietnam" (in Chinese). *Yunnan Academy of Social Sciences, Centre of Southeast Asia Studies (Economic Problems), Yunnan and Southeast Asia Studies* 1 (1995): 1–7.
Xi Chenwen. "A Discussion on the Thoughts of Further Opening Up of Dehong County" (in Chinese). In *Yunnan Provincial Government Report*, pp. 65–68.

Kunming: Yunnan Provincial Government, January 1995.

Xian Shengda. "The Economic Co-operation of Southwest China and Southeast Asia" (in Chinese). *Yunnan Academy of Social Sciences, Centre of Southeast Asia Studies, Yunnan and Southeast Asia Studies* 5 (1992): 17–23.

Zhang Jianzhong (1993). "The Past and Present Situation of Sino-Vietnamese Border Trade in Honghe County" (in Chinese). *Xinhua News Agency*, March 1993, pp. 17–20

The Hmong of the Southeast Asia Massif: Their Recent History of Migration

Jean Michaud and Christian Culas

Over the centuries, the Hmong people have attracted the interest of Asian and Western observers — in particular that of the Han Chinese, the English missionaries in southwest China, and the French colonials in Indochina. It was, however, only after World War II that international interest in the Hmong of Southeast Asia began to intensify, particularly during the Indochina Wars of 1946–54 and 1963–75. American intelligence services produced or commissioned ethnographic studies on highland populations in Laos, Thailand, and both parts of Vietnam, and the Hmong were the subject of several of these studies.[1]

In the 1990s, after the period of political seclusion that followed the communist take-overs in Vietnam and Laos in 1975, the minority regions were rapidly being re-opened, and this could also soon happen in southern China. The possibilities today of doing field research will surely contribute significant additions to the information that has existed ever since the mid-1970s or, in the case of northern Vietnam, for more than five decades. With the present pace of modernization and acculturation of highland societies, along with the forced sedentarization process taking place over the last few years, the task of collecting information is urgent. This chapter provides an account of the migration of the Hmong from China into peninsular Southeast Asia — a critical moment in their history.

WHO ARE THE HMONG?

The ancient history of the Hmong is intimately linked to that of today's Miao of southern China. It is, however, quite another story to pretend that the earlier history of the Hmong is linked also to that of the historical "Miao" as they appear in ancient Chinese texts. The Chinese term *Miao* was for a long time used in a broadly generic sense and referred to many non-Han ethnic minority groups. In much the same way, no definitive conclusions can be made to ascertain the real identity of the groups called Miao by the earliest Western writers.

But today, there is no doubt that the term *Miao*, as it is used in China and elsewhere, designates a specific, although large, set of ethnic groups, which all come from the same linguistic family, the Miao-Yao, from which the Hmong of the Indochina peninsula originate and to which they are still related. The Mandarin term *Miao* applies to the whole of the population from the Miao (*Miáozú*) National Minority group. This group comprises four linguistically (although their languages are not mutually intelligible) and culturally related sub-groups — named, in demographically decreasing order, the Hmong, the Hmu, the Qoxiong, and the Hmau (Haudricourt 1988, p. 43). In 1990, according to Chinese census figures, the total population of all sub-groups of the Miao National Minority was 7,350,000.[2] Ninety-nine per cent of them are distributed among seven provinces, of which Guizhou, Hunan, Yunnan, and Sichuan are the most important ones, with the autonomous Zhuang region of Guangxi province ranking fifth. This number represents 0.65 per cent of the entire Chinese population. Linguistic indications suggest that the total number of Hmong among the Miao in China would be around 2.5 million.

CAUSES FOR RECENT MONTAGNARD[3] MIGRATION INTO SOUTHEAST ASIA

Over a long period, multi-dimensional and, in some cases, powerful human migrations have occurred in the Southeast Asian region. Stronger groups have pushed more ancient settlers further away or higher up into the continental Southeast Asian Massif while keeping themselves to the fertile valleys, the plains, and the coastal areas. All these early highland settlers, precisely because of their earlier arrival in these niches, form societies culturally distinct from those arriving later such as the Akha, the Lisu, the Yao, and the Hmong, who all belong to Tibeto-Burman and Sino-Tibetan language families.

Since the intensification of the European presence and its accompanying geo-political ideology, and since the establishment of modern national borders in the peninsula, only small numbers of migrants from southern China have continued to arrive. Micro-societies of swiddeners, mostly following hilltop paths, have arrived to establish more or less permanent settlements on the last lands yet unclaimed in the higher parts of the Massif in today's Vietnam, Laos, Thailand, and Myanmar. The vast majority of these ethnic minorities — essentially coming from south China and northeastern India — whom we will here call "Montagnard", share cultural, political, and economic characteristics that distinguish them from the earlier mountain societies in the region, such as the Tho in Vietnam or the H'tin in Laos and Thailand. However, it is indisputable that ethnic differences are the most profound with the lowland majorities.

Such a precarious position, either physical, demographical, economic or cultural, could only lead to some form of dependency on, and, often, extortion from, more powerful neighbours. As Tapp has pointed out:

> The reality of the frontier, and the sovereignty of the nation-state which it symbolizes, has led to the increasing vulnerability of ethnic minorities in border areas to manipulation and exploitation by centrist administrations. At the same time it has led to their increasing strategic importance in terms of the power relations between different states. (Tapp 1990, pp. 149–50)

Exceeding by far their demographic importance, the sensitivity associated with the highland dwellers because of their particular habitat, the Massif, has primarily to do with their straddling across several historical as well as modern state borders. In this regard, Lim has rightly stated that in that region:

> The patchwork of hill peoples have in the past been manipulated by groups based in the lowlands to maintain lowland supremacy over the highlands. ... The mountain based "ethnicities" which are an outstanding feature of the geo-strategic map of the region bear an influence on the strategic environment, out of proportion to the numbers of highlanders, who are at the macro-level described as demographic and political minorities in the states where they are found. (Lim 1984, p. 20)

This uncomfortable, at times untenable, position was not achieved out of simple free will. The reasons for these highland ethnic groups migrating across borders are many, but they can ultimately be divided into two categories. One category can be called "cultural", since this is associated primarily with built-in social rules developed over centuries and aimed at regulating the social life in each of these groups. In the case of the Hmong, this aspect has been thoroughly researched and written about and therefore only the main lines will be mentioned here. The other category is "circumstantial", that is, events that are primarily determined by outside factors, such as broad climatic or historical events.

The economy of the highlands provides the primary "cultural" reason for moving. Practising pioneering or rotational swiddening requires frequent shifting, more so if an unsustainable level of demographic increase is reached, or if a crop such as the opium poppy is to be cultivated on a scale that exhausts the land. The cultivation of opium poppy developed among the Montagnards of south China during the second half of the nineteenth century, and its cultivation together with the nearly constant state of rebellion against the Chinese, definitely accelerated the pace of agricultural nomadism.

Health, both physical and spiritual, is another major reason causing group movement. Overcrowded village sites can within a few years get soiled beyond the normal capacity for natural recovery, and consequently, various diseases can rapidly develop among the population of a polluted site. Bad village epidemics, or epizoites among stock, are invariably linked to supernatural forces, and abandoning the village site is often seen as the only way to appease angry spirits. If a whole region is affected by such an ordeal, groups can decide to go a long way in search of a new place where they can find peace.

In times of peace, these and other "cultural" reasons would normally be the major causes for a Hmong individual, household, lineage, village, or whole regional population to seek a better life elsewhere. The movement would be relatively slow, regular, and steady, and it would take a few generations to move several hundreds of kilometres until an auspicious area was found, or until they were stopped by a stronger group, by harsher ecological conditions, or even by famines. However, when exogenous "circumstantial" human factors come to modify this traditional balance, the pattern of movement is altered in proportion to the severity of that outside influence. And indeed, such a trauma occurred in southern China during the nineteenth century, and the aftermath was to be observed deep into the following century. Let us now turn our attention to this question.

THE HMONG MIGRATION FROM CHINA

Han Chinese invasions of the highlands of southern China starting from the sixteenth century constituted one of the most important causes of conflict with highland minorities, who were trying to preserve their access to the land from the impediments of centralized administration and regional rulers. Some minorities responded by simply migrating further south or higher into the mountain ranges of Guizhou, Sichuan, and Yunnan. Other minorities took up arms. A small number even left the Chinese empire altogether to find shelter in the unpopulated mountain ranges, "the Massif", which were later to become incorporated into the modern states of the Southeast Asian peninsula.

Wiens noted that "in the major campaigns in the uprisings of 1698, 1732, 1794, and 1855, the Miao scattered in all directions, initiating the migratory movements of the modern period" (see Wiens 1954, p. 90; see also Lombard-Salmon 1972; and Jenks 1994). This turmoil affected the whole of southern China, resulting in a number of famines and epidemics in the region during most of the second half of the nineteenth century; it contributed significantly to pushing a number of Montagnards of various origins to look for better opportunities further south, even as far as the northern Indochina peninsula. As Geddes states, "the movement which took [the Hmong] beyond the borders of China was a continuation of a process occurring within China" (1976, pp. 25–26). Among these communities, there was a substantial element of the Hmong sub-group of the Miao minority. If we are to believe the figures available today on the demography of the Miao in China and the Hmong in the peninsula, we must conclude that only a fraction of the original group wanted, or was able, to go south. Mottin (1980) estimates that 85 per cent of the Miao stayed in China. Supporting this observation is the decreasing density of Miao/Hmong as one leaves Guizhou and moves down to central Thailand through northern Vietnam and Laos (see Michaud and Culas 1997).

Among the set of factors contributing to the confrontation between the Han state and the minorities in the Massif in the late nineteenth century was the presence of European colonial powers south of the Massif. From the beginning of the 1860s, the French and the British were competing to find and secure a way into South China and its lucrative resources and market potential. However, the Manchu dynasty only reluctantly tolerated this religious, commercial, and military infiltration by foreign powers in the south, and was annoyed that minorities in its own territory were connecting up in one way or another with these foreigners. Strategically speaking, there was no other choice for Beijing but to increase its administrative and military presence in the southern frontier, and clashes became inevitable.

It was in the second half of the nineteenth century that significant numbers of migrating Hmong penetrated the peninsula and rapidly reached as far south as the 17th parallel near Tak in Thailand, following roughly a northeast/southwest route from Tonkin (northern Vietnam). These migrations took the form of small waves of pioneering households grouping together to clear the forest in order to grow upland dry rice and maize. Usually after only a few years, when social and ritual problems appeared or when the soil was no longer capable of sustaining good crops, these groups disbanded, and lineages went looking for other parties further away to join with them in the clearing of new patches of empty forest.

Geddes also emphasized that so-called "pull factors" were incentives for the Hmong to move into the peninsula when noting that "if a new territory appears before [the Miao] their migration speeds up according to its potentialities" (Geddes 1976, p. 29). Supporting this argument, recent ethnographic studies have highlighted a significant factor in the decision of the Hmong to migrate, and in their choice of territory — namely, the particular relationship between the Hmong and the Muslim Chinese caravaners, the "Haw" (Culas 1997*b*). For a long time, the Haw, who originally were from Yunnan, were the only providers of salt and metals, as well as some consumer goods, to the Hmong. These goods were exchanged for medicinal plants and for specialized items of the Chinese pharmacopoeia. The Haw were conducting this trade with many of the populations in the most remote settlements of Burma (now called Myanmar), Thailand, Laos, and northern Vietnam. This relationship between the Haw and the Hmong came to include a very lucrative item, opium, that could thus find an easy transport route out of the villages (Culas 1997*a*). The itinerant trade, about which still very little is known, followed ancient routes which for centuries had linked hinterland cities in China, like Kunming, Dali, Jinghong, and Chengdu, to maritime trading posts and capitals, such as Moulmein, Ayutthaya, and Bangkok, as well as Vinh and Hanoi in northern Vietnam. Thirty years ago, old Hmong living in Laos and Vietnam still remembered their travels with the Haw caravaners in the late nineteenth century. They quite often worked as grooms for the horses and mules loaded with cloth, salt, or opium. Some of them say that they explored new and unpopulated fertile regions, for instance, the Tran Ninh plateau in Laos and the mountains north of Nan in Thailand, and that there were thus possibilities offered to those who wanted to move. The Hmong migration towards the southwest was therefore not made blindly.

This relationship between the Hmong and the Haw was thus a significant factor in the decision to migrate and in the choice of new territory. The blend of fertile and available forest land in proximity to a Haw caravan route was perfectly suited for the Hmong both to escape the Han wrath and to try their luck further away.

Another factor that contributed to the Hmong migration, although this one is rarely referred to in historical studies on the minorities in the region, was directly linked to that activity which until very recently commanded a significant share of the group's energy and focused its labour productivity — the growing and selling of opium. Let us first examine the roots of the problem. Due to the marketing of large quantities of opium in China, first by the Portuguese in the eighteenth century and later by the British and the French, who were bent on raising profits to support their colonial efforts locally, a high level of opium consumption was reached in China in the nineteenth century (15 million Chinese opium addicts in 1870, according to McCoy 1989, p. 63). This trend was significantly stimulated and skilfully maintained by the British, who could have the poppies grown in Bengal and the opium produced at an extremely cheap price, and then distributed through the East India Company network developed throughout Asia in the eighteenth and nineteenth centuries (ibid., p. 60). As early as the eighteenth century, though, Chinese leaders were worried by this growing trade and the huge loss in revenue due to the net importation of thousands of tons of raw opium. Inevitably, as a result of such high stakes, the two main opponents eventually clashed in what were called the Opium Wars (1838–42 and 1856–58), both of which were won by the European colonialists. Following the Opium Wars and the Treaty of Nanking in 1842, China was forced to allow the Europeans, and the Americans too, to install trade posts at a number of locations on the Chinese coast and, subsequently, to allow them to trade almost freely in the huge Chinese market. In order to compete with the intruders and avoid a huge loss in revenue due to the net importation of thousands of tons of raw opium, the only option left to the Chinese was to promote and support the production of opium within its own territory, which the central authorities quickly managed to do. The populations inhabiting the areas suitable for this production, basically the mountains and plateaux of the south, were pressured into growing poppies and producing raw opium for sale to government agents, to be processed and sold in the interior market. The pace was such that, by 1880, opium production in China began to exceed imports from British India (Le Failler 1995, p. 242). Ironically, the French and the British, who were able to reach the southern parts of the Massif through the valleys leading north from Burma and French Indochina, also were pushing these groups of producers in that same direction.[4] Highland minorities in southern China were then caught up in fierce competition, the dimensions of which largely exceeded their usual social circles, their political understanding and, indeed, their military capacities. Locally, having understood the lucrative potential of this new trade and having noticed the competition between the Chinese and the Europeans, the Hmong tried to make the most of it and rapidly went on the road leading to economic war with the Chinese administrators.

THE HMONG IN THE PENINSULA DURING THE TWENTIETH CENTURY

Up to the early twentieth century only Christian missionaries and a few explorers — chiefly British and French, such as Jean Dupuis, in the 1870s, and Archibald Colquhoun in the 1880s, when searching for ways to penetrate the Chinese hinterland — were able to visit the Miao/Hmong in China and northern Vietnam. However, rapidly thereafter the Hmong became the subjects of marked interest to European military authorities, missionaries, administrators, explorers, and, later, researchers. This interest on the part of Westerners in Montagnard societies in the region coincides with the foundation of anthropology and ethnology as scientific disciplines, and definitely fitted in with the cultural trend to explore exoticism. Books, articles, and notes written on the Montagnards are numerous in the early twentieth century — see, for instance, Lefèvre-Pontalis (1892, 1896), Girard (1903), Bonifacy (1904*a*, 1904*b*), Raquez and Cam (1904), Raquez (1909), Lunet de la Jonquière (1906), D'Ollone (1912), and Savina (1924) in French, and Clarke (1911) and Pollard (1919) in English.

These early studies of Hmong society were motivated by missionary action — taking chiefly the shape of linguistic studies aimed at translating the Bible into local dialects (details in Smalley et al. 1990, chap. 11) — and also by the desire to establish control over newly gained territory. In addition, subjects such as physical anthropology (Girard 1903), and security issues like the Pachay revolt of 1918–21 in Laos and northern Vietnam (Savina 1924), were addressed. It was only long after these first steps in general ethnography and the systematic collection of data on Hmong culture that the study and analysis of social organization, religion, and mythology began to develop — but this had to wait until the 1960s before really being able to expand. Such more recent works on the Hmong (that is, those conducted over the last four decades) are both well known and widely available.

The knowledge acquired about the Hmong during this last century allows a few points to be made — in particular, that the population movements recorded during the twentieth century can be localized in space and time. In order to better highlight the dynamic qualities and the principal issues involved in these movements, we will focus on a few zones. First we will seek to explain the massive support of the Viet Minh by the Hmong in the region of the western part of northern Vietnam, which is largely dominated by the Tai. The process of division within the Hmong society in Laos will then be discussed. The division took place during the international historical events which led to the exile of many Hmong to Thailand after 1975. In a zone on the Thai-Lao border, we will also see that migratory flux could be reversed within a few years. Finally, in Thailand, the backlash from the two Indochina wars meant that the Hmong and the Thai state looked upon each other with a notable lack of trust.

BURMA (NOW KNOWN AS MYANMAR)

In the case of Burma the British policy was to maintain the long-established opposition between the Christianized minorities and the majority, the Buddhist Mons, in order to better control local politics as well as to efficiently exploit the colonized kingdom. This aggravated further the rift between highlanders and lowlanders. However, the small number of Montagnards involved in the late immigration to Burma, in contrast to the more ancient highland migrants like the Shan and Karen, precludes us from devoting more space here to the Burmese situation. Recent arrivals might have included only a very small number of Hmong, or perhaps none at all.

VIETNAM

Historically speaking, the French colonial grip on the highlands where the Hmong lived was first officially marked in 1883, when the Hue treaty made Tonkin and Annam French protectorates. In 1885 the

Tientsin treaty signed with China gave France the upper hand over other European colonial powers to build a presence in Yunnan. France then began to take control over and to occupy the Red River Basin and its principal adjacent valleys. The northern Lao principalities, which would become the northern part of Laos, were then freed from Siamese occupation and became a French protectorate in 1893. A unified Laos thus became the fifth member of the *Union indochinoise* in 1896, with the (however reluctant) approval of the British and the Chinese.

The French colonial policy towards mountain minorities in the north of French Indochina varied, following the local policies and alliances contracted by the colonial administrators on the ground. A significant example is the early relationship established between the French and the Tai (especially the White Tai) in the Black River valley, a large region called Sip Song Chau Tai in the western parts of northern Vietnam between the Upper Red River valley and the Laotian border. Several Tai groups inhabited the alluvial plains and certain foothills of that region. For around 1,000 years they had had a hierarchical social and political organization with powerful landlords and an exploited peasantry. For the French administration, as for the Vietnamese representatives from Hue before them, this stable traditional structure was seen as an attractive chain of command for colonial institutions. Having the ear of the indigenous leader was thus the key to control.

A major figure with whom the early French administration allied was the White Tai leader Déo Van Tri, who died in 1909. This traditional Tai leader in the Black River valley, lord of Lai Chau, and former officer of the Black Flag army, participated in the conquest of Luang Prabang in 1887. He then allied with the French, becoming a close collaborator of Auguste Pavie, who in return made him the official and fully fledged leader of the Sip Song Chau Tai in 1890. This alliance worked extremely well — for example, it secured a stronghold for the French troops fleeing the Japanese in the spring of 1945.

By treaty, Pavie also confirmed the principle of the hereditary transmission of power. This recognition constituted the juridical basis upon which was to be founded, decades later, the Tai Federation of Tonkin. In reaction to the unilateral proclamation of independence of the Democratic Republic of Vietnam by the Viet Minh in September 1945, a French-Tai temporary accord was promulgated in 1948, creating an independent Tai Federation inside the *Union française* that grouped together the provinces of Lai Chau, Phong Tho, and Son La under the presidency of the Tai, Déo Van Long, a descendant of Déo Van Tri. The legal status of what was called the "sub-minorities" inside the Federation was claimed to be one of *adhésion de fait*, or *de facto* inclusion (Nollet 1953, p. 43).

The Tai of the Federation took advantage of the French support to exploit further the "sub-minorities" in their neighbourhood, of whom the Hmong formed the largest element. Teaching in the Tai language and script was quickly organized with the help of the *Ecole française d'Extrême Orient*. No other minority population in that region enjoyed such privileges. With the full development of Viet Minh activities at the end of the 1940s, the Tai of Déo Van Long drew closer and closer to the French while, understandably, the Hmong, exploited by the former, sided with the communists to challenge the might of the Tai rulers. After the Dien Bien Phu defeat in 1954, in which numerous Hmong from Sip Song Chau Tai were instrumental as allies of the Viet Minh, several White and Black Tai from wealthy families fled to Laos, followed by other Hmong families who had collaborated with the French east of the Red River, particularly in the production of opium. These families were outside the influence of the Tai Federation and, consequently, had no particular reason to fight the French. Occasional clashes between Hmong and Viet Minh fighters occurred over the decade following the year 1946. Deprived of French support after the Geneva Accord of 1954, anti-communist Hmong rebels were severely repressed until their complete submission in 1957, which in turn led to a second wave of refugees from Vietnam pouring into Laos. As in China earlier, those who stayed were clearly and irrevocably submitting to the central power under a general policy of complete Vietnamization (Viet 1968).

The political behaviour of the Hmong in northern Vietnam during the wars, which might appear surprisingly volatile and inconsistent, is however easily explainable. The Hmong, like most Montagnard societies in the region, have a stateless, kinship-based social organization, the simplest form of political organization. This gives each head of household the full right to make every decision regarding the course of action he and his immediate family should be taking, regardless of what other non-related Hmong might choose to do or not to do. In the true fashion of independent nomadic swiddeners, there are no political ties between the Hmong above this level. This explains why the Hmong from different clans in different locations have taken radically different political options depending on the region, on the individual actors, and on the specific pressure put on them,. This was the case in northern Vietnam, and it has been even more so in Laos.

Living in upper northern Vietnam outside the main combat zones during the second Indochina war, or the American Vietnam War, the Hmong seem to have had a relatively stable relationship with the communist state in the Democratic Republic of Vietnam.[5] The authorized growing of opium — officially stopped only after 1993 — guaranteed them a regular cash income and also contributed significantly to the coffers of the Viet Minh. Moreover, the near-absence of Kinh settlers in the mountains where the Hmong live — namely, the provinces of Cao Bang, Ha Giang, Lao Cai, Lai Chau, Son La, Hoa Binh, Thah Hoa, and Nghe An — and the active participation of some Hmong in local and regional administration[6] allowed them to switch relatively smoothly from a subsistence to a commercial economy. In 1989 the Vietnamese authorities estimated that 558,043 Hmong lived in the country (Nguyen 1995, p. 103), accounting for 0.9 per cent of the national population.

LAOS

In the Laotian mountains, the relations between the Hmong and the French developed somewhat differently. It was after the arrival of the Japanese forces in Laos in 1945 that contacts intensified between French parachutists, responsible for the organization of the resistance in the hinterland, and some Hmong clans on the Xieng Khouang plateau (in Vietnamese: Tran Ninh). Touby Ly Fong, of the Ly clan, sheltered and guided these French soldiers in the mountains for several months. In September 1946, he was rewarded by being nominated *Chao Muong*, district governor of Xieng Khouang province, by the King of Luang Phrabang. It was in this region that the Hmong of Laos would keep the most regular links with the French, be they colonial administrators, missionaries, or military authorities.

In deciding whether or not to collaborate with one or another of these outsiders, the Hmong of the region again took different directions. The traditional rivalry between members of the Lo clan and those of the Ly clan turned into an open opposition, the former collaborating with the Japanese while the latter opted for the French. Internal division crystallized rapidly between these two clans, and also divided those who were allied to them through kinship, economic, or ritual ties. This division came to influence the future of practically all of the Hmong in Laos. They would, directly or not, be obliged to take sides in the military conflict between the French and the Japanese, and also later between the Americans and the communists.

Several thousand Hmong thus participated, more or less closely, in the war against the spread of the Pathet Lao and Viet Minh communists in the mountains, while other Hmong, perhaps as numerous, were enrolled in the ranks of the People's Liberation Army. However, the number of Hmong in Laos who had genuinely tried not to get drawn into taking sides in the conflict were also numerous. But the very difficult material conditions they lived under during the war — the impossibility of cultivating under shelling, displacement of populations fleeing the combat zones, and so forth — did not allow them to provide for their basic needs in the way they were accustomed to. With the war, social and economic inequalities soared. The income of a Hmong swiddener growing mountain rice, or even opium, did not match that of a soldier fighting in the Royal Army under Hmong General Vang Pao, who was heavily supported by American funding. Thus, social pressure exerted through lineage or clan obligations did not allow access to the food supplies provided by the Americans unless one had a close kin ready to help in the administration of the army. This form of collaboration directly or indirectly touched practically every family and ignored their desires, often very strong, not to get involved in the conflict. In the regions under American/Laotian control, as well as in the "liberated zones" of the north, royalists and communists were equally unhappy about the lack of commitment to one side or another by many Montagnards, and these "pacifists" were therefore suspected of sympathizing with the enemy and had to suffer the consequences.

Today, of the eleven Laotian provinces where Hmong live, four are home to more than 70 per cent of the Hmong population. These provinces are Xieng Khouang, Vientiane, Sayaburi, and Luang Prabang. In Xieng Khouang province (one of the most affected by war) alone, the total population decreased by more than 40 per cent between 1961 and 1985, with a large proportion of them from the Hmong group. In the Huaphan, Luang Namtha, and Sayaburi provinces, the decrease amounted to 23 per cent in the same period, while the figure was 8 per cent in Phongsaly, Udomsai, and Luang Prabang (Taillard 1989, p. 192). More precisely, between May 1975 and June 1985, 309,694 persons left Laos to take refuge in Thailand. Of that number, 194,220 were classified as *Lao lum*, or Lowland Lao, also including Chinese and Vietnamese living in Laos. The remaining 115,474 refugees were broadly identified as Montagnards, including *Lao theung*, or Mountain Slope Lao, and *Lao sung*, or Highland Lao. The Hmong essentially belonged to the latter. Thus, Taillard estimates that approximately 30 per cent of the Hmong in Laos fled the country after 1975. All we have records of, however, is that the number of Hmong from Laos and Vietnam who took refuge in Thailand up to 1990 is 116,000 individuals. In 1994, the Hmong in Laos were believed to number 260,000 individuals (Chazee 1995, p. 111), while their number was estimated to be between 300,000 and 500,000 in 1972 (Whitaker et al. 1985).

THAILAND

In Thailand, the situation evolved in yet another manner. Ever since Montagnard groups had first arrived in the peninsula, they had been tolerated by the Siamese monarchs. Most of these groups were practising pioneering or rotational swiddening, Actually, the kingdom and its northern principalities did not have, and made no attempt to gain, a clear knowledge of the highland minorities dwelling in the mountains. Unlike their neighbours in Burma, Laos and northern Vietnam, under firm British or French colonial control since the end of the nineteenth century, the Siamese/Thai were not yet attuned to the political ideology of administrative centralism and hermetic territorial and border control (Lim 1984; Thongchai 1994, chap. 3). For the kings of the modern Thai monarchy, the Chakkri dynasty, the traditional existence of buffer spaces on the northern kingdom's periphery was easily tolerable and served multiple objectives in connection with safe isolation and trade. The fact that peripheral mountainous and forested space was inhabited by non-Thai semi-nomadic agriculturalists was not of much importance, as long as they did not pose a threat to the kingdom's security and wealth (ibid., chap. 5). In some cases, for centuries and certainly up until the 1950s, highland minorities of northern Siam/Thailand could peacefully live their own lives without major conflicts with or hindrance from Lowland Thai.

In the early 1950s, however, the Thai state initiated a certain number of activities aimed at establishing "pacific and specific" links with the Montagnards in a few mountain villages especially targeted.[7] Why did the state at that very moment suddenly become aware of the existence of these mountain dwellers to the point of designing programmes for their specific inclusion in the Thai nation? After all, the Montagnards accounted for — then, as they still do today — only 1 per cent of the national population, and spoke languages and had religious practices dramatically different from the majority of Thailand's population.

The answer lies in the troubled regional political situation of that time. The extension of decolonization movements, whether or not supported by communist ideology in neighbouring countries, was conducive to proclamations of independence. Moreover, in 1953–54 several autonomous regions, based on various highland ethnic minorities in Yunnan, were created in southern China (Thompson and Adloff 1955, p. 222). Quite understandably, these political and ideological changes in neighbouring countries worried the Thai state.

In response to the communist advance, the American pressure on the Thai government became ever stronger in the early 1950s. The Americans were anxious that the Thai take active control over their northern frontier, a mountainous area suspected to be a potential source of instability. The United States feared the infiltration of "hostile agents" from north Vietnam, through Laos. It was due to their major financial, material, and technical support that the Americans succeeded in orientating, even managing, the various programmes aimed at controlling the land and the people in highland Thailand. Such externally funded policies targeting the Montagnards — then, and still often today, generically called "hilltribes" — in particular, addressed anti-insurrectional activities and the suppression of opium production and circulation (Huff 1967; Amara et al. 1993, p. 4). Armed opposition in northern Thailand started in 1967, following the destruction of numerous opium fields and a few Hmong villages in the Nan region.[8] As late as 1982, there was occasional fighting in four border areas — in Nan, Tak, Chiang Kham, and Loei-Phitsanulok. In spite of the important and multi-faceted American support, the Thai army did not totally succeed in suppressing the insurrection in the mountains.

In 1980, Thailand unofficially agreed with China to supply the Khmer Rouge — who, in spite of Beijing's support, were being severely pressured by the Vietnamese inside Cambodia after the 1979 invasion — with the possibility of retreating into Thai territory, where the Vietnamese would not follow them. In support of its new Thai partner, China totally cut off its support of the Communist Party of Thailand (CPT), which it had helped for decades. China also asked the communists in Thailand to cease all military activities against the Thai state. Thus, communist guerrilla warfare was not militarily defeated, but rather was diffused through an international conjunction of events that rendered it henceforth pointless (Dassé 1993, p. 95).

As in Laos, most of the Hmong in Thailand avoided taking sides in the conflict either with the Beijing- or Hanoi-supported guerrillas or with the Thai military. The violence of the conflicts and, occasionally, the shelling of mountain villages, however, forced many of them temporarily to take refuge in the neighbouring Laotian province of Sayaburi. As in 1967, several thousand Hmong from Nan province took their goods and families to the more peaceful highlands of Laos, but finally, in 1975, the maximum spread of the war reached the Sayaburi region, and a reverse movement took place, with many of the Hmong returning to the neighbouring Thai provinces.[9]

Life having finally resumed a more peaceful course in the Indochina Massif, the worries of the Thai state concerning security issues on the highland frontier have today largely subsided. Throughout most of the 1980s and part of the 1990s we can, nevertheless, easily detect a disposition by Thai experts to hold the highlanders, and the Hmong in particular, responsible for one national problem or another, in particular for problems concerning deforestation and soil erosion (cf. Arbhabhirama et al. 1988, pp. 174–75; critical analysis in Michaud 1994) — even where this tendency has more ancient roots (see Wanat 1989, p. 3). The priority is now to settle Montagnard villages permanently, to introduce commercial agricultural practices, and to implement national education *in situ* (Wanat 1989), with the objective of finally and definitely integrating these non-Thai animists into the national identity, which is Thai, Buddhist, and monarchist.

In 1995, according to the Tribal Research Institute of the Ministry of Interior, the Hmong population numbered 124,000 individuals living in 233 villages in thirteen of the northern provinces, the most important of which are Chiang Mai, Chiang Rai, Tak, and Nan. This represents 17.8 per cent of the Montagnard population in Thailand (total number of individuals: 696,629) and 0.2 per cent of the country's total population.

BEYOND ASIA

A review of Hmong migrations would not be complete without mentioning an important movement of populations from Laos within what has since been called the "Hmong diaspora". Following the communist take-over in 1975, a wave of Montagnards, formed largely of Lao and Hmong but also containing several other ethnic denominations (Lua, White Tai, Yao, Haw, Lahu, Khmu, and so on), fled to Thailand, where the United Nations High Commissioner for Refugees (UNHCR) had temporarily assumed responsibility for them until they could officially migrate to a third country.[10] This exodus from Laos, as mentioned earlier, was linked to Lao and Hmong collaboration with the pro-American forces. Those who had collaborated preferred to flee the country rather than to have to endure retaliation, and sometimes severe "re-education", by the Pathet Lao. The majority of them have been able to leave Thailand and migrate to a third country.

Currently, the most important Hmong community in the West is in the United States (approximately 100,000 individuals according to North and Yang 1988, and Sherman 1988, p. 594). California is home to almost half of them, while the rest are to be found in Minnesota, Wisconsin, Washington, Pennsylvania, and North Carolina (Supang and Reynolds 1988, p. 239). The number of Hmong in France is approximately 10,000, including 1,400 in French Guyana.[11] Canada accepted approximately 900 individuals, while another 360 are in Australia, 260 in China, and 250 in Argentina (Supang and Reynolds 1988, p. 17, citing UNHCR sources of December 1986).

POLITICAL PERSPECTIVES

In the light of what we know today of the various dimensions of Hmong culture and social organization, it has become evident that during the two Indochina wars, regional and foreign governments, institutions, and armies misunderstood the motivation of the Hmong in the region. What was interpreted then as opposition and a siding with the enemy was in fact the precise reflection of a very strong will for independence and for the maintenance of an age-old isolation, both of which characterize Hmong identity.

Let us recall a few basic points. The Hmong have a kinship-based society. They are related to each other primarily through blood ties and alliance, not through geographical proximity or political affinities. A Hmong from the province of Guizhou in southern China who belongs to the same patronymic clan as a Hmong from Laos is sure to get shelter and assistance from his kin. On the other hand, two Hmong from neighbouring villages in the same country, who belong to different clans, will not feel any obligation whatsoever to provide each other with help and support. This has far-reaching consequences. One of the most obvious is that stateless and landless societies like the Hmong cannot readily organize into a political body based on supra-clanic ties or on territorial claims. The concept of ethno-nationalism is not relevant here. This concept belongs to a body of political theorization that has often been associated — at times hastily — with many minorities in Southeast Asia in attempts to explain their behaviour during the Indochina wars.

A further predicament in their relationship to a more formalized political organization is the considerable geographical spreading of the Hmong over four, perhaps five, countries. As Tapp states:

> Much of the trade conducted across these (admittedly permeable) borders is classified as illicit, as is also much of the human movement across them. In the discourse of modern nationalism, one is dealing with economic phenomena classified as "smuggling" and human mobility categorized as "refugee" or "illegal immigrant". (Tapp 1990, pp. 149–50)

Great efforts to get large numbers of Hmong under the same banner in Laos during the second Indochina war had neither lasting nor overwhelming effects in spite of crafty "social engineering". The mere idea of a Hmong military organization is not consistent with the segmentary tradition of the group. Some organizational formalization has materialized, but only temporarily, as a result of outside manipulation of certain internal antagonisms, and of a recurrent and always latent messianic ideology,[12] particularly among the Hmong of Laos (Tapp 1989; Culas 1997b).

The major cause of Hmong insurrections — without the catalyst of a foreign military command or the temporary emergence of a messianic leader — was direct aggression by a national army, for example, in Thailand between 1967 and 1982. When the Hmong took up arms, it was not to follow a political ideology — as suggested by some American authors such as Hamilton-Merritt (1993) — but to defend their lives, their families, their houses and their crops, including the right to carry on with the only cash crop that really generated profits — opium — a cash crop, be it noted, which these same regional powers forced on them in the nineteenth century, when the profits generated were more than instrumental in supporting the colonial ventures of the era.

As was the case in southern China during the nineteenth century, history has once again caught up with the swiddener in his forest and severely encroached on his traditional life cycle — but this time to the point that flight is no longer possible. Human waves literally climb the mountain slopes in China, Vietnam, and Thailand. Concurrently, in Thailand and Laos the state orders the mountain agriculturalist to abandon his last refuge and settle down in the foothills in order to empty the higher altitude forests of "unproductive" swiddeners, whose practices are said to be damaging to the entire ecosystem. The meeting with the Other, postponed for such a long time, has become inevitable. What follows is a path where massive acculturation is to be confronted, thanks to the military draft, national schooling, international market forces, and television.

No doubt, the only solution left for the Hmong, if they are to try to organize into a supra-national and cross-clanic unified body, is both a politically promising and a culturally undermining one. This involves education and literacy. The struggle to get education in vernacular languages in each of the national contexts where the Hmong live has been simmering for several years, but has not yet yielded any substantial results. Each state is eager to bring its minorities into the national identity; in general, only lip-service is paid to the promotion of minority languages and their cultures. Education in the national language is the rule, and this invariably leads to an increased fracture between young Montagnards who are attracted by the promise of modern life and the elders holding on to old ways.

Unexpectedly, support for a collective self-consciousness and, perhaps, some sort of collective political action, might come from returning Hmong refugees who are now citizens of Western countries. There is a noticeable tendency among the second generation of Hmong refugees, particularly in America and France, to come back in search of their origins. All are educated, and many want to get involved politically, although their agendas may still be tainted with the old anti-communist rhetoric. However, their impact must not be underestimated, and it could be revealing to monitor their actions and analyse the consequences of them in the near future, especially in Laos.

NOTES

This chapter is a revised version of a French article published by the authors (Michaud and Culas 1997).

1. For research done on the region as a whole, see, for example, Lebar et al. (1964), Kunstadter (1967), and Schrock et al. (1970, 1972). Several other authors who studied the Montagnards or highland populations in one country or one area in particular can be added. For instance, studies on Laos and Thailand have been done by Keen (1966), Binney (1968), Moréchand (1968), Walker (1970), Dessaint (1972), Lemoine (1972), Yang (1975), Bertrais (1977), and Mottin (1980).
2. *Tabulation from the 1990 Population Census of the People's Republic of China* (1993).
3. We here call "Montagnard" the ethnic groups belonging to two linguistic families: (a) the Tibeto-Burmese branch of the Sino-Tibetan family: Karen, Lisu, and Lahu

(Lolo or Yi group), and Akha (Hani group); and (b) the Miao-Yao branch of the Austric linguistic family, including Hmong (Miao group) and Yao. We would also like to state here that, despite the historical and largely unjustified association of the French word "Montagnard" with very specific Austronesian highland minorities in South Central Vietnam, the term is given here in its original meaning of "mountain people", as used by most French ethnographers in the late nineteenth and early twentieth century.

4. The extension of French involvement in the opium trade both in China and in their colony is clearly illustrated in many economic articles of the early twentieth century, such as several articles by H. Brenier and W. Lichtenfelder in the 1903 issue of the French Indochinese *Bulletin Économique*.

5. "The provisions of the 1960 Constitution of the Democratic Republic of Vietnam regarding the status of national minorities are virtually identical with those of the Popular Republic of China Constitution. They provide for equality and autonomy within a unified, multinational state. Prior to the promulgation of the 1960 Constitution, a decree concerning the establishment of autonomous areas in the DR of Vietnam had been issued on April 29, 1955. On May 7, 1955, there came into being the Tai-Meo Autonomous Region, the name of which was subsequently changed to Tay Bac (Northwest) Autonomous Region. The Tay Bac AR embraces an area equivalent to three provinces in the mountains between the Red River valley and the Laotian frontier. In the north, it borders the province of Yunnan. Its area of over 36,000 square kilometres is one fifth of that of the entire area of the DR of Vietnam [North Vietnam]; its population of 500,000 includes 25 different nationalities, the most important of which are the Thai (T'ai) and the Meo (Miao)." (Moseley 1973, pp. 157–58).

6. For instance, in 1995 a Black Hmong woman was head of the Sa Pa district in Lao Cai province, a district where the Kinh, comprising 10 per cent, are largely outnumbered by the Hmong, at 60 per cent (provincial data collected in Lao Cai by Michaud in May 1995).

7. In the Nan region, for instance, Lee (1981) and Kesmanee (1991) give details of this early activity by the Thai state.

8. About the impact of the war and the national opium policy on the Hmong communities in Nan province, see Culas (1997*b*, chap. 3 part 2).

9. According to the 1986 CCSDPT Handbook (Committee for Coordination of Services to Displaced Persons in Thailand), the camp [of Ban Nam Yao, Nan province] was left open to 1,350 Htin and 750 Hmong displaced persons claiming to be Thai citizens. They had moved into Laos in the 1960s but re-entered Thailand with the influx of Laotian refugees between 1975 and 1979 (Supang and Reynolds 1988, p. 30).

10. On the problems of refugees in Southeast Asia, see Phuwadol and Chongvatana (1988) for data on Thailand, and Condominas and Pottier (1982) for case studies.

11. See Hassoun (1983). On the Hmong in French Guyana, see Géraud (1993).

12. Sometimes, when social and religious crises run very deep, a man — usually one

who is poor and discreet — can be recognized by the people as being a "Saviour". His father is the mythical "King of the Sky". According to historical context, this Messiah can lead these followers in war or in a peaceful expectation of the coming of the "Great Peace" for the Hmong.

REFERENCES

Amara Pongsapich, Suriya Veeravongse, and Phinit Lapthananon. "Natural Resources Management Policy and Ethnic Minorities: Conflicts and Resolutions in the Huay Buffer Zone". *Proceedings of the 5th. International Conference on Thai Studies.* London: School of Oriental and African Studies, 1993.

Arbhabhirama, A. et al. *Thailand: Natural Resources Profile.* Natural Resources of South-East Asia series. Singapore: Oxford University Press, 1988.

Bertrais, Yves. *Le Mariage traditionnel chez les Hmong blancs du Laos et de la Thaïlande.* Chiang Mai: Siosavath, 1977.

Binney, George A. "The Social and Economic Organisation of Two White Meo [Hmong] Communities in Northern Thailand". Ph.D. dissertation. Washington, D.C.: Wildlife Management Institute, 1968.

Bonifacy, Auguste Louis-M. "Les groupes ethniques de la Rivière Claire". *Revue Indo-Chinoise*, 30 June 1904*a*, pp. 813–28.

Bonifacy, Auguste Louis-M. "Les groupes ethniques de la Rivière Claire, suite". *Revue Indo-Chinoise*, 15 July 1904*b*, pp. 1–16.

Brenier, Henri. "Appendice I: note sur la production et le commerce de l'opium en Chine". *Bulletin Économique* 6ème année, 1903, pp. 763–76.

Chazee, Laurent. *Atlas des ethnies et des sous-ethnies du Laos.* Bangkok [published by the author], 1995.

Clarke, Samuel R. *Among the Tribes in South-West China.* London: China Inland Mission, Morgan and Scott, 1911.

Condominas, Georges and Richard Pottier, eds. *Les réfugiés originaires de l'Asie du Sud-Est. Arrière-plan historique et culturel. Les Motivations de départ.* Paris: La Documentation Française, Collection des Rapports Officiels, 1982.

Culas, Christian. "Les usages de l'opium chez les Hmong en Asie du Sud-Est: tolérances et contraintes sociales". In *De l'épice à l'extase. Excitants et substances du rêve en Asie du Sud-Est,* edited by Philippe Le Failler and Annie Hubert. Collection Grand Sud. Songkla: Prince of Songkla University Press, 1997*a*.

⎯⎯⎯⎯⎯. "Le Messianisme hmong en Asie du Sud-Est. Rituels et représentations du monde". Ph.D. dissertation, Université de Provence at Aix en Provence, France, 1997*b*.

D'Ollone, H. *Ecritures des peuples non chinois de la Chine.* Paris: Ernest Leroux, 1912.

Dassé, Martial. *Les guérillas en Asie du Sud-Est: les stratégies de la guérilla asiatique.* Paris: L'Harmattan-Fondation pour les Études de Défense Nationale, 1993.

Dessaint, Alain Y. "Economic Organisation of the Lisu of the Thai Highlands". Ph.D. dissertation, University of Hawaii, 1972.

Geddes, William Robert. *Migrants of the Mountains: The Cultural Ecology of the Blue Miao (Hmong Njua) of Thailand.* Oxford: Clarendon Press, 1976.
Géraud, Marie-Odile. "Les Hmong de Guyane française. Étude ethnologique du changement social et des représentations de la tradition dans une communauté en exil". Ph.D. dissertation, Université de Montpellier III, France. 1993.
Girard, Henri. *Les Tribus sauvages du Haut-Tonkin: Mans et Méos. Notes anthropométriques et ethnographiques.* Paris: Imprimerie Nationale, 1903.
Hamilton-Merritt, Jane. *Tragic Mountains: The Hmong, the Americans, and the Secret Wars for Laos, 1942–1992.* Bloomington: Indiana University Press, 1993.
Hassoun, Jean-Pierre. "Hmong réfugiés: Trajectoires ethno-spatiales". Ph.D. dissertation, Ecole des Hautes Etudes en Sciences Sociales de Paris, France, 1983.
Haudricourt, André Georges. "Les langues Miao-Yao". In *Le Riz en Asie du Sud-Est* edited by N. Revel, vol. 1, pp. 43–46. Paris: Éditions de l'École des hautes études en sciences sociales, 1988.
Huff, L.W. "The Thai Mobile Development Unit Programme". In *Southeast Asian Tribes, Minorities and Nations*, edited by Peter Kunstadter. Princeton, N.J.: Princeton University Press, 1967.
Jenks, Robert Darrah. *Insurgency and Social Disorder in Guizhou. The "Miao" Rebellion, 1854–1873.* Honolulu: University of Hawaii Press, 1994.
Keen, F.G.B. "The Meo of North-West Thailand: A Problem of Integration". MA dissertation Victoria University of Wellington, New Zealand, 1966.
Kesmanee, Chupinit. "Highlanders, Intervention and Adaptation: A Case Study of a Mong N'jua (Moob Ntsuab) Village of Pattana". MA thesis (Geography), Victoria University of Wellington, New Zealand, 1991.
Kunstadter, Peter, ed. *Southeast Asian Tribes, Minorities and Nations.* Princeton, N.J.: Princeton University Press, 1967.
Lebar, F.M., G.H. Hickey, and J.K. Musgrave, eds. *Ethnic Groups of Mainland Southeast Asia.* New Haven: Human Relations Area Files, Yale University Press, 1964.
Lee Gar Yia. "The Effects of Development Measures on the Socio-Economy of the White Hmong". Ph.D. dissertation, University of Sydney, 1981.
Le Failler, Philippe. "Le coût social de l'opium au Vietnam. La problématique des drogues dans le philtre de l'Histoire". *Journal Asiatique* CCLXXXIII, no. 1 (1995): 239–64.
Lefèvre-Pontalis, Pierre. "Notes sur quelques populations du nord de l'Indo-Chine". *Journal asiatique* 8 (1892): 237–69.
———. "Notes sur quelques populations du nord de l'Indo-Chine". *Journal asiatique* 12 (1896): 1–43.
Lemoine, Jacques. *Un village Hmong Vert du Haut Laos. Milieu technique et organisation sociale.* Paris: Éditions du Centre National de Recherches Scientifiques, 1972.
Lichtenfelder, W. "Le pavot à opium". *Bulletin économique* 6ème année (1903): 597–614; 689–709; 752–62.
Lim Joo-Jock. *Territorial Power Domains, Southeast Asia, and China. The Geo-Strategy of an Overarching Massif.* Singapore: Institute of Southeast Asian Studies, and Canberra: Australian National University, 1984.
Lombard-Salmon, Claudine. *Un exemple d'acculturation chinoise: la province du Guizhou*

au XVIIIe siècle. Vol. LXXXIV. Paris: Publication de l'École Française d'Extrême-Orient, 1972.

Lunet de Lajonquière, Emile. *Ethnographie du Tonkin Septentrional*. Hanoi and Paris: E. Leroux, 1906.

McCoy, Alfred W., with C.B. Read and L.P. Adams III. *The Politics of Heroin in Southeast Asia*. Singapore: Harper Torchbooks, 1989.

Michaud, Jean. "Montagnes et forêts frontalières dans le Nord thaïlandais: L'État face aux Montagnards". In *Le défi forestier en Asie du Sud-Est/The Challenge of the Forest in Southeast Asia*, edited by R. De Koninck. Document no. 7. Québec: Groupe d'Études et de recherches sur l'Asie contemporaine (GÉRAC), Université Laval, 1994.

Michaud, Jean and Christian Culas. "Les Hmong de la péninsule indochinoise. Histoire et migrations". Les Cahiers des Sciences humaines. Paris: Office de la recherche scientifique et technique outre-mer, 1997.

Moréchand, Guy. "Le chamanisme des Hmong". *Bulletin de l'École Française d'Extrême-Orient* 54, no. IIX (1968): 53–294.

Moseley, G.V.R. *The Consolidation of the South China Frontier*. Berkeley: University of California Press, 1973.

Mottin, Jean. *History of the Hmong*. Bangkok: Odeon Store, 1980.

Nguyen, Van Thang. "The Hmong and the Dzao [Yao] Peoples in Vietnam: Impact of Traditional Socioeconomic and Cultural Factors on the Protection and Development of Forest Resources". In *The Challenges of Highland Development in Vietnam*, edited by Terry Rambo et al. Honolulu: Hawaii East-West Center Program on Environment; Hanoi: Center for Natural Resources and Environmental Studies, Hanoi University; and Berkeley: Center for Southeast Asia Studies, University of California, 1995.

Nollet, R. "Une Minorité du Vietnam: les Thais". *L'Afrique et l'Asie* [C.H.E.A.M.] 21 (1953): 38–47.

North, David S. and Doua Yang. *Profiles of the Highland Lao Communities in the United States. Final Report*. Washington: Office of Refugee Resettlement, Department of Health and Human Services, 1988.

Phuwadol Songprasert and Noppawan Chongvatana. *Thailand: A First Asylum Country for Indochinese Refugees*. Asian Studies Monograph no. 38. Bangkok: Institute of Asian Studies, Chulalongkorn University, 1988.

Pollard, Samuel. *The Story of the Miao*. London: Henry Hooks, 1919.

Raquez, A. "Variétés. Chez les Méos du Tranninh". *Revue Indochinoise*, 1909, pp. 924–27.

Raquez, A. and Cam, compilers. "Mémoires de Déo-Van-Tri". *Revue Indochinoise*, no. 4 (31 août) (1904): 256–75.

Savina, François-Marie. *Histoire des Miao*. Hong Kong: Imprimerie des Missions Étrangères, 1924.

Schrock, Joann L. et al. *Minority Groups in Thailand*. Ethnographic Study Series. Washington: Headquarters of the Department of the Army, 1970.

―――. *Minority Groups in North Vietnam*. Ethnographic Study Series. Washington: Headquarters of the Department of the Army, 1972.

Sherman, Spencer. "The Hmong in America". *National Geographic Magazine* 174, no. 4 (1988): 586–610.
Smalley, William A., Chia Koua Vang, and Gnia Yee Yang. *Mother of Writing: The Origin and Development of a Hmong Messianic Script.* Chicago and London: University of Chicago Press, 1990.
Supang Chantavanich and Bruce E. Reynolds, eds. *Indochinese Refugees: Asylum and Resettlement.* Asian Studies Monograph no. 39. Bangkok: Institute of Asian Studies, Chulalongkorn University, 1988.
Tabulation of the 1990 Population Census of the People's Republic of China. Beijing: Population Census Office, State Council and Department of Population Statistics, State Statistical Bureau, 1993.
Taillard, Christian. *Le Laos. Stratégies d'un État-tampon.* Montpellier: RECLUS, 1989.
Tapp, Nicholas. *Sovereignty and Rebellion: The White Hmong of Northern Thailand.* Singapore: Oxford University Press, 1989.

———. "Squatters of Refugees: Development and the Hmong". In *Ethnic Groups across National Boundaries in Mainland Southeast Asia*, edited by Gehan Wijeyewardene. Singapore: Institute of Southeast Asian Studies, 1990.
Thompson, V. and R. Adloff. *Minority Problems in Southeast Asia.* New York: Russell and Russell, 1955.
Thongchai Winichakul. *Siam Mapped. A History of the Geo-Body of a Nation.* Chiang Mai: Silkworm Books, 1994.
Tribal Research Institute (TRI). *The Hill Tribes of Thailand.* Chiang Mai: TRI, Technical Service Club, 1995.
Viet, Chung. "National Minorities and Nationality Policy in the DRV". *Vietnamese Studies* 15 (1968): 4–23.
Walker, Anthony R. *Lahu Nyi (Red Lahu) Village Society and Economy in North Thailand.* Chiang Mai: Tribal Research Centre, 1970.
Wanat Bhruksasri. "Government Policy: Highland Ethnic Minorities". In *Hill Tribes Today*, edited by J. McKinnon and B. Vienne. Bangkok: White Lotus-ORSTOM, 1989.
Wiens, Herold J. *China's March Toward the Tropics: A Discussion of the Southward Penetration of China's Culture, Peoples, and Political Control in Relation to the Non-Han-Chinese Peoples of South China and in the Perspective of Historical and Cultural Geography.* Hamden, Conn.: Shoe String Press, 1954.
Whitaker, D.P. et al. *Laos, a Country Study.* Washington: Foreign Area Studies, the American University, 1985.
Yang, Dao. *Les Hmong du Laos face au développement.* Vientiane: Siaosavath, 1975.

Regional Trade in Northwestern Laos: An Initial Assessment of the Economic Quadrangle

Andrew Walker

A GOLDEN OPPORTUNITY

"The Economic Quadrangle" is now the focus of Asia ... as the economic place for consumers who demand more choices for shopping and excursion. Also investors, businessmen and manufacturers who are intent to expand their trading, and investment can aim at increasing their benefits. ... We are ready for those investors, who are aiming for success, and profits, by cooperating with the Lao People's Democratic Republic. This is a golden opportunity in doing business, in the area full of natural resources and labour with lower wages. Therefore we can assure you of stability and achievement in business. (*The Economic Quadrangle Joint Development Corporation*, promotional brochure, 1996)

The Economic Quadrangle has become a popular motif in discussions of Southeast Asia's northern borderlands. For its proponents in international development organizations, national governments, and regional chambers of commerce, the Quadrangle is an ambitious vision of liberalized economic integration across national borders and rugged terrain. Creation of transport linkages between the expanding economies of northern Thailand and southern China via the hinterlands of Myanmar and Laos is promoted as a sure path to regional development and prosperity. In the tawdry tourist stalls where the borders of Thailand, Myanmar, and Laos meet on the Upper Mekong, Economic Quadrangle tee-shirts (four flags and a river of blue) are now sold alongside the

6. Regional Trade in Northwestern Laos: The Economic Quadrangle 123

opium memorabilia and Golden Triangle kitsch (three flags and a poppy) of an earlier socio-geometric era. A new frontier, we are told, is opening up: a deregulated Upper Mekong corridor, a new era for the borderlands.

The Economic Quadrangle Joint Development Corporation — a joint venture between the Lao government and a northern Thai construction firm — is one of the most ambitious and optimistic proponents of this new era. It is marketing an extraordinary future for northwestern Laos, one of the "quarters" of the Quadrangle and the focus of this chapter. The company's latest promotional brochure features a glowing, golden map of northwestern Laos, flanked by glossy pictures of investment opportunities, laid out to tempt the Thai entrepreneur. Service stations, warehouses, chemical plants, and shopping centres mingle with charming thatched-roofed villages nestled in verdant highland valleys. Artists' impressions of cruise boats, trains, tour buses, and airlines are arrayed in formation, ready for the transport infrastructure that will dissect and liberalize the region, a resort hotel, complete with a glistening swimming pool, glows in the setting sun against the backdrop of a blood-red sea. As even the most cursory cartographic inspection will show, for northwestern Laos this is a formidable vision indeed.

But in the Thai Mekong River town of Chiang Khong — the main trading point between northern Thailand and northwestern Laos — there is a sense of weariness about the Quadrangle hype. Visiting in late 1996, I heard endless stories of the problems of doing business across the Mekong in Laos. These ranged from the trivial — regular harrassment of the cross-border petty traders, as they sit and wait for orders from tardy customers, by the Lao immigration police — to the more significant — the summoning of Thai timber traders to a meeting in Luang Namtha, where Lao military brokers demanded a multi-million baht payment in return for timber price stability in the coming year. And there are also problems in the Thai sector of the Quadrangle. The recent arrival of a Thai river navy unit in Chiang Khong — with machine-gun mountings on metal speedboats and allegedly overactive libidos — has hardly encouraged a sense of borderlands liberalization. At the southern end of the town, Chiang Khong's 40 million baht cargo port — jutting out into the Mekong on a forest of concrete pylons — is busiest at night when small mobile restaurants move in to sell hot food, cool beer, and whisky. No doubt, it is a pleasant view looking across the Mekong towards the Lao provincial capital of Houayxay — lit up like never before, courtesy of a new power line running from Chiang Khong. But, when the frequent black-outs come, it is very dark. "That's the Economic Quadrangle," one customs officer told me. "When there's a black-out in Chiang Khong, the lights go out in Laos."

The aim of this chapter is to provide an assessment of the Quadrangle's uneven and partial development in northwestern Laos. To place Lao developments in context, the first section briefly examines some of the regional components that make up the Economic Quadrangle. The chapter then focuses on trade liberalization within Laos and argues that the changes to date have been relatively modest and represent a resumption of long-standing trading connections. Despite the rhetoric of regional integration and liberalization, these connections are now more firmly under the control of Lao traders and transport operators than they have ever been. While ambitious plans for transit trade between Thailand and China signal more dramatic changes, progress to date has been very limited, in large part due to the slow progress on transport infrastructure. In the final section, I examine the argument that the development of "trans-border economies" — such as the Economic Quadrangle — represents a threat to the authority of the region's states. Indications to date are that, in fact, the Economic Quadrangle is providing numerous opportunities for reinvigorated state intervention. In brief, the chapter argues that while the rhetoric of the Economic Quadrangle emphasizes transformation, co-operation, and liberalization, the current reality has as much to do with continuity, competition, and regulation.

COMPONENTS OF THE QUADRANGLE

The "vision splendid" of an Economic Quadrangle in the northern borderlands of Southeast Asia first emerged in the early 1990s (Chapman and Hinton 1994, p. 1). As with "growth triangles" and "growth areas" elsewhere in Asia, the main idea underlying the Quadrangle is that opportunities for economic growth and development will arise if the border regions of adjoining countries are permitted and encouraged to exploit co-operatively their complementarities (Hasnah 1996; Ohmae 1995). "Located within the same economic space it would make good economic sense if areas in these sub-regions could harness their economic potential for the mutual benefit of the region" (Hasnah 1996, p. 1). These trans-border zones are, according to Ohmae (1995, p. 5) the new "regional economies ... where the real work gets done and real markets flourish". In the case of the Upper Mekong, these arguments are seductive: they represent a formula for trans-border prosperity based largely on the indisputable reality of geographic proximity. As a prominent Thai banker argued at a conference in Beijing:

> The resources from Myanmar and Laos can be given added value with the help of technology, funds and other necessary infrastructure from Thailand and China. (*Bangkok Post/Reuters Textline*, 6 July 1993)

Given the poor state of communications in the Upper Mekong region, infrastructural development has been the highest priority in Economic Quadrangle discussions to date (Asian Development Bank 1996). In the creation of what has been called a "Mekong corridor" (Chapman et al. 1992), most interest has been expressed in road links between Thailand and China. The main proposal is that a circular road be developed, linking northern Thailand and the Yunnanese capital, Kunming, via both Laos and Myanmar. As early as 1993, work had started on the link through Myanmar — via Keng Tung — but the project was abandoned by 1995, a legacy of lingering military insecurity and corporate bankruptcy. Most attention has now shifted to the road links through Laos. One proposed route runs from Chiang Rai through Luang Namtha while the second route attracting attention runs north from Nan through Hongsa, Pak Beng, and Oudomxai. There has also been considerable interest in reviving French colonial dreams of a river route to China and — following several survey missions along the Mekong River — a series of plans have been developed for improving Upper Mekong navigation. Even the ambitious nineteenth century plans for rail links between Thailand and Yunnan have been reborn, despite the massive cost of the project and uncertainty about the future level of traffic (*Bangkok Post*, 7 September 1994; *Bangkok Post*, 13 December 1994). Finally, some improvements have been made to regional airports and air services, with the lavish airport at Chiang Rai a potent symbol of that town's desire to become the Quadrangle's air-transport hub (*Bangkok Post*, 4 August 1994).

The main aim of these transport projects is to promote the flow of goods, capital, and labour between the Quadrangle countries. To this end, there have also been sustained calls for liberalizing reform to take place alongside infrastructural development. As Ohmae (1995, p. 4), one of the most active proponents of the new "regional economies", has argued, state regulation and mediation is an impediment to the development of new trans-border markets which, if given the opportunity, will "work just fine on their own". Economic growth, he writes, will be much more rapid if traditional nation-states — "unnatural, even impossible, business units in a global economy" — greatly limit their intervention in the new trans-border economies (see Ohmae 1995, p. 5; see also Hasnah 1996, p. 1). A survey sponsored by the Asian Development Bank (ADB) of firms with interests in the Mekong region found that "bureaucracy and nontransparent regulations" were the most serious impediments to trade (Brimble 1994, p. 7). Commercial and political interests in Thailand, in particular, have lobbied hard for the reduction and "harmonization" of financial and non-financial trade barriers and the development of regionally standardized trade and investment laws (*Bangkok Post*, 16 September 1994, 31 August 1996). Officials in Laos have also lobbied for the reduction of Thai tariffs on agricultural products in an attempt to address the substantial trade imbalance between the two countries (ibid., 21 July 1994, 3 January 1995). There have even been ambitious, though poorly developed, plans for the Quadrangle to become a "quasi free trade zone" (ibid., 7 January 1994).

In the climate of the late 1970s and early 1980s, this level of liberalized co-operation seemed unlikely, but in the following decade a series of international and domestic developments has laid the groundwork for an Upper Mekong Quadrangle. First, there was a general decline in regional tension coinciding with the end of the Cold War. In Thailand, this geo-political shift was symbolized by Prime Minister Chatichai's 1988 call to turn the region's "battlefields into marketplaces" and given practical effect with political and commercial diplomacy in Laos, Myanmar, and China (Pasuk and Baker 1995, p. 351; Mayoury and Pheuiphanh 1994, pp. 34, 77–78). There were still some points of tension — such as a bitter border dispute between Thailand and Laos (ibid., pp. 56–80) — but these were increasingly subordinated to the broader goal of economic co-operation. Relations between China and Laos were also placed on a more stable footing in the early 1990s and, together with Myanmar, they signed an agreement that their Upper Mekong borders would be a frontier of "peace, friendship, and co-operation" (*Bangkok Post*, 19 April 1994).

Factors within the four Quadrangle economies were also important in restructuring the region's interconnections. In Thailand, highly politicized environmental constraints were encouraging a search for non-domestic sources of timber, minerals, and energy (Hirsch 1995). After the national Thai logging ban in 1988, Thai loggers and sawmillers began beating a path to Vientiane and Yangon to negotiate access to

6. Regional Trade in Northwestern Laos: The Economic Quadrangle

cross-border resources. In northwestern Laos, they became active in reviving the sawmilling industry. Thailand's domestic power needs were also a pressing concern, and Thai consortia became involved in lignite mining at Viangphoukha and Hongsa — where a coal-fired power station is also planned — and in reviving old plans for hydro-electric projects on the Mekong and its tributaries. Some Thai businesses also saw an increasingly open southern China as a lucrative market for their manufactured goods. With wage growth in Thailand, this area was also considered as an alternative production site that could make use of cheap Chinese labour (Chapman and Hinton 1993, 1994). Upper Mekong tourism opportunities were also attractive to some Thai businessmen (though less attractive than the breathless accounts in the Thai media would suggest). In some sections of the Thai business community, the old concept of *sawanaphuum* (heavenly land) was revived: "they imagined a prospering mainland Southeast Asia dominated by Thai capital emerging as a major force in the economy and politics of Asia" (Pasuk and Baker 1995, p. 351). In northern Thailand, widespread property development and land speculation occurred in border districts as small and large investors sought to secure a strategic position in the hoped-for "golden" Quadrangle.

In China, the southern province of Yunnan was also experiencing sustained economic growth (Chapman et al. 1992; Feng 1993). Liberalized and revitalized state and private enterprises in Yunnan were said to be keen to secure southern outlets for their growing industrial output, with millions of tonnes of goods stockpiled there due to bottlenecks at Chinese east-coast ports (*Nation*, 15 December 1993). A major Mekong river port near Simao was constructed to facilitate the downriver trade, and border trading-posts were carved out of the jungle at a number of locations further south. In the southern districts of Yunnan there was rapid economic growth and social transformation as immigrants from other regions arrived to exploit commercial opportunities along the border (Chapman et al. 1992; Evans 1996). A new class of southern Chinese entrepreneurs also looked across the border to investment opportunities in both Myanmar and Laos. Like Thailand, China is also interested in the hydro-electric potential of the Mekong, and by the early 1990s had commenced construction of a major Mekong dam, with long-term plans for a cascade of dams along its section of the river.

In northeastern Myanmar, the domestic environment for investment, infrastructure development and trade was made more attractive by the 1989 collapse of the Communist Party of Burma and the signing of a raft of ceasefire agreements between Rangoon (now known as Yangon) and rebellious ethnic groups (Porter 1995, pp. 15–20). There has been significant growth in trade and investment in Myanmar districts bordering China, though the more westerly routes towards Mandalay and Yangon are developing much more rapidly than the "Quadrangle routes" towards Thailand (Porter 1995, pp. 48–67). Though there is a busy commercial life on the Thai-Myanmar border at Mae Sai-Tachilek, development in the eastern districts has been compromised by the ongoing activity of Shan rebel groups (*Bangkok Post*, 23 March 1995).[1] Possibly concerned about their degree of control in the Mekong hinterland, the Myanmar government has been the least active party in Quadrangle discussions.

Laos, the fourth country in the Quadrangle, has also experienced important domestic developments. These are discussed in detail in the following section.

RE-ESTABLISHING TRADING CONNECTIONS

The incorporation of Laos into the Economic Quadrangle has been facilitated by a series of policy initiatives that have encouraged a more open and market-oriented economy. The package of policies, usually referred to as the "New Economic Mechanism" (NEM), has been described in detail elsewhere and need only be summarized here, highlighting some of the important implications for the northwest (Bourdet 1996; Ljunggren 1992; Pham 1994; Vokes and Fabella 1995). There is no doubt that the effect of the policies has been liberalizing, but they have also provided incentives and opportunities for new forms of domestic control and state regulation.

When the NEM was introduced in 1986, one of its main aims was to dismantle the widespread restrictions on internal and external trade that had been imposed since the Pathet Lao victory in 1975. Some loosening of rigid controls on private sector involvement in trade had occurred in the early 1980s, but there was still considerable uncertainty and much of the trade, while officially tolerated or ignored, was often, in fact, illegal (Vokes and Fabella 1995, p. 108). In early 1987, private traders were officially permitted to compete with state enterprises on internal trade and, soon after, they were also permitted to participate in many areas of import and export trade, though some "strategic goods" were excluded (Vokes and Fabella 1995, p. 109; Government of the Lao People's Democratic Republic (PDR) 1988*b*, 1988*d*). In the following year, the remaining restrictions on inter-provincial trade and travel were abolished, the government declaring that "[l]egal commodities can be sold over the country without any form of restriction" and ordering the eradication of "all commodities checking points along various communication lines within the country" (Government of the Lao PDR 1988*a*). Other reforms encouraging private involvement in trade included relaxation of controls on currency exchange, elimination of subsidies to state and co-operative stores with the adoption of market pricing arrangements, and expansion of the banking sector (Government of the Lao PDR 1988*c*). Between 1988 and 1990, the number of privately operated shops increased by almost 55 per cent, while the state and collective sector declined by almost 70 per cent (Government of the Lao PDR 1991, p. 5):

> There are many stores and some department stores established in urban areas, which gradually improved the quality of services to customers. In rural areas they have reorganized the old market centers and constructed new market centers to answer the requirement of local people. (Ibid., p. 8)

Not only did the private sector share of retail activity increase — from 46 per cent in 1986 to 76 per cent in 1990 — but the overall level of retail activity increased more than 300 per cent (ibid., p. 10; Vokes and Fabella 1995, p. 115).

In northwestern Laos, the expansion in private trade was facilitated by improved border trading conditions with both Thailand and China. The Upper Mekong Thai-Lao border had been closed in 1976 as part of the Thai economic blockade of the newly communist Laos. By 1987 the border crossing between Houayxay and Chiang Khong was being opened on a temporary basis to enable the operation of occasional border markets on the Lao side of the river, and by 1988 substantial import and export trade had recommenced, though there were still numerous restrictions on free passage. After vigorous lobbying by provincial chambers of commerce, the Thai government resolved to address problems of border trade with Laos and, in early 1989, border crossings at both Chiang Khong–Houayxay and Chiang Saen–Tonpheung were officially re-established (Tanyathip et al. 1992, p. 236). In late 1993 the crossing at Chiang Khong–Houayxay was upgraded to an international border crossing, having little effect on Thai-Lao trading conditions but serving as an important symbol of Upper Mekong co-operation and enabling international tourist entry and exit. In 1994, provincial authorities on both sides of the border entered into an agreement that allowed for longer hours of border passage — though this was still not implemented in late 1996 — for minimization of provincial taxes and charges and, most importantly, for the sale of electricity from Chiang Khong to Houayxay. A part-time border crossing was also established at the Lao village of Bandan some 20 kilometres downstream from Houayxay — to enable the operation of a weekly border trading market. A border crossing was also established with considerable fanfare to the south of Hongsa, mainly to service the large lignite-mining development taking place there, but also to open up an alternative trading route between northern Thailand and northern Laos.

Since the recommencement of cross-border interaction, there have been significant increases in both import and export trade passing through Chiang Khong–Houayxay. Pent-up demand for Thai manufactured goods resulted in a mini-boom in imports from Chiang Khong between 1988 and 1990, followed by something of a slump in the following two years, and a return to rapid growth since 1993 (Table 6.1). Lao exports had a more modest start, largely a reflection of the parlous state of northwestern Lao sawmilling, but experienced sustained growth in the following years. In 1992 and 1993, the balance of trade at Chiang Khong–Houayxay was about equal but, by 1995 the value of imports to Laos from Thailand was outstripping Lao exports by about 80 per cent, a

Table 6.1
Import and Export Trade,
Chiang Khong–Houayxay, 1988–95
(in baht)

Year	Imports to Laos	Exports from Laos
1988	30,610,000	6,640,000
1989	50,086,000	16,254,000
1990	83,113,000	28,590,000
1991	44,319,000	24,689,000
1992	36,851,000	37,564,000
1993	63,003,000	63,499,000
1994	110,430,000	86,176,000
1995	154,790,000	86,340,000

Note: The figures should be taken as indicative only, and are likely to understate trading volumes given frequent evasion of customs taxes and other charges.
Source: Fieldwork 1994–95, 1996; Chiang Rai Office of Commerce.

pattern common throughout Laos. There has also been growth in trade at Chiang Saen–Tonpheung, but this border crossing is much less strategically placed and has experienced only a fraction of Chiang Khong–Houayxay's trading volumes. Informal reports from customs staff at the new border crossing south of Hongsa also suggest that current trading volumes are low. There are, however, indications that this could increase substantially if road links south to the Thai city of Nan are improved.

The trade that now passes through Chiang Khong and Houayxay is managed in several different ways. Fuel, the major export commodity, is sold by production companies in Thailand to the Lao State Fuel Company, with a local trading company in Chiang Khong preparing the customs paperwork and arranging for the trucks to cross the Mekong on the vehicular ferry. During 1994, fuel pumped into river tankers at Houayxay supplied all of the towns in northwestern Laos and, when the road north from Vientiane was impassable, Luang Prabang as well. Several other trading companies in Chiang Khong are involved in the sale of construction materials (for infrastructure projects in Laos) and occasional large consignments of manufactured goods. Despite the liberalization of the NEM, Lao regulations usually require these Thai companies to work in conjunction with Lao companies in Houayxay. These enforced partnerships are not without their problems, with regular disputes over the allocation of tasks and profits. "The Lao company ... invests nothing. All it does is sign the papers," one Thai trader complained (quoted in Supalak 1993).

Most of Chiang Khong's export trade in manufactured goods, construction materials, and processed food is, however, conducted by independent Lao traders from towns throughout northwestern Laos. These traders make regular trips to Chiang Khong, where they are supplied by a revived and active wholesale shopping sector and a large "dry goods" market that is held in Chiang Khong each Friday. The majority of them are women, an unusual situation given that long-distance wholesale trade in Southeast Asia is usually dominated by men.[2] A large number of them come upriver to Chiang Khong from Luang Prabang, returning with boatloads of cement, corrugated iron, condensed milk, and washing powder. Smaller-scale traders make the four-hour speed-boat trip from Pak Beng, returning with stock for the retail shops that sprawl along the dusty road that climbs up from the port. Others come from Oudomxai, Luang Namtha, Muang Sing, and Hongsa, their vinyl handbags stuffed with thousand-baht notes and crumpled orders from the shopkeepers in the markets that dominate the commercial lives of the towns. Finally, there are the long-distance traders in Houayxay itself, strung out along the river bank opposite Chiang Khong. Using and creating far-flung connections, they have established a regular trade with the other towns of northern Laos, in particular the important northern entrepôt of Oudomxai — a rough seven-hour journey north of Pak Beng in the Russian-built trucks that wait patiently at the port for boats from Chiang Khong. These long-distance trading networks that distribute Chiang Khong's merchandise throughout northern Laos are exclusively Lao. Chiang Khong's residents are heavily involved in small-scale cross-border trade with Houayxay, but Lao regulations prevent them from travelling farther afield.

Lao exports at Houayxay are comprised mainly of timber, non-timber forest products, and agricultural products. Seed, fruit, bark, grass, and resin accounted for over 40 per cent of exports during 1994, a percentage substantially higher than in other parts of Laos. These are collected and cultivated by villagers throughout northern Laos and pass along an extensive chain of small-scale traders and larger trading companies to ports at Pak Beng, Luang Prabang, and Houayxay before being shipped to Thai buyers. Many boatloads of forest products are said to pass upstream, beyond Chiang Khong–Houayxay, to Myanmar river ports, where the cargo is unloaded and then smuggled into Thailand near Mae Sai. The timber trade is much more concentrated, with the 12,000 cubic metres of sawn timber passing through Houayxay during 1994 deriving almost entirely from three northwestern Lao sawmills, all operated by Thai entrepreneurs. During 1995, additional Thai investment saw three new sawmills commence operation in northwestern Laos, increasing the flow of timber across the Mekong to Chiang Khong's busy timber yards.[3]

Cross-border trading relationships have also improved with China. The Chinese-Lao border was closed in the late 1970s as regional tensions heightened over the Vietnamese invasion of Cambodia. However, by the late 1980s, southern districts in Yunnan were increasingly looking southward for commercial opportunities. In the early 1990s, provincial authorities in Houayxay entered into an agreement with the Simao district in Yunnan to provide facilities for trade and tourism along the Mekong River (*Reuters Textline*, 7 October 1992). Simao had constructed a major Mekong River port and was keen to secure downstream facilities. Other provincial agreements have provided for Chinese involvement in infrastructure projects in the northwest — roads and a small hydro-electricity dam to supply Oudomxai — and for co-operation in relation to "mineral survey, agriculture, trade, tourism and health" *(Bangkok Post,* 5 July 1994). These agreements have been accompanied by a revival in border trade. By the late 1980s, the border crossing at Boten was open for local trade between Mengla district and Luang Namtha, and in late 1993 it was upgraded to an international border crossing, serving as the mainland trading point between China and Laos (*Vientiane Times,* 23 December 1994). A second northwestern border crossing has also been established near Muang Sing. Though this is officially only a local border crossing, it serves some long-distance trade that heads down the old caravan route to Xiangkok and onward to Myanmar and Thailand.[4] The old Lue settlement of Mengla is still the predominant Chinese-Lao trading town, though it has been radically transformed by central Chinese investment and immigration. A border trading village, with neatly laid out rows of concrete shophouses, has also been established at Mohan, just a few kilometres north of Boten.

It is difficult to assess the level of trade with China in the absence of reliable customs figures. One report, quoting official Yunnanese sources, suggests that Lao-Chinese border trade was in excess of US$7 million — approximately 180 million baht — in 1993 (*Reuters Textline,* 13 February 1994). This is about 50 per cent higher than the level of trade at Chiang Khong–Houayxay during the same year, but this Lao-Thai trade has increased substantially since, while local reports are that Lao-Chinese trade has plateaued or even decreased as a result of unfavourable currency movements. A large proportion of Lao-Chinese border trade is conducted via the border crossing at the village of Boten but, unlike Chiang Khong–Houayxay, only a relatively small percentage is trade with northwestern Lao provinces. Most of the border trade at Boten is directed to provinces in central and southern Laos, which have no common border with China. This very long-distance trade is conducted mainly by Lao trading companies that deal in Lao coffee and scrap metal and buy Chinese machinery and electronic goods. There is also some export of Lao timber and forest products, but at a relatively low level. Northwestern Lao trade with China is mostly undertaken by independent traders, many of whom are also involved in trade with Thailand (Walker 1997*b*).

What, then, has been the effect on trade of the regulatory changes that have occurred since the late 1980s? Essentially, their impact has been to re-establish and strengthen the long-standing connections between northwestern Laos, northern Thailand, and southern China. I have written elsewhere about the history of trading linkages between northern Laos, China, and Thailand, and I therefore reject the view that what we are witnessing now is an emergence of northern Laos from a long-standing state of isolation (Walker 1997*b*). During the nineteenth century, northern Laos had complex and multi-faceted trading relations with neighbouring states, with the main trading axis running between Chiang Khong in Thailand and Mengla in southern China, as it still does today. There was intensive regional trade in rice, forest products, cotton, opium, salt, and European manufactured goods. During the colonial period, the French made some attempts to re-orient northern Lao trade towards Vietnam, but the realities of geography defeated them. As transport and trading networks in northern Thailand developed, northern Laos was increasingly drawn into the commercial orbit of Bangkok, Chiang Mai, and Chiang Rai. Cross-border interactions flourished during the war-torn 1960s and 1970s in what is remembered by local residents as a golden era of trans-Mekong trade and sociality. More research needs to be done on this period but there are strong indications that levels of cross-border economic interaction may have been even higher than they are today. Even during the brief period of "closed" borders between 1976 and 1988, alternative and informal trade routes were actively pursued and the borders were probably much more porous than we have been led to believe. In brief, the re-establishment of cross-border bilateral trading relations in the post-socialist age probably represents much less of a socio-spatial revolution than the proponents of the Quadrangle are suggesting.

However, there has been one important change in northwestern Lao trading and transport systems, an ironic change given the regional emphasis on liberalization, openness, and integration. Now, most cross-border trading systems are dominated by Lao traders and transport operators rather than by the ethnic Chinese and Thai entrepreneurs of the past. The origins of this change lie in the period following the communist victory in 1975 when many of the established merchants and transport operators left Laos or, in the case of Thai Mekong riverboat operators, were excluded from it. This allowed small-scale Lao operators to gain a foothold in the restricted — but often lucrative — trading economy that was in place up until the mid-1980s. In the more liberal trading environment of the late 1980s and 1990s, these Lao traders and boat operators have prospered, as have Lao truckers following the privatization of state-owned trucking fleets in 1990. While the reforms of the NEM have opened Lao borders to trade, there are still sufficient restrictions (in most areas) to hold Thai and Chinese traders and trans-

6. Regional Trade in Northwestern Laos: The Economic Quadrangle

port operators at bay. Thai trading companies have made some inroads, but they too are caught up in a bewildering array of deals, disputes, and compromises with commercial counterparts in Laos. Even in the timber industry, where Thai capital has made significant inroads, there are indications that Lao interests are being vigorously reasserted, with the recent allocation of national logging rights to three state-owned military enterprises. Lao liberalization appears to be managed in a way that gives domestic traders, transport operators, entrepreneurs, and officials an important stake in the external trading connections.[5]

Of course, the main hope of the Quadrangle promoters is that transit trade between Thailand and China will increase dramatically. In 1992 and 1993, things looked hopeful, with the value of transit trade booming as hundreds of imported cars were despatched by trading companies in Chiang Khong to eager buyers and agents in the Chinese trading town of Mengla. Customs records in Chiang Khong indicate that cars valued at over one billion baht were exported via Laos in 1993. Some good profits were made, and the trade became an influential motif in Quadrangle promotions, but when the Chinese government enforced heavy duties and import restrictions on their remote southern border, almost 900 luxury cars were left to gather dust and mud in fields throughout northwestern Laos. By early 1995, two of the companies that had been most involved in the trade with China had closed their offices in Chiang Khong and there were many reports of large financial losses and unpaid debts. Losses incurred by the Lao banks that provided credit to car traders also prompted the Lao government to place restrictions on vehicle imports (Sundberg 1994, p. 88). In 1994, there was very little transit trade heading north to China, though a number of Chinese vessels came to Houayxay to pick up Thai cargoes, including 2,000 tonnes of dried fruit from Chiang Mai and 200 tonnes of rubber from southern Thailand. Some Lao traders also sold consignments of Thai manufactured goods and rice when they travelled to Mengla.

Thai imports from China are also at a low level. During 1994, some machinery, technical equipment, construction materials, and agricultural products came down the Mekong in Chinese boats, and some Chinese imports were also trucked to Pak Beng and then brought upriver in Lao boats. In late 1996 I witnessed several boatloads of Chinese apples being unloaded at Chiang Saen and was told that there had been some increase in Chinese river traffic since 1994. However, an elaborate showroom established in Chiang Khong to sell high-quality imported Chinese merchandise is now closed due to lack of business — it has become a Toyota car yard. In the first six months of 1995, the value of Thai-China trade passing through Chiang Khong–Houayxay was reported to be only 13 million baht and the Thai consul in Yunnan has recently expressed concern about the sluggish activity in this new trading corridor (*Bangkok Post/Reuters Textline*, 12 September 1995; *Business Day*, 13 September 1996). There are, however, indications that senior Lao trade officials are less concerned, conceding that they place greater priority on developing bilateral trading ties (*Nation*, 15 December 1993).

The disappointing level of transit trade can be attributed to the painstakingly slow progress of transport infrastructure. To date, the main transport improvements in northwestern Laos have been relatively short lengths of road from the Thai border to the lignite mines at Viangphoukha and Hongsa, and there are even considerable doubts about the quality of the work done on these roads. Progress on the widely promoted transit routes has been limited. In part this is a product of the failure to agree on a single priority transit route through northwestern Laos. The competing transit routes each have their own set of corporate, provincial, and political backers who are keen to promote the merits of their own proposal and undermine confidence in their rivals (Walker 1997*b*). This rivalry — which continues despite the valiant efforts of national governments and international agencies to resolve it — has undoubtedly undermined investor confidence, and the flow of capital into the transit projects has consequently been slow. Investors may also be waiting to see if recent improvements in security in the Myanmar borderlands enable a resumption of work on the more lucrative Thai-Chinese transit route through Keng Tung (*Nation*, 9 November 1996).

However, the broader regional context of infrastructure development must also be considered. Recently, Quadrangle discussions have been increasingly incorporated within the Asian Development Bank's "Greater Mekong region" vision (which also includes the Lower Mekong nations of Cambodia and Vietnam). Within this vision, there is a bewildering Greater Mekong wish-list of roads, railways, airports, and fibre-optic cables (Asian Development Bank 1996). With a total cost of over US$40 billion — and the Asian Development Bank itself foreshadowing relatively limited support — the competition for private-sector Mekong investment will be intense. With such an array of investment opportunities, the benefits of large-scale investment in the relatively undeveloped and impoverished northwestern region of Laos may be difficult to promote, especially as the centre of gravity for interest

6. Regional Trade in Northwestern Laos: The Economic Quadrangle   137

and investment shifts south towards the much more populous Vietnam. At a recent conference in Melbourne, there was a sense of desperation in the Yunnanese delegation's attempt to revive flagging interest in the Upper Mekong Quadrangle (Stensholt 1996).

At this stage, it appears that "fraudulent" transit trade through northwestern Laos is somewhat more active than the legitimate Thai-Chinese trade. During 1994 and 1995, some of the most active trading companies in both Chiang Khong and Houayxay were involved in despatching regular cargoes of cigarettes, cloth, and electrical goods upriver to the small village of Muang Mom, where they were transferred across the river to Myanmar. The goods travelling along this route were goods originating from outside of Thailand, mainly from Singapore. They are imported duty-free at Bangkok as transit cargoes, then exported to Laos — where no duty is paid because the goods are in transit to Myanmar — and once they are in Myanmar the goods are spirited back into Thailand at the busy border crossing at Mae Sai where they are sold for a handsome profit. Tourists buying cheap cigarettes from touts in the busy Mae Sai market are undoubtedly unaware of the level of cross-border economic integration that has contributed to their good fortune. Sometimes the journey through Myanmar is dispensed with altogether: if the traders receive word that there will be no customs patrols, the goods are shipped just a short distance upstream from Houayxay and unloaded into trucks waiting in the small Thai villages dotting the river bank. There are also rumours that a prominent Thai businessman is active in the "export" of boatloads of water upriver from Chiang Saen to China. Of course, he claims that the water is fuel, but it is likely that the fuel — imported into Thailand tax-free as a transit cargo — is profitably sold on the domestic market through his network of service stations. It seems that some of the most profitable Quadrangle trade is based on the manipulation of tariff regimes, rather than on their eradication.

CONCLUSION: THE DEMISE OF THE STATE?

To date, the Economic Quadrangle has not lived up to its ambitious plans in northwestern Laos. Bilateral trading relationships with Thailand and China have been resumed but patterns of trade have not been transformed. As in the nineteenth century, and for most of this century, manufactured goods sold in the markets and shops of northwestern Laos are imported predominantly from Thailand, and Chiang Khong has resumed its long-standing role as an important Upper Mekong trading centre. The main change has been that most imported goods are now manufactured in Thailand itself, rather than in Japan or Europe. Chinese goods are also again flowing across the northern borders, especially into the nearby markets in Luang Namtha and Oudomxay. As in the past, Mengla is the primary border trading town, with the Lao village of Boten being the main border-crossing point. Although promotional hopes are high, there are some doubts that trading volumes will continue to increase, with reports, for example, of a significant decline in cross-border trade between Laos and China. "This is probably the peak," one shopkeeper in Chiang Khong told me.

What, then, of the popular argument that emerging regional economies — such as the Quadrangle — pose a threat to the authority of the state? The business consultant, Ohmae, is a popular advocate of this view. He argues that trans-border regions are the "natural economic zones" in a borderless world (Ohmae 1995, p. 80). States, by contrast, are a "fiction" and a "transitional form of organisation for managing economic affairs" that have now outlived their usefulness (ibid., pp. 80, 136). Referring to the Mekong's "baht defined zone of influence", he suggests that the "nation-state focused policy may be intentionally blind to these developments" (ibid., p. 109). The Thai scholar, Chai-Anan, is a supporter of Ohmae, but casts a more gentle and nostalgic gaze north from Bangkok. He has suggested that recent economic, social, and cultural opportunities in the borderlands amount to a "bypassing of the state". He argues that the resumption of "age old" trans-border networks "implies a breakdown of the authority of the nation state because it opens more room for non-state actors" (Chai-Anan 1995). Both arguments resonate with recent discussions in social theory which highlight the increasing irrelevance of the state in the face of globalization. Summarizing a large body of recent work, Eade (1997, p. 3), for example, writes that "the significance of national state boundaries and institutions declines as global and local social relations interweave and worldwide social relations intensify".

The evidence from the Economic Quadrangle — albeit one of the most remote and least-developed regional economies — suggests that there may be some confusion in this uneasy coalition of free-marketeer, liberal nostalgic, and post-modern views. To date, the Quadrangle has provided substantial opportunities for renewed and reinvigorated forms of state intervention. The basis for the confusion appears to lie in a widespread preoccupation with states as *bounding, enclosing,* and *restricting* entities (Ohmae 1995, p. viii; Chai-Anan 1995). This focus on exclusive sovereignty, as Foucault argued (Foucault 1980, pp. 121–22), is an oversimplification of the complex field of power and can only deal with the state's engagement with external flows by declaring its increasing irrelevance. A more realistic approach lies in recognizing the role of states in *regulating* and managing trans-border flows rather than in *preventing* them. While states may seek to establish exclusive sovereignty within their territory, they are also actively involved in creating *overlapping* and *ambiguous* spheres of economic, social, and cultural influence. In particular, state power is crucial to the initiation, maintenance, management, and protection of external trading networks. In the light of this more open and regulatory approach to the state, contemporary developments represent much less of a threat to state authority. The ongoing relevance of the state is reflected in several different aspects of the Economic Quadrangle's development.

In most general terms, the rhetorical emphasis on liberalization and deregulation sits uneasily with hopes that the Economic Quadrangle will provide opportunities to regularize, formalize, and eradicate the illegal practices of the infamous Golden Triangle. At a Myanmar trade fair I attended in Tachilek, government and corporate organizers were explicit in their hope that the fair would be a first stage in the conversion of smuggling into formal trade (Walker 1994, p. 8). In Thailand, customs officers spoke to me of their regular meetings with village leaders, where they tried to persuade them to use the official trading points in Chiang Khong or Chiang Saen rather than to ship timber, cattle, and forest products between the small villages that are scattered along both banks of the Mekong. The establishment of Upper Mekong navy units represents a less gentle crackdown on such practices. Similarly in Laos, there are regular border-commissions with both China and Thailand, aimed at developing a co-ordinated approach to the "bad elements" who are said to congregate in border districts. Publicly, Lao officials also make much of their attempts to restrict borderland trade in opium and heroin. Of course, it would be nonsense to suggest that state authorities have had substantial success in these initiatives, or even that the popular distinction between formal and informal trade is a legitimate one. My argument is that alongside the rhetoric and practices of liberalization there are equally important elements of regulation and control. The opening of border crossings and the construction of infrastructure are liberalizing processes, but they often aim to regularize and channel the flows of trade.

Infrastructure development — "one traditional ... mainstay of state activity" — represents a dilemma for those who advocate or predict the demise of the state in regional economies (Mann 1996, p. 304). Even Ohmae (1995, pp. 126, 136) recognizes a need for states to act as "catalysts for the activities of regions" and lists infrastructure as one area where state intervention may be appropriate, even if only to maintain common standards. In the infrastructural development of the Economic Quadrangle, state officials and agencies have been the *most* active participants in a bewildering programme of meetings, inspection tours, feasibility studies, and public relations stunts. State enthusiasm and endorsement is one part of the strategy of mobilizing reluctant investors. State co-ordination and brokerage have also been necessary to prevent Quadrangle planning deteriorating into bitter rivalry between competing provincial and commercial interests (Walker 1997*b*).

Yet, state involvement in infrastructure has gone beyond facilitation and co-ordination, and state officials, commercially minded politicians and even national governments are active participants in major projects. In northwestern Laos, the proposed transit route from Houayxay to Luang Namtha is a collaborative project between the state and private enterprise. Thai investors in this project are said to have close connections with senior political figures in Laos and at least one provincial deputy governor has been recruited to an "advisory team" for the project (*Bangkok Post/Reuters Textline*, 25 July 1995). Formally, the Lao government has secured a 40 per cent share in any revenue that the road will generate, if ever it gets beyond a series of concrete bridges linked by mud and dust. This is a mutually beneficial arrangement: state revenue will be enhanced and the central government will maintain some degree of control over a major development in one of its more remote regions; at the same time, Thai investors have secured wide-ranging rights to land, natural resources, and commercial licences, rights that could not have been obtained without substantial state backing. The nature and extent of collaboration on this project has alarmed even the Asian Development Bank (Nonis 1994), despite its enthusiasm to see private-sector funds make some inroads into its Mekong wish-list. Given the level of state intervention around Hongsa — where the military is heavily involved in logging and lignite-mining — it would be very surprising if similar collaborative arrangements were not developed for the road north from Nan.

There is no clearer illustration of renewed state intervention in the borderlands than the fiscal transformations that are occurring in Laos. The dramatic increases in private-sector trade have provided a rich harvest for state tax collectors and revenue embezzlers. The percentage of Lao state revenue derived from import and export taxes increased from 19 to 48 per cent between 1987 and 1990 (Vokes and Fabella 1995, p. 32) and there is no doubt this "broadening of the tax base" (Bourdet 1994, p. 38) has continued since. The NEM reforms did not affect high tariffs on many items and, though there have been some small changes in the new 1994 customs law, "they could not reasonably be described as a significant trade liberalisation" (Warr 1997). No wonder, then, that Lao officials have vigorously, and successfully, resisted Chinese proposals that Upper Mekong navigation be made free of all taxes and charges (*Bangkok Post*, 18 October 1994). No wonder also that provincial regulators, who were granted substantial financial independence in the mid-1980s, have resisted Vientiane's attempts to bring their budgets under central control and have continued to levy taxes and maintain internal checking points that have been abolished by central decree (Bourdet 1994, p. 43; Vokes and Fabella 1995, pp. 31–32; Warr 1997, pp. 5–6). In this fiscal resistance, and in the active participation of provinces in pursuing cross-border economic agreements, there are, indeed, signs of challenges to state power — conceived in centralized terms — but the challenges represent tensions within the state rather than a by-passing of it. States have never exercised monolithic control in the borderlands, but have relied on a spatially dispersed and volatile network of collaborations:

> ... the state does not exist as a fully constituted, internally coherent, organisationally pure, and operationally closed system but is an emergent, contradictory, hybrid and relatively open system. (Jessop 1990, p. 316)

While the relationships between components of the state may be experiencing some renewed tensions in Laos, there is no indication that they are going to break.

Finally, the role of the military in the Economic Quadrangle must also be considered. In Thailand, during the 1960s and the 1970s, the army played an important role in the economic development of many provinces (Pasuk and Baker 1995). Many traders and entrepreneurs commented to me that Laos is now entering a similar phase. Commercial companies run by the military were quarantined from the privatization of the early 1990s, and are now expanding into many "formal" and "informal" sectors of economic life. In October 1994, for example, the central government revoked logging concessions throughout Laos and transferred them to the three main military corporations. These corporations now sell timber quotas to the sawmills at ever increasing prices, impose heavy taxes on the export of sawn timber, and manage the illegal export of unprocessed logs to Thailand. Their intervention has dramatically changed the balance of power in Laos' largest export industry.[6]

In his recent assessment of the NEM in Laos, Bourdet has suggested that "[t]here is a clear dichotomy in Laos between the comprehensiveness of the economic reforms and the inertia of the political system" (Bourdet 1994, p. 92). My observation of the Economic Quadrangle suggests that this dichotomy may, in fact, be very blurred with persistent and substantial state/political penetration of the economy. The rhetoric of the Economic Quadrangle liberalization ignores the extent to which revived cross-border trade is providing numerous opportunities for re-invigorated state intervention in trading systems. One of the ironies of cross-border relations in the post-socialist age is that "open" borders can provide more opportunities for regulation than the "closed" borders they have replaced.

NOTES

1. The important border crossing between Mae Sai and Tachilek was closed for almost a year after an attack by Shan rebels in March 1995.
2. Some of the reasons for this are discussed in detail in Walker (1997*a*).
3. For a detailed discussion of the northwestern Lao timber trade, see Walker (1997*b*).
4. World Bank funds have been allocated to upgrade the rough track between Muang Sing and Xiangkok.
5. These issues are discussed in detail in Walker (1997*a*, 1997*b*).
6. For a detailed discussion, see Walker (1997*b*).

REFERENCES

Asian Development Bank. *Economic Cooperation in the Greater Mekong Subregion: An Overview*. Manila: Asian Development Bank, 1996.
Bourdet, Yves. "Budget Policy under Transition in Lao PDR". In *Economic Development in Lao PDR: Horizon 2000*, edited by Do Pham Chi, pp. 72–81. Vientiane: Bank of the Lao People's Democratic Republic, 1994.
──────. "Laos in 1995: Reform Policy, Out of Breath?" *Asian Survey* 31, no. 1 (1996): 89–94.
Brimble, Peter. *Promoting Subregional Ccooperation among Cambodia, the People's Re-

public of China, Lao People's Democratic Republic, Myanmar, Thailand, and Viet Nam: Trade and Investment (Interim Report). Manila: Asian Development Bank, 1994.

Chai-Anan Samudavanija. "Bypassing the State in Asia". *New Perspectives Quarterly* 12, no. 1 (1995): 9–14.

Chapman, E.C. and Peter Hinton. "The Emerging Mekong Corridor: A Note on Recent Developments (to May 1993)". *Thai-Yunnan Project Newsletter* 21 (1993): 12–16.

———. "'The Mekong Corridor'/'Economic Quadrangle': Who Benefits?" Paper presented at the Conference on Asia's New Growth Circles, 3–6 March 1994, Chiang Mai Orchid Hotel.

Chapman, E.C., Peter Hinton, and Jingrong Tan. "Cross-Border Trade between Yunnan and Burma, and the Emerging Mekong Corridor". *Thai-Yunnan Project Newsletter* 19 (1992): 15–19.

Eade, John. "Introduction". In *Living the Global City: Globalization as a Local Process*, edited by John Eade, pp. 1–19. London: Routledge, 1997.

Evans, Grant. "Transformation of Jinghong, Xishuangbanna, P.R.C.". Paper presented at the Conference on South China and Mainland Southeast Asia: Cross Border Relations in the Post-Socialist Age, University of Hong Kong, 4–6 December 1996.

Feng Yuan Lun. *Promote Friendship, Strengthen Cooperation and Seek Common Development on a Mutually Beneficial Basis*. Kunming: Yunnan Provincial Border Economic Relations and Trade Administration, 1993.

Foucault, Michel. *Power/Knowledge: Selected Interviews and Other Writings, 1972–1977*. Brighton: Harvester Press, 1980.

Government of the Lao People's Democratic Republic (PDR). *Decree No. 12 of the Council of Ministers on Directives and Measures to Increase the Circulation of Commodities and Currencies*. Vientiane: Vientiane International Consultants, 1988*a*.

———. *Decree No. 13 of the Council of Ministers on State Monopoly of Import-Export Management*. Vientiane: Vientiane International Consultants, 1988*b*.

———. *Decree No. 14 of the Council of Ministers on State Price Policy*. Vientiane: Vientiane International Consultants, 1988*c*.

———. *Decree No. 18 of the Council of Ministers on the State Monopoly of Strategic Goods Import-Export*. Vientiane: Vientiane International Consultants, 1988*d*.

———. *Trade Statistics for 1986–1990*. Vientiane: Ministry of Commerce and Tourism, Statistics Division, 1991.

Hasnah Ali. "Growth Triangles in the ASEAN Region: Issues, Challenges and Prospects". Paper presented at the Asian Studies Association of Australia Conference on Communications with/in Asia, La Trobe University, 8–11 July 1996.

Hirsch, Philip. "Thailand and the New Geopolitics of Southeast Asia: Resource and Environmental Issues". In *Counting the Costs: Economic Growth and Environmental Change in Thailand*, edited by Jonathan Rigg, pp. 235–59. Singapore: Institute of Southeast Asian Studies, 1995.

Jessop, Bob. *State Theory: Putting the Capitalist State in Its Place*. Cambridge: Polity Press, 1990.

Ljunggren, Carl Börje. *Market Eeconomies under Communist Regimes: Reform in Vietnam, Laos and Cambodia.* Ann Arbor: University Microfilms International, 1992.
Mann, Michael. "Nation-States in Europe and Other Continents: Diversifying, Developing, Not Dying". In *Mapping the Nation*, edited by Gopal Balakrishnan, pp. 295–316. London: Verso, 1996.
Mayoury Ngaosyvathn and Pheuiphanh Ngaosyvathn. *Kith and Kin Politics: The Relationship between Laos and Thailand.* Manila: Journal of Contemporary Asia Publishers, 1994.
Nonis, Eustace A. "Economic Linkages through New Highways: Implications of Different Land Routes". Paper presented at the Conference on Asia's New Growth Circles, 3–6 March 1994, Chiang Mai Orchid Hotel.
Ohmae, Kenichi. *The End of the Nation State: The Rise of Regional Economies.* New York: The Free Press, 1995.
Pasuk Phongpaichit and Chris Baker. *Thailand: Economy and Politics.* Kuala Lumpur: Oxford University Press, 1995.
Pham Chi Do. *Economic Development in Lao PDR: Horizon 2000.* Vientiane: Bank of the Lao People's Democratic Republic, 1994.
Porter, Doug J. "Wheeling and Dealing: HIV/AIDS and Development on the Shan State Borders". Mimeographed. United Nations Development Program, 1995.
Stensholt, Bob. *Development Dilemmas in the Mekong Subregion. Workshop Proceedings 1–2 October 1996.* Melbourne: Monash Asia Institute, Monash University, 1996.
Sundberg, Mark. "Trade Policy and Lao Development". In *Economic Development in Lao PDR: Horizon 2000*, edited by Chi Do Pham, pp. 82–92. Vientiane: Bank of the Lao People's Democratic Republic, 1994.
Supalak Ganjanakhunda. "Cross-Border Traffic". *Manager* 58 (1993): 56–59.
Tanyathip Sriphana, Watcharin Yongsiri, and Maana Maalaphet. *Kaan kha thaj indoociin.* Bangkok: Chulalongkorn University, 1992.
Vokes, Richard and Armand Fabella. "Economic Reform in the Lao People's Democratic Republic". Unpublished manuscript, 1995.
Walker, Andrew. "The Myanmar Trade Fair: Tachileik 21–31 December 1993". *Thai-Yunnan Project Newsletter* 24 (1994): 8–9.
————. "Women, Space and History: Long-Distance Trading in North-Western Laos". In *Lao Culture and Society*, edited by Grant Evans. Chiang Mai: Silkworm Books, 1997a.
————. "The Legend of the Golden Boat: Regulation, Transport and Trade in North-Western Laos". Ph.D. thesis. Canberra: Australian National University, 1997b.
Warr, Peter. *Impacts of Market Reforms on Agricultural Development in Laos.* Canberra: Australian National University, 1997.

7

Lue across Borders: Pilgrimage and the Muang Sing Reliquary in Northern Laos

Paul T. Cohen

The Muang Sing reliquary is known locally as Thaat Muang Sing or Thaat Chiangteum. It is situated at the top of Doi Chiangteum mountain about 4 kilometres southeast from Muang Sing town, the market and administrative centre of Muang Sing district, Luang Namtha province, northern Laos. The reliquary has long been venerated by the Tai Lue and Tai Neua people of Muang Sing and by the Tai Lue of the neighbouring area of Xishuangbanna in China. There are twenty-six Lue and five Neua villages in the Muang Sing district, with all but three being located in the fertile Muang Sing valley where wet-rice cultivation is the dominant form of agriculture. The surrounding mountains are inhabited by non-Buddhist Akha and Yao tribes dependent on swidden cultivation of dry rice and opium.

The aim of this chapter is to explore several issues with reference to the Thaat Chiangteum reliquary of Muang Sing. These are:

- the relation between Buddhist universal values, as represented in pilgrimage, and moral communities which cut across political boundaries;
- the effect of physical factors (for example, geographic distance, terrain, and transport) and political factors on pilgrimage, particularly in the post-socialist context of the "open-door" policy in the central Mekong region;

- the relation between the Muang Sing reliquary and the mission of the contemporary charismatic Buddhist saint, Khruba Bunchum Yaansuamro, and his role in Buddhist revival, especially among the Tai Lue of Xishuangbanna in China.

THE RELIQUARY

The religious site consists of a central stupa, 12 metres high, capped by metallic parasols and surrounded by four smaller replica stupas. Recent renovations (*burana*) were carried out in 1950, 1960, and early 1996. Two additional stupas, also smaller than the central one, were constructed on the eastern end of the rectangular base at the beginning of 1996.

Lafont (1957, p. 2) notes that the reliquary is of Myanmar style, reflecting its geographic proximity to Myanmar and closer political orientation of the local Tai Lue and Tai Neua to Myanmar than to Laos. Lafont refers to the reliquary as "That Xieng Tung" and then in a long footnote (ibid., p. 14) expresses bewilderment as to why it should be so called, given that Xieng Tung (Chiangtung) is 200 kilometres away and that local texts make no reference to this principality or to its founder, the legendary Tungaraja. However, a local Buddhist text on the history of the reliquary consistently refers to it as "Thaat Chiangteum" and so do local villagers (though occasionally the name "Thaat Chiangteung" is used). Moreover, villagers are adamant that the reliquary has no connection with Chiangtung. There is less certainty about the meaning of the word "Chiangteum". Some simply do not know and others give seemingly contrived answers. The most plausible explanation is offered by Saengthong Photibupbaa, a provincial official who is writing a history of Luang Namtha and Muang Sing. He claims (n.d., p. 1) that the first period of settlement of Muang Sing was initiated in 1792 by Naang Khemmaa, who fled Chiangkhaeng (a small principality on the Mekong River) with her six sons together with commoners (*phrai*). Saengthong (personal communication) also claims that Khemmaa established a *lak meuang* ("pillar of the principality") and a Buddhist temple (Wat Luang Paa Fang) in the vicinity of Doi Chiangteum. She built the reliquary, which she named after her son who, when ordained as a monk, took the name of Phra Chiangteum, in 1794. When he left the order (*sik*) he changed his name to Cao Saengsii and when he succeeded as ruler his name was changed yet again to Cao Khatiyawong.

However, local villagers attribute the building of the Chiangteum reliquary not to Naang Khemmaa but to Panyaa Tanhai, who is now the pre-eminent guardian spirit of the reliquary and a key personage in a Buddhist chronicle, *Tham Tamnaan Thaat Luang Chiengteum Muang Sing*, which provides a mythical history[1] of the reliquary.

THE MYTHICAL HISTORY OF THAAT CHIANGTEUM

The following is an abbreviated version of the mythical history of the reliquary:[2]

> When the Buddha was alive He left one day on a journey and arrived at the city of Alavi, accompanied by his disciple Ananda Thera, and resided at the top of Doi Chiangteum. Here Buddha was offered water by a Naga (*Panyaa Naak*) for drinking and bathing. After eating, Buddha rinsed his mouth out with water and spat it towards the north-east, thereby creating a well (*bor thip*). He then threw water to the south-east and created a pond (*norng*) nearby.
>
> The Buddha then instructs Ananda that upon His demise, His stone knife sharpener (*mak hin sai kham lapfaa*), and His razor for shaving his head (*phamiit khuut kan kham*) and Adam's Apple (*duk tom khor hoi*) should be buried on top of Doi Chiangteum so that it would become a place of worship and veneration for men and gods.
>
> The Buddha died and many years after his death the Dhammaraja Asoka conquered the entire world and built, amongst other things, 84,000 Buddha reliquaries (*mahaacetiyathaat*) in 14,000 different towns and cities. During this period the monk, Sariputra Thera, deposited Buddha's relics on Doi Chiangteum and asked Asoka to build a reliquary there. The Dhammaraja then built a *phasaat*[3] in which he placed the relics, dug a pit so deep that it reached sea level, and constructed a stupa in which he placed the *phasaat*.

For hundreds of years, successive kings maintained the reliquary but it was eventually abandoned after the city was devastated by war. Then a Dhammaraja called Panyaa Tanhai established a city at Doi Chiangteum and ordered his officials to build monasteries in the centre of the city. As the men were digging, a white crow (*kaa pheuak*) prevented further work by pecking at their heads. When the king, Panyaa Tanhai, was made aware of this, he ordered that a net be used to catch the crow, and that the crow be caged with a child. The crow told the child that the place where the king had made his men dig was the site of a Buddhist reliquary. However, the deeper the workers dug, the deeper the reliquary sank into the earth. The king then abandoned the project and ordered the reliquary to be built above the ground in its present location.

THE GUARDIAN SPIRITS OF THE RELIQUARY

The reliquary is protected by four spirits: Panyaa Tanhai, Theewabut Luang, Panyaa Naak, and Sa Buakham.[4] Three of the four are mentioned in the Buddhist chronicle *Tham Tamnaan Thaat Luang Chiengteum Muang Sing* mentioned above.

Panyaa Tanhai is the pre-eminent guardian spirit of the reliquary and its site. He is a key personage in the above-mentioned chronicle (though as a devout Buddhist ruler rather than a tutelary spirit); he is not only guardian of the large pond to the southeast of the reliquary but is also generally considered the protector of the whole of Doi Chiangteum; and he is the only one of the four spirits who is included in the thirty-two guardian spirits (*phii meuang*) of Muang Sing. His stone shrine is located at the foot of a large Bo tree and overlooks the pond.

The second guardian spirit, Theewabut Luang, has a shrine similar in structure to that found at all local Buddhist temples, at the northwest corner of the reliquary base. However, the above-mentioned chronicle states that the god Indra appointed a goddess (*theewabut*) called Bunyalaekanthasiri to protect the reliquary. One of my informants, widely considered very knowledgeable on matters concerning the reliquary, affirmed that Bunyalaekanthasiri and Theewabut Luang are one and the same, though I have never heard villagers use the former name.

The abode of the third guardian spirit, the Naga spirit (*Panyaa Naak*), is at the edge of the pathway leading up to the reliquary and his domain covers a good part of the surrounding forest. This serpent spirit is said to dwell in a small and ancient well (*bor thip*) in a cave under a boulder a few feet away.[5]

The shrine of the fourth guardian spirit, Sa Buakham, is located immediately west of the reliquary, a short distance down the side of the mountain. Buakham is an historical figure, a wife of Cao Faa Sirinor, who actually preceded her husband to initiate the second period of settlement of Muang Sing in the 1870s (Saengthong n.d., p. 4). It is said that she was responsible for the restoration of the Chiangteum reliquary and presumably for that reason was elevated after her death to the status of guardian spirit.

THE THAAT CHIANGTEUM FESTIVAL

The Chiangteum reliquary is the focal point of the major festival in Muang Sing called simply *Bun Thaat*. The festival is attended not only by local Tai Lue and Tai Neua villagers from Muang Sing but also by Lue from other districts in Luang Namtha province as well as Lue from Xishuangbanna in China. Local tribal people — Akha and Yao — also attend, but as onlookers not as devotees.

The festival is held between the thirteenth and fifteenth days of the waxing moon of the first month of the Lue year (November). The final day is that of the full moon. The festival is simultaneous with the Thaat Luang festival in Vientiane, which also commemorates the erection of 84,000 Buddha reliquaries by Emperor Asoka. The Buddhist features of the two festivals are fundamentally similar, including the key rite of *pradaksina*, that is, the triple circumambulation of the reliquary by the faithful.

The Thaat Chiangteum festival, which I observed in 1996, was restricted, by decision of the local committee charged with organizing it, to two days (24–25 November), though it lasted into the early morning of the 26th.

The first day was given mostly to cleaning the reliquary and precincts and to decorating it (for example, with *tung chai* or "victory flags" around the surrounding walls). At night a number of elderly men slept near the reliquary to keep vigil.

On the second day, from early morning to late afternoon, pilgrims climbed the steep pathway up the side of the mountain to the reliquary. About half way up, they stopped to present offerings to the Naga spirit at the edge of the well. On reaching the plateau on top of the mountain they made similar offerings to two more guardian spirits, Sa Buakham and Panyaa Tanhai. Then, on entering the precinct of the reliquary, water was poured on the ground to transfer merit to the dead and to call upon the Earth Goddess (*Naang Thoranii*)[6] to witness the act. They then proceeded to a small temple (*aaraam*) adjoining the eastern side of the reliquary, and presented offerings to Buddha statues within. This was followed by offerings outside the temple to a Buddha image, to a flat stone (on which it is said Buddha sat when offered water by the Naga spirit) and to an image of Phra Uppakrut ("Lord of the Nagas").[7] Finally, offerings were presented at the shrine of Theewabut Luang at the western end of the reliquary. The offerings to the guardian spirits, to the Buddha images, and to Phra Uppakrut were all the same and comprised of sticky rice, fruit, flowers, and candles.

Some devotees also presented more lavish offerings of tree-shaped structures (adorned with paper money, flowers, and flags) called *cong tham*.[8] Some years even more expensive offerings were made by individuals in the form of large, ornate *phasaat* made of bamboo and banana trunks. This spire-shaped canopy is, as noted above in the mythical history of the reliquary, a replica of a palace, a temple, or a sacred mountain in which Asoka had placed the relics of Buddha deep within Doi Chiangteum.[9]

For the pilgrims the most important rite in the festival, the *pradaksina*, locally known as *wian thian* (literally, "circling with candles"), followed next. The devotees, one by one, circumambulated the reliquary (comprising the central and four smaller stupas) three times in a clockwise direction, each holding a leaf-cone (*suai dork*) containing a candle or candles, flowers (a type called *hon kai* or "cock's crest") and paper money. Notably, men and women were separated, the men encircling the reliquary at a higher, interior level. This contrasts with the *pradaksina* at the Thaat Luang in Vientiane where there is no separation of the sexes. After completing the circumambulation, the pilgrims knelt before the reliquary, clasped their leaf-cones of offerings head-high in salutation, lit a candle, and uttered a spontaneous prayer or wish.

As the *Bun Thaat* is essentially a Buddhist festival, Buddhist monks and novices attended — the latter in large numbers — and participated in the religious ceremonies. During the second day of the festival, novices joined lay devotees in making the triple circumambulation of the reliquary. In the late morning of that day a monk and a lay congregational leader (*acaan wat*) led a group of faithful in prayer and presented offerings of money trees to the Buddha relics within the central stupa (*taan thaat*). In the early evening, six monks chanted (*suat*) at the eastern side of the reliquary. Later, nine monks chanted at one of the four smaller stupas until midnight and then again from 3 to 4 o'clock in the morning. It is said that until 1962, four or eight monks, representing the four sub-districts (*taseng*) of Muang Sing, used to chant at each of the four smaller stupas.

The festival ended at about 8 o'clock in the morning of the third day, with offerings of sweetmeats, cooked sticky rice, curried pumpkin, and cooked pork and buffalo meat, all on separate trays, to the four guardian spirits of the reliquary. This took place in front of the Buddha images in the small temple adjoining the reliquary. Later the trays of offerings were taken and placed at the abodes of the guardian spirits.

Finally, despite the solemnity of most of the rituals described above, there was generally a festive atmosphere during the second day: hundreds of female vendors sold a variety of foodstuffs (especially a popular sweet sticky rice called *khaaw laam*), Akha girls strutted in their colourful and ornate tribal costumes and willingly posed for photos, many young men, mainly Lue, consumed copious amounts of alcohol in the late afternoon and throughout the night (though at a site set aside at a respectful distance from the reliquary), and at dusk there was a fireworks display.

BUDDHIST PILGRIMAGE, UNIVERSAL VALUES, AND POLITICAL BOUNDARIES

It is, however, important to emphasize that for the devotees the primary purpose of this festival is to make merit (*bun*), as is apparent from the name of the festival, *Bun Thaat*. Merit-making is in fact the main purpose of all Buddhist reliquary pilgrimage. Thus Keyes, commenting on Buddhist pilgrimage in northern Thailand, states:

> One significant way to produce merit is to make a pilgrimage to a shrine associated with the actual person of the Buddha. Such shrines are believed to "possess merit" (*mii bun*) which can be tapped by those who perform the pilgrimage. (1975, p. 83)

Lafont, furthermore, claims that offerings are a "symbol of faith and the more onerous the making of offerings is, the more merit is acquired" (1957, p. 44).

Merit-making is an expression of the universal moral values (*dhamma*) of Buddhism and is closely linked to the theory of karma. As Keyes puts it:

> In the northern Thai tradition, as in other Theravada Buddhist traditions, one's relative degree of suffering is determined by one's karma, that is, by human acts and their consequences. By the "law of karma" (*kod haeng kam*), good acts produce "merit" (*bun*) and evil acts produce "demerit" (*bap*) ... While a good Buddhist hopes eventually to escape the working of karma altogether and to attain nirvana, thus emulating the Buddha, he can reap more immediate benefits, in the form of reduced suffering in this existence or the next, through the pursuit of merit. (1975, p. 83)

The paper by Keyes focuses on the Northern Thai or the Yuan tradition of pilgrimage to Buddhist shrines linked to the twelve-year cycle. What is of special relevance to my argument are Keyes' comments on political boundaries and moral communities. The twelve shrines (reliquaries) are: Phra Thaat Com Thong (Chiang Mai), Phra Thaat Lampang (Lampang), Phra Thaat Cho Hae (Phrae), Phra Thaat Chae Haeng

(Nan), Phra Thaat Wat Phra Sing (Chiang Mai), Si Maha Pho (Bodh Gaya, India), Phra Thaat Takong (Yangon, Myanmar), Phra Thaat Doi Suthep (Chiang Mai), Phra Thaat Phanom (Nakhon Phanom, N.E. Thailand), Phra Thaat Haripunchai (Lamphun), Phra Thaat Doi Tung (Chiang Rai), Phra Ket Kaeo Culamani (heaven).

According to Keyes, these twelve shrines together constitute a sacred topography which "articulates with, but is not isomorphic with, the political topography of traditional northern Thailand" — only two of the shrines are located in capitals and four of the shrines are not even in Thailand. Keyes then reiterates Turner's argument (Turner 1973):

> The sacred topography of pilgrimage centres creates bonds across political boundaries; it serves to create inclusiveness, disinterestedness, and shared values as against the exclusiveness, selfish and sectional interests, and conflict over these interests stressed by political divisions in space. Whereas the political topography of northern Thailand was fragmented into a number of small discrete principalities (*muang*), the sacred topography, defined by the twelve shrines, united people into successively larger moral communities. (Keyes 1975, p. 85)

At the widest levels this includes the whole of the Buddhist world (including India) and, by the inclusion of the Culamani shrine, Buddhists in heaven and on earth (all sentient beings bound by the law of karma).

Keyes, however, makes the point that in practice, Northern Thai pilgrims were unlikely to have ventured beyond the political boundaries of the Northern Thai principalities and adds: "Only the most religious would have crossed these boundaries to make pilgrimages to more distant shrines in another principality or country" (ibid., p. 82). It seems to me that this is a statement about the practical obstacles (distance, terrain, time, physical danger, and so forth) to pilgrimage rather than the limits of the moral community. The rituals of traditional Tai principalities (*muang/meuang*) marked their territorial limits and, in some cases (for example, among the Lue), ritually sealed off the political community against outsiders (Tanabe 1988). By contrast, the long-distance pilgrim who penetrates beyond the narrow confines of his home community and overcomes numerous hardships to travel to far-flung shrines is considered, in Buddhist terms, exemplary.

LUE ACROSS BORDERS

Having raised the issue of the relation between pilgrimage, wider moral communities, and the transcendence of political boundaries, I turn now to look specifically at the Lue of southern Xishuangbanna in China, who come from villages of the former principalities of Muang La, Muang Phong, Muang Yuan, and Muang Mang. They annually cross the border into Laos for the purpose of pilgrimage to the Muang Sing reliquary.

Muang Sing has never been politically incorporated into the kingdom of Xishuangbanna, at least not since the second period of settlement beginning in the 1870s. Cao Faa Sirinor, the ruler of Muang Sing, was from Muang Yu on the west side of the Mekong River in Burma (now Myanmar). However, many of the early settlers during the second period were from southern Xishuangbanna.[10] Sirinor ruled Muang Sing as a semi-autonomous principality, paying tribute to Siam (now Thailand) but also having close political connections to Chiangtung. He later sided with the French in a long-standing border dispute with the British which culminated in the incorporation of Muang Sing into French Laos in 1904.

Lafont, in his 1957 paper on the reliquary festival, makes no mention of Lue pilgrims outside the Muang Sing valley, implying that the festival in that period was a purely local one.

However, old men in Muang Sing report that Lue from Xishuangbanna have made the annual pilgrimage to the Chiangteum reliquary for as long as they can remember, albeit in small numbers. One seventy-year-old informant said that before World War II, and even in the 1950s, only nine to ten Lue from Xishuangbanna attended the festival. He claimed, as did other elders, that the main reasons for the small number of pilgrims were poor roads, the time spent on travelling (three days from Muang La, two days from Muang Phong, and one day from Muang Mang), and the physical danger of being killed by robbers. Given these obstacles, it is likely that, to repeat Keyes' phrase: "Only the most religious would have crossed these boundaries to make the pilgrimage to more distant shrines." The only periods during which pilgrimage to the reliquary ceased altogether were during World War II and the local war of 1964–68, the U.S.-backed Yao rebellion.[11]

During the political turmoil of the Cultural Revolution (1966–76) as well as during the political tension between Laos and China and consequent border closure between 1979 and 1986, the Lue from southern Xishuangbanna continued to attend the reliquary festival in Muang Sing, though in small numbers. In these periods, it is said, the Lue of Xishuangbanna came by stealth (*lak maa*), crossing the border secretly via the forest and Akha villages. This also applied to inter-village visiting by Lue on both sides of the border for other religious and social occasions such as Buddhist holy days, funerals, marriages, and so forth. In the 1979–86 period, according to one informant, Lue from both Xishuangbanna and Muang Sing, if accosted by Chinese or Lao officials, would simply defend their intrusion with the subterfuge that they were in search of stray cattle. He also likened people to cattle as having a natural tendency to intermingle freely with their own kind — in the case of the Lue, their kin across the border.

Local informants from Muang Sing estimate that since 1992 up to 2,000 Lue from the southern Xishuangbanna have attended the Chiangteum reliquary festival each year. How does one explain the substantial increase in the number of Lue pilgrims from Xishuangbanna to the Muang Sing reliquary in recent years? I consider the main factors to be improved cross-border accessibility between China and Laos and a Buddhist revival in Xishuangbanna.

CROSS-BORDER ACCESSIBILITY

Since the border agreements between the Lao People's Democratic Republic (PDR) and China in 1992, traffic across the China-Laos border has increased greatly. Most of the large-scale trade has been via Oudomxay and Boten, while trade via the border crossing 12 kilometres from Muang Sing is mainly local petty trade focused on Muang Sing, Muang Mang, and Muang La.[12] The trade is dominated by young Lue women from Muang Mang, a short distance across the border in Xishuangbanna. They deal in goods such as rice, fruit, beer, cigarettes, batteries, and clothes. Nowadays, cross-border visiting between the Lue of Muang Sing and southern Xishuangbanna is frequent and includes inter-village visiting for housewarmings, marriages, funerals, and village-based Buddhist festivals.

In addition to the opening up of the border and the increased freedom of movement, improved transport has facilitated access to the reliquary festival. There has been a rapid increase in vehicular transport since 1992, particularly in the number of Chinese-built tractors. These tractors are known locally as *tek tek* and are used both for ploughing and for transporting goods and passengers. As the distance from the border is only 16 kilometres, it is now relatively easy for pilgrims from Xishuangbanna, on the day of the festival, to get there by late morning and return to China on the same day. They thereby also avoid the additional expense of 500 kip (50 U.S. cents) per day imposed by Lao border officials.

BUDDHIST REVIVAL AND THE BUDDHIST SAINT, KHRUBA BUNCHUM YAANSUAMRO

Since the mid-1980s, the restoration of Buddhism in Xishuangbanna has accelerated, following the period of decimation caused by the Red Guards during the Cultural Revolution in China.[13] The revival has taken the form of the remaking of temples and Buddha images, the rebuilding of the monastic order, and the renaissance of the traditional Lue writing system — a variation of a script once shared with the Northern Thai, Lao, and Khoen. There was also a cultural revolution, Lao style, in Muang Sing, but of a much milder form. Thus, the Chiangteum reliquary festival was never prohibited by the Pathet Lao or Lao PDR government. Nevertheless, many senior monks left the district and young men were discouraged from joining the monastic order. The legacy of the flight of senior monks is that there are now only twenty-five monks (*phra*) in the twenty-one Buddhist temples of Muang Sing and most of these are very young. On the other hand, since the late 1980s there has been a proliferation in the number of novices (*saamaneen*) to more than 300 and this is linked to the study of the Lue script in monasteries.

According to Keyes (1992), the revival of Buddhism in Muang Sing has been part of a general revival of Buddhism taking place simultaneously in Laos as a whole, whereas for the Lue of Xishuangbanna the revival is associated with their status as a threatened minority in China and with a passive resistance to the state. Evans (1996) also notes the inexorable expansion of Han population and commerce in Xishuangbanna and the widespread view that the Lue are "culturally backward". It is difficult, he adds, for the Lue "to counter the relentless pressure of Han civilisation — which has intensified with the opening of the border" (ibid., p. 24). In this context, Buddhist revival is surely empowering — a process in which the charismatic Buddhist monk, Khruba Bunchum Yaansuamro, has come to play an important role.

In early January 1996, Khruba Bunchum left his residence in Bangsa on the Mekong River in Myanmar (not far from Tachilek and close to the intersection of the Laos, Thailand, and Myanmar borders) and then travelled by boat and road to Chiangkok, Muang Long, and Muang Sing. Local reports claim that Bunchum's presence attracted as many as 10,000 Lue pilgrims, with about 5,000 coming from Xishuangbanna.

On 5 January 1996, Bunchum built two small stupas on the eastern side of the Chiangteum reliquary to commemorate his birthday. The stupas were built between the central stupa and the small temple (*aaraam*), and were called Hor Phra Kaew and Kesa Thancai. Under these new stupas were placed Bunchum's shaven hair, a magical formula (*yantra*) inscribed by Bunchum on bronze, a stone, and a brick and two of his monks caps. The two stupas have now become reliquaries (*thaat*) and it is worth noting that the relics of Buddhist saints are also venerated as sacred receptacles of merit (Taylor 1993, p. 175–80).

The following day, Bunchum gave a long sermon in the Lue dialect to the thousands of fervent devotees who had flocked to see him and to make merit. During the two days, he spent long periods in meditation (*samathi*), mostly inside a makeshift monk's hut (*kuti*) at the edge of the pond.

A pamphlet, written by Khruba Bunchum in memory of his mother, traces his exemplary religious career. He was born in 1965 into a farming family in a place called Bandaai.[14] When his father died, his mother moved with her children to Sankampaeng near Chiang Mai. Bunchum spent most of his early Buddhist career as a novice in northern Thailand. As a novice and a monk he made pilgrimages to Nepal, India, and Sri Lanka to practise meditation.

Khruba Bunchum records that between the years 1976 and 1995 he built in total twelve reliquaries at the following places: Chiang Saen (northern Thailand), Muang Phong (Myanmar), Muang Yong (Myanmar), Phrao (northern Thailand), Muang Yu (Myanmar), Chiangtung (Myanmar), Mae Sai (northern Thailand), and Muang Cae (Xishuangbanna). Following the construction of the two reliquaries at Doi Chiangteum in January 1996, he travelled northwards, building reliquaries at Wat Chiangcai in the town of Muang Sing and at Muang Wen and Muang Cae in Xishuangbanna.

Khruba Bunchum's religious career and achievements certainly make him a candidate for the title of a Buddhist saint, not as an *arahan* but as a more inner-worldly *nak bun* (or *ton bun*). Keyes defines a *nak bun* as "one who is so endowed with merit himself that he can, through compassion towards others, serve as a means for them also to acquire merit" (1982, p. 149). One expression of this compassion is to build and repair Buddhist monuments (such as reliquaries), as those who contribute their wealth and labour are believed thereby to acquire great merit. The exemplar of the *nak bun* tradition in northern Thailand is Khruba Siwichai.[15]

Bunchum, in his autobiographical pamphlet, is not reticent in identifying with this saintly tradition and claims that by the time of his ordination as a novice he had already been recognized by many as a *ton bun*. The Lue of Muang Sing and Xishuangbanna seem not to have any doubts in this regard and normally refer to Khruba Bunchum as simply *cao bun*.

It seems as if Khruba Bunchum has given special attention to the Lue of Xishuangbanna, having made two journeys there in the last two years. The evidence, however, suggests that Bunchum's religious mission is not confined to the Lue of Xishuangbanna or the Lue from any other region but rather encompasses a multi-ethnic and, indeed, multi-national following. What better headquarters to launch such a mission could be found than the liminal, interstitial tri-border region near Tachilek and Mae Sai? Khruba Bunchum has built reliquaries in northern Thailand, Laos, China, and Myanmar and in areas inhabited not only by Lue but also by other Tai-speaking groups such as Northern Thai, Khoen, and Shan. Bunchum has certainly attracted a large number of devotees among the Northern Thai. His photograph now adorns many restaurants and homes in northern Thailand and busloads of Northern Thai pilgrims regularly cross the border at Mae Sai to make merit by presenting offerings to Bunchum at his residence at Wat Dornreuang near Bangsa. Furthermore, a number of Northern Thai I have spoken to claim that Bunchum is the reincarnation of Khruba Siwichai. It is also said that Bunchum has converted to Buddhism a large number of Musur (Lahu) tribal people in the Bangsa area.

The religious perspective of his Lue followers is more limited. The Lue of Muang Sing and Xishuangbanna claim that Khruba Bunchum is Lue: he is not only a Buddhist saint but a Lue Buddhist saint. The Lue of Xishuangbanna seemed to have developed an especially close identification with Bunchum. Cao Mahaakanthawong, a well-known Lue intellectual from Chiangrung whom I met in Chiang Mai recently claimed, for example, that Bunchum's birth-place, Bandaai, is located near Muang Cae and Muang Hai in Xishuangbanna. This is a claim that has no basis in any facts.[16] Furthermore, a large proportion of the faithful who attended the Muang Sing reliquary during Bunchum's visit in early 1996 were Lue from Xishuangbanna. For them the Chiangteum reliquary is likely to take on added sanctity and fame in the future. The two new stupas (Hor Phra Kaeo and Kesa Thancai) have become the receptacles of Khruba Bunchum's charisma, an enduring and abundant source of merit and a powerful spiritual magnet for Lue pilgrims across the border.

CONCLUSION

This chapter has been concerned with the Chiangteum reliquary of Muang Sing in northern Laos, with special reference to the annual *Bun Thaat* festival. Merit and karma are fundamental universal values of Buddhism and pilgrimage to stupas containing the relics of Buddha or Buddhist saints are ranked highly as means of acquiring merit.

Following Turner and Keyes I have argued that Buddhist pilgrimage transcends the narrow and particularistic confines of political boundaries and creates wider moral communities. While the Lue of Muang Sing and the Lue of the former principalities of southern Xishuangbanna have been linked by migration and kinship ties they have not been united politically, at least not over the last two centuries. As far as the Chiangteum reliquary is concerned, that wider Buddhist moral community, which transcends political boundaries now comprises mostly Lue from Muang Sing and Lue across the border in China. It is therefore in a sense an ethnically bound Buddhist moral community.

Pilgrims, especially long-distance pilgrims, must contend with the mundane and practical obstacles of distance, time of travel, fatigue, and physical danger, so that often only the most devout would have travelled to more distant reliquaries. In the case of the Chiangteum reliquary this is exemplified in the period before 1960 when only a trickle of pilgrims from southern Xishuangbanna tackled the poor roads and braved attacks by robbers to make the pilgrimage to the reliquary.

This trickle of pilgrims from Xishuangbanna has increased to a stream in recent years which, I have argued, is related to the political and economic changes of the "post-socialist" era. These changes culminated in the 1992 border agreements between Lao PDR and China, which have increased cross-border traffic for trade, social, and religious purposes. Improved roads and vehicular transport have also facilitated access, including access to the Chiangteum reliquary.

However, accessibility alone cannot explain the recent increase in pilgrims from Xishuangbanna. Another significant factor has been the Buddhist revival which has taken place in both Xishuangbanna and Muang Sing. For the Lue of Xishuangbanna this revival is related to their status as a threatened minority and provides a powerful counter to Han Chinese hegemony.

The Buddhist monk, Khruba Bunchum Yaansuamro, has emerged on the scene to play a unique role in this revival. Although his mission is not confined to the Lue, he is regarded by them as a Lue Buddhist saint.

The sanctity of the Chiangteum reliquary has now been augmented by Bunchum's own reliquaries and the reliquary has become inextricably linked to Bunchum's religious career. As such, the reliquary has become an abundant store of merit to be tapped by pilgrims. The Chiangteum reliquary is also the focus of a transnational Lue moral community. The identification of Khruba Bunchum as a Lue Buddhist saint can only reinforce this orientation.

ACKNOWLEDGEMENT

I would like to thank Director Houmphanh Rattanavong of the Institute for Research on Culture and Society, Vientiane, for his support for the research on which this chapter is based. I am also indebted to Khampeng Thipmountali, also from the same institute, for his research assistance in the field.

NOTES

1. I have borrowed this term from Lafont, who refers to the chronicle as an *histoire mythique*. However, it is doubtful whether villagers, including monks, regard the story as mythical in the sense of being untrue.
2. My translation is from a ten-page-long version written in Lue *Tham* script, which was lent to me by an elder of Ban Sor village in Muang Sing. Lafont provides a translation from a version obtained from Wat Chiangcai in the centre of the town. My translation and Lafont's French translation differ in a number of details but I was unable to locate the Wat Chiangcai version to check.
3. A simulacrum of a palace, temple, or sacred mountain.
4. Lafont (1957) makes no mention of Sa Buakham. The other three he asserts are pre-Buddhist spirits who have been appropriated by and subordinated to Buddhism.
5. Lafont (1957, p. 14) simply refers to this spirit as a "stone-spirit" (*pierre-genie*) who, he says, is guardian of the pathway to the reliquary and is presented with offerings to avoid accidents and excessive fatigue en route. This differs from a local legend often recounted to me: the cave under the boulder was once full of jewellery which female pilgrims used to borrow to adorn themselves for the *Bun Thaat* festival. However, some failed to return the jewellery to the cave and so the Naga spirit, in retribution, closed off the cave by moving the boulder over the opening.
6. A beautiful goddess in Buddhist mythology who destroys the forces of the demonic Mara by wringing her long hair and causing a flood.
7. This image was built as recently as in early 1996 by the request of Khruba Bunchum.

According to Buddhist beliefs, Phra Uppakrut or "Lord of the Nagas" has the power to subjugate Mara, the enemy of Buddha. Villagers are familiar with Phra Uppakrut, and they are also unanimous that he has never had any association with the Chiangteum reliquary and its site as a guardian spirit. Nor do they confuse Phra Uppakrut with Panya Naak (one of the four guardian spirits of the reliquary).

8. According to Tambiah: "In popular Buddhism *cong tham* are said to represent the four trees that will blossom at the four corners of the city in which the next Buddha, Maitreya, will be born. They will then produce all kinds of delicious fruits in fabulous quantities." Tambiah also notes the link between these trees and merit-making rites (1970, p. 165). Among the Lao they are called *ton kalapheuk*, from the Pali *kapparukkha*.

9. According to informants, *phasaat* are not presented every year due to the expense. In 1995, the District Officer of Muang Sing had one made for the Bun Thaat festival, but in 1996 he gave a large donation as a contribution to the building of a new cement stairway to the reliquary instead.

10. The most recent large-scale migration from southern Xishuangbanna to Muang Sing was in 1958, following the collectivization campaigns in China.

11. The festival was still held but, because of the danger of night attacks by rebels, finished at 6.0 p.m.

12. Muang Sing is more likely to be a conduit for large-scale trade in the future with the completion of a new road from Muang Sing to Chiangkok on the Mekong River. Construction of the road began in November 1996.

13. Nearly all the Buddhist temples and images were either severely damaged or totally destroyed.

14. In his autobiographical pamphlet Khruba Bunchum does not identify the location of Bandaai. I have not been able to locate Bandaai on any map, but as far as I can ascertain from the reports of my informants it is situated in the Chiang Saen district of Chiang Rai province, northern Thailand.

15. Khruba Siwichai is northern Thailand's most famous monk. He was born in 1878 in the northern province of Lamphun. After ordination as a monk he soon gained a reputation for his strict asceticism and for the construction and repair of religious monuments (activities which provided laymen opportunities to make merit). This was at a time when northern Thailand was being politically and administratively incorporated into the Siamese state. This process included the integration of northern monks into a single, national monastic order (*Sangha*). On this issue Khruba Siwichai ran foul of the Siamese authorities by insisting on his right, derived from Northern Thai tradition, to perform ordinations without the permission of district ecclesiastical and civil officials. His defiance soon made him the focus of anti-Siamese regional sentiment. Between 1919 and 1935 he was called to Bangkok three times to respond to charges of violating *Sangha* regulations. During the final visit he assented to recognize the authority of the Siamese *Sangha* and thereby averted a possible regional rebellion (see Keyes 1982, pp. 154–57).

16. See note 14.

REFERENCES

Evans, Grant. "Tranformation of Jinghong, Xishuangbanna, P.R.C.". Paper presented at the International Conference on South China and Mainland S.E. Asia: Cross Border Relations in the Post-Socialist Age, 4–6 December 1996, Centre of Asian Studies, University of Hong Kong.
Keyes, Charles F. "Buddhist Pilgrimage Centres and the Twelve Year Cycle: Northern Thai Moral Orders in Space and Time". *History of Religions* 15, no. 1 (1975): 71–89.
Keyes, Charles F. "Death of Two Buddhist Saints in Thailand". *Journal of the American Academy of Religion, Thematic Studies* 48, nos. 3, 4 (1982): 149–80.
Keyes, Charles F. *Who Are the Lue? Revisited Ethnic Identity in Lao, Thailand and China*. A Working Paper from the Center for International Studies, Cambridge. Massachusetts, Cambridge: Massachusetts Institute of Technology, 1992.
Lafont, Pierre-Bernard. "Le That de Muong-Sing". *Bulletin, Societe des Etudes Indochinoises* 32, no. 1 (1957): 1–15.
Saengthong Photibupha. "The History of Singharajathani" (in Thai). Mimeographed. n.d.
Tambiah, S.J. *Buddhism and the Spirit Cults in North-East Thailand*. London: Cambridge University Press, 1970.
Tanabe, Shigeharu. "Spirits and Ideological Discourse: The Tai Lue Guardian Cults in Yunnan". *SOJOURN: Journal of Social Issues in Southeast Asia* 3, no. 1 (1988): 1–25.
Taylor, J.L. *Forest Monks and the Nation-State: An Anthropological and Historical Study in Northeastern Thailand*. Singapore: Institute of Southeast Asian Studies, 1993.
Turner, Victor. "The Centre Out There: Pilgrims Goal". *History of Religions* 12 (1973): 191–230.

Transformation of Jinghong, Xishuangbanna, PRC

Grant Evans

The opening up of the land borders between China and the mainland Southeast Asian states has not only involved economic processes, but also social and cultural ones, such as shifts in ethnic composition along the border. In some cases it has seen the re-establishment of a previous status quo, such as the return of ethnic Chinese (Hoa) traders to the northern borders of Vietnam. During the conflict with China along the border in the late 1970s and early 1980s, the Hoa were compelled to move away from the border for "security" reasons, and many fled Vietnam as refugees. Today, they have moved back in strength, and border towns like Mong Cai or Lang Son once again have large and thriving Hoa populations (see Chapter 12).

By comparison, the towns inside Laos along its border with China have always been small, and the volume of trade low. The ethnic Lao are in a minority in the provinces of Phongsaly, Oudomxay, and Luang Namtha, all of which have ethnically very mixed populations of Khmu, Lue, Hmong, Goh (Akha), Phu Noi, Haw (Yunnanese Chinese), and others. While Haw have always played an important trading role and tended to base themselves in the towns, the boundary between ethnic Chinese towns and ethnic "other" rural areas has been blurred. For example, Haw (who are sometimes thought of as a "hilltribe") also engage in slash-and-burn upland cultivation. Many Chinese left Laos after the 1975 communist take-over, including a significant number of Haw from the north, and the subsequent conflict with China in the late 1970s caused more to leave, although they were not compelled to do so, as they were in Vietnam. Some, in fact, remained, and they have formed a core for the return of Chinese to the border, including Chinese who have never lived there before. For example, a Lao-Chinese from Pakse in the south of Laos, who had studied Chinese in China, moved to Luang Namtha with his wife from Hubei to act as an interpreter in Lao-Chinese trade, at the same time setting up a small coffee-shop in the main street. Luang Namtha, nevertheless, remains an ethnically mixed town, with many Lao, Black Tai, Lue, and others living there. The town of Phongsaly has always had a predominantly Haw and Phu Noi population, and this remains true today. Oudomxay is quite simply ethnically mixed, although there is a growing Chinese trade presence. A survey by Khampheng Thipmuntali and myself of the Oudomxay market in mid-1995 found that about one-third of the traders were Haw, one-third Phu Noi, and one-third were Hmong. In the long term, however, we may see the Chinese move into a position of clear dominance in such markets through their ability to manipulate ethnically based regional trade networks.

Towns along the Myanmar side of the border were similar to those in Laos, but the much greater proportion of trade between Myanmar and China is changing the situation there quickly. "In 1996, Yunnan's trade with Burma (excluding smuggling) totalled $362 million ... Trade with Vietnam, Thailand and Laos totalled $85 million" (Forney 1997, p. 55). This makes the stakes along this border higher and drives Chinese migration into Myanmar, something the government has less control over than in Laos. Bertil Lintner writes:

> In Mandalay, in northern Burma, Yunnanese are buying up shops, restaurants, hotels and karaoke bars — even citizenship. "When a person dies in Mandalay, his identity card is sold to a broker across the border in Ruili, who resells it. The picture is then changed and the new owner has become a Burmese citizen who can settle and buy property in Burma," explains a Chinese in Ruili who is involved in the business. I have come across no instances of this in northern Laos. (1997, p. 58)

SIP SONG PANNA/XISHUANGBANNA

Across from Laos lies the Dai (Tai Lue) Autonomous Region of Xishuangbanna (or what is known in Tai as the Sip Song Panna[1]), established by the People's Republic of China (PRC) in 1953. Its capital is

Jinghong, which is also the name of one of the three counties of the region. The other two are Menghai and Mengla, the former leading into Myanmar, the latter into Laos. The population of the region is under one million, of which one-third are Han; one-third Dai; and one-third other ethnic groups, the largest being Hani, with approximately 153,496 persons, other groups having less than 50,000 — such as Bulang, Jino, Yao, Lahu, Miao, and so on. In the 1950s the Han made up only 2.3 per cent of the population, the Dai 47.3 per cent, and the other groups 50.4 per cent (Hsieh 1989, p. 61).

For several hundred years this region had a variable tributary relationship with the Chinese empire in which the latter increasingly exercised its power through a *tusi* system (that is, a form of indirect rule). In the twentieth century with the gradual formation of a modern Chinese state obsessed with borderlines and total control over every inch of claimed territory, we have seen a growing Han political presence in what became designated "minority regions" by the modern state. Definitive Han colonization of Xishuangbanna only begins after the communist revolution in 1949,[2] despite the establishment of "autonomous regions" for minorities, a historical peculiarity of Marxist-Leninist "nationalities" policy implying no lessening of Han political control of these regions, only some concessions to some local customs.[3] Han political control was exercised from the cities and towns, while the rural areas remained exclusively populated by Dai and other groups. This pattern begins to change in the late 1950s with the creation of state farms for growing tea, and in the 1960s, state rubber plantations, all of which were overwhelmingly staffed by Han immigrants (Hill 1989; Henin and Flaherty 1995).[4] Thus the Han population rapidly grew from 5,708 in the 1950s to 229,083 in the 1970s. Yet during this time of communist austerity and "self-sufficiency", these large state farms were like small towns — separate and distinct Han nodes in the countryside.

JINGHONG

Xieng Hong, now called Jinghong in Mandarin, was the seat of the most powerful *muang* in Xishuangbanna in the nineteenth century. It was presided over by a lord or king, the Chao Fa. The American missionary W.C. Dodd, who travelled through the region in 1919, left this description of the city:

> It is situated on a steep western slope overlooking the [Mekong] river. It is so hidden by trees that little can be seen of it from the river excepting

the numerous temples and the long sloping roof of the palace of the Chao Fa, or Lu chief of the Sipsawng Panna. This is a big barn-like structure, solidly built of beautiful woods of different kinds, once the pride of the country, now weather beaten and blackened by exposure and the touch of many soiled fingers. (1923, p. 183)

He goes on to describe the establishment of the Chinese administrative headquarters:

The Chinese officials are building a new town three or four miles up the river from the old one, which is locally called Chiengmai [new city in Tai]. It is really on the site of the old city, decimated so many years ago that there is scarcely a trace of it now except portions of the wall and moat. The Chinese yamen or court is built of burned brick and is quite imposing for this wilderness place. It was about eight years in building; is the regular Chinese establishment, somewhat in the nature of a fort, as there are holes in the walls for guns ... The city is open to the Tai as well as the Chinese, and probably few Chinese will come to live here as it is too hot for them. At present there are only the officials, the soldiers, and a few merchants. (Ibid., p. 184)

When the Chinese established the autonomous region in 1953 they appropriated the name of the city of the old Chao Fa, who had been deposed, and the Chinese administrative town became known as Jinghong. The transfer of power was made complete when the old palace was torn down during the Cultural Revolution, and the old town converted to a rubber plantation. Dai informants have led me to houses now occupied by Sichuanese rubber workers and pointed to large foundation stones at the corners of these houses and explained that these were once the foundation stones of the palace. They are all that is left of the once proud structure described by Dodd, and the stones have become an almost sacred relic in the ethnic memory of the Dai.

One official publication describes the city in 1949 as having "only a few brick houses for the local government, four Western-style buildings for foreign missionaries and a street of less than 100 metres flanked with some 30 shabby cottages" (An and Liu 1985, pp. 10–11). Information on the development of Jinghong up until the 1980s is difficult to find because it was a region which remained closed to foreigners until the mid-1980s. But by the early 1980s it had become a city of approximately 30,000 people, most of whom were Han administrators, shopkeepers, transport workers, soldiers, and the like. At the time of his fieldwork in the late 1980s, Hsieh Shih-chung observed that the "Dai who live in town are usually civil servants. A majority of them are former aristocrats and their relatives and descendants" (1989, p. 275). Hsieh claims most of these seemed determined to assimilate into the dominant Han culture and to shake off their "stigmatized" Dai ethnicity. Incorporated into the city at its edges were Dai villages such as Man Jinglan and Man Ting,[5] the paddy fields of which were interspersed between city buildings.

BOOMTOWN

From 1949 up until 1978 there was almost no foreign trade with Yunnan, which lived up to its reputation as a "mysterious land beyond the clouds". Following Deng Xiaoping's declaration that China must modernize, this situation began to change rapidly. Initially it was the coastal provinces which opened up to the outside world, but then in the 1980s the slogan "gateway into Southeast Asia" marked Yunnan for development in the region. In 1985 the provincial government released the "Yunnan Province Temporary Provisions on Border Trade", and trade growth along its southern border has accelerated ever since. Matt Forney's description of a briefing given by a senior Yunnan economist in 1997 captures the mood well:

> Che Zhimin whacks his pointer onto a wall-size map of Asia and drags it noisily from Hong Kong to New Delhi. After a contemplative pause, he repeats the operation from Rangoon to Moscow. Then he glares at his guests, exasperated, as if only an idiot could still miss his point. "Look where the lines cross!" he yells. "Yunnan! ... It will make the Strait of Malacca obsolete. It will be like uniting Canada and Mexico! (1997, p. 54)

Chapter 1 (by Peter Hinton) in this volume deals wonderfully with such rhetoric.

Xishuangbanna is Yunnan's border "doorstep", and Jinghong its natural frontier development headquarters. It provides the Chinese anchor for the so-called "economic quadrangle" incorporating China, Laos, Myanmar, and Thailand, the southern Thai anchor of which is Chiang Rai. Plans for this region include massive transport infrastructure projects of roads and river transport, with Jinghong developing into a major port on the Mekong River as well as a centrepoint for road transport to Kunming, the capital of the province. In 1991 an international airport was opened at Jinghong, which will be a crucial hub in inter-regional air transport. In the mid-1990s, as a further step in this direction, Yunnan Airlines acquired a 60 per cent state in Lao Airways. Promoters of the concept speak brashly of being able to drive all the way from Singapore to Kunming, and in response to this local entrepreneurs are preparing snares along the way for the modern Asian businessman. In sleepy Luang Namtha I have heard of a Thai company's plans for a golf course, although I am sure golf is a game none of the locals have even heard of, let alone the Lanten and Akha hillpeople who occasionally visit the market there. One can only wonder at what they will make of well-dressed men in their dark spectacles hitting, and then following, a small white ball around wide open spaces, and then zooming off in their limousines! But this will be one of the least troubling challenges facing the peoples of this region which is now on the fast track into the modern world.

Tourism is planned to be one of Yunnan's biggest money earners, playing on the province's reputation in China as being full of natural forests and populated by colourful minorities, of which there are claimed to be twenty-four. And Xishuangbanna, it could be said, has become the jewel in the ethnic-tourism crown of the province.

All of these developments have caused a building boom in Jinghong for office space and for large, modern hotels, and, of course, for housing for the growth in governmental administrators, businesspeople, and ordinary workers. The multi-storeyed Banna Mansion Hotel loomed up into the skyline in the early 1990s, a huge clockface at its pinnacle seeming to announce "Jinghong, your time has come!" Other large international hotels have since sprung up. In the past ten years the population of Jinghong has quadrupled, from 30,000 people to 130,000 in 1996, and there are projections that it will reach 230,000 by the year 2006. In what was already a Han-dominated city, almost all of this growth is accounted for by Han immigrants from other provinces. Thus one consequence of the opening of the borders has been the definitive Hanification of Jinghong City.

TOURISM

Ironically, or perhaps predictably, along with this irrevocable Hanification of Jinghong has gone its embellishment with "ethnic characteristics" to make it attractive to tourists. This is most apparent in the ubiquitous use of yellow to mark something as Dai — yellow roofs on buildings which may also try to imitate the roof of a temple, yellow walls, and so on. This style has been repeated throughout Xishuangbanna.[6] When tourists first look out of their aircraft windows at Jinghong airport they are greeted by its expansive and striking yellow roof, and they know they have reached another, "wondrous", part of China. But, as Hsieh (1989, p. 251) has remarked, the Dai themselves "feel nothing toward the yellow symbolism of Jing Hong, because it is based on a Han image of Dai culture". Another key symbol that is promoted is that of palm trees. These are planted along the roads even as the foundations of new buildings are being set. They suggest the "tropical paradise" promised in the tourist brochures.

Since the opening up of China, foreign tourism has skyrocketed from 1.88 million tourists in 1978 to 43 million in 1994, and it is still increasing. Less noticed, but much more spectacular, has been the massive growth in Chinese domestic tourism over the same period, and especially since the early 1990s following the government's implementation of a nation-wide holiday system granting each employee seven to fifteen days' annual leave. This, combined with rapidly rising incomes especially in the coastal provinces, has led to a "travel craze", according to the *Beijing Review* (17–23 October 1994). In the main cities of China (as already in Hong Kong and Taiwan), culture has taken a modernist turn. Far-off places are no longer associated with banishment or viewed with fear and trepidation, and many Chinese tour companies promote their tours with the slogans: "go to the boundary areas!", "Frontier Tours", and "Minority Nationality Tours". According to Zheng and Wang:

> Chinese tourists mainly focus on sightseeing, and the richness and uniqueness of natural resources ... In general, the frontier cities have much richer resources for nature tourism, more unique and spectacular than inner regions. (1996, p. 29)

But they also argue that "the essence of tourism is the pursuit of cultural difference and similarity" (ibid.). Domestic and Overseas Chinese tourists travel, say, to the Confucian temple, and this will reinforce their sense of cultural "similarity" as Han; when they travel to minority areas, it is to experience cultural difference. All of this fits very neatly with Gladney's (1994) argument about modern Chinese nationalism and the creation of a unified Han ethnicity this century by the Chinese state. Minorities, as he has argued, receive an inordinate amount of publicity in the People's Republic of China (PRC). Why? Because by looking at minorities (however their image is actually constructed), "Han" people can say "that is not us". Tourism, therefore, helps to consolidate the idea of a unified Han ethnicity in modern China.[7] Thus travel does not take one further away from home, but paradoxically consolidates one's identity with home. In this sense one can perhaps talk about the "domestication of the frontier" in contemporary China.

Figures provided by tourist officials in Jinghong show that in 1994 the region received 10,000 foreign tourists, and 1.2 million domestic tourists; in 1995, 30,000 foreign tourists and 1.5 million domestic tourists. Most of the foreigners were from Southeast Asia, probably Thailand. These officials said that for a short time, over 1992–93, there were many Japanese tourists, and this appears to have been associated with speculation about the origins of the Japanese people.[8]

The main attractions for tourists in Xishuangbanna are tropical rainforest sights and products from the rainforest, especially medicines (whether they be herbal or from endangered animal species), and Dai culture. While one attraction of internal tourism for Chinese is the lack of problems with language and with travel documentation, a trip to the frontier in Xishuangbanna also allows a brief, visa-free, one-day international excursion into Myanmar, mainly to buy jade. When late morning comes down in Dalou, for example, the place is suddenly choked with mini-buses which have travelled from Muang Hai or Jinghong to carry Chinese tourists across the border into Myanmar for shopping.

The image of the Dai promoted among the Chinese is that they are "safe", non-violent, and not "primitive", signalled by the fact that they have their own writing system and an institutionalized Buddhist religion. But perhaps the dominant image peddled is that of illusive, beautiful Dai women in their long colourful dresses. The sexualization of Dai women in the Han imagination can be seen in the ubiquitous imagery of Dai women bathing half-naked in the rivers. Originally promoted by the so-called Yunnan school of painting, this image is reproduced photographically in all tourist promotion, and on billboards. The viewing of Dai women bathing has become a tourist treat for Han, and when we were in Muang Han in the middle of 1996 we saw a banner stretched across the road saying: "See women bathing down by the river after 5p.m.!" We enquired from the local Dai about this and they claimed that it was Hani women hired by tourist promoters. These Hani women would pretend to be Dai and allegedly did not mind exposing their breasts, in contrast to the modest Dai.[9] Because of voyeuristic Han tourists many Dai women around main tourist centres have had to find new bathing locations.

This sexualization of Dai women is consonant with a sense of "lawlessness" on the frontier which is, in imaginary terms, at the edge of cultural constraints. Hence the Han have fantasies of sexual freedom and licence among minorities, and among the Dai in particular. Such fantasies also grow out of a Confucian society's incomprehension of the status of women in non-Confucian societies, where relative female freedom in mate choice is mistaken for sexual libertarianism. When Han, men in particular, travel to this frontier, they move to the edge of their own cultural constraints and seek sexual adventure among these allegedly "sexually wild" women.[10] A recent sexual "adventure" which has been added to the frontier has been the promotion of transvestite cabarets just over the border from Dalou in Mong La, Myanmar, which are put on by "girls" from Thailand. Thus one aspect of tourism to Xishuangbanna is the development of a variety of sex tourism such as is seen in other parts of Asia, the growth of prostitution there, and the attendant problems of sexually transmitted diseases. It is estimated that Jinghong has around 500 prostitutes, most of them Han immigrants, some of whom pretend to be Dai, and a small number of Dai and other minority women. For a time the authorities blamed the spread of AIDS (acquired immune deficiency syndrome) on the "sexually irresponsible" Dai, but recently it has been shown that there are more Han AIDS cases in Jinghong than Dai.[11]

MAN JINGLAN

Man Jinglan is an old established Dai village which lies just south of the main city centre of Jinghong. Until the 1980s it was not much different from most other Dai villages in Xishuangbanna, except of course for its access to the services, such as medical care and some commodities, offered by the city, but until the policy changes of the late 1970s, the economic and social differences between the countryside and the city were not great, as all people were absorbed into some kind of state or cooperative sector.

Collectivization of Man Jinglan's land began in the late 1950s. Forest land and grazing land considered by custom to belong to the village was expropriated, and on these lands now stand the Institute of Medicine State Farm, the Tropical Crop Institute, and the Nationality Park. Forest land which was left to the south of the village (around 500 *mu*) was converted to a rubber plantation in the late 1960s and managed by the collective. In the 1970s and 1980s, management of both this plantation and of the village's paddy fields was gradually de-collectivized and came under the Household Responsibility System. The population of the village in 1980 was 665 persons distributed into 138 households, which by 1995 had grown to 806 persons in 194 households. Paddy land held by the village in 1990 was approximately 717 *mu*.

When tourists started coming to Jinghong in the mid-1980s the Dai of Man Jinglan, and the other Dai village to the south, Man Ting, were inevitably drawn into the tourist trade, and some Dai restaurants began to appear along Man Ting Road, which ran through the centre of Man Jinglan. Today the road through the village is wall-to-wall restaurants, hotels, bars, and cafes, and every evening is invaded by scores of buses carrying tourists to restaurants featuring primarily Dai hostesses, or hostesses dressed as Dai, while one or two have their hostesses dressed as Hani. There they are fed and entertained by "traditional" Dai (or Hani) dances and songs. Outside, gaggles of girls dressed as Dai with flowers in their hair, powdered faces and bright lipstick, or others in the short black skirts of the Hani,[12] beckon to customers as they walk along the street.

Many Dai, especially young women, in Man Jinglan are now heavily dependent on the tourist trade for their income, and no one in the village grows rice anymore. How did this come about?

When plans began for the expansion of the city the first problem was land, which was what the residents of Man Jinglan had. The Economic Development Committee of Xishuangbanna therefore compelled the village to sell their 717 *mu* of paddy land to the committee for the "socialist development of the city". Not surprisingly, the committee did very well out of the transaction: buying the land from the village for 30,000 yuan per *mu* and reselling it to developers for 150,000 yuan per *mu*. The problem for the villagers then was what to do with the money paid to them by the committee, and who had rights to this money. A formula which divided the villagers into six ranks (largely based on residence and ancestry) was devised, and then villagers received a lump sum payment of one-third of what they were entitled to; another third was placed in a bank to earn interest, and the final third invested in development projects to be managed by the village leadership. Soon the committee had invested in a hotel, the Lancang, in Man Ting Road, and a parking lot. Subsequently, they invested in a joint-venture hotel and a joint-venture gas station with the army. By 1994, management of the funds was in turmoil, with the leadership being accused of corruption. For example, the thickness of the concrete in the parking lot for tourist buses was less than claimed, leaving several hundred thousand yuan unaccounted for; 180,000 yuan was also unaccounted for in the construction of the Lancang Hotel. Much of the suspicion for this corruption fell on the woman accountant Gaew, a Communist Party member and a member of the Congress of Xishuangbanna. An investigation through the court recovered 360,000 yuan, but suspicion reigns that much more went missing. Gaew was not penalized, and now works in the city government. A new leadership was elected in 1994, but its head was put in jail in 1996 for taking a 120,000-yuan bribe.

While a small number of people in the village have become at least a little wealthy through these changes to Man Jinglan, either through bribery or entrepreneurial skill, most feel powerless in the face of events. Table 8.1 provides a breakdown of the income of thirty houses surveyed in Man Jinglan in 1995. It can be seen that returns from the sale of land provide a significant income for only a small number of the villagers, and these tend to be the poorer ones. For most people their main income comes from household rent, and from other activities, such as small business, working in the tourist restaurants, and so on. The Dai of Man Jinglan are now totally dependent on a money economy, including buying their rice in the market.

Perhaps the most interesting category in this breakdown is "household rent". When one walks behind the tourist façade which has been thrown up along Man Ting Road and down through the village of large traditional Dai houses raised on stilts, one quickly notices a significant difference between these houses and those of Dai in rural villages. In the latter the space under the houses may be used to tether pigs or house chickens at night, and to store ploughs and other agricultural equipment. In Man Jinglan all of these bottom areas have been walled in and broken up into little cubicles which are rented out to Chinese immigrants from Hunan, Sichuan, and elsewhere who have streamed into Jinghong to work as cyclo drivers, labourers, bar girls, and so on. One gets an idea of the scale of immigration when one realizes that the population under the floorboards of the main houses is four times that of the official village population. That is, in 1995 official residents of Man Jinglan numbered 806 persons, while immigrants numbered more than 4,000 persons. The importance of this income to the villagers is indicated by the fact that thirteen households out of thirty in the survey gained half or more of their income from rent, with another six gaining between a quarter and a half. Pressures to rent appear to be offset by income from either rubber or the sale of land. Nevertheless, a significant number of Dai households in Man Jinglan have become dependent on rental income. While some may joke about the fact that they now house Chinese where they used to house the pigs, the Dai grip on this extra income is vulnerable to a sudden change of heart by the city

Table 8.1
Transformation of Jinghong: Household Survey of Income per Household in Man Jinglan, 1995
(renminbi/yuan)

Family	People	SPFSL	Rubber	H-rent	Others	Total
1	7	4,400	2,250	840	11,510	19,000
2	4	2,200	0	3,600	10,740	16,540
3	5	4,000	0	1,920	7,300	13,220
4	2	1,600	0	10,800	0	12,400
5	7	4,400	2,250	840	16,965	24,455
6	4	2,100	0	3,600	7,100	12,800
7	5	4,000	0	1,920	7,000	12,920
8	6	4,400	0	3,600	12,400	20,400
9	2	1,600	0	5,760	1,800	9,160
10	4	3,200	0	6,000	0	9,200
11	7	3,800	0	18,000	70	21,870
12	4	2,000	17,450	8,160	0	27,610
13	3	2,400	0	6,000	1,000	9,400
14	6	1,400	0	5,760	10,895	18,055
15	6	4,800	0	5,760	0	10,560
16	4	2,600	0	6,720	3,300	12,620
17	6	3,000	0	6,720	3,600	13,320
18	3	2,400	0	0	5,028	7,428
19	4	3,000	0	8,400	2,400	13,800
20	5	4,000	0	3,600	80	7,680
21	5	4,000	10,000	0	2,000	16,000
22	2	1,600	0	360	0	1,960
23	2	1,400	0	0	6,300	7,700
24	3	1,600	8,000	9,360	3,700	22,660
25	2	1,600	0	7,920	3,700	13,220
26	4	2,200	0	4,200	3,600	10,000
27	4	0	0	7,200	9,200	16,400
28	6	4,000	0	10,800	36,200	51,000
29	4	3,200	72,000	0	3,000	78,200
30	4	0	3,200	19,600	25,800	48,600

Notes: SPFSL = "Share Profit From Sale of Land". "Others" includes small business, part or full-time job incomes, the sale of pigs and chickens, the selling of skills, and so on.

government, which could quickly crack down on this informal arrangement, which has evolved out of necessity. And if one walks beyond the houses and towards the Mekong River one finds market gardens, which have also been rented by the people of Man Jinglan and Man Ting to immigrants from the north — but this land too is targeted for development.

SOCIAL CONSEQUENCES

While many of the Dai in Man Jinglan are, financially, reasonably well-off at the moment, certainly compared with the poor Chinese who live under their houses, there is an air that they are living in a "fools paradise", and a little probing quickly reveals foreboding about the future, especially among parents for the future of their children. Within one generation the village has gone from being a rural-oriented "traditional" Dai village to become a suburb of the ethnically Chinese city, Jinghong. No longer rice growers, they now buy their rice in the market, and this has meant a change from sticky rice — an ethnic marker among Dai — to plain rice. Young people, they say, do not like sticky rice, and the latter (like Han) complain about sticky rice being too heavy and indigestible. The young must seek work within a Han world and therefore are under pressure to change culturally in food, in dress, and in speech. Young Dai face a significantly different social context from that of young Lao or Thai in this regard. For example, if a young Dai woman puts on jeans, she immediately looks "Chinese", whereas in Laos or Thailand she would simply look young. There are no ethnic complications or implications in this simple shift in attire for the latter.

To compete in a Chinese world, however, requires a knowledge of spoken and written Chinese, if one does not want to end up a poor, second-class "Han", not unlike the people living under their parents' houses. Most young Dai, however, are not good at written and spoken Chinese, while their Dai is simply the language of the household.

The young Dai of Man Jinglan are suspended between a Dai rural past and the Chinese present, which looms over them. They are suspended in another way too. Below them poor Chinese take the roughest and most poorly paid jobs, while above them the Chinese also take the most well-paid and prestigious positions. Dai have few places to go — but for the moment, while there is income from investment and rent, there is little pressure on young Dai from their families either to study hard or to seek work. Meanwhile, many of the older ex-farmers sit at home and gamble and gossip, watched by their children.

Observing their predicament, the Dai are quick to describe themselves collectively as "lazy" — *khi khaan* — and compare themselves unfavourably with the "hard-working" Chinese. I have been struck by this self-description, for I have also come across it in Laos in several contexts. In the north of Laos today, gangs of Chinese labourers have been employed to push through the roads which will make up the

"Golden Quadrangles" network. Lao, I have observed, take some perverse pleasure in seeing Chinese do the heavy, dirty work while they sit back and watch — in much the same way as the Dai get a perverse pleasure out of living "above" Chinese in Man Jinglan. But the Lao will also say that "the Lao" are too *khi khaan* to do such hard work, not like the Chinese. Yet my observations are that Lao peasants work hard and value hard work,[13] and it is true that the Lao I have heard making these comparisons have invariably been urban Lao.[14] The description of "hardworking Chinese" and "lazy Dai" (or "lazy Lao") has obvious common-sense attractions in that it provides an easily comprehensible "explanation" for the economic success and power of the Chinese.[15]

Chinese hegemony also propagates this view. It is well known to the Dai (at least in places like Man Jinglan) that the Chinese consider them lazy and they have accepted both the self-description of the Chinese that they are hardworking as well as adopting the Chinese description of themselves as lazy. One of the main transmission points for these ideas is the school system, where Dai do less well than Han and are compared unfavourably with the latter. Here Chinese are at an obvious advantage because they are working in their own language, and they are also advantaged by the strong emphasis on educational success in Han society, something which is not part of traditional Dai culture.[16] For Dai who remain farmers, this problem is not acute and they are less affected by feelings of inferiority. However, it is a problem felt and faced by Dai, such as those in Man Jinglan, who have to compete directly with Chinese in an urban context. The problem is partly one of the structure of the labour market. Dai women who function as touristic icons can often find work in the tourist industry as waitresses or hostesses, whereas there are fewer openings for men.

While we do not have time to go into this important cross-cultural contrast in detail here, the differences between Chinese and Dai/Lao also lie in family and community structures. Dai in Man Jinglan will remark on parental indulgence towards children as one explanation as to why they do not put pressure on their children with regard to study or work.[17] Studies of child development in Tai communities[18] have shown how the strong sense of hierarchy inculcated during socialization entails respect and deference as one looks up the hierarchy, and indulgence and nurturing as one looks down and deals with *nong* (younger sibling) relationships (Eberhardt 1993). Furthermore there is a cultural assumption that boys will leave the home (partly a product of the tendency to matri-local residence) and hence they are "loved" in order to tie them to their maternal home. Stricter discipline is partly allocated to other cultural institutions, such as the monkhood, which boys are expected to enter at least temporarily and where they are supposed to learn restraint and self-discipline. This contrasts with the Chinese family where, although boys are highly valued, they remain in the patrilocal family and live their lives under the strict discipline and tutelage of their fathers. The family bears full responsibility for discipline and socialization, and claims total and often harsh control over its members, who are expected to work/study for the family's benefit.

There are, however, important gender differences in socialization patterns, as well as a signal gender blindness, in the various perceptions of either hard work or laziness. Chinese women, of course, are subsumed within the general description of hardworking Chinese, just as they are subsumed within the patriarchal structure of family businesses.[19] Most observers of Tai societies, on the other hand, are well aware of the economic diligence of women and their important role in trade. But this economic activity generally confines itself to petty trade, and rarely expands into major, public economic activity comparable to male public economic activity. For the Chinese patriarchal family, there is no tension between the private and public economic roles of the family because the activity is clearly dominated by males, whereas in the female-centred family structure of the Dai there is always a potential tension, and female economic activity is oriented towards family provision rather than capital accumulation *per se*, and hence their "success" or hard work is not acknowledged in the public sphere because of the problems it would pose for gender relationships.[20]

Broader social structural features have also been seen to contribute to the Chinese work ethic. Steven Harrell (1985) has argued that the theoretical openness of the traditional Chinese social structure, with its "ladder of success" through the Confucian examination system, produced a culture which stressed that effort and hard work would pay off. This cultural attitude was adaptive in the modern context as well, especially wherever it was open and rewarded hard work. So, for example, structural *disincentives* under communism produced a great number of "lazy" Chinese. Dai traditional culture contained no similar "ladder of success", and the presence of open, rather than closed, corporate institutions has bequeathed a cultural stress on broad social relationships. Thus while studies in Thailand have shown that Thai respond positively to structural incentives, and work hard for material rewards, in attitudinal surveys "all Thai, without exception, ranked hardworking achievement value much lower than the group of social relationship values" (Suntaree 1991, p. 199).[21] The structure of Theravada Buddhist societies also encourages a system of generalized exchange for creating social solidarity (Strenski 1983), rather than the more restricted exchange of corporate systems, and this produces an outwardly oriented sociability and a high valuation of situations that are *sanuk* (fun).[22] The contrast between the festivities of the Dai/Lao New Year and the Chinese New Year could not be more marked — the former stresses outwardly oriented, public partying in the community, whereas during their New Year each Chinese family locks itself away and only receives visits from (mainly patrilineal) kin.

Thus, to almost state the obvious, some central features of traditional Chinese culture have been much more adaptive to modern capitalism (at least in its early phases) than Tai culture.

The Thai or the Lao, whatever feelings they may have *vis-à-vis* the economic success of the Chinese, at least know that the latter must publicly defer to Thai or Lao culture, because it is the former who control the state; but Han are under no such constraint in Xishuangbanna. Dai may take some heart from Thailand's economic success to counter Han claims that they are culturally backward and cannot achieve success in the modern world, and the touristic promotion of "Dai culture" may generate some residual pride; but this seems hardly sufficient to generate the sense of confidence required to counter the relentless pressure of Han civilization — which has intensified with the opening of the border.

The Dai of Jinghong are in a *cul-de-sac*, and future plans for the city will submerge them. Some women will marry "up" to more educated Han and become Han, while some men will become poor, newly Hanified, proletarians. Whether a core of Man Jinglanians can retain their Dai identity for more than another generation remains to be seen.

JINGHONG FANTASYLAND

The most extraordinary plans for the future of Jinghong are in the hands of the Management Committee, Xishuangbanna Tour Vacationland, who will transform the city beyond recognition. Currently they are in charge of building hotels and office blocks on the former paddy land of Man Jinglan. But they have plans for the development of a further 10 square kilometres to the south, a development which will swallow up Man Ting, the next Dai village down the road. Approved in September 1993,

Figure 8.1
Perfection of the Scenic Spot at Jinghong: A Reconstruction of the Golden Palace of the Former Kingdom Is Included in the Plan

the development will see the creation of a large golf course, a race course, an elephant performance area, a tropical plants garden, a "thousand birds" garden, a Waterworld (a section of which has been completed), and a service area and shopping centre for Thai, Lao, and Myanmar food and products. Also to be built will be an ethnic park, like those one sees in other areas of China, to display the thirteen different ethnic minority groups in Xishuangbanna. According to the committee's brochure "it will be a wonderful, fantastic garden to show off the different cultures". But perhaps the *piece-de-resistance* is the creation of a "Southeast Asian Paradise" along "the river Danube in the Orient" (the Mekong) where there will be displays showing the geographical location and cultures of the peoples in ten countries of South East Asia.[23] The committee is still in search of foreign investors to help realize the whole plan.

But perhaps the crowning moment of the Han transformation of Jinghong will be the so-called "re-construction" of the old royal palace area — described by Dodd and torn down during the Cultural Revolution — as a "scenic spot" designed according to the specifications of the board members of Vacationland rather than those of the historical city. Thus will the Han have created their own Dai Disneyland (see Figure 8.1).

ACKNOWLEDGEMENT

I would like to thank Brian Su and Khamngern for their help with much of the fieldwork on which this chapter is based, in particular for the economic survey reproduced in Table 8.1. Of course, they are not responsible for the opinions expressed in the text.

NOTES

1. "Sip Song Panna" can be translated as the twelve Tai principalities (*muang*), although it literally means the 12,000 ricefields. It should not be mistaken for the Sip Song Chau Tai of Vietnam. In the drawing of the borderline by the French, British, and Chinese earlier this century, one of the principalities centred on Keng Tung fell to Myanmar, while two others partly fell to Laos, one centred on Muang Sing in Luang Namtha, the other in Phongsaly.

2. Wiens (1954, p. 314) writes: "Aside from the officials, a few soldiers, and individual tradesmen, and aside from a few villages of Han-Chinese mountain farmers [Haw] who paid tribute to the T'ai rulers, there were no Han Chinese in the land in 1943."

3. The fragility of these structures was shown by their abolition during the Cultural Revolution, experienced in minority areas as a radical outburst of Han chauvinism. The Xishuangbanna Autonomous Region was abolished in 1966 and re-established in 1984.
4. The ecological effects of this were equally dramatic. Over this period virgin forest decreased from 66 per cent to 26 per cent of the region (Hsieh 1989, p. 220, citing a mainland source).
5. *Man* means the same as *Ban* in Thai or Lao, that is, "village". It is indicative of one of the slight dialect shifts in Lue.
6. Hsieh (1989, p. 249) speculates that the idea of yellow was struck upon because of its association with the colour of Dai Buddhist monks' robes. Theravada Buddhism is one clear cultural feature which marks Dai off from the Han.
7. Gladney (1994) puts an argument for the modern construction of Han ethnic consciousness.
8. Emiko Ohnuki-Tierney in her book *Rice as Self* (1993) talks of how some Japanese folklorists, after hearing about Dai rituals for the rice goddess, speculated that Japanese may have had their origins among the Dai. Some of this speculation may have filtered through to the tourist trade which then sponsored tours to Xishuangbanna. However, this bizarre episode in "roots" tourism seems to have petered out rather quickly.
9. In Hani villages, exposed breasts are a common sight and are not sexually problematic.
10. For a discussion of similar issues in a Miao area in China, see Schein (1997).
11. For some of this information I would like to thank Sandra Hyde, a medical anthropologist who has been working in Xishuangbanna.
12. These very short skirts when seen in a village context are sexually neutral or normal, but in this city context they take on the flirtatious connotations of the "mini-skirt".
13. William Klausner (1981) many years ago wrote an excellent essay ("*Nak Aw, Bao Su:* The Work Cycle in a Northeastern Thai Village") demonstrating all the different tasks carried out by northeastern peasants during the dry season when, according to ignorant outsiders, they were supposedly simply lying around loafing.
14. Indeed, it is among peasants that one is most likely to hear the use of the perjorative term *jek* to describe Chinese, and fewer descriptions of grudging admiration.
15. By common sense, I mean an ahistorical explanation inasmuch as it is not based on an understanding of, for example, state favouritism of Chinese traders in Thailand in the past, which is one reason why they are wealthy today (Pannee 1995), or even obvious state-favouritism in China today. Commonsensical explanations are also unanalytic — in the sense that they are not based on, for example, some sociological analysis of patterns of reciprocity. Chinese are simply seen as people who keep things to themselves, are "mean" or "stingy", *khi tii*, which is also "the reason" why they are rich. And, so on.

16. This also applies to Lao culture and I think the Lao description of themselves as lazy is also partly acquired in schools where Sino-Lao also have a reputation for working hard and doing well, as this cultural stress on education is retained within these families.
17. I have observed exactly the same phenomenon in Vientiane where people also discuss openly "the problem" of parental indulgence of their children's wishes. I asked a male friend of mine who lives in a female-centred cluster of houses, why one of the younger sisters of his wife is just allowed to sit around, while still receiving money from her mother. "She's been talked to, but she just doesn't listen," he replied. "She takes a job for a few weeks, and then just leaves it. I think she's *khi khaan*, but it's not for me to tell her." I should say, also, that my friend is an extremely hard worker.
18. "Tai" here refers to a broad ethno-linguistic group which includes the Thai, Lao, Dai, and others.
19. Susan Greenhalgh (1994) in her very interesting critique of "orientalist" perspectives on the Chinese family firm, among other things, points out how common views subsume the role of women.
20. Andrew Walker (1998) has explored the role of long-distance female traders in northern Laos, arguing that the peculiar conditions of war and revolution there opened a space for long-distance, as against localized, female trading and suggests that this has allowed the negotiation of a modified gender identity, at least for the women engaged in this trade. This does not appear to have modified the gender blindness that I am referring to, however. Furthermore, the ethnic and gender space opened up for women in Laos by the fleeing of Chinese merchants did not, of course, occur for the Dai in China.
21. It is worth noting that "it was farmers who preferred 'work' the highest" (Suntaree 1991, p. 200).
22. An extensive literature has also grown up which purports to show how Buddhism's "other worldliness" is supposedly a drag on economic action. In fact, it can be argued that merit-making is a spur to economic action, although it is sensitive to political context (socialist or capitalist, for example). For an argument along these lines, and a brief survey of the literature, see Evans (1993).
23. The Dai of Man Jinglan are oblivious to this plan, as are, surely, the Dai of Man Ting.

REFERENCES

An Chinning and Liu Bohua. *Where the Dai People Live*. China's Nationalities Series. Beijing: Foreign Languages Press, 1985.

Dodd, William Clifton. *The Tai Race: Elder Brother of the Chinese*. Cedar Rapids, Iowa: Torch Press, 1923.

Eberhardt, Nancy. "The Cultural Context of Moral Reasoning: Lessons from the Shan

of Northern Thailand". *Crossroads* 8, no. 1 (1993).
Evans, Grant. "Buddhism and Economic Action in Socialist Laos". In *Socialism: Ideals, Ideologies, and Local Practice*, edited by Chris Hann. London: Routledge, 1993.
Forney, Matt. "Yunnan Rising". *Far Eastern Economic Review*, 11 September 1997.
Gladney, Dru. "Representing Nationality in China: Refiguring Majority/Minority Identities". *Journal of Asian Studies* 53, no. 1 (1994).
Greenhalgh, Susan. "De-Orientalizing the Chinese Family Firm". *American Ethnologist* 21, no. 4 (1994).
Harrell, Stevan. "Why Do the Chinese Work So Hard? Reflections on an Entrepreneurial Ethic". *Modern China* 11, no. 2 (1985).
Henin, Bernard and Mark Flaherty. "Ethnicity, Culture, and Natural Resource Use: Forces of Change on Dai Society, Xishuangbanna, Southwest China". *Journal of Development Studies* X (1995): 219–35.
Hill, Ann Maxwell. "Chinese Dominance of the Xishuangbanna Tea Trade: An Interregional Perspective". *Modern China* 15, no. 3 (1989).
Hsieh Shih-chung. "Ethno-Political Adaptation and Ethnic Changes in Sipsong Panna Dai: An Ethnohistorical Analysis". Ph.D. dissertation, University of Washington, 1989.
Klausner, William J. *Reflections on Thai Culture: Collected Writings*. Bangkok: Suksit Siam, 1981.
Lintner, Bertil. "Reaching Out". *Far Eastern Economic Review*, 11 September 1997.
Ohnuki-Tierney, Emiko. *Rice as Self: Japanese Identities through Time*. Princeton: Princeton University Press, 1993.
Pannee Auansakul. "Chinese Traders and Thai Groups in the Rice Business". *Southeast Asian Journal of Social Science* 23, no. 1 (1995).
Schein, Louisa. "Gender and Internal Orientalism". *Modern China* 23, no. 1 (1997).
Strenski, Ivan. "On Generalized Exchange and the Domestication of the Sangha". *Man* 18 (1983): 463–77.
Suntaree Komin. *Psychology of the Thai People: Values and Behavioral Patterns*. Bangkok: Research Center, National Institute of Development Administration, 1991.
Walker, Andrew. "Women, Space and History: Long-Distance Trading in Northwestern Laos". In *Lao Culture and Society*, edited by Grant Evans. Chiang Mai: Silkworm Books, 1998.
Wiens, Harold J. *China's March toward the Tropics*. Hamden, Connecticut: Shoe String Press, 1954.
Zheng Hongfang and Wang Hongxiao. "Establishing Tourism as a Precursor Industry and Developing Frontier Cities" (in Chinese). *Minority Research*, no. 3, 1996.

9

The Hell of Good Intentions: Some Preliminary Thoughts on Opium in the Political Ecology of the Trade in Girls and Women

David A. Feingold

> *Silver (money) grows in the "virgin room".*
> — Brothel owner
>
> *If I can sell her virginity twice, I double my investment.*
> — Brothel owner
>
> *Sometimes, I have to teach them with the stick.*
> — Woman owner of "sex coffee shop"
>
> *We think: if she's young, she's clean — no AIDS.*
> — Customer in a massage parlour
>
> *U.S. anti-drug assistance to the Burmese government has failed ...*
> — Robert S. Gelbard,
> U.S. Assistant Secretary of State for
> International Narcotics and Law Enforcement Affairs
>
> *The road to hell is paved with good intentions ...
> and it's the best paved road in Bangkok.*
> — Anonymous

This chapter is a preliminary attempt to share some thoughts on two topics that have compelled attention — public or private — in most human societies: sex and drugs. Or more precisely, the relationship *between* sex and drugs; not as conjectured (or remembered) by the worried parents of teenage daughters, but as commodities in international trade. In the specific case of mainland Southeast Asia and China, what is the relationship through time of opiate production to the production of sexual services?

The mythic narrative of narcotics and sexual degradation (and like many mythic narratives, it embodies elements of "reality") can be read in newspapers, quoted from non-governmental organization (NGO) reports, or seen on TV:

> Miba, innocent and simple hill tribe girl from the "colorful" Akha tribe, is rescued from a brothel (often by the BBC, CH-4, ABC, or "60 Minutes" film crew). She has been sold by her father, who is an unrepentant heroin addict. Desperate for money to feed his vile habit (but not, the implication goes, desperate enough to work for it), he (supposedly) sees his daughters as a crop to be harvested when they are ripe.

There frequently follows a learned interview that calls for the reform of patriarchal societies and explains that "Asian Cultures" (all of them!) have always devalued daughters, which was why Miba was sold in the first place. The piece generally closes with hope for a new life for Miba, thanks to the sewing skills that she has been taught — preferably, for a Western TV audience, by nuns, missionaries, or fresh-faced NGOs. Lest we become complacent, however, a sober male or compassionate female voice reminds us — over shots of happy girl children — of "all the other Mibas" awaiting the sweaty embraces of panting paedophiles from Peterborough or their American equivalents.

Of course, it is easy to mock the voyeuristic and sentimentalized conventions of television (or their print counterparts), and stories similar to Miba's can certainly be documented. Moreover, the problem of minority girls and women in the Thai "sex industry" is an extensive one: today, there are estimated to be up to 30,000 from Myanmar alone, growing by some 10,000 per year.[1] Yet the explanations given for this seem inadequate in the face of one fact: twenty years ago there were virtually no minority girls or women in the Thai "sex industry". The current research project is aimed at answering a deceptively simple question: What changed?

To this end, we are examining the relationship of changes in the patterns of opiate production, trade, and use, to the process of the commodification of girls and women. The aim is to investigate the implications for regional development of a traffic in persons which contravenes numerous provisions of international humanitarian law, and threatens the physical and cultural survival of populations stretching from southern China across the Shan states of Myanmar through northern

Thailand to Laos. The focus will be on the primarily upland minority peoples — Akha, Lahu, Lisu, Yao, Hmong, Shan, and so forth — most at risk from this trade.

INTRODUCTION

The past decade has witnessed an exponential increase in the traffic in girls and women from Myanmar and Yunnan into Thailand for the sex industry. Moreover, with the opening of borders and improved transportation routes, Laos stands poised to become a supplier and transshipper of girls to Thailand. Boys are not — as yet — a major factor in *this* trade. Both Myanmar and Han Chinese women and girls flow into this traffic, stocking the brothels of Yangon or massage parlours and brothels of the north (Asia Watch 1993). Tragic as are these individual cases, the greatest collective impact is on the upland minority groups of the Thai-Myanmar-China periphery, who are disproportionally represented in the trade, and whose cultural and physical survival are most directly threatened. Networks of recruiters reach into remote mountain villages to buy, abduct, or lure young women and girls into the pipeline that feeds the lowest levels of the Thai sex industry. Poverty, warfare, forced labour, and repression also bring whole families across the Myanmar border, and make entry into the sex industry a rational (if dangerous) choice for young women eager to contribute to the well-being of their households.

THE SEX INDUSTRY

The term "industry" is carefully chosen. Sex — gay as well as straight — is big business in Thailand. Professor Pasuk Phongpaichit, an economist from Chulalongkorn University who specializes in research on corruption and money laundering, estimates that the income from prostitution and trafficking in women abroad alone exceeds the income from drugs and illicit arms trafficking combined. Tourism has boomed in Thailand over the last three decades. According to figures supplied by the Tourism Authority of Thailand, in 1960, 81,340 persons visited the kingdom, staying an average of three days. In the year 1996, 7,192,145 persons arrived as tourists, staying an average of 8.23 days. It is estimated that of the 7 million who enter Thailand on tourist visas, between 1.8 million and 2.2 million are tourists.[2] Tourism revenues grew from US$10 million in 1960 to nearly US$8.7 billion in 1996. It is the largest source of foreign exchange, earning nearly eight times the value of Thailand's rice exports in 1996.

The majority of tourists visiting the country are "single" (though not necessarily unmarried) males. In fact, as of 1996, 62 per cent of tourists were male. Easily available, relatively inexpensive commercial sex has long been one of the appeals of Thailand as a tourist destination, and Thailand has certainly reaped rich economic rewards because of it. Yet various Thai governments, concerned about the image (if not the reality) of the country, have sought to conform appearances to Western rectitude, while still catering to Western desires. From 1960, when Marshal Sarit first "outlawed" prostitution to "clean up" Thailand's image, through 1987 ("Visit Thailand Year") to 1998 ("Amazing Thailand Year"), this tension has reasserted itself each time a new strategy has been put forward to market the country (Cohen 1996).

However, despite the partially successful attempts to market Thailand as a "cultural" and "family" tourist destination, and despite the expected chilling effect of acquired immune deficiency syndrome (AIDS), "sex tours" continue to come from the United States, Germany, Britain, Scandinavia, and Japan. An advertisement for a package tour from England promises air ticket, hotel, meals, transfers, and "a selection of beautiful and exotic ladies", all included in one low price — easy terms available. Many of these tours have brochures that feature obviously pre-pubescent girls, and guidebooks are available which advise on how to avoid extra-territorial laws. Yet most of the sex service industry caters to local men and intra-Asian travellers, the establishments of which are quite different from the bars of Patpong and Soi Cowboy, so well known to tourists and TV cameras that senior citizens are now shown them through the windows of air-conditioned buses on their tours of Bangkok.

The precise number of commercial sex workers in Thailand is an issue hotly debated, with force and not a little ideological fervour, by researchers, government officials, NGOs, politicians, and pressure groups. An article in the *Nation* newspaper entitled "Prostitution: Looking Beyond the Numbers" (11 July 1993), noted an "official" estimate of about 500,000 "registered" prostitutes. This seems quite low, however, since the Police Department gave a figure of slightly over 400,000 as long ago as 1964 — before the expansion of the industry to meet the "rest and recreation" (R&R) needs of the Vietnam War or the massive upsurge in tourism in the late 1970s and 1980s. Given that most women and children in brothels are not registered, Thai NGOs currently estimate that the correct number is closer to 2 million.

However, were this number correct, it would mean that 24 per cent of the female population of Thailand between the ages of ten and thirty-nine were engaged in commercial sex work. Even allowing for greater than observed influxes from other countries, this appears unlikely on its face.

At the other end of the spectrum, the Ministry of Public Health each year conducts a census of all sex service establishments in Thailand. This is done every January to obtain comparable data from year to year. In 1997, for the first time, they differentiated between self-identified sex workers (65,983) and the total numbers of workers potentially available for sex (105,454). They believe the latter figure to be the more accurate. They are also aware that although they try to sample for "street walkers" and so forth, there is an undercount. However, it is not clear how this could possibly reach a level of nearly two million.[3] A number of researchers have settled (for not altogether clear reasons) on figures between 200,000 and 250,000.

These commercial sex workers (CSWs) work in a wide spectrum of establishments which vary greatly in terms of remuneration, working conditions, coercion, and autonomy. The Ministry of Public Health of Thailand has classified twenty-four different types of sex service establishments, including brothels, hotels or motels, tea houses, nightclubs, beer bars, dancing bars, a-go-go bars, discotheques, restaurants, coffeeshops, cafes, cocktail lounges, pubs, massage parlours, traditional massage services, beauty salons, barber shops, escort services, call girls, and "others" (Thanprasertsuk 1991).[4] They range from upper tier bars in which women can choose their customers, decide the services which they will offer, and retain their earnings from those services to brothels where young girls are literally chained to beds and forced to service up to thirty men a day.

Distinctions are made among CSWs between direct sex workers (DSWs) who work in brothels or other establishments that only provide sex services, and indirect sex workers (ISWs) who work in bars or massage parlours, and so forth, and have greater selectivity with regard to sexual activity. Research to date has shown (not surprisingly) that DSWs are more likely to become infected by human immunodeficiency virus (HIV), to suffer from other sexually transmitted diseases (STDs), and to have lower earnings. Minority girls and women, whether from the hills of Thailand or Myanmar or China, almost all end up as DSWs — stocking the lowest rungs of the sex trade. While some may move up, most do not.

It is currently estimated that between 20,000 and 30,000 of these are girls and women from Myanmar, increasing by 10,000 each year. These figures do not distinguish between Myanmar and minority peoples, nor do they include women and girls who come from Yunnan and pass through Myanmar on their way to Thailand. Furthermore, despite a net increase each year in the aggregate number of these women engaged in sex work, some women drop out of sex work in Thailand, either returning to their home villages, or finding alternative employment. In addition, these figures do not take into account seasonal fluctuations in sex work, during which women enter (or re-enter) sex work for a limited period of time. One indicator of this was pointed out by a Thai health worker in Mae Sai, a town on the northern Thai border with Myanmar, which is a major entrance point for sex workers and migrant agricultural labourers: brothels in Mae Sai use, on average, a total of 6,000 condoms per month; in February, they use 10,000. It is likely, therefore, that total figures at any one time under-represent the number of girls and women affected by the trade.

While it is obvious that any such statistics are imprecise at best, it is clear that the participation of women and girls from Myanmar in the sex industry in Thailand has burgeoned rapidly over the last decade. Most recently, it has been estimated that 25 to 35 per cent of those entering the sex industry in northern Thailand are from northern Myanmar (Lintner and Hseng 1996). In fact, an unpublished study reported that 97 per cent of the workers in brothels in the town of Mae Sai on the Thai-Myanmar border were minority women from Myanmar or the Thai hills.

It is also clear that while these minorities still represent a relatively small percentage of total sex workers in Thailand, they are particularly vulnerable to exploitation and maltreatment. This special vulnerability has implications not only for the girls and women themselves, but also for the very existence of the communities from which they come.

In particular, the physical and cultural survival of upland minority groups on both sides of the Thai-Myanmar border, extending up into China, are threatened as never before. By 1990, there were already significant HIV infection rates among both the Dai and Jingpo in Yunnan (Yu et al. 1996). More recently, tests on minority women in Simao (Yunnan) have confirmed the presence of HIV-1 sub-type E (Cheng et al. 1994). This HIV sub-type is characteristic of Thailand (Hu et al. 1996), and can be taken as an indication of trans-border migration. The documented spread of HIV/AIDS back from concentrations in Thailand to relatively isolated upland communities in Myanmar and China could result in the wholesale destruction of these peoples, in a manner not seen in this century. Moreover, as large infection pools are established in China (in particular) and Myanmar, increased migration will fuel the epidemic in Thailand and contribute to infection rates in the Lao People's Democratic Republic (PDR) as well.

It seems clear that, with the opening of major transportation routes, the expansion of trekking tourism and development projects, and the planned displacement and resettlement of highland populations, Laos will play an increasingly important role as a source of supply of minority girls for the Thai sex industry. At present, there are relatively few highland girls and women from Laos engaged in sex work either in Laos or in Thailand. However, many of the preconditions exist for the rapid expansion of the sex industry in Laos (Lyttleton 1996), as well as for an increased flow of women into Thailand. In fact, Thai businessmen have already set up brothels along the Mekong (on the Lao side), and are ferrying customers across from Thailand. The women are paid in Lao currency (kip), but the customers pay in Thai baht, increasing the profit for the owners. The women in these brothels are, for the most part, Lowland Lao. However, in areas of northern Laos where Chinese construction workers are building roads and Koreans have a dam project, highland girls and young women are starting to come down to the roads to offer themselves to the workers.

Laos is a very poor country (the United Nations International Children's Emergency Fund, UNICEF, places it among the lowest group in Asia for infant mortality and life expectancy), and the upland regions are under increasing economic and social pressure. Large areas, particularly in the northwest, are extremely dangerous to farm because of Unexploded Ordnances (UXOs) left over from the war. Unexploded cluster bomb sub-munitions have made Laos to UXOs what Cambodia is to land mines.

In addition, there is increasing pressure from the international community on the Lao PDR government to curtail the opium production — which has been central to the economic survival of many of the hill peoples for the last century (Feingold 1970). Moreover, despite a documented record of the failure of lowland resettlement programmes in Laos (among other countries) (Westermeyer 1982), the Lao PDR is planning to relocate a large percentage of its highland population. Precisely how large the percentage will be is as yet unclear, but what is clear —

and unsettling — is that the plan has the avid support of the Asian Development Bank (ADB). The director of ADB's programmes department, Noritaka Morita, was quoted thus in the *Nation* newspaper in Bangkok:

> We may need to reduce the population of people in mountainous areas and bring them to *normal life* [emphasis added]. They will have to settle in one place ... but don't call it resettlement. It is just migration. (Nantiya 1996)

Past experience has shown that resettlement of highland people into lowlands is accompanied by increased mortality, decreased nutritional status, breakdowns of social controls on domestic violence and theft, increased problems with drug and alcohol abuse, transition from opium to heroin use, and dependence on low-wage occasional labour. While clearly it is possible in theory to construct programmes that will prevent or mitigate these negative outcomes, in practice successes have been rare (Tapp 1989).

There are also subtler, but no less destructive, processes which undermine traditional constraints on certain deleterious behaviours. Increased exposure to a broad spectrum of material goods (which become newly valued) coincides with diminished resources to acquire them. This is not to imply that hill people live in some sylvan idyll, contemplating the beauty of the land, free of material desires. Farming in the mountains is hard, and most people would like more rice or more opium or more pigs or a new silver neck ring or a new gun. However, the range of useful consumables is limited; satisfactions can be obtained in other ways.

Rapid immersion in the market system tends to reduce all values to market values. Commodification is not an event, but a process; and while sex among Southeast Asian highlanders (or Americans, for that matter) has always had economic aspects, it has not generally been reducible to an economic transaction. A Thai scholar, Professor Vitit Muntarbhorn (1996), has correctly noted that "many societies that are poor do not have a high degree of prostitution, so prostitution does not necessarily follow from poverty". However, while poverty alone may not be a sufficient condition for commercial sex, it is often a necessary one in the transformation of women into transnational commodities.

Mr Morita of the ADB has stated that "there is a need to build road networks to enable governments to reach remote areas and introduce them [the highlanders] into the market system" (Cohen 1996). Others

9. Opium in the Political Ecology of the Trade in Girls and Women   191

advise greater caution. Experts of the Joint United Nations Programme on HIV/AIDS (UNAIDS) believe that the projected road network linking China, Vietnam, Laos, Thailand, and eventually Myanmar will make Laos a major transshipment route for HIV as well as goods. In terms of HIV/AIDS, "Laos seems headed where Thailand has been".

SUPPLY AND DEMAND FACTORS INFLUENCING THE TRAFFIC IN GIRLS AND WOMEN

Prostitution is not new in Thailand, nor (as is sometimes maintained) is it some unexploded cultural ordinance left over from the Vietnam War. In the sixteenth century, throughout the trading ports of Southeast Asia, there were systems of "temporary wives", who would contract with foreigners to "marry" for the length of their stay, for a negotiated price (Reid 1988, pp. 155–56). Variations on this institution were reported by Chou Ta-kuan, the famous Chinese visitor to Angkor, in the thirteenth century. A custom of "hired wives" was reported by the *Bangkok World* in Udon on 1 September 1969.

When the British sent an embassy to the Kingdom of Ava in Burma (the previous name of Myanmar) in 1795, Michael Symes notes, the system was in place at the time (1827, vol. I, pp. 252–53). He also notes in Rangoon (the previous name of Yangon) an entire "village of prostitutes". These women were "slaves", as were many of the prostitutes in Southeast Asia during this period. However, as there were many categories of persons loosely designated by the English word "slave", it is unclear to what extent (if any) these women exercised any degree of social or economic autonomy and if they had any control over their earnings.

In Thailand, the involvement of the state in prostitution dates at least from the Ayutthaya period. A monopoly and licence system was put in place so that by the 1680s, a designated Thai official controlled all prostitution in the capital on a warrant from the King. This official oversaw some 600 women who were purchased or had lost their freedom for various criminal offences. (La Loubère 1969, pp. 74, 85). At the time, this clearly represented a significant source of revenue to the state.

Western visitors to Bangkok in the first half of the nineteenth century remarked on the large number of brothels in the city. The *Siam Free Press* (2 May 1900) carried complaints about rampant prostitution and police inaction. However, prostitution continued to be sanctioned and taxed by the state, and was seen as a vital source of revenue for the country as it attempted, by rapid modernization, to shield itself from colonialism. Under the Contagious Disease Control Act of 1908, brothels and prostitutes were required to register, with the aim of controlling venereal disease. They were also required to pay fees to the government. (Rayanakorn 1995).

The first clinic for venereal disease opened in Bangkok in 1937. In the same year, an important Thai novel — *Ying khon chua* ("The prostitute") — presented a sympathetic portrait of a village girl lured into prostitution. Written by the now famous woman author K. Surangkhanang (1949), the book was widely read at the time and was the first portrayal of the context of prostitution in Thailand for a Thai audience.

Nevertheless, there is little doubt that the influx of large numbers of Americans on R&R from Vietnam changed the economics and social context of sexual services in Thailand. It is important to note, however, that despite the notable expansion of the sex industry during this period, the participation in the trade of hilltribe women and Myanmar (whether actually Myanmar or otherwise) was negligible. Moreover, the age of the young women was generally close to that of the young men who sought them out (though, of course, there were many exceptions).

DEMAND FACTORS

Economic expansion in Thailand and development in much of Asia has generated increased demand for sex workers (Muecke 1992).[5] In the past decade, the large increase in disposable income for Thais, as well as the expansion of the tourist trade has expanded the effective demand for sexual services at precisely the time when alternative employment opportunities (for example, factory work) have become available. Thai women from poor areas of the north and northeast are still drawn into the sex trades (as in the thirty years following World War II), but factory work and foreign employment (even including moving into the upper end of the sex trade in Japan and Hong Kong) are competing with older patterns. This has resulted in a need to expand the pool of potential recruits beyond the Thai and Chinese who have traditionally worked in the sex industry. As yet, it is unclear what effect the recent devaluation of the Thai baht and the ensuing economic crisis will have on this pattern. More and more women are likely to be laid off from factories, and new jobs will be hard to come by. It may well be also that the aggregate demand for sexual services will drop, since men will have less disposable income. However, because of the baht's weakness versus foreign currencies, Thailand may once again become something of a bargain for tourists, bringing more foreign patrons. Nevertheless, it is clear the pattern will continue whereby the differential economic growth of lowland Thailand, in comparison to those of neighbouring countries and of her own upland minorities, has pulled upland minority, Myanmar, Cambodian, and Lao women into the sex trade in increasing numbers.

Moreover, the rapid spread of HIV/AIDS in Thailand has resulted in an increased valuation of younger girls from remote areas. Virginity, always highly prized by Chinese and Japanese customers in particular, holds out not only the promise of restored youth and virility but the "guarantee" of safety as well. Safety is not a minor consideration. The Ministry of Public Health of Thailand has started distributing condoms in brothels,[6] and gave away about 60 million of them in 1996. In the past ten years, condom consumption had climbed from 10 million to 170 million annually. Nevertheless, 46,000 Thais died of AIDS in 1996 alone. The epidemic may kill up to 800,000 within ten years (National Economic and Social Development Board Working Group on HIV/AIDS Projection, 1994). Dr Jennifer Gray (1993), an Australian AIDS researcher, in a paper delivered at the School of Oriental and African Studies (SOAS) in London, called AIDS in the uplands of Thailand "a crisis just waiting to happen". Although new infection rates for HIV are presently declining for Thailand as a whole, the crisis has happened.

Myanmar, which came late to the AIDS epidemic, is thought to have 400,000 cases of HIV infection, but no one really knows. What is known is that condoms are not easily available (until recently, they were illegal), and that the government is neither willing nor able to undertake a significant prevention campaign. I learned from sources inside Myanmar, however, that although the government is no longer enforcing the law and is attempting some AIDS prevention activities, a woman found with condoms is taken, *prima facie*, to be a prostitute. Furthermore, the association of condoms with prostitutes causes many Myanmar women to accuse their husbands of using prostitutes or treating them like prostitutes if they attempt to use condoms. Needless to say, this does not encourage widespread condom use.

A report to the United Nations International Drug Control Programme summarized the problem: "Condom use is so rare as to be virtually non-existent and at present is playing no role in the prevention of HIV in Myanmar" (Stimson 1994).

The first HIV case was reported in 1988. Each year since has seen a dramatic increase in HIV infections. By the end of 1993, 7,152 people had been identified as HIV-positive. However, compared with Thailand, there is little hard data for Myanmar. The Myanmar authors of one of the very few scientific articles on HIV/AIDS in Myanmar point out that "the relatively low number of HIV infections reported in the country compared with neighboring countries reflects the limited screening conducted" (Htoo et al. 1994).

In northern Myanmar, in particular, AIDS is reported to be "out of control" as a result of girls and women returning from the brothels of Thailand and of injection drug users (IDUs) (Lintner and Hseng 1996).[7] It should be noted, however, that HIV has started to be detected in lowland Myanmar villages among people with none of the obvious risk factors.

From the point of view of the procurers and brothel owners, young girls are cheaper to obtain and more docile — particularly if they have entered Thailand illegally, lack language skills, and have no local contacts. A girl's virginity can be sold for more than her family was paid for her in the first place. Moreover, she may be sold as a virgin more than once. Although subsequently the price for her services drops to less than 10 per cent of the initial value, the profits to the brothel owner remain very high indeed. The maintenance costs for the girls are minimal, and they are forced to pay off the original money given to their families — often at extortionate rates of interest. The heaviest expenses for brothel owners are payments made to police and recruiting agents.

Unfortunately for both their customers and themselves, young girls are more susceptible to HIV infection. In the first place, sexual intercourse is more likely to cause vaginal lesions in an immature girl than in an adult woman, especially when (as is often the case) force is used. Secondly, a young girl, often barely able to communicate in the language of her customer, is less able to enforce or cajole condom use — even if she were aware that it was important to protect herself. Condoms are virtually never used the first few times she "loses her 'virginity'". In fact, health workers have explained in interviews that girls are most likely to be infected with HIV during their first six months of sex work. This leads to the displacement of the AIDS epidemic onto those least able to protect themselves or cope with the results.

Chilling empirical confirmation of these factors comes from an important study, which followed 800 CSWs, finding an overall HIV-1 prevalence rate of 22 per cent. However, when the age of the start of commercial sex work was between twelve and fifteen, prevalence was 36 per cent; while when the age at starting was twenty-one and over, the rate dropped to 11 per cent (Van Griensven 1995). The same study found that another major risk factor, in addition to youth, was being non-Thai.

SUPPLY FACTORS

In addition to the pull of the expanding economy of lowland Thailand, there have been a number of economic, social, and political elements which have pushed increasing numbers of girls and women into the sex trade from the Thai hills, Myanmar, and the border regions of China in the last ten years. The past two decades have seen the impoverishment of the upland economies in Thailand, and a shift in the balance of trade between the highlands and the lowlands.

The frontier areas of highland Southeast Asia are both politically and economically interstitial. They were (and are) the regions in which social systems rub against one another, and where networks of cultural and social identity interpenetrate. The cultural discontinuities between hill and valley, swidden and paddy field, tribesman and peasant have never been as sharply contrastive as their symbolic representation. A complex network of relationships has long extended from the lowlands into the highlands, not merely across them. Nor is this simply intrusive exploitation. The highlanders also extend their influence into the plains through trade networks and military alliances. Opium and cattle, in particular, lend themselves to such extensions of influence.

In the case of cattle (including buffalo), the hills have a comparative advantage for raising them. For example, in northern Thailand until quite recently it was common for lowland farmers to make cattle purchases in hill villages. The animals were purchased after birth and left to be cared for by the hill people until they were full grown. The payment for this care was on top of the purchase price. British district officer records from the Shan states show that this practice was frequently followed there as well, at the end of the nineteenth century and the beginning of the twentieth. From the point of view of the hill person, livestock is one of the few possibilities for productive investment, because of its low labour costs. An old Yao man once said to me: "[T]o grow poppies, you must plant and harvest the fields; pigs plant and harvest themselves."

In the past, the balance of trade between the highland and lowland economies tended to be approximately equal. Upland people traded forest products (resins, medicinal plants and animals, wild honey, and so forth), vegetables, and opium — most of which had a high value per unit of weight, and therefore low transport costs — for a generally small range of goods desired from the lowlands (Feingold 1981).

Thirty years ago, relatively few products from the lowland were seen as necessities for the "good life". To cite a case in point, in 1967 the Akha villagers with whom I lived used kerosene, kerosene tins, matches, woks, kettles, shoes, plastic rope, some decorative beads, some tools, salt, plastic sheeting, and a few other things that caught their fancy in the local lowland market. However, I had the only radio in the village, and while this was considered an amusing toy good for a few moments' diversion, no one would have sold a pig (or even, a chicken) to obtain one. Similarly, my watch was seen as primarily ornamental, and certainly less desirable than even a lightweight silver bracelet. Over the past ten to fifteen years, the desire for a broad range of lowland consumer goods has increased in the hills, while the demand for upland products has dropped in the lowlands.

Land degradation, lowland incursion, and the loss of opium production in Thailand, and warfare, over-production of opium, and impressment of labour in Myanmar have led to economic and social breakdown in many minority communities.

Thailand is the rare country to significantly reduce its drug crop production. During the two years I studied opium production while living in an Akha village on the Thai-Myanmar border (1967–69), Thailand produced about 167 metric tons per year. This year, it will produce at most around 35 tons. Interestingly, most of the drop took place by 1972, before either suppression or crop replacement programmes were much in evidence. One unintended consequence of this modest victory in the oft-declared "War on Drugs" was that highlanders who smoked opium no longer grew enough of it for their own use. This meant that they lost control over their supply. They now had to buy what they used to produce, with less cash available to do so. The result was that heroin (derived from opium, but much more potent) was relatively cheaper than the raw product. There has also been a breakdown in the cultural constraints that ordered and limited drug consumption (Falk and Feingold 1987). Well-meaning, but often ill-conceived, detoxification programmes brought relatively benign opium smokers out of the hills and placed them in treatment programmes with heavy lowland heroin users. A cynic might well call this a "study tour". Heroin use (previously rare among many hill groups) increased — first through smoking, more recently by injection. Needle-use facilitated the transmission of HIV at the same time as the need for cash pushed more daughters into the sex trade, making them likely to return infected to the villages.

In Myanmar, thirty years of warfare have taken a dreadful toll in the minority areas. When I first worked with Shans in 1964, Myanmar never produced more than 450 tons of opium per year. By the end of the U.S.-sponsored suppression programme in 1988, production had risen to 1,200 metric tons (United States Department of State, Bureau of International Narcotics Matters 1988). (Ironically, it can be said that this was the most successful agricultural development programme any place in the world.) This year, the U.S. government estimates that Myanmar will produce about 3,000 metric tons — a record crop. It must be noted, however, that many United Nations International Drug Control Programme (UNDCP) officials as well as knowledgeable Shans are sceptical of this figure, given what is known of labour supply and yields.[8]

However, production of a highly labour-intensive crop at anything near these levels benefits smugglers and impoverishes farmers. My own studies have shown that (among the Akha) it requires a minimum of 387 man-hours to produce 1.6 kilograms of opium (1.6 kilograms = 1 viss or joi, the standard unit of opium). This is about 80 per cent more than the labour input into upland rice. Opium is also a delicate crop: not enough rain or too much rain at the wrong time of year and the entire crop can be wiped out. This accounts for the fact that a single field can show up to 300 per cent variation in yield from year to year. There are strong indications that current returns to the farmer per unit of labour are significantly lower than they were twenty years ago, while the costs of lowland goods deemed essential to village life have risen precipitously in both absolute and relative terms during the same period.

While opium is a crop that requires considerable labour and expertise to grow well, it has certain important advantages for the upland farmer. First, the hills have a significant comparative advantage *vis-à-vis* the valleys; in Southeast Asia, the poppy does not grow well below 1,000 metres. Second, in regions with high transport costs such as the upland regions of Thailand and Myanmar, opium is desirable because it has a high value per measure of weight. Thirdly, it is more forgiving of land than rice is. In other words, it is possible to grow poppies on land that could not be put under rice. Areas such as Kokang and the Wa states, which are poor rice producers, have been major opium producers for more than a century. The evidence for this continuity of regional specialization is clear. In the nineteenth century, the Wa states and Kokang produced the vast bulk of the opium grown in what is today Myanmar. This year these same two regions produced about 45 per cent of the total illicit opium production.

Furthermore, as in other situations of political and social instability, the warfare and repression in Myanmar leads to heightened liquidity preferences among both highland and lowland peoples. (In simple terms: how would you rather hold your wealth during a war — in gold coins or in real estate?) This favours the production of drug crops over food crops, and (in a choice no one should have to make) the conversion of daughters to cash.

It is also true that, given the documented proclivities of the Myanmar army to use rape and atrocity as a major element in pacification policy,[9] keeping girls at home is no guarantee of protection against sexual abuse (Smith 1994, pp. 110–16). Many parents believe that girls will work in factories or as maids or waitresses. While some may "sell" their daughters without compunction, many are duped or faced with the anguished choice of sacrificing one child so that the rest of the family might not starve (Images Asia 1997).

The permanent overvaluation of the Myanmar kyat (about 6.7 kyat = US$1 at the official rate, versus some 100 kyat = US$1 at the black market rate some time ago) has meant that relatively small sums of Thai baht can seem huge to a poor family. This has continued, despite the recent fall in the value of the baht by some 30 per cent. In fact, the situation has been growing steadily worse. In the last eighteen months, the kyat moved to 170 to the dollar and then to 200. The recent open market rate has been 240. However, even this figure does not give a true picture of the degree of uncertainty and instability in Myanmar. In mid-July of this year (1997), the kyat collapsed from just over 200 to the dollar to 340 in one day. Trading came to a standstill. It was widely rumoured that the military threatened key dealers at gunpoint to make them exchange at 170. There were also rumours that the State Law and Order Restoration Council (SLORC) government would demonetize large bills, as had been done before in Myanmar.

Furthermore, this recent plummet of the kyat further exacerbates the condition of poor households, so that even the meagre payment given to the young women themselves often allows them to contribute significantly to the support of their families.

Recent political and military activities have also increased the economic and social pressures on the upland minorities in Myanmar. The recent "surrender" of Khun Sa (the well-known "King of Opium") has led to a new expansion of forced labour and an attempt by the Myanmar to eradicate Thai influence in the Shan region. This will have the effect of pushing more refugees across the border. The attempt to enforce the circulation of the Myanmar kyat at the expense of the baht will have the perverse effect of further devaluing girls in terms of Thai currency at precisely the time when their families will be most strapped for cash.

Another change in the north of Thailand that will influence the trade is the movement from direct to indirect sex service establishments. It is clear that the profit margins are extremely high, depending on the nature of the establishment. It appears that brothels (in general) show a higher rate of return than so-called "indirect" sex establishments (bars and so forth). However, brothels are more vulnerable to police action — either to enforce laws, or to extract bribes. Because of pressures from the central government on the police to take action, many brothels have converted to "coffee-shops", karaoke bars, and similar operations. While this has resulted in better working conditions for many women, it has made it more difficult for health officials to maintain monitoring programmes. In addition, concerned about domestic and international attention on the issue of child prostitution, the police have advised brothel owners to treat the girls better so they will not be forced to take action. The director of the Centre for the Protection of Children's Rights told us that this has resulted in a significant drop in the number of complaints which would have allowed them to take action.

Increased forced relocations and economic hardships in the Shan states are changing the pattern of recruitment in some areas. Instead of daughters being bought in villages and entering Thailand in a condition of debt bondage, more households are crossing the border, often with the aid of traffickers. The parents and boys seek agricultural work, while the girls gravitate to sex work. Again, the trend towards indirect sex establishments makes this transition easier.

As yet, it is not clear whether these trends evidence a significant shift in the sex industry in northern Thailand, or are merely temporary. What is clear is that the sex industry will continue to be fed by cheap labour escaping intolerable political and economic conditions in Myanmar, and more and more girls and women from the hills of Laos will cross into Thailand as, despite the present economic crisis in the country, Thailand is still far wealthier than her neighbours.

If villages are not sustainable, neither the "War on Drugs" nor the newly declared war on sexual exploitation will have very much impact. International supply control drug policy can best be characterized as often in error, but never in doubt. In drug policy, nothing ever fails, even if it never succeeds. Many of the policies which failed in Thailand, Myanmar, and even Peru are now being pushed on the Lao PDR. It would be well to be aware that flawed plans of bureaucrats can have unexpected and devastating consequences for the women (and men) of the Southeast Asian highlands.

ACKNOWLEDGEMENT

Research for this project was conducted under grants from the John D. and Catherine T. MacArthur Foundation, the Else Sackler Foundation, and the Spunk Fund, Inc. The project has received additional support from the United Nations Educational, Scientific and Cultural Organization (UNESCO).

Earlier research was conducted under grants from the U.S. National Institute of Mental Health (NIMH), the National Institute on Drug Abuse (NIDA), and the National Endowment for the Humanities (NEH).

The author wishes to acknowledge the generous support of these organizations. It must be noted, however, the ideas presented in this chapter do not purport to represent the views of any of these institutions.

NOTES

1. These figures are consensus figures derived from interviews with a range of researchers, officials, and journalists — both Thai and Western. In general, they do not account for return migration and seasonal sex work. Moreover, women will often be identified by nationality or ethnonym, but rarely by both.

   Precise figures are difficult to obtain, which is hardly surprising in light of the fact that virtually all of the women have entered Thailand illegally, making them vulnerable to arrest, imprisonment, and deportation. The situation is further complicated by the fact that the Ministry of Health, which conducts a census of commercial sex workers in Thailand every January, does not ask questions regarding ethnicity or national origin. To do otherwise, health officials maintain (with justification), would limit compliance and impair the accuracy of their survey.

2. The discrepancy is due to the fact that many business and other travellers use tourist visas for convenience.

3. In an interview, the head of a very responsible and effective Thai NGO said that he had arrived at the 2 million figure by extrapolating from police entertainment

establishment registration figures for 1989. He says that these figures from the police include many sites not included on the list of the Ministry of Public Health. However, the figure still appears extremely high.
4. In 1991 there were nineteen categories; in 1997 there were twenty-four.
5. Marjorie Muecke (1992), in a perceptive article on the cultural underpinnings of prostitution in Thai society, asked the question, "Why is the rapid growth of female prostitution not culturally problematic for the Thai?" She goes on to point out that "the sanctions of prostitution provide a resource, young women, that contribute to the development of the national economy through their labour in sex tourism and the sex entertainment industry".
6. I have been informed by a health official, however, that this programme will be curtailed or ended because of budget cuts.
7. According to the Myanmar Government, Department of Health AIDS Prevention and Control Programme, *Sentinel Surveillance Report for September 1993*, HIV rates for injection drug users (IDUs) ranged from 27 per cent in Taunggyi to 95 per cent in Myitkyeena.
8. For example, the United States seems to use a yield figure of 10 kilograms of opium per hectare (an unusually high *average* yield over a large area), while the United Nations prefers a figure of 7 kilograms per hectare.
9. As long ago as 1964, Shans reported (during interviews) specific incidences of punitive rape carried out by Myanmar soldiers against villagers.

REFERENCES

Asia Watch. *A Modern Form of Slavery: Trafficking Burmese Women and Girls into Brothels in Thailand.* New York: Asia Watch, 1993.
Bangkok World. "US Withdrawal Effect Being Felt in Udon", 1 September 1969.
Cheng H. et al. "HIV-1 Subtype E in Yunnan, China" (letter). *Lancet* 344 (1994): 953–54.
Cohen, E. "Sensuality and Venality in Bangkok: The Dynamics of the Cross-Cultural Mapping of Prostitution". In *Thai Tourism: Hill Tribes, Islands and Open-Ended Prostitution*, by E. Cohen, pp. 293–304. Studies in Contemporary Thailand, no. 4. Bangkok: White Lotus, 1996.
Falk, John L. and David A. Feingold. "Environmental and Cultural Factors in the Behavioral Action of Drugs". In *Psychopharmacology: The Third Generation of Progress*, edited by Herbert Y. Meltzer. New York: Raven Press, 1987.
Feingold, D. "Opium and Politics in Laos". In *Laos War and Revolution*, edited by N.S. Adams and A.W. McCoy, pp. 322–39. New York: Harper & Row, 1970.
Feingold, D. "Money, Myths, and Models: Opium, Economics, and History on the Thai-Burma Frontier". In *Opiate Drug Consumption Patterns in Asia*. Penang, Malaysia: National Drug Centre, U.N./WHO Collaborating Centre for Research and Training in Drug Dependence, 1981.

Gray, J. "HIV/AID in The Hills: A Crisis Just Waiting to Happen". Paper presented at the 5th International Thai Studies Conference, School of Oriental and African Studies, University of London, 1993.
Htoo, M.T. et al. "HIV/AIDS in Myanmar". *AIDS*, 1994, pp. S105–S109.
Hu D.J. et al. "The Emerging Genetic Diversity of HIV: The Importance of Global Surveillance for Diagnostics, Research, and Prevention". *JAMA* 275 (1996): 210–16.
Images Asia. *Migrating with Hope: Burmese Women Working in the Sex Industry*. Chiang Mai: Images Asia, 1997.
La Loubère, S. de. *A New Historical Relation of the Kingdom of Siam*. London: Tho. Horne, 1691, 1693. Reprint ed. Kuala Lumpur: Oxford University Press, 1969.
Lintner, B. and Hseng Noung Lintner. "Blind in Rangoon: AIDS Epidemic Rages, but the Junta Says No to NGOs". *Far Eastern Economic Review*, 1 August 1996, p. 21.
Lyttleton, C. "Sexual Negotiation in Downtown Laos". Paper presented at the 6th International Thai Studies Conference, Chiang Mai, 1996.
Muecke, M. "Mother Sold Food, Daughter Sells Her Body: The Cultural Continuity of Prostitution". *Social Science and Medicine* 35 (1992): 891–901.
Muntarbhorn, V. "International Perspectives and Child Prostitution in Asia". In *Forced Labor: The Prostitution of Children*. Washington, D.C.: U.S. Department of Labor, Bureau of International Labor Affairs, 1996.
Myanmar Government, Department of Health AIDS Prevention and Control Programme. *Sentinel Surveillance Report for September 1993*. Yangon: Myanmar Government, 1993.
Nantiya Tangwisutuit. "Relocation in Sight for Hill People". *Nation*, 4 August 1996.
National Economic and Social Development Board (NESDB) Working Group on HIV/AIDS Projection. *Projections for HIV/AIDS in Thailand: 1987–2020*. Bangkok: Human Resources Planning Division, NESDB, 1994.
Rayanakorn, K. *Special Study on Laws Relating to Prostitution and Traffic in Women*. Bangkok: Research and Action Project on Traffic in Women, Foundation for Women, 1995.
Reid, A. *Southeast Asia in the Age of Commerce — 1450–1680, The Lands Below the Winds*. Vol. I. New Haven: Yale University Press, 1988.
Smith, M. "Ethnic Groups in Burma: Development Democracy and Human Rights". A report by Anti-Slavery International, London, 1994.
Stimson, G. "HIV Infection and Injecting Drug Use" (Final Report). A report to the United Nations International Drug Control Programme, Bangkok, 9 February 1994.
Surangkhanang K. *Ying khon chua* [The prostitute]. 4th ed. Bangkok: Khochittamet, 1949.
Symes, M. *An Account of an Embassy to the Kingdom Ava in the Year 1795*. 2 vols. Edinburgh: Constable, 1827.
Tapp, N. *Sovereignty and Rebellion: The White Hmong of Northern Thailand*. Singapore: Oxford University Press, 1989.
Thanprasertsuk S. "AIDS and the Sex Service Business" (in Thai). In *NIC — Prostitu-*

tion Free Zone. Proceedings of the Conference Celebrating the 20th Anniversary of IPSR, publication no. 148. Bangkok: Institute of Population and Social Research, Mahidol University, 1991.

United States Department of State, Bureau of International Narcotics Matters. *International Narcotics Control Strategy Report*. Washington, D.C.: Department of State, 16 March 1988.

Van Griensven, G.J.P. et al. "Socio-Economic and Demographic Characteristics and HIV-1 Infection among Female Commercial Sex Workers in Thailand". *AIDS CARE* 7 (1995): 557–65.

Westermeyer, J. *Poppies, Pipes, and People: Opium and Its Use in Laos*. Berkeley: University of California Press, 1982.

Yu, E.S.H. et al. "HIV Infection and AIDS in China, 1985 through 1994". *American Journal of Public Health* 86 (1996): 1116–1122, August 1996.

Cross-Border Mobility and Social Networks: Akha Caravan Traders

Mika Toyota

The development of new infrastructure linking the northern margins of Southeast Asia with the southern perimeter of China is retracing historical trade routes that once connected the indigenous peoples of the region. This chapter is an attempt to provide some empirical evidence of Akha[1] cross-border trading activities between southwest China, Myanmar,[2] and Thailand. Trade and commerce activities are found to be important components of Akha society and they especially illuminate the dynamics of Akha mobility and social networks. Trade activities also shed light on the way in which the Akha interact with other ethnic groups and the way in which their ethnic identities are manipulated in such a context.

The image of highlanders, particularly the Akha in Thailand, as "egalitarian", "self-sufficient", and "the least contacted hill tribes" is widely pervasive. Researchers tend to view them as subsistence farmers,[3] and the ideology and ritual practices associated with this pursuit have intrigued anthropologists. Consequently, little attention has been paid to their non-farm activities. Few studies have focused on the trade and commerce activities of the Akha.[4]

There is no doubt that agricultural activities are a prominent part of life among the Akha and that their ritual practices follow the agricultural cycle. But the Akha have always been aware of other economic possibilities, because agriculture did not always supply enough food. Food shortages are nothing new and the fear of hunger is chronic. It was often the case in the past that, in order to survive, the villagers would inevitably be involved with trade and commerce. Indeed, the Akha have been trading for centuries.[5]

Therefore, in order to explore the effects of economic development in the Mekong region on the local society, it would be misleading to assume that Akha society has moved from an "egalitarian" situation to one of unequal class stratification, from a subsistence economy to a market-oriented economy, and from "homogeneous" to complex ethnic relations. In contrast to these nostalgic images of Akha society — images reinforced by the tourism industry and by the recent movement to preserve indigenous "traditional" culture — economic differentiation, in fact, seems to be a distinctive element among the Akha. As Alting von Geusau (1983, p. 258) points out, the opposition between poor and rich is an often repeated theme in Akha oral texts. There are several Akha love songs describing the lover's poverty as compared with the wealth of the beloved or of others. Economic differentiation among Akha and its implication should not be underestimated, as it helps to reveal the meanings of status and prestige in Akha society.[6]

As economic differences and commercial activities among the Akha are not products of the penetration of Western capitalism, but are embedded in trade and commerce activities that run deep in Akha history, I agree with Bowie (1992, pp. 797–823) that to romanticize or to glorify the past in order to dramatize the deleterious impact of capitalism underestimates important facets of Akha history.

Akha trade relations with the "Cin-Ho" (Yunnanese Chinese), Tai Yai, Tai Lue, and other ethnic groups were detected in the course of my research.[7] These cross-ethnic relationships must have existed for centuries. Old Akha oral texts reveal that Akha ancestors gained their practical wisdom through the interactive relationship with other ethnic groups.

It is not surprising to find that inter-ethnic marriages also took place. Although the ideal in Akha society is to marry another Akha, it should be recognized that what actually happens and what is supposed to happen are rather different. In anthropological studies it has long been pointed out how ambiguous, flexible, situational, and multiple ethnic identities are, particularly in the ethnic mosaic of south China and mainland Southeast Asia (Conrad 1989; Leach 1954; Lehman 1979; Moerman 1969). This is particularly true in the context of inter-ethnic marriages. Inter-ethnic marriage among Akha traders is evident from the research, indicating that trading activity is a means of structuring social relations and networks.

The purpose of this chapter is to show how identities and multi-ethnic relations have been manipulated within the context of the trade and commercial activities of the Akha in the past as well as in the current situation. It will comprise three parts. Firstly, the historical evidence of Akha caravan trading activities will be illustrated. Secondly, I will report how Akha entrepreneurs are currently taking the opportunity to improve their informal cross-border trading activities as a result of the open economic policy of the Chinese government. Lastly, I will analyse these phenomena with reference to the way in which Akha organize their fluid social networks by utilizing their ability to use the Chinese language and their inter-ethnic marriage relations.

1. HISTORICAL EVIDENCE

AKHA ORAL TEXTS

Akha oral texts reveal the fact that the Akha have been associated with different ethnic groups with whom they exchanged practical wisdom through trading interaction. Though it is difficult accurately to identify periods of time from oral records, such records clearly mention that there were many traders in Akha villages in former times. Yunnanese Chinese mule caravan traders came regularly to exchange silk thread and gold and silver for Akha rice wine and white cotton. They also associated with Tai cattle caravan traders from lowlands to the south.

The oral texts also describe how Akha learned to organize markets from other ethnic groups. Moreover, they contain stories of mixed marriages between Yunnanese Chinese traders and Akha women. Although it cannot be proved to what extent these are historical facts, it is apparent that these experiences of their ancestors' trade and commercial activities have for centuries been cherished and memorized by Akha oral text reciters.

CHINESE SOURCES

According to Chinese literature sources, the Akha have been involved in horse caravan trading since the eighth century, during the Tang dynasty, although horse caravan trade by minorities is sparsely documented in the Chinese official documents. Such documents should be critically investigated, particularly in reference to the Akha, who do not have a written language system of their own, as they often represent the official perspective of the central government, rather than local points of view. Moreover, as ethnic categories are a creation of historical political processes, it cannot be assumed that those identified as "Akha" in the Tang dynasty are categorically homogenous with those who at present call themselves "Akha".

According to Reid, inland trade from AD 1450 to AD 1680 must have received a great stimulus from the boom in sea-borne trade, even though carrying goods through the interior was far more difficult and robbery was far more common (Reid 1993, pp. 53–54). After the Ming dynasty (1368–1644), the imperial government's priority was to develop maritime commerce to the West, and little attention was paid to Yunnan routes. However, it should not be assumed that informal cross-border trading activities in the Yunnan region in fact declined. On the contrary, Yunnan routes remained in use in the Lower Mekong region, as goods traded in the Shan states of Myanmar, in northern Laos, and in northern Vietnam still had to be carried out by horses and boats. The opium trade, which has played a significant role in the regional trade economy, has maintained this basic spatial pattern.

Research conducted by Wang (1993) analyses the geographical, social, and political conditions under which the horse caravans emerged and gives a brief review of this historical development from the Qin dynasty (221 BC) up to the present day. Unfortunately, he only covers the region around Dali, Lijiang, and Baoshan in the northwestern part of Yunnan province. Little information or documentation can be found on horse caravan trading activities in the "Lower Mekong" areas, where most of the Akha traders were involved.

GEOGRAPHICAL SITUATION

Along the caravan routes, water passages were taken wherever possible. Thus the four rivers which connect south China with mainland Southeast Asia — the Red, the Mekong, the Salween, and the Irrawaddy — were intertwined with the main trade routes. According to Chananont's study (1986, p. 40), it took only fifteen to seventeen days to go between Moulmein (Myanmar) and Chiang Mai, while the trade routes between Chiang Mai and Bangkok took two to three months. It is evident that northern Thailand and Burma (now known as Myanmar) were actually a coherent part of a broad upland zone within which socio-economic networks expanded to southern China, northern Laos, and North Vietnam. As the Tibetan Plateau almost cut off the greater part of Yunnan province from the rest of China, close socio-cultural and politico-economic relations were established between Yunnan and mainland Southeast Asia. By contrast, the zone connecting Chiang Mai and Bangkok is a rather recent invention. It was only after the turn of the century that arbitrary demarcations of the region were created as a result of the emergence of the nation-state. Until then, inhabitants along the Yunnan frontiers used to pay tribute to both the Burmese king and the Chinese emperor, while never completely absorbing the politico-economic system of either.

CHINA PRIOR TO 1949

Prior to the Chinese Revolution in 1949, Akha traders' caravan routes went over mountains as well as along and across rivers and were quite extensive, leading to northern Vietnam as far as Hanoi; to Luang Prabang, Xieng Khouang, Phongsaly in Laos; to Keng Tung, Mandalay, Rangoon (now Yangon) in Burma (now Myanmar); and to Mae Sai and Chiang Mai in northern Thailand. Some even extended as far as Taiwan and Hong Kong.

In the Honghe area the majority of the population were Akha[8] and Yi, and at present this area is designated an autonomous county. According to a key informant (male, fifty-one years old) whose grandfather used to be a well-known chief leader of caravans to Laos and Vietnam, Akha involvement in horse caravan trading was the largest among the ethnic minorities. The Akha horse caravans seldom contained fewer than one hundred horses, as all long-distance caravan routes traversed densely forested mountainous areas, where there was a constant danger of encountering wild animals and bandits. They usually consisted of 300 to 400 horses, and of around twenty persons per 100 horses. The main items traded were: cotton, cloth, dye, farm implements, forest products, opium,[9] tobacco,[10] salt,[11] Yunnanese tea,[12] silver,[13] tin — as well as the small, beautifully embroidered Qing dynasty (1644–1911) shoes for women which were valued by the Chinese female immigrants in Laos and Vietnam who practised "foot-binding" and who, considering themselves as "sojourners" abroad with the intention to return "home" some day, believed that if the Chinese shoes were put on after death, the soul could go back "home".

Bernatzik (1970, pp. 568–78), on his expedition in 1936–37, saw the Akha selling opium, cotton, pepper, pigs, and forest products such as honey and the wax of wild bees at Shan market. In exchange, they bought salt, betel, pepper, and silver ornaments. He observed that principal articles of Akha trade were raw cotton and sturdy standing-baskets, and that they also bred buffaloes exclusively for sale to the Lao. Looking at their successful trade activities, he stated that "next to the Lisu, the Akha are among the richest of the mountain tribes" (ibid., p. 572). He also came across Akha villages whose inhabitants neglected all agriculture other than the cultivation of poppies.

> They were devoting themselves entirely to the smuggling of opium, exchanged the drug for food with the neighbouring Lahu, and thus lived incomparably better than their fellow tribesmen who had remained faithful to agriculture. (Ibid., p. 523)

Interestingly, Bernatzik records that the Akha were familiar with the weights and balances used by the Chinese, and used a special cotton-weighing machine. For measuring maize and rice they used a sort of measuring basket, and for measuring liquids they used bottles which they bought from the Lao or Shan, although they had their own terms to measure quantity.

Horse caravans were well organized: division of labour and status stratification were rigidly defined. The caravans had a chief leader, who often gave the caravan its name. There was also a sub-leader, a chef, a military officer, watch guards, and porters. A chef was needed because the caravan normally had to carry its own food, and some of the horses carried food supplies such as oil, dried meat, salt, and rice. The military officers carried guns made in the United Kingdom, Italy, Germany, France, Belgium, and China. The guards normally followed at the back of the horse caravan. Porters were not allowed to ride on the horses, so that the speed of the caravan was governed by the pace of walking.

According to Reid (1993, p. 57), "a hardy Shan porter could carry 36 kg about 24 km a day". The Han Chinese or the "Cin-Ho" (Yunnanese Chinese) were often the ones that took the initiative to do caravan trading. If the caravan chief was a "Cin-Ho", then the caravan train was identified as such, which does not necessarily mean that all of the members were exclusively "Cin-Ho".[14] A few prestigious chief leaders were Akha who had become independent enough to organize their own horse caravans after years of experience with other caravans.

Horse caravan trading among the Akha was considered a profession rather than a part-time or seasonal job, unlike the situation among the ox traders in northern Thailand, most of whom, according to Chuusit, were peasants who worked as traders for about six to seven months during the dry season after harvesting their fields. Their trading activities were thus rather limited, and they "did not dare to expand their business into other towns and the business could not be different from their ancestors" (Chuusit 1981, pp. 1–2). Horse caravan trading, however, expanded across borders and created trade specialists, making reciprocal exchangers into trade dealers who gained profit from transit trade margins.

Each horse caravan had specialized routes and areas.[15] The fifty-one-year-old informant mentioned above, for example, told me that his grandfather, who specialized in trading in Laos and Vietnam under the French colonial regime, often brought home French goods, such as soap, matches, flashlights, and sweet candy, which he had obtained from Hanoi. Another informant (male, fifty-two years old) told me about his father, an Akha from the Xishuangbanna area in the southwestern part of Yunnan province, who specialized on the Kunming–Simao–Jinghong–Menghai–Ken Tung–Mae Sai route. His father had died when his caravan came in conflict with the British Army in Burma around 1942–43.

It is interesting to note that the horse caravan took a prominent role as a means of communication, as there were no established postal systems in these cross-border areas. Both merchandise and information were exchanged at the market centres.[16] The traders were esteemed by the home villagers not only because they possessed uncommon items and were economically well-off but also because they brought news and information from far away.

Men involved in trading were generally viewed as prosperous and sophisticated, having knowledge of different cultures. According to a fifty-three-year-old female informant whose father and husband were traders, the traders' wives stayed behind in the village, raising children while the husbands travelled for a few months. A woman often had no idea when her husband would return home, and normally he would spend more time travelling than at home. If the husband had a good position in the horse caravan, the wife did not have to bother to work as a farmer as she could afford to purchase everything she needed.

Family members of the traders had more opportunities for formal education, not only because of the father's wealth, but also because of his extensive social networks and access to information. This was particularly true in China. Since people with higher education have better access to higher positions in society, trade and commerce activities were influential not only economically, but also socially and politically.

2. THE AKHA AND THE MEKONG BASIN GROWTH AREA

With China's "open door" economic policy of the last few years, the influence of Yunnan's economic growth is extending rapidly into cross-border areas, and particularly to Thailand. Moreover, the border region of Thailand, Myanmar, Laos, and Yunnan where the Akha reside, has been designated as the "Great Mekong Development Area" and the Asian Development Bank is promoting a huge investment in infrastructure.

With the recent involvement of various multinational investors in this region, there is a growing concern for the social effects of rapid economic development on the local ethnic minorities in this area. The general tone of this discourse is often sympathetic towards local residents, who are viewed as poor exploited ethnic minorities. However, I propose that it is too simplistic to apply the dichotomy of powerful majority and vulnerable minority in this context. It should be remembered that these ethnic minorities have been active participants in cross-border trading activities for centuries, as we have seen. Over time, they have established cross-border trade networks which go beyond the rigid political boundaries of nation-states. Their social network is highly flexible. This informal network might be better able to adjust to the current situation than initially envisaged, and it might be misleading to lump all the local ethnic minorities together as victims of development.

It is not only large business groups that are in the position of exploiting new opportunities in the area. Small unofficial entrepreneurs cannot be overlooked in this region. From field research near the border between Thailand and Myanmar, it is clear that some Akha entrepreneurs have slipped in to exploit new opportunities by reviving their trading routes between Xishuangbanna and northern Thailand. They are fully utilizing multiple language skills and extended trade networks developed over many years of history.

Of course, the Akha who are able to take advantage of such new business opportunities are far from representative of the Akha generally in Thailand. Due to exposure to the rapid deterioration of their environment and to considerable political and economic pressures, the majority are, in fact, in a fairly destitute and depressed condition.[17] Drug addiction among highlanders has recently grown at an alarming rate. The recent replacement of opium smoking by heroin injection and amphetamine use is causing even more serious damage to the health of individuals and society as a whole. Prostitution is not an uncommon choice among young Akha girls from broken families.

On the other hand, there are also some remarkably successful Akha entrepreneurs in Thailand, though they are few in number and have had hardly any attention paid to them by previous researchers. Here I would like to present some evidence of how the Akha traders are retracing their trade routes in the current context.

First of all, they have altered their means of transportation from horses to ships and trucks. Because they passed the Mekong River in fleeing from China to Thailand, they were fully aware of its significance as a trade and transportation route, and as soon as the Mekong River routes between Jinghong in China, and Chiang Saen in Thailand opened, they started to trade along them. Travel from Jinghong to Chiang Saen takes two days. When the ships arrive at Chiang Saen, the cargo is sent off to Mae Sai, Chiang Mai, and Bangkok by truck. The return takes three days from Chiang Saen to Jinghong, from where trucks send the cargo on to Kunming. When the river is high, 40–60 tonne ships are used; when the river is low, 20-tonne ships. Eight ships are used altogether, going back and forth on the Mekong River four to ten times a month.

Traders deal in varied merchandise, as they operate a carrier agency, acting as brokers to connect local enterprises in China and Thailand. The main merchandise observed during field observations in 1996 was as follows (although I suspect this may be subject to rapid change):

- from China to Thailand: apples, pears, fireworks, plastic toys, dolls, telephones, blankets, lighters, silk, personal organizer, chestnuts, nylon stockings, garlic;
- from Thailand to China: biscuits (Imperial, Nissin, Euro), tinned fruits (Malee), dried beef, instant noodles (Mama), Thai fragrant rice, fresh lichee, palm oil, rubber, rubber sandals.

During field observations, I was most impressed by the usage of mobile telephones. Under conditions where they cannot rely on stationary communication systems, mobile phones have become crucial items among the traders. The mobile phone dialogues are frequently highly skilful inter-ethnic negotiations between trade partners in different countries. Finding Akha traders who can speak four or five different languages is not difficult — one informant (male, thirty-two) can communicate in Tai Lue, Cin-Ho, Myanmar, Standard Thai, Northern Thai, Mandarin, Hokkien, English, and Akha; another trader (male, thirty-eight) can communicate in Tai Lue, Cin-Ho, Myanmar, Northern Thai, and Akha. Though they lack writing and reading skills in these languages, nevertheless, in terms of oral skills for negotiating with trade partners and for making trade network connections, they are remarkably able, independent entrepreneurs.

The trade partners' close affinity with "Cin-Ho" and Tai Lue has also been observed. It is obvious from Akha oral texts that inter-ethnic marriage between "Cin-Ho" or Tai Lue and Akha traders did take place. In some cases, it seems that there were strategic elements in choosing such marriage partners. Even today multi-ethnic marriages between trade partners are not uncommon, either in Thailand or in China. Despite the Akha ideal of marriage with other Akha, it is not unusual to find male Akha traders who marry more than once[18] — perhaps in China, Myanmar, and then in Thailand, along trading routes. For example, the father of an informant (male, forty-four years old) has married seven times (twice in China, four times in Myanmar, and once in Thailand), and the informant himself has married three times (in Myanmar, Mae Sai, and Chiang Mai). In the case of Akha women, too, it is not uncommon of them to marry other traders (Cin-Ho, Tai-Lue), who are often better off. In their words, "the traders eat rice with meat and fish while the poor eat rice with salt". Marriage is a practical survival matter rather than an idealistic romantic matter for young Akha girls, and the first priority is to escape from poverty and hunger.

In addition to earlier relations with Tai Lue and "Cin-Ho" in China, Myanmar, and Thailand, some successful traders now have marriage connections with Overseas Chinese in Singapore, Malaysia, Taiwan, and Hong Kong. Here are the marriages of one family's eight children:

1. Female (fifty)* married to an Akha (in China)
2. Male (forty-seven) married to a Cin-Ho
3. Male (forty-four) married to an Akha (in Myanmar)
4. Male (forty) married to a Tai chuu (in Thailand)
5. Female (thirty-six) married to an Akha (in Thailand)
6. Male (thirty-two) married to a Taiwanese
7. Female (thirty) married to a Hakka (in China)
8. Female (twenty-five) single graduate from a university in Bangkok and working there

This family has evidently established kinship networks which coincide with trade networks crossing geographical boundaries, political units, and ethnic categories — networks which were constructed during the move from China to Thailand. Such marriages weave personal social relations into powerful trade networks.

Parents involved in trade consider the Chinese language vital for the expansion of trade networks, especially for the future, and so are very keen to send their children to study Chinese, and then to Taiwan for higher education, if they can afford to do so. A few schools in northern Thailand provide Chinese language education from Taiwanese text books. Classes last for two or three hours, beginning after Thai school hours, at 5 p.m. These schools are often financially supported by Taiwanese, and scholarships to study in Taiwan for five years more are provided annually.

Another dimension to the connection with Taiwan is the recent success of Taiwanese Christian churches among the highlanders residing along the borders of Thailand. It is an interesting dimension of the rapidly growing cohort of Christian highlanders in Thailand today. Previous studies of Christian conversion among Akha have focused on Western missionaries (either Protestants or Catholics), but although a number of foreign missionaries are still active in the region (Kammerer 1990, 1996), there are also a growing number of Asian Christian missionaries in northern Thailand. Thus, Christianization does not always mean the penetration of alien Western cultural values, as used to be the case.

Taiwanese churches often provide Chinese-language lessons during the evening or at the weekend under the guise of "Bible study". This is an undeniable motivation for conversion, especially among the young generation whose parents cannot afford to send them for private Chinese lessons. Thus, converting to Christianity provides an opportunity to find a better job and a better life.

At present, Taiwan is also one of the most popular destinations for migrant workers from Thailand, and particularly for the Akha. According to one informant (male, twenty-three), it costs 75,000 baht to arrange for work in Taiwan, and those with the language ability obviously have an advantage. Those who can speak Chinese dialects can obtain a Thai passport free of charge from a Taiwanese broker.

3. ANALYSIS

MULTI-ETHNIC SOCIAL NETWORKS

As described above, Akha oral records claim that the Akha have had a long history of interactive trade relations with other ethnic groups through which they have accumulated cultural knowledge which has been passed down to their descendants. Although historical documents written by scholars and late nineteenth century British travellers give us an impression that long-distance caravan trading activities around this region were dominated by Cin-Ho, this does not necessarily mean that other ethnic groups were excluded from these activities. In fact the components of these trade systems were multi-ethnic groups of people — "Cin-Ho caravan train" in these documents simply means that the chief was Cin-Ho; the rest of the members could have been from other ethnic groups. Such a multi-ethnic make-up of caravans would have been effective in expanding traders' networks and broadening their language abilities. Recent observation of Akha entrepreneurs in the Mekong Basin Growth Area shows that they are highly flexible and hungry to utilize any social networks available, and that they consider multi-lingualism a critical ability for enhancing their trade networks.

Among the Akha, it is clear that one set of cultural elements used to define group membership is kinship, but this is not the sole criterion. Close residence, shared experiences, proximate age, and potential profit can all provide bonds as strong as genealogical proximity. For example, during field observations I have come across certain Ubya Akha traders who felt a much closer affinity with Cin-Ho, who might be potential trade partners, than with Ulo Akha, who are not likely to be such. Ubya Akha and "Cin-Ho" sometimes called each other "brother". They explained their behaviour in this way: "Cin-Ho are from south China. We Ubya Akha are also from south China. The origins of our ancestors are the same anyway", and they put me into the same category by saying "a Japanese is also of the same origin a long time ago". This kind of justification reveals the fact that at the end of the day, what counts most is a shared interest rather than some fictional ethnic category. There is not much difference between the manner in which they claim Akha ethnic group identity — by ancestry — and the manner in which they claim brotherhood with the Cin-Ho.

The dynamics of multi-ethnic networks have not received adequate attention because of limitations imposed by the conventional anthropological approach of conducting research among people restricted within the static unitary notion of a single village. However, in fact it seems that a pragmatic fluidity in trade and commercial activity, combined with situational membership criteria, enables the Akha to be flexible and durable in adjusting to constant hardship and the ever-changing circumstances of their environment.

AKHA AND THE CHINESE IDENTITY

Trade and commerce activities disclose the way in which the Akha manipulate their identification. The category of "hilltribe", considered a low-class social group in Thai society, was created through the slogan of hilltribe development "to improve the standard of living of those backward people". The Akha, in particular, tend to be viewed as the lowest among the hilltribes. As a result, some Akha traders are reluctant to be considered "Akha". The Akha élite, who stand out because of economic success or higher education, prefer to differentiate themselves from other Akha, and one option is to identify themselves as Chinese traders.

This phenomenon is to some extent a result of recent changes in China. China is no longer the ideological threat that it used to be, and is now generally viewed as offering great economic opportunities. Consequently, the prestige of Chinese within Thai society is being revived (see for example, Vatikiotis 1996). In the past, people of Chinese origin were discouraged from projecting their Chinese identity in order to encourage their integration into Thai society; but this is no longer an issue, as their descendants have already been assimilated and are no longer "sojourners", but "settlers". Since today Chinese identity has a positive connotation among the Thai middle class, the Akha often categorize themselves as descendants of Chinese traders. It is worth noting in this case that the occupational identity is more significant than ethnic group identity.

With this growing prestige of Chinese, Akha traders often accentuate their identity as Chinese traders by burying their parents in the Chinese way, praying for business success as Overseas Chinese do, carrying business cards with Chinese characters on the back, and so on. At first glance it may not be possible to differentiate them from other Chinese traders, though this may not be necessary: ethnic identification is an ever-changing historical and political process, and clear-cut ethnic group boundaries were early academics' illusions. It is not surprising to find highly ambiguous, flexible representations of identity in real life.

Looking at this present situation, it is not too difficult to imagine that Akha traders who worked with Cin-Ho traders in the past might have identified themselves as Cin-Ho, or behaved as Cin-Ho. In outsiders' eyes they might have looked like Cin-Ho traders. Sir J.G. Scott, who became Superintendent for the northern and later the southern Shan states of Myanmar, observed that Chinese and Akha mixed well freely, that it was quite common to find half a dozen Chinamen with

Akha wives living in an Akha village, and that there were also villages entirely of mixed Akha-Chinese (Scott 1932, p. 274). In such cases, there might have been no way, and no need, to discern between the "real" Cin-Ho and the others.

CONCLUSION

This chapter demonstrates how the Akha have interacted with other ethnic groups through their trade and commerce activities and how they construct their identity in both the past and the present. It should be noted that the current projection of Chinese identity by Akha traders is just one consequence of circumstance, that this identity mirrors changes in different socio-political and economic environments, and that it will be continuously reshaped through changing times. The Akha traders demonstrated in this chapter may not typify the Akha in general — however, the issue I am concerned with in this chapter is not how to illustrate the collective representation of the Akha, but to understand their dynamic social relations, which go beyond village boundaries and ethnic categories, and to examine the process of how their identity is constructed in response to their immediate social and economic relations.

The conventional presumption of an ethnic group with a clearly bounded society within a single village with a shared ethnic identity is challenged in the context of trade and commerce activities in the ethnic mosaic that consists of the area between China and mainland southeast Asia. More attention to the compelling emergence of occupational identities in this region may clarify the complex situation of multi-ethnic relations.

NOTES

1. The Akha language falls within the Tibeto-Burman group. The Akha (called "Hani" in China) are widely scattered in the border areas between southwest China and mainland Southeast Asia — Vietnam, Laos, Thailand, and Myanmar. The total population of the Hani/Akha was roughly estimated to be about 1,820,000 in 1996. According to a personal conversation with Professor Shi Jun Zhui (an Akha researcher at the Yunnan Academy of Social Science), the distribution of the population is suggested as: 1,260,000 in southwest China (the third largest minority in Yunnan province), 60,000 in North Vietnam, 70,000 in northern Laos, 50,000 in northern Thailand, and 380,000 in Myanmar. The author is aware of the issues of

ethnic identification as a symbolic process of historical and political construction, and that ethnic boundaries are ambiguous, changeable and situational; thus, the indication of the population is simply a matter of convenience.

2. "Burma" and "Myanmar" are used interchangeably in this chapter. In June 1989 the name of the state was changed from "Burma" to "Myanmar", and the adjectival form changed from "Burmese" to "Myanmar". Other names have also been changed to conform to Myanmar spelling, for example, Rangoon to Yangon. These uses conform to the editorial style of the Institute of Southeast Asian Studies and do not necessarily represent the contributor's preference.

3. Akha in Thailand as shifting cultivators; Hani in China as irrigated terrace farmers.

4. Alting von Geusau (1983) points out the hundreds of years of involvement of the Akha in market systems. Among the studies on the trade and commerce activities of the highlanders in Thailand, there are two articles on the Lahu by Sanit Wongsprasert (1975, 1983). There are also remarkable works on Cin-Ho Caravan Traders in this region (see, for example, Forbes 1987*a* and 1987*b*; Hill 1982).

5. Another common practice among the Akha was to sell their labour to more powerful, prosperous neighbours.

6. Other elements which differentiate power stratification would be age, sex, the level of knowledge or education, access to property or natural resources, information, valued social connections, and so forth.

7. The data were collected during the course of field research on "the Urban Migration and Social Networks of the Akha in Chiang Mai", conducted from July 1994 to October 1996. This was part of a Ph.D. dissertation and was made possible by a grant from the Institute for the Culture of Travel (Japan). This chapter is based on occasional participant observation and on in-depth interviews with nine key informants (six males, three females) about life histories. I have selected these nine key informants out of 343 informants with whom I have conducted semi-structured interviews, including the Ubya Akha in Phami village (sometimes also called Phami Akha). This is because there is a relatively higher involvement with cross-border trade and commerce activities among the Ubya Akha. Despite their small number and the fact that they have come to Thailand more recently, some of them are relatively successful economically. Previous Akha studies have been conducted mostly with Ulo Akha (see Alting von Geusau 1983; Hansson 1983*a* and 1983*b*; Kammerer 1986).

My research findings contradict the statement "While the Akha have traditionally been involved in the market economy ... they lacked a class of middlemen and traders" (Alting von Geusau 1983, p. 265). This is probably because his research was conducted only among Ulo Akha in Thailand, whereas my informants included Ubya Akha in Thailand and Myanmar as well as Hani/ Akha in China.

8. The term "Hani" instead of "Akha" is used in Chinese official ethnic classification.

9. It was sold to Europe, via Shanghai, Taiwan, Hong Kong, and Hanoi, until the Chinese government banned its trade in 1949.

10. Tobacco was produced in southeast China, Burma, Laos, and Vietnam. It was

valued because of its different harvest time in southern China and north mainland Southeast Asia.

11. Salt was produced at Simao, and valued especially in inland Vietnam, Laos, and Burma.

12. One of the famous Pu-erh teas from the southern Yunnan frontier, called "Akha tea". It is considered a first-class quality tea. There are no other minority groups in Yunnan after which a tea has been named.

13. Silver was highly prized not only for its ornamental and cash value, but also for its cultural significance. A piece of silver was often put in the mouth of a dead person as it was believed this would enable him to have enough money to spend in heaven.

14. Forbes and Hill also argue the possibility of many other Yunnanese being involved in the trade as entrepreneurs, horse-boys and porters (Forbes 1987a, pp. 25–26; Hill 1982, pp. 114–15).

15. Some Akha caravan traders in Burma shifted the means of transportation from horses to trucks after they obtained second-hand automobiles from the American Army. This made it possible to trade more efficiently between Ken Tung, Mandalay, and Rangoon.

16. Literally, "horse stations" in Chinese. The trade partners were Hani, Yi, Tai, Haw, Han, and so forth. Yunnanese Chinese was mainly spoken among them.

17. See, for example, the situation of the Akha in Thailand (Alting von Geusau 1992; Kammerer 1989). See also the situation of the Akha in China (Henin 1996).

18. In Akha society, if the first wife does not have a son, it is legitimate to have a second wife.

REFERENCES

Alting von Geusau, Leo. "Dialectics of Akhazang: The Interiorizations of a Perennial Minority Group". In *Highlanders in Thailand*, edited by John McKinnon and Wanat Bhruksasri. Kuala Lumpur: Oxford University Press, 1983.

———. "The Akha: Ten Years Later". *Pacific Viewpoint* 33, no. 3 (1992): 178–84.

Bernatzik, Hugo Adolf. *Akha and Miao: Problems of Applied Ethnography in Farther India*. New Haven: HRAF, 1970.

Bowie, Katherine. "Unraveling the Myth of the Subsistence Economy: Textile Production in Nineteenth Century Northern Thailand". *Journal of Asian Studies* 51, no. 4 (1992): 797–823.

Chananont, Plai-Auw. "The Role of Merchant Capitalists in the Rise and Expansion of Capitalism in Northern Thailand 1921–1980". M.A. thesis, Department of Economics, Chulalongkorn University, 1986.

Chuusit Chuuchat. "Ox Traders: Pioneer of Village Trading in Northern Thailand 1855–1960" (in Thai). Research Report, Department of Teacher Training, Ministry of Education. Mimeographed. 1981.

Conrad, Yves. "Lisu Identity in Northern Thailand: A Problematique for Anthropology". In *Hill Tribes Today: Problems in Change*, edited by John McKinnon and Bernard Vienne. Bangkok: White Lotus-Orstom, 1989.

Forbes, Andrew. "The 'Cin-Ho" (Yunnanese Chinese) Caravan Trade with North Thailand during the Late Nineteenth and Early Twentieth Centuries". *Journal of Asian History* 21, no. 1 (1987*a*): 1–47.

——— . "The Role of Hui Muslims in the Traditional Caravan Trade between Yunnan and Thailand". In *Marchants et hommes d'affaires asiatiques dans l'Ocean Indienne et la Mer de China 13-20 siecles*, edited by D. Lombard and F. Aubin, pp. 289–94. Paris: Editions de l'Ecole des Hautes Etudes en Sciences Sociales, 1987.

Hansson, Inga-lill. "Death in an Akha Village". In *Highlanders in Thailand*, edited by John McKinnon and Wanat Bhruksasri. Kuala Lumpur: Oxford University Press, 1983*a*.

——— . "The Marginalization of Akha Ancestors". *Pacific Viewpoint* 33, no. 2 (1983*b*): 185–92.

Henin, Bernard. "Ethnic Minority Integration in China: Transformation of Akha Society". *Journal of Contemporary Asia* 26, no. 2 (1996): 180–200.

Hill, Ann Maxwell. "Familiar Strangers: The Yunnanese Chinese in Northern Thailand". Ph.D. thesis, University of Illinois, 1982.

Kammerer, Cornelia Ann. "Gateway to the Akha World: Kinship, Ritual, and Community among Highlanders of Thailand". Ph.D. dissertation, University of Chicago, 1986.

——— . "Territorial Imperatives: Akha Ethnic Identity and Thailand's National Integration". In *Hill Tribes Today*, edited by John McKinnon and Bernard Vienne. Bangkok: White Lotus-Orstorm, 1989.

——— . "Customs and Christian Conversion among Akha Highlanders of Burma and Thailand". *American Ethnologist* 17, no. 2 (1990): 277–91.

——— . "Discarding the Basket: The Reinterpretation of Tradition by Akha Christians of Northern Thailand". *Journal of Southeast Asian Studies* 27, no. 2 (1996): 320–33.

Leach, Edmund. *Political Systems of Highland Burma*. London: Bell, 1954.

Lehman, F.K. "Who Are the Karen, and If So, Why? Karen Ethnohistory and Formal Theory of Ethnicity". In *Ethnic Adaptation and Identity: The Karen on the Thai Frontier with Burma*, edited by Charles F. Keyes. Philadelphia: Institute for the Study of Human Issues, 1979.

Moerman, Michael. "Ethnic Identification in a Complex Civilization: Who Are the Lue?" *American Anthropologist* 67 (1965): 1215–30.

——— . "Kinship and Commerce in a Thai Lue Village". *Man State and Society in Contemporary Southeast Asia*. New York: Praeger Publishers, 1969.

Reid, Anthony. *Southeast Asia in the Age of Commerce 1450–1680*. Chiang Mai: Silkworm Books, 1993.

Scott, J. George. *Burma and Beyond*. London: Grayson & Grayson, 1932.

Vatikiotis, Michael. "Sino Chic—Suddenly, It's Cool to Be Chinese". *Far Eastern Economic Review*, 11 January 1996.

Wang, M.D. *Horse Caravan Culture* (in Chinese). Kunming: Yunnan People Publication, 1993.
Wongsprasert, Sanit. "Lahu Trade and Commerce". *Journal of the Siam Society* 63, no. 2 (1975): 199–218.
───────. "Lahu Agriculture and Trade in North Thailand". In *Highlanders in Thailand*, edited by John McKinnon and Wanat Bhruksasri. Kuala Lumpur: Oxford University Press, 1983.

Cross-Border Links between Muslims in Yunnan and Northern Thailand: Identity and Economic Networks

Jean Berlie

Islam is the second largest religion in the People's Republic of China (PRC), including about 20 per cent of all religious worshippers. Thailand, which nearly borders China's Yunnan province, is a Buddhist kingdom where Islam is accepted.

Administratively, China's near-twenty million Muslim population, 600,000 of which is Yunnanese, is divided into ten minorities. Islam in China is an irregular mosaic of nationalities and cultures. Since the Tang dynasty, the dominant Han have tried to sinicize Islam and integrate the Muslims; present Muslim identity reflects this historical fact (Berlie 1996, p. 213).

According to Joseph Fletcher (1934–84), three Islamic waves flowed into China (Gladney 1996, pp. 36–62). These three tides can be termed those of the "Old Religion" (*laojiao, gedimu*), mystic Sufism, and "New Religion". The present complexity is a result of these three tides. The orthodox Sunni "Old Religion" is the main pillar of the state Chinese Islamic Association and dominates also in northern Thailand (although there is also a Pakistani influence). In dialectical Yunnanese, *laotou* ("Old Head") is still a common self-designation of the Muslims, showing clearly that "Old Religion", orthodox Islam, is predominant.

Most of the "New Religion" (*xinjiao*) reformers are also Sunnites and members of the Islamic Association through the network of mosques and other structural institutions.

Formerly involved in the trade with Thailand and Laos, the Sufi group (also Sunni) is divided into Naqshabandi *tarîqa* or *pai* ("schools" or "sects" in Chinese). Some follow the Islamic Association and the Party, while others are by tradition against the concept of non-Islamic governments.

Yunnanese Muslims are present in Keng Tung and Mae Sai in Myanmar, and in Chiang Rai and Chiang Mai in Thailand, where they are known as *khon Islam* or simply "Ho" (a Dai Lüe name for "Chinese" which has no religious connotation). In China, their common and official designation "Hui" (*minzu* or *huizu*) is a puzzling name; the character also means "return". The general and shorter term *huimin* designates all the Muslims in China, but the "Hui" often prefer the term "Muslim Chinese".[1]

The ethnonym "Hui" was probably mentioned for the first time in 917, in the records of the Liao (Couling 1917, p. 244). Later publications mention this ethnonym in the eleventh century, during the Northern Song dynasty; and then two centuries later, during the Yuan dynasty (1279–1368) (Yang 1991, p. 11), when the ancient Chinese links with so-called "mainland Southeast Asia" developed through maritime and also land relations. Later still, the Chinese Muslims Ma Huan and Admiral Zheng (Ma) He (1371–1435) sought trade in Southeast Asia.

Like the above, Yunnanese "Hui", when they migrate to Southeast Asia, are not only Chinese Muslims but also Overseas Chinese, and no economy in the region functions without Chinese involvement. In colonial northern Vietnam, as in modern Thailand, a Southeast Asian pattern of separation was to be observed. In inner mainland Southeast Asia, Islam was under Yunnanese influence, while in Malaysia, Singapore, south Thailand, Cambodia, South Vietnam, and (partly) in ancient Hainan, originally Malay and Cham populations constituted the dominant Muslim group.

Around 10 per cent of the population of Thailand today is ethnically Chinese; they are divided into two main categories: a powerful and rich élite and a "middle class". Islam is well documented in the Thai- and Malay-speaking southern Muslim provinces of Thailand, but in northern Thailand the significant former influence of Yunnanese Muslims is little reported. The Muslims involved in the cross-border trade before 1950 were usually organized into guilds (Forbes 1987, pp. 25–26) and there was certainly an Overseas Chinese solidarity in Thailand in which the "Ho" were included.

During the Cultural Revolution (1966–76) some Muslims from Dali and Mojiang escaped a dangerous situation and, following the old path of Muslim caravans, moved southwards to Simao and other places. Is there now a tendency to recreate links from Yunnan south to northern Thailand?

In the following paragraphs I explore the identity and economy of the Muslims in northern Thailand and their links with Yunnan; sources include those of my fieldwork (between 1986 and 1996) and others, such as the publicized court decisions in Yunnan, which give names and minority identifications.

YUNNAN AND FORMER CARAVANS

Steles, of interest for the early history of Islam in Yunnan, have largely disappeared or are illegible, but some are still existent inside the perimeter of Kunming's oldest mosque (in Zhengyi Road).

The first Muslims recorded in Yunnan came after the conquest of Dali in 1253 (Yang Zhaojun 1994, p. 7), and after the Islamization of Kunming and Weishan (the former Mangshi, southern principality of Nanzhao) in 1257. Kublai Khan appointed a Muslim governor, called the King of Xianyang in Chinese (Sayyid Ajali [Aijal] Omar Shams ud-Din in Arabic), who was born in Bukhara and buried in Songhuaba, north of Kunming (Yang Zhaojun 1994, p. 372). Although Guangdong and Fujian provinces had had an earlier maritime Muslim network, and although some Muslims in Yunnan suggest earlier contacts, this period was a turning point for the inland Islamic influence in south China and Southeast Asia, and according to our present knowledge there are no records available of earlier Islamic economic relationships between Yunnan and Siam.

In Chiang Mai, during the nineteenth and early twentieth centuries, the average economic impact of the former cross-border caravan trade was significant: during the winter and dry seasons, 700 to 1,000 laden mules came yearly from Yunnan (Forbes 1987, p. 18). Yunnan exported tea, opium, silk, iron, and lead bars, silver bullion, copper utensils and pans (from Sichuan), salt, jackets, and cloth. Yunnan and Keng Tung together imported cotton, ivory, gums, European goods, gold dust, and bird's nests (Forbes 1987, p. 22).

On the ancient caravan route from Kunming to Chiang Mai we see that a network of mosques, which often sat on dominant hills (Mojiang, Simao, Menghai), were the cultural and logistic anchorages along the route — that is, this network of mosques was not only religious but also economic. The starting points of the former cross-border trade towards Burma (now Myanmar) and Siam (now Thailand) were Dali and Kunming. In Dali there are three mosques, plus an old one in the modern city of Xiaguan (south of the Erhai Lake). Georges Cordier has pointed out that the number of mosques in the former Yunnanfu (now Kunming) was six; and in fact there were still six *qingzhenxi* in 1996 (Cordier 1927, pp. 112–17). These mosques in Yunnan province formerly had strong links with mainland Southeast Asia, and in particular with Chiang Mai, although at present they are no longer directly linked with north Thailand.

Other mosques located along the route were those at:

- Yuxi, an important Muslim centre situated 100 kilometres south of Kunming with old relationships as far as Guangzhou;
- Tonghai, a Muslim centre southwest of Yuxi, off the main caravan route to Chiang Mai but also significant;
- Mojiang, a centre of the Naqshabandiyya Sufi *Zhehelingye*, 100 kilometres northwest of Simao;
- Puer, 50 kilometres north of Simao, famous for its customs check-point and for the well-known Xishuangbanna tea, which bears its name;
- Simao (formerly [Da] Mengla; Ssu-mao), a former Dai market, now an administrative centre oriented towards the Mekong River;
- Menghai, unique in Yunnan as before 1950 the Muslims there were commonly fluent in Dai, Shan, Northern Thai, and Lao;
- Keng Tung, in the Shan states of Myanmar, a key city on the old caravan route to Tachilek and Mae Sai; and
- Chiang Rai, in northern Thailand, the last stage on the Yunnanese Muslim caravan route before Chiang Mai.

From Nan another road leads to Phrae and Uttaradit, with lesser and poorer villages off the main route.

In previous enquiries in central Yunnan, we interviewed Yunnanese Muslims who had formerly plied between the mosques of Keng Tung in Burma and Mojiang, where the mosque, and formerly a Sufi family, owned a small sandalwood forest. The tomb there, of Ma Mingxing's sister, is the centre of a local Muslim cult for a *Zhelingye* Sufi *menhuan* or branch (Jahariyya Sufism). Mojiang was linked to Keng Tung, and the sons of a related Yunnanese Imam in Keng Tung's *masjid* were *mafu* (guides of caravans). Dru Gladney insists on the cruciality of identity for this particular Banqiao Naqshabandiyya (Gladney 1996, p. 53), which contributes to explaining their former favourable trading network. These

Sufi Muslims were successfully plying with their mules[2] between Mojiang, Keng Tung, and Chiang Mai, until they became sedentary in the 1950s.

Opportunities for caravan trade, however, were not the only forces which brought Yunnanese Muslims to Southeast Asia. The "Panthay rebellion" and the Muslim state in Dali (1855–73) ended with the execution of the Muslim hero Du Wenxiu (Sultan Suleiman); afterwards, many of his supporters escaped to northern Burma. The beginning of the twentieth century witnessed the development of cross-border ties between these Muslims and their kin back in Yunnan.

Just after the turn of the century, the French (a Lyon-based company) built up the cross-border trade with a railroad; it was the first modern attempt to solve the problems associated with Yunnan's landlocked position. When the Kunming-Hanoi Railway was under construction, many interpreters were Yunnanese Muslims who had learnt French.

Following the establishment of the People's Republic of China (PRC) in 1950, there was a commercial decline along the caravan route, and Muslims in Yunnan became isolated from those in northern Thailand. The near-closure of the Yunnanese borders between 1950 and the 1980s allowed only one check-point between China and the bordering countries: Ruili was, for many years, the only customs and immigration point between Yunnan and Myanmar (and, indirectly, Thailand).

After the opening of China, mainly in the late 1980s, the traditional Muslim caravans from Kunming, Mojiang, and Keng Tung to Mae Sai and Chiang Mai were replaced by maritime trade through Beihai (which played the former role of Moulmein and Hanoi) and Bangkok. These modern relations disadvantaged the Muslims (Dobbin 1994, pp. 86, 97) and favoured Chinese companies (particularly those in Kunming and Jinghong), and also the rich Chaozhou merchants in Thailand who control the more highly capitalized trades.

In Kunming the Muslim bazaar of Shuncheng Jie, one of the oldest streets of Kunming, is at risk today from property development (including that of Han-Muslim companies), which has transformed a city of 1.5 million people (in 1986) into a modern metropolis of more than 3 million inhabitants.

In Jinghong (Cheli), formerly one of the main Dai economic centres on the caravan route, the impact of recent economic changes is also evident. During the economic reforms of the 1980s more and more Han came to reside in the Dai Autonomous Prefecture, and in the last ten years they have developed their own trading network and prosperous businesses, with boosts from Thai investments. The small airport of Simao was replaced by an international airport at Jinghong in the 1990s, during which period also the PRC opened the first regular flights to Thailand, Laos, and Vietnam.

Similarly, the former discreet influence of the Yunnanese Muslims in the cross-border trade between China and Vietnam is now non-extant; neither are Muslims involved in the entrenched drug trade between Myanmar, northern Thailand, and Yunnan.

ISLAM, IDENTITY, AND ECONOMIC CHANGE IN YUNNAN

There is no Muslim identity, and there are no Muslim economic relations, without a network of mosques or *qingzhensi*, a term which translates literally as "pure and true temples". Behind the concept of purity (*halâl* food is also called *qingzhen*), however, this term also demonstrates Sinicization, as its origin is neither Arabic nor Qur'anic (Broomhall 1987, p. 306).

Identity and purity are related, and purity is an important part of Islamic rituals, such as the Muslim ultra-purity of Ramadan and the Pilgrimage (Charnay 1994, p. 159). According to Dru Gladney, the question of purity becomes paramount in the context of an ethnic nationalism (Gladney 1996, p. 15) such as that of the "Panthay Rebellion" mentioned above, as well as when the "Hui" are exposed to different interpretations of Islam from the outside world (ibid., p. 59).

The influence of the economic opening of China and the creation of the so-called *shehuizhuyi shichang* (socialist market economy) on Yunnanese Muslim religio-cultural affairs through the Chinese Islamic Association, with which the maintenance of good relations is a *sine qua non* for combining economic success with Islamic revival, can be illustrated by the following example: in Ruili, the main inland commercial gate between Yunnan and Myanmar, a foreign Muslim became *imam* in 1992. This religious man is Arakanese; his sons and cousins are traders, and together they have built a typical cross-border relationship. This is a rare case of a foreigner taking advantage of the weakness and lack of diplomacy of a "Hui" predecessor and succeeding to responsibility for a Chinese mosque, where he could propagate his religious as well as economic ideas in a severely restricted national domain. During our different enquiries on Friday *jumma*, the mosque of Ruili was full and there were no "Hui" complaints concerning the *imam's* use of the Myanmar language or the announcements in Urdu. The "Hui" *guansi* (attendants of the mosque), who were linked to the Chinese Islamic Association, more or less accepted (formally, at least) the Arakanese network and its religious and trade connections with the Pakistani and Bangladeshi Islamic worlds. Yet our main informant in Chiang Mai, an *ahong* (from the Persian *akhun*, a "master" able to read Arabic and to comment on the Qur'an), gave his ideas concerning this action of the Chinese Islamic Association with a smile: "Well, you know, this association, like many other official institutions, has good and less good achievements."

In the 1980s the creation of a new mosque in Kunming fit the theory of a "Fourth Islamic tide" in the PRC (Gladney 1996, pp. 62–63).[3] A revival of Islam is currently noticeable in Yunnan and also in Chiang Mai,[4] but so far it does not seem to have a direct impact on the cross-border relations between China and the kingdom of Thailand.

CHIANG MAI

Chiang Mai is the end of the former main caravan route from Yunnan to Thailand. In the significant, new structural context of the old cross-border route which was created by the Deng Xiaoping reforms, what economic roles are Yunnanese Muslims playing in mainland Southeast Asia, and in particular in Chiang Mai?

At present, in Chiang Mai as in Bangkok and many other cities of Thailand, *chaozhou* (Teochiu) Chinese play a major role in the economy. In Chiang Mai, for example, they dominate the Chinese medicine sector. According to our fieldwork of December 1994, the products come through Bangkok rather than directly across the border from the great reservoir of Chinese medicine which is Yunnan. In Chiang Mai the products are rinsed very clean, losing a part of their Yunnanese qualities; they are very similar to Chinese medicinal products sold in Hong Kong and London, and of course in Bangkok.[5]

Tea, an important product of Yunnan, gives us an example of the relationships between trade, social change, and consumption (Berlie 1995). In 1895, Davies mentioned a trade of 900 tons, or 15,000 mule loads, in Simao (Forbes 1987, p. 23). In 1984, in the corresponding Xishuangbanna, the official production exceeded 3,000 tons[6] (Yang 1989, p. 62); but this production, because of the restrictions imposed on commercial cross-border relations between Yunnan and northern Thailand since 1950,[7] does not cross the border.

As do other Yunnanese, the Muslims in Yunnan drink green tea. In Chiang Mai, however, the *habitus* patterns of Yunnanese Muslims, because of their marriages with Thai young women, have come to reflect the former Muslim maritime trade (which gave the Fujian name *tee* [tea] to this beverage) instead of the traditional pre-1950s inland business relations with Yunnan. Thus, the Yunnanese Muslims in Chiang Mai currently do not drink tea from Yunnan but instead prefer Indian, Malay, or Thai black tea with milk. This acculturation in food habits shows a new modern Thai culture influenced by Indian and Pakistani Muslims, as opposed to a traditional Yunnanese Muslim culture.

Today, the largest Muslim community in Chiang Mai is under the supervision of a Chinese *ahong*, who holds the title of *imam*. In 1938 the first recorded *imam* was Ma Yuting, who was replaced in 1957 by Li Renfu (1957–77). The third *imam* was Yang Genhua (1977–84); he was followed by Haji Na Shunxing (1984–94), who was born in Tonghai in 1919.

In Chiang Mai there are four mosques, one of which has a Qur'anic school. The oldest mosque is called *qingzhen gusi* (the "Old and Pure Temple"). This old Yunnanese mosque was founded around 1915 by a rich Muslim from Yunnan surnamed Cheng (1871–1964), who also donated the land for the city's airport (Mote 1967, p. 491). He was knighted in Thailand and died in Mecca.[8]

The main mosque of Chiang Mai is very close to the night market (bazaar); and, in addition to the *qingzhen (halâl)* restaurants, the Yunnanese Muslims of Chiang Mai have some shops (for example, a precious-stone business called Omega, which deals in rubies, jades, and sapphires) close to the old mosque.

The second "Yunnanese" mosque of Chiang Mai was founded in 1950, partly for the numerous Muslims in the Kuomintang (*Guomindang*) armies, who built the small mosque of Mae Sai (where there are two Yunnanese Associations) after entering Thailand.

The third mosque was founded by the Moulmein community. This is not surprising, as Moulmein was the main harbour linked with Yunnan in the former caravan trade. In this mosque, the Bengali *imam* is like the majority of his followers, who can only speak Thai and Urdu because of the long acculturation of their ancestors in Burma, their country of origin.[9]

Also in Chiang Mai there is a Pakistani mosque and a recent *madrasah* (Islamic school), as there are a significant number of Urdu-speaking Muslims in Chiang Mai.

A DOUBLE IDENTITY: CHIANG MAI CASE STUDIES

It is the family which is the important institution within which we may identify the *dunya/guansi-renqing* (Islamic "terrestrial life"/Chinese "relationships and their ethics") of the Yunnanese Muslims. It seems that, for a Chinese Muslim, the bonds of reciprocity and mutual aid, based on familial and emotional attachments, imply a strong sense of obligation and indebtedness (Yang Mayfair Mei-hui 1994, p. 68). These personal relationships and networks of mutual dependence are part of the Chinese identity and, according to a Muslim Chinese informant, are more Chinese than Islamic.

IMAM NA AND HIS FAMILY

Following an old Muslim pattern, many male Yunnanese Muslims in Chiang Mai are married to Thai women who have converted to Islam. The new "double identity" of the "Hui" becoming "Ho" in Thailand is partly a consequence of the lack of communication between Yunnan and Chiang Mai between 1950 and 1980.

One example is Imam Na, born in Tonghai in 1919. He has his Yunnanese links with his elder brother's and sister's families in Xinping and Eshan and with his son's family in Kunming. The comradeship of Imam Na and three friends who entered Thailand together during the hardships at the end of World War II shows a Yunnanese Muslim identity, a Chinese ethics, and a Muslim identity through the community and the network of mosques. The four followed the pre-1950 route from Kunming through Simao, Jinghong, Menghai, Mengban, and Keng Tung to Mae Sai in 1946, from which a relative's truck took them to the Yunnanese mosque in Chiang Rai and then to Chiang Mai, where Imam Na now resides.

In 1955 Imam Na married his second wife, a Thai Muslim born in Chiang Mai — his first wife had remained in Kunming, where she died in 1980. Imam Na had five sons and two daughters by his second wife. In the second generation his younger, favourite daughter married a Yunnanese Muslim who, although born in Chiang Mai, was able to speak the Kunming dialect. Although this marital link demonstrates a preferred Yunnanese relationship and strengthens the "Ho" identity, the present second and third generations are Thai Muslim or Thai-Yunnanese Muslim and are more integrated into Thai society. After living many years in Thailand, these Muslims have a "double identity" — yet they are Muslim citizens of Thailand, and their sons and daughters and grandsons are more Thai than Yunnanese.

However, identity is never rigidly established, and the importance of the Yunnanese tradition was demonstrated by Imam Na in the role he played during a funerary ritual for the Yunnanese Muslim leader, Yuan Xinchang (1917–96), five days after his death, on 13 October 1996. Yuan had been a rich man; his two widows were present at the funeral.

Although Imam Na had given up his position as leader of the Yunnanese Muslim community in 1994 because of back problems and had been replaced by Ma Qinzheng, an *imam* in his mid-forties from Weishan and Mandalay, Haji Na's good knowledge of Chinese — of a quality difficult to find among the younger generations, who are primarily educated in Thai — as well as his integrity and the fact of his having made the pilgrimage to Mecca (in 1982), all continue to function to give him considerable credibility. At this ritual he participated jointly with the acting Imam Ma, who represents a modern and more "Thai" Islam.

PEARL DUCK AND HER SISTERS[10]

The father (died: 1982) of the five sisters was from Kunming. Although the cradle of our informant, Pearl Duck, born in 1929, was the Yunnanese tobacco capital of Yuxi in central Yunnan, Pearl Duck's parents had gone to Chiang Mai with their two eldest daughters (who died in 1990 and 1982, respectively) in 1928, just before the great economic crisis. We can imagine that, with five daughters, life was not easy.

In 1948 Pearl Duck, then nineteen, was married to a forty-three year-old Muslim from Kunming.[11] According to our informant, her husband was a very good man, and one can imagine the chaos in her heart when only twenty days after his death in 1982 her second eldest sister passed away.

In October 1996 Pearl Duck, her two daughters of ages forty-one and twenty-eight, and her youngest son of thirty-one were working in the same Muslim restaurant in Chiang Mai, close to the old mosque; while another — the elder daughter — was a nurse, and a daughter-in-law was a teacher in Chiang Mai. In Lampang, a son works in a bank. The eldest of Pearl Duck's sons has a son of twenty-one who is in the army (showing a "Thaization" of the family); and two daughters, sixteen and six years old. Pearl Duck's two elder sons are married, as are two daughters, the fourth daughter living in Virginia (United States) where her husband studied and later worked: his family name is Ma, a common Muslim surname. The modern Overseas Chinese pattern of migration is clearly indicated here and consequently minimizes the cross-border links with Yunnan.

These facts do not contradict the existence of the new "double identity" Hui/Ho, shaped by Thai culture and education, in the context of an original Yunnanese Muslim identity. As in the case of Imam Na's genealogy, a loose cultural link, without any commercial links, appears to exist between Yunnan and Chiang Mai. The professional activities show a tendency towards conservation of the Islamic faith (the *halâl* restaurant being a family source of income) but demonstrate no relationship with cousins in Yunnan: nevertheless, one of Pearl Duck's dreams is to return once to Yuxi, which she perceives to be her native town, to see her cousin Chen Zhongyi. Because the link between Thailand and Yunnan was cut in the 1950s we only know the name of this cousin. We will try to advertise the existence of Pearl Duck and her strong desire to return to Yuxi to see her cousin in the local newspapers in Yunnan.

INDICATIONS OF THE FUTURE

The current economic failure of the Muslim "Ho" is related to the closure of the borders for an extended period, but it is also caused by their lack of intergration into the modern Sino-Thai trading system, by their position outside the dominant Chaozhou business network and by competing Thai investments in Yunnan. Consequently, new Chinese trade networks between Yunnan and Thailand have replaced the ancient, traditional Muslim ones. Although Muslim trading delegations from the Middle East are often formally welcomed, with Chinese hospitality, in the main mosques of Kunming on Shuncheng Street, the numerous Thai delegations which have been coming since the 1980s are not Muslim: the first foreign bank to open a branch in Kunming is Thai. Landlocked Yunnan could be developed by the Myanmar, and/or may be developed by the Indian and Arakanese Muslims in Myanmar, but there seem to be few possibilities for development by Hui and Yunnanese Thai-Muslims (Ho). In similarly land-locked Laos, the Muslims of Vientiane, centred as they are on a single mosque, are too small a community to have much possibility of economic growth involving Yunnan, and are not likely to reactivate former relations with Muang Sing (where, currently, small-scale Han and Dai trade is taking place), Phongsaly (where there is a Chinese community), and Luang Prabang.

Relevant developments are occurring on the Chinese side of the frontier, however. Yunnanese businessmen who manage, after difficult administrative formalities, to obtain passports, are free to travel in Southeast Asia if they belong to registered, well-organized companies linked with the region. The booming tourist industry in China also tries to target Muslims in Yunnan, and the travel agencies, mainly governmental, advertise their tours to Bangkok and Chiang Mai in the main mosques. The current economic impact of these types of travel is not yet clear.

CONCLUSION

Yunnanese Muslims in northern Thailand have managed to retain their religion and, in part, their culture (in particular their Kunming dialect) in spite of the disruption in economic relations between Yunnan and northern Thailand between 1950 and 1980. Yet in Chiang Mai, the network of mosques, which plays an economic role, is becoming more Thai-Muslim and Pakistani than Yunnanese, and the lack of present significant cross-border trade links with Yunnan is clear. As a result, the cultural and economic system of the Yunnanese Muslims, under the combined pressures of a globalized economy, the Thai Buddhist national education system, and an internationally double-sided aspect to Islamic revival, is at risk.

ACKNOWLEDGEMENTS

Our special thanks goes to our informants in the different communities where we carried out our research, and we also thank Professor Donald C. Baker and Dr G. Wade for their precious comments. I assume full responsibility for the content of this account.

NOTES

1. Mote defines the "Ho" (also written Haw, Hor, or Chin-Ho) as: representatives of a "High Culture", relatively prosperous for a short time, who are remnants of a civil war and who might contribute to the modernization of other peoples in north

Thailand (Mote 1967, pp. 487–89). "Hui" is one of the fifty-five rigidly limited names for minorities in China. In this article "Hui" in China and "Ho" in Thailand are originally the same Muslim group now living in two different countries. Chinese words and names are transliterated in *pinyin* in this article; personal names mentioned are protected.

2. The Muslim muleteers were sometimes associated with Yi (ex-Lolo), who currently use mules to reach their isolated villages; and also with Dai, which explains the existence of a mosque in Menghai. The pack-saddles used were typically Yunnanese: they had four feet for stability on the ground after being released from the backs of the mules (the best animals for these caravans), ponies, or slow-humped oxen. The Yi, Lisu, and Bai minorities in Yunnan, and the Yunnanese in Myanmar enlisted in the different armies in the Golden Triangle region, currently use these extremely convenient pack-saddles.

3. In the 1920s, according to Cordier, the average annual number of *haj* pilgrims from China was twenty (twenty-three in 1923); these included five or six from Yunnan, who travelled via Burma or Hanoi. After 1987 the number increased to more than 2,000, and we are now close to a figure of 6,000.

4. In November 1996 the election of Wan Mohamad Nor Matha (New Aspiration Party) as the Speaker of the Thai Parliament, the first Muslim to have such a high post, demonstrates both the long tradition of religious tolerance in Thailand and a certain Islamic revival.

5. In modern Kunming itself, Western medicine seems to be preferred. This whole subject invites medical-anthropological enquiry among Thai-Yunnanese Muslims.

6. Or 62,500 *dan*; the *dan* is a unit of 50 kilograms.

7. Concerning which there is some evidence of slow progress in the frequent international talks on the Mekong River, the "Asian Danube" (the author attended the two related international conferences in Kunming in 1994).

8. According to a Yunnanese informant in Hong Kong who had stayed in northern Thailand for five years, there are other rich "Ho" in Chiang Mai (and in Chiang Rai, where there are two mosques as well), showing the importance of the former trade and their connections with the "Yunnanese Associations" in northern Thailand.

9. In Myanmar, Hindustani (a spoken language in between Hindi and Urdu) is currently the second language, after the official Myanmar language.

10. Their surname, Chen, is Chinese; "Pearl Duck" is an English translation of the informant's Thai nickname.

11. We do not know if he left a first wife in Kunming, but his sister still lives there.

REFERENCES

Berlie, Jean. "Le thé: son hypothétique origine chez les Hani et sa préparation chez les

Bulang du Yunnan" [Tea: Its possible Hani origin and village manufacturing among the Bulang, in Yunnan]. *Journal d'agriculture tropicale et de botanique appliquée* (Paris) 37, no. 2 (1995): 115–28.

_____ . "Sinisation: A la limite de trois provinces de Chine, une minorité qui devient chinoise" [Sinicization: A minority becoming Han-Chinese in Hunan, Guizhou, and Guangxi]. Mimeographed. 1996.

Broomhall, Marshall. *Islam in China: A Neglected Problem.* 1st edition. London: Darf Publishers, 1987.

Charney, Jean-Paul. *Sociologie religieuse de l'Islam* [A sociology of Islam]. Paris: Hachette, 1994.

Cordier, Georges. *Les Musulmans du Yunnan.* Hanoi: Imprimerie Tonkinoise, 1927.

Couling, Samuel. *The Encyclopaedia Sinica.* London: Oxford University Press, 1917.

Dobbin, Christine. "Accounting for the Failure of the Muslim Javanese Business Class: Examples from Ponorogo and Tulungagung (c. 1880-1940)". *Archipel* 48 (1994): 87–101.

Forbes, Andrew D.W. "The "Cin-Ho" (Yunnanese Chinese) Caravan Trade with North Thailand during the Late Nineteenth and Early Twentieth Centuries". *Journal of Asian History* 21, no. 1 (1987): 1–47.

Gladney, Dru C. *Muslim Chinese: Ethnic Nationalism in the People's Republic.* 1st. ed. 1991. Cambridge, Massachusetts, and London: Harvard University Press, 1996.

Mote, F. W. "The Rural "Haw" (Yunnanese Chinese) of Northern Thailand". In *Southeast Asian Tribes, Minorities, and Nations*, edited by Peter Kunstadter, pp. 487–524. New Jersey: Princeton University Press, 1967.

Yang Mayfair Mei-hui. *Gifts, Favors, and Banquets: The Art of Social Relationships in China.* Ithaca and London: Cornell University Press, 1994.

Yang Yucai. *Yunnan Geminzu Jingji Fazhanshi* [A history of the economic development of different minorities in Yunnan province]. Kunming: Minorities Press, 1989.

Yang Zhaojun et al., eds. *Yunnan Huizu Lishi* [A history of the Hui in Yunnan]. Kunming: Yunnan's National Minorities Press, 1994.

Yang Zhijiu. "Yuandaide Huihuiren" [The Hui-Yuan dynasty]. *Zhongguo Huizu Yanjiu* [Studies on the Hui nationality, Ningxia] 1 June 1991, pp. 11–18.

Trade Activities of the Hoa along the Sino-Vietnamese Border

Chau Thi Hai

Since the opening of the border at the end of the 1980s, diplomatic relations between Vietnam and China have improved and Sino-Vietnamese trade in the border regions has gained momentum. This chapter will explore how the Hoa (ethnic Chinese in Vietnam) use their social and economic networks to further their trading activities along the border. It will also discuss the reasons for their success.

The Hoa have many advantages in trading which other groups lack. Their main advantage is their networks, which have made it easier for them to mobilize capital and to gain access to the sources of goods, and to the transfer of technology. The strength of these networks has given the Hoa community a high degree of competitiveness in terms of capital, technology, prices, and product quality — not only in the border area but also throughout the country and elsewhere in Southeast Asia. This fact helps to explain why the Hoa have risen so rapidly, and why they have proved themselves to be among the region's top businesspeople.

THE HOA IN VIETNAM

The Hoa (*nguoi Hoa*) are the ethnic Chinese who have settled in Vietnam. They are one of the fifty-four ethnic groups, and are Vietnamese citizens with full citizenship rights. However, through their language and their customs they are distinguishable from the ethnic Vietnamese, the Kinh, and other ethnic groups. In towns and cities inhabited by the Hoa, they have established Chinese-language teaching centres, especially in the southern part of Vietnam. The Chinese language is also often taught in the families. They also observe Chinese customs and worship Chinese gods.[1]

Besides the Hoa, there is also a small group called Hoa Kieu (literally "Overseas Chinese") residing in Vietnam. They are citizens of China, Taiwan, Hong Kong, or Macau whose primary objective in Vietnam is trading and business.

The Hoa do not represent a large segment of the population. There are about 1 million Hoa, which is less than 1 per cent of Vietnam's total population of 75 million people. Eighty-five per cent of the Hoa live in the southern provinces, notably in Ho Chi Minh City and in the towns of Dong Nai, Soc Trang, Can Tho, Kien Giang, Minh Hai, and An Giang, while in North Vietnam, there is another 15 per cent. They live mainly in the cities of Haiphong and Hanoi and only a few thousand of them live in the border region (Chau 1992, pp. 44–45).

HISTORICAL BACKGROUND

Vietnam and China have a 1,347-kilometre-long shared border, linking the two Chinese provinces of Guangxi and Yunnan to six of Vietnam's northern border provinces. The various ethnic groups who live on both sides of the frontier have long-standing ties and share many cultural traits. They often understand each other's languages and many of them enjoy ties of kinship and friendship, all of which facilitates cross-border trade.

The border crossings of Dongxing–Mong Cai, Pingxiang–Dong Dang, and Hekou–Lao Cai serve as links between southern China and the commercial centres of Vietnam. The advantages of border trade have always constituted an important element in the external economic policy of the Chinese government.

When the People's Republic of China (PRC) achieved independence in 1949, one of its first priorities in establishing diplomatic ties with Vietnam was bilateral trade. An initial protocol concerning this issue was signed in April 1952, followed in 1955 and 1957 by protocols on "Small-scale border trade between China and Vietnam", "Exchange of goods between Vietnam and China", "Exchange of goods between local state-owned trading enterprises along the border", and "Measures to regulate small-scale trade along the Sino-Vietnamese border". The main objective of these agreements was to permit markets located on both sides of the border to operate. Each country established twenty-six trading posts, nineteen of which were for overland trade and seven for coastal trade. In addition, trading posts outside the jurisdiction of these twenty-six sites were allowed to continue operations.

Sino-Vietnamese border trade was most vigorous during the period between 1956 and 1969, benefiting from the participation of many different ethnic groups. When the borders were first opened, the value of trade was tens of thousands of renminbi and by the end of the 1960s it had risen to millions of renminbi. During the late 1970s, trade and other ties, however, were disrupted for a long time. Relations between the two countries were poor, especially after the border conflict broke out on 17 February 1979.

The attack by Chinese forces on Vietnam's six northern border provinces in 1979 destroyed 330 villages, 735 schools, 428 hospitals and clinics, 41 farms, 38 tree farms, 81 industries and mines, and 80,000 hectares of food and other agricultural crops. Roughly half of the 3.5 million inhabitants of these provinces lost their homes, and thousands of Vietnamese lost their lives. Three provincial capitals (Lao Cai, Cao Bang, and Lang Son) and a district capital (Cam Duong in Lao Cai) were also completely destroyed. All activities along the border came to a halt as people had to flee the area. This situation lasted until the end of the 1980s (Nguyen and Vu 1996, p. 89).

In 1986, when Vietnam had just emerged from the "subsidy period" (that is, the centrally planned economy), the Vietnamese people were "starving" for goods. Meanwhile, China had a surplus of consumer goods, produced by "township enterprises" that tried to get their products into the markets of neighbouring countries such as the Lao People's Democratic Republic (PDR), Myanmar, Pakistan, India, and Russia — and, particularly, into Vietnam. But at the time an official agreement between Hanoi and Beijing concerning border trade had not yet been signed. In Vietnam, border activities were mainly regulated by Communiquè 118-TB/TW from the Party Secretariat, dated 19 November 1988, which allowed the people in villages directly adjoining the frontier to travel back and forth in order to visit relatives and to exchange goods. Residents of other areas were not granted this privilege.

Between 1985 and 1987, before the release of Communiquè 118, border trade was forbidden. Nevertheless, due to the demands of the local people, Chinese goods managed to slip into the Vietnamese market through border points such as Kho Da, Boundary Marker 16, and Tan Thanh (in Cao Loc district of Lang Son province), through Lung Vai, Muong Khuong, and Ban Lau (in Lao Cai province), and through Hoanh Mo and Po Hen (in Quang Ninh province). The local name for these goods was *hang tam ly* ("mental" or "psychological goods" — in other words, smuggled goods).

NORMALIZATION OF SINO-VIETNAMESE RELATIONS

In September 1990, Secretary Linh, former Premier Pham Van Dong and the Council of Ministers' Chairman Do Muoi held talks with Jiang Zemin, then General Secretary of the Chinese Communist Party, and Premier Li Peng, in Chengdu, Sichuan. The summit led to an improvement of bilateral ties (*Vietnam News Agency*, 15 October 1990), resulting in the normalization of Sino-Vietnamese relations. In November 1991, at the invitation of Jiang and Li, a high-level Vietnamese government delegation, led by Do Muoi (now Party General Secretary) and Vo Van Kiet (who succeeded Do as Chairman of the Council of Ministers), paid an official visit to the PRC. In their communiqué, the two sides affirmed that "[we] are pleased at the gradual improvement and development of relations between our two countries". They stated that Vietnam and China would develop close and friendly neighbourly ties based on five principles: "respect for each other's sovereignty and territorial integrity, non-aggression, non-interference in each other's internal affairs, equality of interests, and peaceful co-existence" (*Nhan Dan*, 6 November 1991).

A Trade Agreement was signed on 7 November 1991, and following that, provincial authorities from both countries met frequently. Talks between a delegation from the Guangxi Zhuang Autonomous Region and a delegation from the three border provinces of Lang Son, Cao Bang, and Quang Ninh, and from the Municipality of Haiphong, led to an agreement suggesting that "each government open twenty-five markets at border crossing points for border residents" and that non-state-owned companies and "other economic entities" be allowed to become involved in cross-border trade. "Other economic entities" refers to different ethnic groups which conducted private economic activities.

As a follow-up, Li Peng paid a visit to Vietnam in October 1992. Commenting on the significance of the normalization of relations, Jiang Zemin observed that "After a period of twists and turns, the high-level meetings between China and Vietnam play a very important role in closing the book on the past and opening a new chapter for the future. These meetings will have a profound influence on the long-term bilateral relations between our countries (*Quan Doi Nhan Dan*, 11 November 1991).

Between 1990 and 1992, the Council of Ministers in Hanoi promulgated a number of directives setting down the rights and responsibilities of the people engaged in border trade. Directives for the organization of currency exchange, exchange rates, and for border control were also issued. The Council also worked to implement agreements on various other border issues such as commercial activities; communication by air, sea, or land; telecommunications; and scientific, technological, and other forms of co-operation; as well as the establishment of consular operations. One significant policy, relating to the organization and management of border trade, was passed on 25 March 1992 and followed on 27 March by a permission to open twenty-one border crossing points (see Appendix Table 12.1).

The normalization of Sino-Vietnamese relations through the protocols signed between the two nations, together with the specific directives from the Council of Ministers regulating the opening of border crossing points, has encouraged the revival of border trade. What were "ghost town" areas along the frontier between 1979 and 1985 gradually became bustling markets during the late 1980s and early 1990s, attracting many different ethnic groups. Of these, the Hoa have been the most significant as far as business activities are concerned.

CROSS-BORDER TRADE BY THE HOA

Once the military activities ceased along the borders in the mid-1980s, and particularly after the normalization of Sino-Vietnamese relations, the Hoa were allowed to return to their former homes and could begin to stabilize their lives in various ways. Trade activities were one of the principal means of doing so. They began by re-establishing contacts with relatives, who had left during 1978–79 and who now lived in China or in a third country. Through these contacts they could get capital and also information about the needs of the market on both sides of the boundary line.

After the 1991 trade treaty and other agreements had been made between national and provincial authorities in Vietnam and China, trade evolved very quickly and spread beyond the actual border area. At this stage, it was spontaneous and guided by the laws of supply and demand. There were no official regulations, and signed contracts were mostly based on good faith. These conditions favoured the Hoa more than other groups, since they were fluent in both Vietnamese and in the local Chinese dialects of the southern provinces. They were also familiar with the maze of routes back and forth across the frontier. It was easy for them to find partners and to earn people's trust and they were consequently in a good position to serve as middlemen, interpreters, guides, contractors, and agents, as well as to handle the transportation of goods.

MONG CAI AND OTHER MARKETS

Among the border markets, Mong Cai, in Quang Ninh province, is the site where most of the Hoa and the Chinese, including the Hoa returnees from the PRC,[2] are engaged in trading activities. Because of its key location in the Dongxing–Mong Cai inter-market system, Mong Cai has become the only market that draws businesspeople from all over China.[3] Every day hundreds of people cross the bridge with their border passes, and some of them actually live at the market for a period of time. Not counting tourists and people who come in search of business partners, there are four or five hundred people who, every day, bring goods from China to sell in Mong Cai. They get off the boat at the Ka Long landing, shouldering heavy baskets full of goods from different parts of China, and then queue up to buy tickets to enter the market.

There are about 1,200 businesses in the Mong Cai market. Out of these, more than 300 stalls are run by people from China, who some days earn up to 30,000 to 50,000 renminbi.[4] The market is also a gathering place for people from twenty-one different Vietnamese provinces, and trade goes on non-stop day and night, with large quantities of goods for sale.

Small-scale trading represents the most common form of cross-border commerce. All sorts of building materials, different kinds of machinery and spare parts, chemicals used in farming, medicine, ready-made clothing and sewing materials, foodstuffs including sugar and monosodium glutamate (MSG), household items and many other consumer goods are brought in from China by the Hoa. Goods purchased on the Vietnamese side include items such as rice, cashew nuts, rubber, crude oil, coal, iron and steel, rattan products, tea, fruits (green bananas, mangoes, lychees, longans), wood, spices, handicrafts, medicine, and seafood. The Hoa also trade in rare animals such as snakes, golden turtles, golden monkeys, pangolins, tortoises, and sea-horses.

In addition to products that are brought for direct retail sale in the market, a huge volume of wares is passed along through channels which run deep into both Vietnam and the PRC. Mong Cai is a typical example of the cross-border market known as "one market, two countries" (*nhat thi luong quoc*; Chinese: *yi shi liang guo*).

Along the frontier there are many other similar markets, such as the "Vietnamese" market in Hekou (in Yunnan province), Muong Khuong (in Lao Cai province), and Tra Linh (in Cao Bang province). None of these places, however, are as nice, clean, and modern as Mong Cai, nor do they attract as many Chinese traders from across the border. Dong Dang is another lively border market, which links the commercial area of Pingxiang with Lang Son. Unlike the Mong Cai market, the main role of the Dong Dang market is to transport goods, an activity in which the Hoa are actively involved.

SMUGGLING: THE EXAMPLE OF THE AUTOMOBILE "CAMPAIGN"

The geography of each province facilitates different forms of trade. When, for example, the provinces of Cao Bang and Lang Son are mentioned, the first thing one immediately thinks of is the cross-border automobile "campaign" in 1990–91. This "campaign" became even more aggressive in 1992 and the first half of 1993. What happened was that, by night, group after group of cars bearing false registration plates were driven to gathering points in the markets of Tra Linh (in Cao Bang province) and Dong Dang (in Lang Son province). The Hoa played an important role in this, as many of them acted as middlemen in the bargaining between the Chinese (*nguoi Trung Hoa*) and Vietnamese merchants.

At this time Vietnam was not producing automobiles but was nevertheless able to "export" many cars to China. How was this possible? To answer this question, we must follow the tracks of these Toyotas, Nissans, Hondas, Mercedes, and Peugeots from their gathering points to the border markets. The decision made by the government of the PRC to assign preferential tariff rates to goods imported from Vietnam had a significant effect on the border trade. The tariff was reduced from 30 to 15 per cent. This policy made it very lucrative for car dealers in China to sign contracts directly with their counterparts in Hong Kong and Taiwan involving transshipment through Vietnam. Each group of cars that crossed the Lao-Vietnamese or Lao-Cambodian borders originally came from Taiwan, Thailand, or Hong Kong and then passed through a border crossing point along the Sino-Vietnamese border or through the ports of Haiphong or Quang Ninh. Thanks to a bit of "tipping", the cars would slip past the customs posts and would then arrive safe and sound at the border markets. From there the latest models of Japanese, German, and French cars would reach the hands of traders in China and penetrate deep into the Chinese markets (Bui 1992).

A point worth mentioning here is the fact that no matter which border crossing these cars passed through, they were all controlled by the Chinese. Consequently, these transshipments represented a tremendous loss of foreign exchange to the Vietnamese government. The amount of dollars needed to move so many cars across the border during the first six months of 1992 alone was more than twice the sum of overseas capital invested in six fisheries and banking projects. The ones getting rich were individual businessmen and companies that were specializing in the transfer service of automobiles (Bui 1992).

These vehicles are used for business purposes — to transport goods from collection and distribution points into the Vietnamese market, to and from places as far away as Ho Chi Minh City. Goods are also gradually beginning to be moved further into China, as far away as Beijing. In Lang Son province, approximately 10 per cent of Hoa enterprises have their own vehicles. Some families have four or five trucks, such as the families of Mr Liu, Mr He, Mr Quan, and Mr Hwang (see below). Each son of a rich Hoa family usually has his own truck.

Field research carried out among the Hoa in the border market town Dong Dang in Lang Son province shows that there are a number of families (who will remain anonymous) whose business activities run into the tens of billions of dong (that is, millions of U.S. dollars).[5]

FINANCE AND BANKING

Currency exchange activities are widespread along the border and constitute an important form of trade which has attracted various ethnic groups. The Hoa played a significant role in this, especially in the early stages when the Vietnamese and other ethnic groups were still rather baffled by the market economy and were unable to find partners. Many kinds of currency are being exchanged. The money is kept in bags or baskets or, where things are more organized, in iron boxes inside exchange booths, for example, in the market at Mong Cai. Money-changers have access to telephones and can therefore find out the daily exchange rates. An average of two to three hundred million dong (US$20,000 to US$30,000) changes hands daily, and some days this figure reaches four to five hundred million dong.[6] These transactions have to a large extent facilitated the movement of goods by traders, but they have also caused the State Bank many headaches in its attempts to regulate the money flow — especially that of counterfeit currency — in the border area.

In the more formal financial and banking sector, also, currency activities have extended as far as the border provinces. Hoa-owned banks in Ho Chi Minh City are gradually opening branches in towns along the border. In early 1995, for instance, a branch of the Viet-Hoa Bank was opened in the border crossing town of Mong Cai. In Lang Son province, there is an office of the Que Do Company which belongs to the Hoa Association and which functions as an intermediary, moving currency between the Que Do Bank in Ho Chi Minh City and Hoa businessmen in Lang Son province. Funds are transferred from branches of the State Bank of China, particularly from those in the south, to the State Bank of Vietnam, and then to Chinese banks in Ho Chi Minh City such as Que Do, Viet Hoa, Phuong Nam, De Nhat, and Dong A. From there the money goes to Hoa businesses around the country.[7] These financial transactions are linked to remittances sent to the Hoa by their relatives overseas, as discussed below.

Quite a number of joint ventures are active in Lang Son province and operate mainly in the service sector, especially as restaurants and hotels, as these businesses can make quick profits and need little start-up capital and are also less vulnerable to problems in the border zone. In fact, almost all of the companies, including the joint ventures, run restaurants and hotels. Examples include the Loi Lai Hotel in Mong Cai town (a joint venture between Hong Kong and Vietnam), the Kim Son and Thanh Tung Hotels, and the A Chau Restaurant (joint ventures with the Nanfang Company of Guangxi province), and the Thai Binh Duong Restaurant (run by the Vietnamese Lang Son provincial labour union with Chinese partners).[8]

In the border provinces, particularly in Lang Son, there are a number of investments in the name of individuals from Hong Kong and Macao who are actually fronting for people in China. Other projects are registered in the name of Vietnamese investors but are really joint ventures between Hoa in Vietnam (including returnees from China) and Hoa elsewhere. Consequently, it is difficult to measure with any kind of accuracy the size and proportion of businesses that are Hoa or to determine their economic positions compared with those of other ethnic groups involved in border trade.

SOCIAL AND ECONOMIC NETWORKS OF THE HOA

Working through links based on family and clan ties, the Hoa carry out trade on a "buy now, pay later" basis, which means that the amount of "start-up capital" required is not large — anyone can engage in trade. For this reason, the Hoa are able to accumulate capital faster than other ethnic groups and, following the signing of the bilateral trade agreement in 1991, many of them have moved up to large-scale business activities like contracting, acting as sales agents, and transporting goods.[9]

The Hoa rely on networks of acquaintances and on "trust" to recruit and use squads of porters to carry the goods across the border to places from where they will be sent off along distribution routes, which are also based on their networks of relationships. This goes on day and night, especially in the border provinces of Quang Ninh, Lang Son, and Cao Bang. One such route runs overland from the border crossing point of Dongxing–Mong Cai down to the cities of Haiphong and Hanoi and continues further south. Another route stretches from the Pingxiang–Dong Dang border crossing point in Lang Son province through to the cities of Ha Bac and Hanoi, continuing further south. A third route goes from the border crossing point of Hekou in Yunnan province through Lao Cai province to Hanoi via Vinh Phu province and the city of Viet Tri, and then also heads south.

The Hoa networks of relatives encompass almost every city and province in Vietnam, as well as many areas on the Chinese side of the border. Most of the Hoa who went back to China in 1978–79 live in Guangxi and Guangdong provinces, and a few also live in Hainan and other provinces. Out of the 200,000 in Guangxi province, a few thousand are living in the town of Pingxiang. Because this is a border crossing point, the Hoa there have been given preferential treatment by the Chinese government in order to encourage their involvement in trade, and are, for example, given an 8 per cent reduction in taxes. Those with special expertise and a high level of education are particularly favoured and often employed by companies (Do 1995).

The following examples from Pingxiang represent only a few typical cases of business networks:

Wei Zhengqing is a former instructor at Vietnam's Foreign Trade University. He returned to China in 1978–79, and is now the Head of the "Association of Overseas Chinese"[10] (*Hoi Kieu Lien*; Putonghua: *Qiaolianhui*) in Pingxiang. Wei is also the Director of the town's Border Trade Company. His son, Wei Zhenxing, is the Office Head of the People's Committee in Pingxiang Town. Since the normalization of Sino-Vietnamese relations, Wei has also made numerous trips to Vietnam to seek out business partners.

Li Xinhua is a second example. Li formerly taught at the University of Hanoi and, after going to China, at Xinan University. His father is a former Vietnamese Vice-Minister of Foreign Trade. Although Li is now retired, he acts as a go-between for Vietnamese-Chinese businesses, supplying them with up-to-date information through his network of relatives and old friends. He is also doing business with his younger brother who is living in Vietnam.

The Hoa have a particular talent for developing "symbiotic" relationships with local authorities, so that all of their operations run smoothly. Making such symbiotic ties is a traditional skill of the Hoa; they are quite easy to make in the border area, since a number of those who left in the late 1970s had formerly worked in the Vietnamese government. As mentioned above, there were even individuals who had held important posts and who therefore still had ties [in Vietnam] when they returned to look for business partners.

Hoa business networks enable the Hoa to act as agents for Hoa-run companies in large cities such as Ho Chi Minh City, Hanoi, and Haiphong. For example, the Binh Tien Plastics Company of Duc Khai Thanh (De Kaicheng) in Ho Chi Minh City has 200 representatives throughout Vietnam. Its activities stretch to the Chinese border and even beyond, to locations such as Dongxing, Fengcheng, and Pingxiang in Guangxi, and Hekou in Yunnan. In 1995, the Binh Tien Plastics Company was able to send 80,000 pairs of sandals to China to test the market, thanks to a network based on kinship and other ties (Vietnam News Agency, 2 May 1996).

REASONS FOR THE HOA'S SUCCESS

How have the Hoa been able to become so rich so fast? The most obvious factor is their ties with relatives in other countries such as Britain, the United States, Canada, Australia, Germany, Hong Kong, and Taiwan. Each year the Hoa receive funds through postal money orders or through visits from those who have emigrated — money and gifts totalling approximately 10 million dong (US$1,000) a year.[11] Through the exchange of "psychological" (smuggled) goods between 1986 and 1990, they were also able to get some money and have thus amassed enough funds to successfully engage in various kinds of trade during the open-door period.

Li, Mo, Wu, and Liu are typical examples of wealthy Hoa businessmen in Lang Son. They have been able to make fortunes quickly through financial remittances from relatives in other countries and through the business channels constituted by these relationships. The strength of these networks has given the Hoa community a high degree of competitiveness in terms of capital, technology, prices, and product quality — not only in the border areas but throughout the country and elsewhere in Southeast Asia.

Another asset of the Hoa is their ability to organize small-scale business through family and clan ties. Production through these relations is seen as the foundation of initiating business activities. Hoa are thus able to draw on the funds and other resources of close relatives at a stage when they are not yet in a position to operate independently. A number of Hoa in Lang Son and Quang Ninh have enjoyed rapid business successes in this way.

A third factor in the Hoa success is their preservation of "trust" and "reliability" (*tin*; Putonghua: *xin*) in their business activities. They see this as a strategy as well as one of their traditional cultural values. Trust has generated mutual respect in verbal agreements and written contracts — including secret ones during the period when China and Vietnam had yet to normalize relations and when there were no official regulations governing border commerce.

Although Hoa trading associations have yet to be organized in the border areas, networks of business relationships have formed naturally, according to unofficially agreed-upon rules. Before becoming members of a "business network", Hoa business people must go through a probation period and must be sponsored by an individual who has a good reputation and also experience within the network. Any member who is guilty of acting in bad faith will be reprimanded and possibly expelled from the business community.

In addition, regular links between the Association of Overseas Chinese (*Hoi Kieu Lien*)[12] and the Hoa in the border provinces constitute an important advantage enabling the Hoa to guide Chinese business delegations crossing the border into Vietnam. At the same time they supply the delegations with new trading partners and thus new channels for trade.

The fourth secret of the Hoa success is their ability to provide credit. Unlike persons from Western industrialized countries, the Hoa place great emphasis on sources of credit within the family and clan, weighing "trust" in relationships more heavily than administrative procedures, and this helped them to handle trans-border contracts quickly when there were no legal regulations. Even now that such regulations do exist, relations based on trust are more effective and efficient. As a result, in addition to the banking system there is also a system of borrowing and lending through various kinds of credit organizations (*hoi*; Putonghua: *hui*) and "same-year organizations" (*to chuc dong nien*; Putonghua: *tongnian zuzhi*), known in the local dialect as "Ten Sisters" (*xap chia muoi*, Putonghua: *shi jiemei*) or "Ten Brothers" (*xap hinh tay*; Putonghua: *shi xiongdi*). Such organizations, though informal, operate efficiently and enable their members to borrow money from each other, as well as to gain business experience, and to share useful information.

It should also be pointed out that the Hoa are diligent, enthusiastic, and determined and ready to take any risk in their business activities. This is because they believe that poverty and the lack of an opportunity for education will cause their cultural values to decline. Put more simply: they affirm that, for them, there is no other option except to work hard and efficiently.

The Hoa are also able to adjust and adapt to changes in society. They have found ways to make themselves more up-to-date and to maximize the advantages of their own cultural traits, which have helped them to modernize their thinking. Since almost all of the Hoa living along the Sino-Vietnamese border were raised under the old centrally planned subsidy economy, they are not veteran business people, having only emerged during the open-door period. Once the transition towards a market economy with a socialist orientation began, the Hoa were more effective than anyone else in accepting it. They have been able to respond quickly to the needs and tastes of the market, to grasp the pricing system, and to gain rapid access to modern science and technology.

OVERALL IMPACT

The Hoa commercial activities, like border trade in general, have had a significant effect on cultural, economic, and social exchange between Vietnam and China. The Vietnamese have a saying: "Without trade one cannot be wealthy" (*Phi thuong bat phu*; Putonghua: *Fei shang bu fu*).

Before 1989, life in the border areas was very hard and almost everyone was self-sufficient. Now nearly 90 per cent of the population in Dong Dang and Mong Cai, for example, are by contrast dependent on border trade for a living.[13]

Gross domestic product (GDP) in the northern border provinces has increased on average by 7 to 8 per cent annually since 1991. In Quang Ninh province it has grown from 10 to 12 per cent and is expected to reach 15 per cent in the future. Taxation of cross-border trade accounts for 30 per cent of the total revenue in the border provinces; in the Mong Cai area, export and import duties rose from 11.3 billion dong (US$1.13 million) in 1990 to 100 billion (US$10 million) in 1996 (Quy 1997). Such revenue has made Quang Ninh the only border province to have shifted from chronic budget deficits during the closed-door period to a surplus following normalization.[14]

Lang Son has also enjoyed a rapid rate of development thanks to income from border trade. Research by the Institute of Economics and Development in Hanoi shows that there were more than one hundred families in the province who in 1995 were U.S. dollar millionaires, many of them having accumulated tens of billions of dong. Approximately 150 households had from one to three private vehicles, and more than twenty businesses had prospered through joint ventures and links to overseas capital, including to businessmen in China.[15]

Along with economic development, infrastructural modernization has taken place in the towns along the border. The life of the people in the area has improved, and in particular the standard of living of the Hoa has risen a hundred-fold compared with what it was after the conflict in 1979. For 70 per cent of the Hoa population it has reached an average level, and about 30 per cent of the Hoa population are rich.[16] This percentage is higher than that of other groups, including the ethnic Vietnamese themselves. Houses have sprung up everywhere, and most of them are three or four storeys high. All of the town-dwellers and more than 30 per cent of the rural population have electricity and clean water.[17] In the past, towns such as Mong Cai, Lang Son, Dong Dang, and Lao Cai did not have electricity or running water and were even deserted during 1979–80. Now, they are commercial centres. Since normalization, Quang Ninh, Lang Son, and Lao Cai provinces have used hundreds of billions of dong to build roads, schools, and hospitals, the money coming from the taxation of cross-border trade.

For example, Hai Ninh District in Quang Ninh province, poor until 1989, has in recent years become one of the richest districts in Vietnam. Hai Ninh has a population of 40,000. While Hai Ninh in the past had few motorized vehicles it now has about 4,000 Honda motorbikes, 160 cars, and almost 700 motorboats. Furthermore, 95 per cent of the households have radios. The district has also spent 20 billion dong, gained from the taxation of cross-border trade, to build roads (Tran 1994, pp. 26–27).

The border provinces are now linked to an international telecommunications network, and transportation in general has been improved locally as well as between the two countries. In 1993 and 1994 several bridges were opened, linking Vietnam to southwestern China: the two Ho Kieu [Huqiao] bridges between Hekou and Lao Cai and the Bac Luan [*Beilun*] bridge connecting Dongxing and Mong Cai. A railway service from Hanoi to Beijing and to Kunming was inaugurated in February 1996.

Trade has also brought along cultural exchange across the borders. Traditional festivals such as the Lion Dance of the Hoa and the "Down to the Fields" of the Dao, Tay, Nung, and Giay ethnic groups have, for example, been exchanged. Recordings and videos of the music of the Dao, Tay, Nung, and Hmong minorities have reached villages throughout the region, while at the same time the Hmong, Yao, Tay, and Nung people sing along to Chinese music recordings. In short, these new forms of cultural exchange have served to strengthen the already close ties between the various border peoples.

Border trade has, however, also brought with it social, economic, and cultural problems such as gambling, opium addiction, smuggling, trade in women and children, the spread of disease, and the destruction of the environment. The ever-increasing waves of people pouring into the area from both Vietnam and China have brought instability. In addition, the flood of cheap Chinese goods has bankrupted many Vietnamese industries. When the open-door period first began, Chinese products grabbed a 90 per cent share of the total market in the border area.

China is thus in a way encouraging small-scale trade so that excess goods that cannot be sold in China can enter the Vietnamese market — a trade essentially taken care of through smuggling. At the same time, China is draining scarce natural resources out of Vietnam for the benefit of its own markets. This imbalance in trade and its consequences raises the important issue of how to stop the spread of smuggling along the border, which the governments of Vietnam and China are urgently advised to address. If smuggling is stopped a healthy trade environment will emerge, and this in turn will contribute to the security of their common boundary area.

CONCLUDING REMARKS

The open-door period has been significant for the Sino-Vietnamese border trade in general and that of the Hoa in particular.

Once the economic and diplomatic relations between China and Vietnam were normalized, the revival and development of the border trade became possible. Gradually, after five years of the open-door policy, the "ghost town" areas became bustling commercial centres, attracting various ethnic groups. Of these, the Hoa had many advantages when doing business, as well as particular formulas for success which other groups lacked. Their main advantage was their networks based on kinship, which made it easier for them to mobilize capital, form joint ventures, and gain access to sources of goods.

Like other ethnic groups, the Hoa started off with petty trade, gradually expanding their trading activities. Thus, during the first years, the Hoa served as middlemen, interpreters, and guides for customers on both sides of the border. Later on, they became contractors and agents and also handled the transportation of goods.

The Hoa always see "trust" and "reliability" as the core elements of their traditional way of doing business. This element has not only generated mutual respect in verbal agreements and written contracts, it has also created natural networks. Another feature of the Hoa is their ability to respond quickly to the needs and tastes of the market. They have grasped the pricing system rapidly, and are quick to gain access to modern science and technology. With all these characteristics, the Hoa have easily been able to integrate not only into the regional economy, but also into the global economy.

Thus, when looking at the potentials of the Hoa's economic activities, several questions arise. Are the Hoa at the moment contributing more to the international community than to the local provinces? Where will their contributions be made in the future? Will the Hoa be able to use their traditional skills to become a "bridge" between the different areas along the borders? What should the Vietnamese government do to utilize the Hoa networks and their economic resources to better compete in the regional trade? What kind of business networks will the Hoa establish in order to link up with the Hoa in the Pacific Rim economy? These issues are of great concern not only to scholars, but also to policy-makers in Vietnam and other countries in the region.

Appendix Table 12.1
Border Crossings

SRV Crossing	Province	PRC Crossing	Province
1. Mong Cai	Quang Ninh	1. Dongxing	Guangxi
2. Hoanh Mo	Quang Ninh	2. Tongzong	Guangxi
3. Chi Ma	Lang Son	3. Aidian	Guangxi
4. Huu Nghi	Lang son	4. Youyiguan	Guangxi
5. Dong Dang	Lang Son	5. Pingxiang	Guangxi
6. Binh Nghi	Lang Son	6. Ping'er	Guangxi
7. Ta Lung	Cao Bang	7. Shuikou	Guangxi
8. Ha Lang	Cao Bang	8. Kejia	Guangxi
9. Ly Van	Cao Bang	9. Shilong	Guangxi
10. Po Peo	Cao Bang	10. Yuewu	Guangxi
11. Tra Linh	Cao Bang	11. Longbang	Guangxi
12. Soc Giang	Cao Bang	12. Pingmang	Guangxi
13. Sam Pun	Ha Giang	13. Tienhong	Yunnan
14. Pho Bang	Ha Giang	14. Tonggen	Yunnan
15. Thanh Thuy	Ha Giang	15. Tianbao	Yunnan
16. Xin Man	Ha Giang	16. Dulong	Yunnan
17. Muong Khuong	Lao Cai	17. Qiaotou	Yunnan
18. Lao Cai	Lao Cai	18. Hekou	Yunnan
19. Ma Lu Thang	Lai Chau	19. Jinshuihe	Yunnan
20. U Ma Tu Khoang	Lai Chau	20. Pinghe	Yunnan
21. A Pa Chai	Lai Chau	21. Pangfu	Yunnan

Source: *Nhan Dan*, 13 May 1992.

NOTES

This chapter on the forms of Hoa trade activities along the Sino-Vietnamese border represents the first stage of this research and is a contribution to the ongoing work at the University of Hong Kong, supervised by Dr Grant Evans, on the subject of the economic, social, and cultural impact of the opening of China's borders with Vietnam and the Lao People's Democratic Republic (PDR).

1. The following gods are worshipped: Guan Gong, Tian Hou (the Sea Goddess), Tudi Gong (the God of the Earth), Houmen Gong (the Kitchen God), Caishen Ye (the Genius of Prosperity), and Zheng He.
2. Some Hoa returned to China in 1978–79 or later, but have since then moved back to Mong Cai.
3. The businesspeople come from Dongxing (in Fengcheng district, Guangxi province), Beihai, Liaozhou, and Qinzhou in Guangxi province, and from the provinces of Guangzhou, Fuzhou, Hubei, and Hunan.
4. 1 renminbi = 1,300 dong. Fieldwork in Mong Cai, May 1995.
5. Compared with Overseas Chinese businesses in other parts of Southeast Asia, this

is not a large figure, but it is considerable when viewed in the context of the level of economic development in Vietnam.
6. Fieldwork in Mong Cai, February–May 1995; and Lang Son, April–May 1996.
7. Fieldwork in Ho Chi Minh City, June–July 1994; in Mong Cai, May 1995; and in Lang Son, April–May 1996.
8. Fieldwork in Dong Dang and Lang Son, April–May 1996.
9. Fieldwork in Mong Cai, February–May 1995; Lao Cai, July 1995; and Lang Son, April–May 1996.
10. The Association works for the Hoa who returned to China in 1978–80.
11. Fieldwork in the provinces of Lang Son, Mong Cai, and Lao Cai, 1995 and 1996.
12. The Association is set up for the Hoa in Pingxiang who left Vietnam during the period 1978–80.
13. Fieldwork in Mong Cai, May 1995; and Dong Dang, April–May 1996.
14. Fieldwork in Quang Ninh, May 1995.
15. Fieldwork in Lang Son, April–May 1996.
16. Fieldwork in Mong Cai, May 1995; and Dong Dang, April–May 1996.
17. This is true for areas such as Coc Leu and Lao Cai (in Lao Cai province); Na Sam, Dong Dang, and Ky Lua (in Lang Son province); Mong Cai, and Binh Lieu (in Quang Ninh province).

REFERENCES

Bui, Dinh Nguyen. "Phat to trong nghe buon ban oto ai mung ai lo?" [Getting rich in the automobile trade]. *Bao Dai doan ket* [Great solidarity newspaper], 29 August and 4 September 1992.
Chau Hai. *Cac nhom con dong nguoi Hoa o Viet Nam* [Hoa communities in Vietnam]. Hanoi: NXB Khoa hoc Xa hoi, 1992.
Do Tien Sam. "An Open-Door Strategy for the Vietnam-China Border". *Tap chi Nghien cuu Trung Quoc* [Chinese studies review], no. 1 (1995), p. 37.
Nguyen Huy Toan and Vu Tang Bong. *Su that ve nhung lan xuat quan cua Trung Quoc va quan he Viet-Trung* [The truth about China's military expeditions and Sino-Vietnamese relations]. Da Nang: NXB Da Nang, 1996.
Quy Hao. "Mong Cai mo thanh Tham Quyen" [Mong Cai dreams of becoming a *shenquan*]. *Thoi bao Kinh te Viet Nam* [Vietnam economic times], nos. 11–13 (5–12 February 1997), p. 27.
Tran Anh Phuong. "Bien mau Viet-Trung va nhung tac dong kinh te-xa hoi [Border trade between Vietnam and China and its socio-economic impact]. *Kinh te Chau a Thai Binh Duong* [Asia-Pacific economic review], nos. 2–3 (1994), pp. 26–29.

Cross-Border Categories:
Ethnic Chinese and the
Sino-Vietnamese Border at Mong Cai

Christopher Hutton

People on borders, and people who cross borders, people who live on boats, and people who are nomadic may be especially difficult to classify. They are not tied to a particular territory, and do not fit the agrarian model of identity that underlies both much of Western theorizing (ethnic group plus language plus homeland) and nationalist ideologies based on peasant culture. They represent the remnants of pre-modern identities in the sense that the people concerned do not have to have a clear answer to questions such as "What is your mother-tongue?" or "What is your ethnicity?" The questions asked by the ethnographer or linguist symbolize the approaching centralizing-categorization process of the state.

Border areas between modern states are zones of transition and of complex and often bitter identity politics and territorial claims. Ethnographically, borders can seem arbitrary or artificial, and political states are often concerned to contain or deny the transitional or marginal identities found there and to emphasize their control (symbolic and actual) over territory. The role of anthropologists and linguists in this is ambiguous. On the one hand, they often recognize the "artificiality" or contingency of political borders; yet they are frequently (in some sense) the agents of colonial or nationalist states. In contrast with pre-modern polities, empires and post-colonial national states have made it their business to find out who their subjects are. They have undertaken radical labelling enterprises, literal and metaphorical mapping exercises, in which the unknown, the uncharted, and the unclassified have been measured and catalogued.[1] Colonial and nationalist states (unlike pre-modern ones) require a much higher degree of order within their naming and labelling systems. They set up centralized education systems and devise language policies; they register their citizens and carry out censuses. Categories and classifications become a pre-requisite of policy formation and instruments of social control. In return for this increased level of state scrutiny, citizens receive an identity through which they can bargain with the state either as individuals with individual rights or as a group through the assertion of group needs and rights. The existence of "scientific" labelling processes enforced by linguists and ethnographers is predicated on a centralized state within which such labels make sense, acquire political force, or form the basis of secessionist movements.

There is a strong — but not absolute — tendency in the categorization process for linguistic categories to displace gradually other methods of classification. People can be named or classified according to a location or geographical feature (mountain, river, and so forth), a style of dress or other aspect of material culture, or after some physical characteristic or religious affiliation. They may be allocated to a particular group on the basis of customs such as burial or marriage rites, kinship relations, and so on. The boundary between surname and ethnonym is also often unclear. However, the "panoptic gaze" of the modern state and the modern ethnographer cannot deal with the complexity that this engenders; the state cannot deal with thousands of local groups, nor can the ethnic cartographer or the ethnolinguist. What is required is a single viewpoint from which all the diverse phenomena can be organized. A pluralistic method can never give a true sense of order, nor can it be a means of comparing like with like. Group A may be distinguished from its neighbours B by its burial practices; another group C by its clothing from group D. What if A and D have the same clothing, but different burial practices?[2]

This chapter deals with a complex question of ethnolinguistic categorization involving what might be termed the marginal Chinese population of northeastern Vietnam (present-day Quang Ninh province).

NUNG/NGAI/SAN Y/SAN DIU

These reflections arise partly out of my reading of the history of linguistics, but they were also prompted by an experience in June 1990 when Grant Evans and I visited the Nei Ku Chau detention centre on Hei Ling Chau island, Hong Kong. We were going out to visit a group of Nung, and assumed that they would be speakers of a Tai dialect. In fact, these Nung were not Tai-speaking. In the course of the two days we spent there, we uncovered a plethora of categories. The United Nations High Commissioner for Refugees (UNHCR) interpreter, introducing the people in the camp, explained "some speak Cantonese, I mean Nung-Cantonese, some speak Ngai, which we call like Hac".[3] While the majority spoke a Southern Chinese–like dialect with a resemblance to the Southern Yue dialects of Chinese, which they referred to as Ngai, they also termed themselves Nung or Nung people as a group. Some members of the group spoke both Ngai and another language (the labels San Diu and San Y or Xanh Y came up in the interviews).[4] Speakers of San Y/San Diu seemed to be in the process of assimilating into the Ngai, judging by the laughs that were elicited when some of the informants were asked to translate from San Y into Ngai. These "Chinese Nung" were in general either born in Quang Ninh province, in northeast Vietnam, or the children of parents born in North Vietnam or China who had gone south after 1954. They had been denied refugee status, though they claimed family links to the South Vietnamese army.

What was interesting about these "Chinese Nung" was that their identity was under a series of pressures. The status of politically persecuted Overseas Chinese might have made these migrants acceptable to the Hong Kong public. However, any claim to a Chinese identity carried the risk of classification as illegal immigrants (IIs) from mainland China, subject to deportation from Hong Kong. Since many Vietnamese boat people actually passed overland through China and had been born, or their parents had been born, in China, and since many had spent a considerable time in transit, the dividing line between mainland Chinese illegal immigrants and Vietnamese boat people was far from clear. The whole question of whom the Hong Kong government eventually classified as ex-China Vietnamese illegal immigrants (ECVIIs) came to a head in 1993; with large numbers of arrivals from Beihai, a coastal city in Guangxi. These were ethnic Chinese who had fled from Vietnam to China in the late 1970s. An asylum seeker who filed a writ of habeus corpus against the Hong Kong government had left Vietnam on account of the Sino-Vietnamese War in 1979 and settled with other Vietnamese Chinese as squatters in Beihai. He came to Hong Kong when their shanty town was demolished by the Chinese authorities in

1993 to make way for development (Western 1997).

Subsequent research revealed that the category Ngai was a recognized category within Vietnamese ethnography, but one with a complex history. According to Chuong Sau (1978, p. 388), the Ngai are a Hoa (Han Chinese) ethnic group who came to Vietnam from Fengcheng (now in Guangxi province) and who speak a language close to Hakka. I have not been able to find any link between the categories Ngai and Nung in any source, Vietnamese or otherwise. It was not entirely clear whether these Nung saw themselves as Chinese, and if so, in what sense. The ambiguity of their situation *vis-à-vis* illegal immigrants from mainland China might have discouraged any claim to a Chinese identity.

THE DUSTBINS OF HISTORY

The history of the Nung and of the category "Nung" is bound up with a series of migrations. Firstly, there is the southward movement of peoples from China to Southeast Asia, one that has been proceeding for millennia. The second is the migration south within Vietnam after the Geneva Agreement in 1954.[5] Thirdly, there is the return migration by Chinese from Vietnam back to Guangxi province. Lastly, there is the migration of these "Vietnamese" of various kinds to Hong Kong and other ports of asylum in Southeast Asia from 1975 to the present.

After the partition of Vietnam in 1954, the Nung who went south were directed by the authorities to Dalat, Ban Me Thuot, Kontum, and Pleiku in the Central Highlands (Prados 1995, p. 73), though some also settled in Saigon and other urban centres. Many ended up farming in rural South Vietnam. Lewallen (1971, p. 125) reported that members of the Raglai ethnic group in Thuan Hai province, displaced in the late 1960s from the mountains by U.S. free-strike zones, found all the arable land in the lowlands occupied by "Vietnamese, Chams and Nung Chinese".[6]

Intersecting with these two migrations is the complex question of the Chinese in Vietnam. In the post-1954 era, ethnic Chinese made up 5.5 per cent of the population in the south and just 0.5 per cent in the north. The figure of 0.5 per cent, however, appears to omit the rural ethnic Chinese of Quang Ninh province (Unger 1987, p. 609n).[7] The Diem regime in the south took strong measures to curb ethnic Chinese influence, whereas the northern government, its relations with China being cordial, initially left control of Overseas Chinese to the Chinese Communist Party. In the south, Chinese occupied a dominant position in the economy, particularly in the rice trade; in the north, they were workers and technicians in the urban areas, and fishermen, foresters, craftsmen, miners, and factory workers in Quang Ninh province (ibid., pp. 598, 609). However, a visit by Zhou Enlai to Vietnam in 1956 heralded a shift in policy: the Chinese in Vietnam were to regard themselves as Vietnamese and be issued with Vietnamese identity documents. According to an agreement of February 1957, the Ngai and other Hoa minority peoples of Quang Ninh were to become Vietnamese citizens, while the citizenship of the other Overseas Chinese was to be determined later (ibid., p. 609n; Dossier 1978a, p. 24).[8] This whole process provoked a negative reaction from the Chinese, in particular from the Ngai of Quang Ninh (Unger 1987, pp. 602–3). In the early 1970s, the Vietnamese government sought to persuade the Chinese in the north to adopt Vietnamese citizenship, but they were reluctant to do so. They would lose their privileges of being able to visit China easily, and they also feared the military draft (ibid., p. 605).

The collapse of the southern regime in 1975 and the formal reunification in 1976, with the accompanying attack on "comprador capitalists" (Dossier 1978a, p. 80), led to the flight of Chinese from the south, while a deteriorating diplomatic situation in the lead-up to the Sino-Vietnamese War of 1979 led to an exodus from the north. According to Unger (1987, p. 609), 265,000 people crossed from Quang Ninh province into China.[9]

One way to approach the definitional issues raised by categories such as "Nung" is to work backwards from the Hong Kong camp. How did the Nung come to be there? A single case may serve as illustration. Mr V.[10] is sixty-eight, and was born in 1929 of newly migrated parents, in or near Tien Yen in Quang Ninh province. His parents came from Fengcheng in Guangdong (now Guangxi) province, and were involved in domestic paper manufacturing. He served in the French army, and after 1954 went south. Subsequently, he fought in the South Vietnamese army, and was wounded, though he continued to serve as a driver. After 1975 his family lived in Dong Nai province, and was subject to discrimination. They came to Hong Kong in 1989, via China; Mr V. and his family crossed the border at Mong Cai, retracing the journey his parents had made in the late 1920s. In spite of his military service, Mr V. was denied refugee status. However, he is regarded by Vietnam as a non-national and thus cannot be sent back there. He holds the Republic of China (Taiwanese) papers, but these papers do not grant the right of abode in Taiwan.[11] Mr V. is a speaker of what might loosely be termed

Guangxi Cantonese (*baahkwá*), and does not speak Vietnamese well. From a historical-biographical point of view, Mr V. is unambiguously Chinese, and regards himself as such.

The Nung interviewed by Grant Evans and myself in 1990 did not all present themselves unambiguously as Chinese. Of the seventeen we interviewed on our second visit to the camp, only two characterized themselves as Chinese. Fifteen described themselves as Nung, and of those fifteen, nine saw themselves as Chinese Nung, or as both Nung and Chinese. Three who gave their ethnicity as Chinese Nung stated that they had Chinese fathers. Several made the explicit statement that Nung was a form of Chineseness. Only one used the term Ngai as an ethnic designation. In 1954, their families had come south from Hai Ninh province, and had lived in Saigon, Song Mao, or in Xuan Loc.

A document prepared by the group of Nung in the Nei Ku Chau detention centre gives the following version of their history (Nung 1990). The Nung were a minority people scattered through southern China who migrated to Vietnam, chiefly to Quang Ninh province where "they cleared and settled in the wilderness" (p. 1). They served in the French army, and after the 1954 Geneva Agreement they reluctantly migrated south "to pursue their fight against Communism under the leadership of Colonel Vong-A-Sang who had been the commander of the Nung Third Field Combat Division" (p. 1). An "ethnic cadet school" was founded in Pleiku in the Central Highlands, for example. The southern regime had treated them well, and had given Nung special representation in political institutions. They served in the forces of the south, and also as special guards for the southern regime (the presidential bodyguard was, for example, made up of Nung[12]); they also served with the Americans. After 1975 they were dispersed to New Economic Zones in Dong Nai province (Bau Ham, Dinh Quan, Xuan Loc), and they were systematically discriminated against. In the Phu Hoa village (Tan Phu district, Dong Nai province) 98 per cent of the population were Nung, "yet the village secretary, assistant secretary, Chair and Vice-Chair were all Vietnamese" (p. 4). In 1976, Nung participated in the armed opposition to the Vietnamese state with the FULRO[13] in the southern provinces of Dong Nai and Lam Dong. The document contends that "the Communist authority tried to label the Nungs as (Han) Chinese in order to stamp out the Nung race" (p. 5). This last quoted remark stand out in contrast to the self-reporting of the group in Nei Ku Chau, which was far from unanimous in asserting or rejecting Chinese identity. On a tape prepared by the Nung to present themselves, one speaker reported that most Nung speak San Diu; another reported herself to be a Chinese-Vietnamese, but noted that she spoke Vietnamese and San Diu as well. A third contributor to the tape said "we are an ethnic group who speak the Nung language; we are also San Diu people".

On the question of Nung ethnicity, reports by U.S. Vietnam veterans are either vague or make the specific claim that the Nung who fought with them were Chinese. A website[14] sponsored by former Special Forces asks for help for thirty-one Nungs who are "ethnic Chinese who worked with U.S. Special Forces in classified work during the war" (letter from Stephen Feldman, dated 27 April 1997). Among the materials in this website are accounts of the role that the Nung played in guarding U.S. installations, and of the establishment of a Nung Security Platoon in 1964 to guard the headquarters of the Fifth Special Forces in Nha Trang. An essay by Colonel Harry Summers describes them as "ethnic Chinese tribesmen". The Nung we had interviewed and who had previously been screened out, were in June 1997 declared refugees after lobbying by U.S. veterans who agreed to sponsor their entry into the United States (Batha 1997*a*).[15] One of them, profiled in the *South China Morning Post*, was described as "an ethnic Nung, born in Mong Cai" (Batha 1997*b*).

Others have not been so fortunate. In August 1992, sixty Nung were forcibly repatriated from Hong Kong in spite of arguments by Asia Watch that they could face persecution because of their links with the French and U.S. forces (MacMahon and Furlong 1992). In early 1997, the Court of Appeal ruled that ethnic Chinese "who had been stripped of their property and nationality documents", and then held in labour camps in restricted zones in Ha Tuyen province, North Vietnam, had been properly screened out. The Hong Kong government Queen's Counsel, Mr Marshall, had argued that these camps were justified on grounds of national security, and that "the camps were to stop ethnic Chinese acting as spies during the Sino-Vietnamese hostilities". Mr Marshall argued that there was a difference between persecution and "differentiation of treatment", and made a parallel between this internment and the internment of American Japanese by U.S. authorities during World War II (Batha 1997*c*).[16]

THE ETHNOGRAPHIC MORASS

It would not be possible here to review the complex history of the categories that Grant Evans and I were confronted with in the Nei Ku

Chau detention centre. One striking aspect of the scholarly literature on northeastern Vietnam is the appearance and disappearance of particular ethnic and ethno-linguistic designations in the course of the twentieth century.

A French army doctor, Vaillant, who carried out an "anthropological" study — a study of bodily measurements — of the Chinese of the Mong Cai region (Vaillant 1920) speaks of just three other groups: Annamites (that is, Vietnamese), Man, and Tho. These Chinese are described by Vaillant as Hakka, and he makes no mention of other contemporary categories of Chinese in the area. Vaillant dates the migration of Hakka to the Mong Cai region to 1828 and 1832, but chiefly to expulsions of the querulous Hakka from China in 1864 and 1866 (ibid., p. 84). These Hakka arrivals displaced an early Chinese migrant tribe, the "Outong". The Hakka of Mong Cai are Chinese, but "their blood is extremely mixed". They "consider themselves at all events to be Chinese, whose customs they share, and whose language resembles Cantonese to a considerable degree". The peace and order brought by the French presence has given these Chinese a permanent footing in the area (ibid., p. 85).[17]

As Vaillant recognized, the continued presence of these Chinese on the Vietnamese side of the border was dependent on political stability. That has remained true throughout the twentieth century and still applies today. In Mong Cai, for example, the visibility of ethnic Chinese is an index of economic activity and political stability in the wider border region. Another constant of this border region is the question of political loyalty and military service. The Hakka that Vaillant was measuring were recruits into a French militia unit (ibid., p. 83).

This relationship to land has an important place in the ideology of Vietnamese nationalism, for it marks the rural Chinese of the Mong Cai region (present-day Quang Ninh) as different from the stereotypical Overseas Chinese in Vietnam, the rice traders of Saigon. The role that these Chinese played in the economy of Quang Ninh province, in agriculture, fishing, and in mining, made them an organic part of Vietnam and thus paved the way for their naturalization as Vietnamese citizens. An ethnonym such as Ngai marks a symbolic break with the dialect classification normally applied to the Hoa of Vietnam (Cantonese, Hakka, and so forth).

In the French scholarly literature, the Chinese ethno-linguistic categories of Hakka and Cantonese are intertwined in complex ways with Nung, Ngai, and so forth. The category of *baahkwá* (Vietnamese: *Pac*

Va) also appears frequently.[18] When F.M. Savina, for example, was attempting to demonstrate a historical link between the Thai (Tai) and the southern Chinese (1924, p. vi), he chose Nung to represent the Tai dialects in his contrastive dictionary because of its close resemblance to Cantonese.[19] Georges Maspero (1929, p. 67) emphasized the linguistic continuity between the Chinese of northeastern Vietnam and China when describing the presence of Hakka and Cantonese villages near Mong Cai.[20] However, André Haudricourt's post–World War II linguistic survey of the Mong Cai region presented a much more complex picture (1960). Haudricourt gave a range of categories for ethnic Chinese groups, on a continuum from Cantonese to Hakka: Cantonese Nung, San Chi, Ngai, San Giêu (San Diu), Maalao, and Hakka. Nung and San Chi are grouped under Cantonese, while Ngai and San Giêu (San Diu) are categorized as kinds of Hakka. The article ended with the postulation that San Diu was a product of Yao switching to Hakka, and with the now intellectually fashionable assertion that Cantonese and Hakka were the products of sub-stratum influence from Thai (Tai) and Yao respectively (ibid., p. 177).

In Vietnamese writings from the 1970s onwards, the picture becomes still more complex. The linguist Vu Bang Hung (1972) divides the Chinese of Vietnam into two dialect groups, Pac Va and Ngai. Pac Va is categorized as Cantonese, and Ngai as a Hakka dialect.[21] Nguyen Van Ai (1972), in a study of the San Diu dialect in Quang Ninh province, reports that almost all San Diu speak Vietnamese in addition to their own language, and that a number of San Diu also speak Ngai.[22] Further classifications and variations are to be found in U.S. military-sponsored research from the 1970s (Schrock et al. 1972), in Western studies of the Vietnam War (for example, Whitfield 1976; Olson 1988), and in works by (missionary) linguists from the Summer Institute of Linguistics (Vy Thi Be et al. 1982). Now, once again, Western linguists are doing fieldwork in northern Vietnam, as well as in southern China.[23]

An important landmark in the history of ethnic categorization in Vietnam was the implementation of a government directive to social scientists requiring the drawing-up of a definitive list of ethnic groups in Vietnam. As reported in Vietnamese Studies (Vietnamese Government 1978), fifty-four main groups were identified; the Hoa or ethnic Chinese were listed as the fourth largest group, the Nung as seventh, and the Ngai as eleventh. While this survey does not give population figures, this ranking of the Ngai suggests a population of at least 120,000. In this list, the Nung are classified as a Tai group. The Hoa and the Ngai are listed separately, though they are both categorized (along with the San Diu) as speakers of Han languages.

In Vietnamese ethnography from the 1980s onwards, the Ngai are given an extensive set of sub-groups (Dang Nghiem Van et al. 1984, 1993). One can hypothesize that this proliferation of sub-groups is a consequence of the official designation of fifty-four main groups. On the one hand, this sets up an official list of categories; making changes to this may be politically complex. On the other, there are additional ethnonyms which need to be accommodated somehow. This would account for the fact that while the numbers of Ngai continue to dwindle,[24] the number of sub-groups has grown. One group that appears under Ngai is Dan, boat people who live on the northeastern coast of Vietnam.[25] A recently published work on ethnic minorities in Vietnam describes the basic history and ethnic make-up of the Ngai as follows:

> The present day Ngai make up a community comprising elements of several ethnic groups which formerly lived in Southern China before coming to Vietnam at different times in history. The [...] *Annals of the History of the Viet Land* records already long-standing presence in the 10th century of the Dan, who settled along the coast of Vietnam. In fact, the Ngai lived for centuries in Quang Ninh and claimed to be indigenous in the area.[26] The Hac Ca arrived around the first few decades of the 19th century. After 1954, many Ngai moved to Ho Chi Minh City. (Dang Nghiem Van et al. 1993, p. 206)

The San Diu are also defined as having come from Guangdong to Vietnam in the mid-seventeenth century (ibid., p. 202). A further irony is that the Ngai in this description are being given a much longer history in Vietnam than previously (through their association with Dan), at the same time as the category seems to have reached the point of extinction.

In the ethnographic and historical literature a number of positions can be identified. Some writers make no clear distinction between different kinds of Nung, and classify them as an ethnic group or as tribal people from Vietnam. Others only mention the Nung in the context of ethnic Chinese in Vietnam. Vietnamese ethnographers confine the term "Nung" to Tai-speaking groups; Savina (1924) asserts that the Nung were the most Sinitic of the Tai groups. Vy Thi Be et al. (1982) stress that the Tai-Nung and the Chinese Nung are separate ethnic groups that should not be confused. In Chinese sources, the Nung are presented as an ethnic group that has migrated to Vietnam, but with close links to Dai and Zhuang (Hu 1986; Chen 1989).

The 1979 war posed the question of ethnic identity in a particularly powerful and unavoidable way. On the one hand, one might predict that events like the 1979 border war would lead to the demise of transitional identities such as Ngai that lie between Vietnamese and Chinese; this does indeed seem to have happened in the urban areas of northeast Vietnam. On the other hand, what Grant Evans and I saw in the Nei Ku Chau camp was a micro-process of Ngai-ization — since the Xanh/San-Y-Nung spoke Ngai but the Ngai-Nung found the sound of Xanh/San-Y amusing. The linguist Haudricourt would have interpreted this as a continuation of the historical switch from Yao to Hakka. The irony is that in the larger historical context this is a process of sinicization (Yao becoming Hakka), but that the process is taking place within a political context that has declared the Ngai to be Vietnamese.

MONG CAI: THE SEARCH FOR THE SOURCE OF THE NGAI, 1995

My aim in being in Mong Cai was to get an impression of the kinds of people that were there, and to see what, if any, reality there was to the category Ngai in present-day Mong Cai. I did not see myself as trying to trace the "true nature and origins" of the Ngai, but I was using the category as a means of measuring social change. For it struck me, being in Mong Cai, that it was hard enough to find out what the town was like ten years ago, never mind that linguistic reconstructions allegedly reach back thousands or even tens of thousands of years.

Mong Cai was destroyed during the 1979 Sino-Vietnamese War, and was uninhabited until the resumption of trade in the late 1980s. Many of the inhabitants of Mong Cai who did not (have to) flee lived in the near-by town of Ha Coi in that period. Before 1990 there were only soldiers there; by 1991 Mong Cai was once again a trading centre, a transit-point between Vietnam and China. A bridge linking Mong Cai to Dongxing on the Chinese side, a co-operative venture, was opened at the end of 1993 (Womack 1994, p. 501).

Mong Cai, a town on the extreme northeastern tip of Vietnam on the Sino-Vietnamese border, is well known in Vietnam as a cross-border trading town, as well as a pottery centre, and is also near the celebrated beach resort of Tra Co. Mong Cai is linked by ferry to Haiphong, and by road along the coast to Cam Pha, Hong Gai, Haiphong, and ultimately Hanoi. Travel by road in this part of Vietnam is slow-going, and in striking contrast to the roads over the border in Guangxi. Going north from Haiphong up the coast by road, one passes the tourist resort of Halong Bay before hitting the Dickensian coal-mining district around Cam Pha. While Mong Cai is firmly off the Western tourist map, it is a tourist attraction of a sort for Chinese who cross the border to buy Vietnamese jade, Vietnamese lacquer goods, and other souvenirs in the town, and also to visit Vietnamese prostitutes.

Some of the original population of Mong Cai has returned, and many live in the impressive new housing in central Mong Cai. There are also many veterans of Hong Kong Vietnamese camps, some of whom live in semi-temporary housing near the town centre. The UNHCR is a regular visitor.

On a trip to Mui Ngoc, a small coastal village, it seemed that everybody I met had been in a Hong Kong camp. A Vietnamese man from Hanoi who had accompanied me to the village was asked by the young boys how long he had been in Hong Kong, as if a stay in a refugee camp was a rite of passage for all young Vietnamese.

This corner of Vietnam is poor and rough, and Mong Cai is very much the classic border town with a substantial mobile population, from the migrant labourers pulling goods through the streets to the businessmen who come there from Ho Chi Minh City in the south and Shanghai in the north. The more immediate trade-axis is Nanning-Dongxing on the Chinese side, and Mong Cai–Haiphong on the Vietnamese side. But Mong Cai also has links further away. One informant (from Shanghai) told me that Mong Cai was a transit point for heroin to Hong Kong, shipped in Coca-Cola cans. Trade in wild life is flourishing, and some of the rare animals are destined for restaurants in south China and Hong Kong.

In my research I was fortunate to be befriended by the owner of a cafe, a Mr B. In visiting his cafe every day for breakfast I got to meet the other customers who were staying in his guest-house, and he mediated between me and them in explaining my presence. Having been born in New Caledonia, he spoke fluent French. He, like many others, lived a kind of exile's life there, complaining to me that there was no cinema and nothing to do there. His wife seemed to be the driving-force behind whatever business was going on. In general, I found people speaking English, French, broken German (from their time in the former German Democratic Republic), Cantonese, and related Chinese varieties, and Putonghua, as well as Vietnamese.[27] I also asked people I met about the Ngai; Mr B. had not heard much about them, though he knew the label. A returned resident of the town said that they used to be here, but not anymore. They had all left during the Sino-Vietnamese War. Another informant who had been born there said that there used to be Ngai in the district around Mong Cai, but that they had all gone away.

According to Mr B., about half the restaurants in Mong Cai were Chinese-owned. Many of the central properties were occupied by Chinese, particularly from Shanghai, though I had the impression that, in general, they crossed back into China at night. Mr B. told me that there were much fewer now than three years previously, in the real boom days of Mong Cai (1993). The market in Vietnam reached a kind of saturation point, and those with disposable income are now said to prefer goods from Thailand or even goods produced in Ho Chi Minh City to Chinese goods. Mr B. implied that there was a directly proportional relationship between the health of the Mong Cai economy and the number of Chinese established or semi-established there.[28]

Some businessmen I met were very open and talked about what they were doing; others did not invite questions, such as one regular in Mr B.'s cafe from Da Nang. One of the businessmen that I met was a representative of a state enterprise, who was buying cement from China.[29] He crossed the border illegally in the morning for talks and returned at lunch time, then went back in the afternoon, returning in the evening to say that the price of the cement had gone up during lunch and that the Chinese were really ruthless in business. A businessman from Hong Gai who was buying mining equipment in China told me the same, that the Chinese were very *láu cá* (sly, smart). One important group of "businessmen" was made up of returnees from Hong Kong involved in trading raw materials up from Haiphong over the border. The links formed in the Hong Kong camps, particularly Whitehead, were clearly functioning as an old-boy network in various activities linking Mong Cai to Cam Pha and Haiphong. One such young Whitehead returnee, Mr H., took me around and introduced me to others from Whitehead who were based in Tra Co, a small town on the coast next to Mong Cai. They all seemed to be dealing in raw materials. Mr H. said that he preferred speaking Cantonese to Vietnamese, having got into the habit in Hong Kong (he denied that he was Chinese). He also introduced me to his boss, who ran some kind of trading company and obviously worked as an important middleman. Although he denied that he was Chinese, he spoke *baahkwá* (Guangxi Cantonese) and, more unusually, could read and write Chinese. Some traders in the market are the children of Chinese fathers and Vietnamese mothers — that is, they are children of the old Mong Cai — and still have a role as mediators because of their language skills.

Standing in front of his business, with its trading company name, Mr H. confided to me that "this is all fake". I took this as a kind of general commentary on Mong Cai, the shopfronts of which do not necessarily give a clear view of the business that goes on behind them. There were a number of Shanghai businessmen with a base in Mong Cai who, for example, were involved in dealing in the passport business (Cambodian, Thai). Mr H. assumed that since I was British and lived in Hong Kong I could get him a work visa there, and was prepared to offer me about HK$5,000 for my trouble.

As in other contexts, women are very important as local petty-traders and street-level currency traders; the long-distance buyers and dealers tend to be men. I was able to catch a lot of cross-border business and smuggling mobile-phone talk on the FM radio, and this was mainly being conducted by women. This talk was approximately 80 per cent in Vietnamese and 20 per cent in various kinds of Chinese. Mong Cai is thus both a small-scale trading centre and a locus for business meetings of national significance between large state organizations.

Wars between nation-states force people with marginal or mixed identities to choose sides or to flee into exile. What I learned in Mong Cai was that the category "Ngai" is now a vague memory, marginal to the concerns of the people who live there, even if some of the returnees from the Hong Kong camps might be — or speak — Ngai.[30] The Vietnamese state is anxious to stamp its identity on border towns like Mong Cai, and the effect of the upheavals of the last two decades has been an ethnic levelling. The residents of Mong Cai are Vietnamese; the Chinese traders in general cross the border at night back to Dongxing.

CONCLUDING REMARKS: BORDERS AND BORDERLINE CASES

The question of borders has not been fully addressed within linguistics. The classic structuralist work on transitional languages is Uriel Weinreich's *Languages in Contact* (1953), but this work is not concerned with questions of identity and classification. A recent article by Bonnie Urciuoli (1995), with the promising title "Language and Borders", deals with the notion of border more as a metaphor of the problems of categorization than as a geo-political reality.[31]

One way to understand the identity issues discussed in this chapter is to see the categorial "chaos" as a remnant of this pre-modern, unclassified world. The processes that bring the world into categorial order include the classifications of scholars, but also of social and political processes such as war, ethnic cleansing, migration, assimilation, and centralization. If we compare Western European states with Vietnam, we can see a profound contrast in ethnic make-up. In Western Europe, ethnic minorities tend to be linguistically identified with a regional base (for example, the Germans in Belgium), but there are relatively few such groups. Regional ethnic difference is otherwise defined in terms of dialect groups, so that in Germany the population is made up of variants of a common category, German.[32]

One methodological practice that has struck me forcibly in looking at the linguistic analysis of "very small languages" is that the "big" languages (Mandarin Chinese, Thai, Vietnamese, and so forth) or the "medium to small" languages (Cantonese, Hakka, Yao) are, as it were, held constant as parameters of comparison. Thus if we conceptualize Ngai as lying on a continuum between Hakka and Cantonese as Haudricourt does, that explanatory grid is serving to locate a "small" language within the map laid out by the interrelationships between the medium and large languages. In looking at marginal languages and cultures, we behave as if we could define the dominant ones. In this mapping process, there are some categories that need to be held fixed as parameters within which other, smaller, categories can be compared. Thus Chinese is most truly or fully represented as a category by Mandarin, and within the Mandarin dialects most truly by Beijing Mandarin. At the heart of Tai we find Thai. Further down the hierarchy, we find that groups like Hakka have their own core varieties (in the case of Hakka, Meixan dialect); Cantonese and the Yue dialect groups have at their core the Cantonese of Guangzhou and Hong Kong. Mapping becomes then a process of situating smaller language groups within these larger categories. In the case of the Nung-Ngai of Quang Ninh province, the three macro-categories are Chinese, Yao, and Tai. All the categories discussed in relation to Mong Cai (Nung, Cao Lan, San Diu, San Chi, San Chay, San Y, Ngai) can be understood — whatever the details of their historical and linguistic relationships (are the San Diu sinicized Yao or Yao-ized Chinese?) — as being permutations or interactions of these macro-categories. For the sake of the discussion, these are kept fixed. We can decide to call Cantonese a sinicized form of Tai, and Hakka a sinicized form of Yao, but if we raise the indeterminacy to the level of the categories Thai, Yao, and Mandarin the whole enterprise collapses.

One twenty-eight-year-old asylum-seeker from Vietnam who has spent seven years in detention in Hong Kong before being released into an open camp said to me recently: "In Vietnam we were Chinese, but in China we were Vietnamese."[33] She had referred to herself as "Overseas Chinese" when I first talked to her, but also rounded off a discussion of her background with the remark that "I don't know who I am". She took me to Victoria prison to see some of her friends who were being deported from Hong Kong back to Vietnam; it was quite odd to see these young "Vietnamese" in a Hong Kong prison who speak absolutely fluent Cantonese. They use Vietnamese together as they all have grown up in Vietnam and have gone to Vietnamese schools. I had a similar experience of this disjunction when waiting for a bus outside the Pillar Point open camp in the New Territories, Hong Kong, with a group of about thirty "Vietnamese". When the bus appeared in the distance, one of the men called out "It's coming" in Cantonese, and everyone moved towards the stop.

Not knowing who one is is a historical accident, since the doubt arises from being posed the question in a time and place in which one cannot answer it. The question is frequently posed of those who live on borders, or those who cross borders in search of a better life. The Nung/Ngai/San Y/San Diu identity is clearly a borderline one, and arises out of cross-border migration. The Nung interviewed on Hei Ling Chau island did not recognize themselves as Hakka, and in response to a direct question generally denied knowledge of Chinese dialects. But if one as a linguist tells them that they are "really" Chinese (or Hakka or Cantonese), what kind of act is that? Or if the San Diu are informed that they were "originally Yao", what sense does that make, given the ideologically loaded nature of origins?

It is a commonplace in studies of ethnicity that ethnic identities are constructs; it is, however, curious that linguistics — of all the social sciences — remains the most clearly committed to its role as measurer of linguistic variation and identity, as arbiter and therefore creator of horizons of identity. I believe that a careful look at the whole nexus of issues surrounding race, ethnicity, identity, will show that linguistics actually holds the whole intellectual structure together. The message to be learnt from the case of Ngai is that linguistic categories are no less part of the ethnographic morass and of the complex processes whereby groups are named, shaped, and classified.

ACKNOWLEDGEMENT

The author would like to thank Irene Bain, Chau Thi Hai, Grant Evans, Nguyen Van Chien, Karin Smedjebacka, and Geoff Wade. Aouda Tse Lai-hing conducted the interviews in Nei Ku Chau detention centre. My appreciation to her for an excellent job. I would also like to express my gratitude to Director Pham Duc Thanh and the staff of the Institute for Southeast Asian Studies, Hanoi, for their kind hospitality and support during my stay in Vietnam from February to May 1995 and subsequent visits. Translation of the Nung tape was done by Ms V., who has asked not to be named. My warm thanks to her and to her family for their hospitality and help.

NOTES

1. Benedict Anderson (1991) picks out the census, the map, and the museum as central institutions of classification. The dependency of national identities on colonial boundary-drawing was symbolized in the appeal made by Vietnam to France to provide documentation on border agreements made between France and China in 1887 and 1895 (Torode 1997).

2. In Vietnam, studies of ethnic groups using the methodology of physical anthropology were published in the 1970s (for example, Nguyen Dinh Koah 1976); however the official classification of ethnic groups is now done largely by population size and by language group.

3. Presumably from the name of the southern Chinese dialect, Hakka. Hakka is spoken from the Vietnamese border across south China to Fujian province and in Taiwan. It is also spoken in Jiangxi and Sichuan provinces, and in many Chinese communities in Southeast Asia.

4. The label "San Y" presumably derives from, or is related to, the Man San Yi (also Thanh Y) ethnonym. Man is generally defined as the Yao group. Castillon du Perron (1954) records a figure of about 300 Man Xanh Y in the Mong Cai area and a total of 5,000 in Vietnam and China. He states that the Man have their own dialect, but that the men all know a second language, in general, Cantonese. In Vietnam they are found in the region of Mong Cai, west of Tien Yen in the Ba Che district and in Mau Son to the east of Lang Son. "San Diu" is a category associated with Yao sub-groups (Man, Trai), but this group is classified in contemporary Vietnamese ethnography as a "Han" minority (Dang Nghiem Van et al. 1993).

5. Fall (1966, p. 154) gives a figure of 860,000 for those who fled south, of whom 600,000 were Catholics.

6. The *U.S. Army Handbook for Vietnam* gives a figure of about 60,000 Nung, 60,000 Black and White Thai and 40,000 Muong (Harris et al. 1962, p. 57) for this migration.

7. Unger states that 22 per cent of the population of Quang Ninh province was ethnic Chinese before the exodus of 1978 (1987, p. 609).

8. The Dossier, which represents the official position of the Vietnam government, records: "In February 1957, on orders from the Government of the People's Republic of China, the Chinese Embassy in Hanoi came to the following agreement with the Vietnamese side: The Ngai in Quang Ninh will be considered as Vietnamese citizens, and the Vietnamese Government will allow them to enjoy the same rights and fulfil the same obligations as other Vietnamese citizens. As regards the Hoa living in other localities in northern Vietnam, the new guideline will be applied to turn them all into Vietnamese citizens. From now on, political and social work among the Hoa will be entirely done by the Vietnamese authorities. After this 1957 agreement, only in the big cities as Hanoi, Hai Phong, Nam Dinh could one find Hoa people who had not yet acquired Vietnamese citizenship." (1978a, p. 24). A second Dossier (Dossier II 1978b) accused the People's Republic of China of using the Hoa in Vietnam as a fifth column against the government. For fierce criticism of the policies of the Vietnamese government towards ethnic Chinese in this period, see Nguyen Van Canh (1983, pp. 128–36).

9. The *South China Morning Post* gave various figures for the migrants from Vietnam to China in that period (200,000, 250,000, and 280,000; see Ng 1993; Cook 1993; Mackenzie 1993). For further discussion of this exodus, see Chen (1992).

10. Mr V. was interviewed in Pillar Point camp in July 1997.

11. One Cantonese-speaking migrant from Vietnam was reported as having renewed his Taiwan passport for the last time in 1974 at the embassy in Saigon (Wan 1995).

12. In a discussion of the Nung, Buttinger notes cryptically (1958, p. 56): "Some authors think the Nung are not really a Thai tribe. The Diem government of South Vietnam was accused by its critics of having employed only Nung troops of the Vietnamese army to fight the sect rebellions in March and April, 1955."

13. "Front Uni pour la Lutte des Races Opprimeés". On this Montagnard resistance movement to the Vietnamese state, see Prados (1995, pp. 80–87).

14. At http://teamhouse.tni.net/nungs.htm.

15. Other articles in the website document "Chinese Nung" involvement in Civilian Irregular Defence Groups (CIDG), and other projects including Delta, Omega, Sigma, B-36, and the Mike Forces. A report from the *San Jose Mercury News*, 20 June 1997, gives an account of the arrival in California of fifty-one Nung soldiers and their families sponsored by former Green Berets. This website also gives extracts from the biographies of these asylum-seekers, detailing their military careers. Prados (1995, pp. 78, 79) describes the role of the Nung as follows: "The Nung strikers were semiprofessional mercenaries frequently employed by both Special Forces and the CIA. Typically, Nung troops provided defence forces while a tribal militia and strike force was being trained and formed. Later […] the CIDGs [Civilian Irregular Defence Groups] were supplemented with battalion-size Mobile Strike Forces, usually called "Mike Forces". Each corps area in South Vietnam began with one Mike Force while Nha Trang headquarters (after October 1964 redesignated the Fifth Special Forces group) had two Mike Force battalions. The latter units were manned by Nungs."

16. It is extraordinary that this should be an argument *against* the granting of asylum, given the subsequent notoriety of the U.S. government's decision to violate the human rights of its own citizens. The report continues: "Mr Marshall said internal exile was a relatively mild deprivation of liberty and had at least afforded them 'the dignity of labour and self-sufficiency'."

17. Vaillant recorded that most of the Chinese were settled along the coast; however, some lived inland in Than Phun (directly on the Sino-Vietnamese border). Those living inland were in close contact with the Man and the Tho. The conclusion of the study is that the physical characteristic of the Chinese are relatively constant, in spite of the vast area which they occupy, migrations, and intermarriage.

18. This is a term applied to varieties of Southern Chinese that are used as an inter-group *lingua franca*. In Guangdong province it refers to varieties of Cantonese; in Guangxi and in Mong Cai *baahkwá* appears to be a blend of Hakka and Cantonese. This linguistic label is neither actually nor potentially the name of an ethnic group.

19. "If now Thai of all the tribes were to ask me which of their numerous dialects is the closest to Cantonese, not only in virtue of the number of words in common, but also in pronunciation, grammar and syntax, I would not hesitate to reply to them that it is the Nung dialect. Furthermore, that is the reason why I have preferred it to other dialects to show the resemblance that exists between Thai and southern Chinese."

20. "Except for several Hakka and Cantonese villages near Mong Cai, settlements established for less than a century, the Chinese do not form anywhere a base as an indigenous population or even as settlements rooted in the soil. They are traders, originating for the most part from Guangdong and Fukien [Fujian], established in the urban areas for many generations, but in constant contact with their place of origin, the particular dialect of which they continue to speak."

21. The study investigates the language of Song Dong district in Ha Bac, in which the Hoa are reported as mainly speaking Ngai, a few Pac Va, and the language of Mong Cai. In the hills around Mong Cai such as Loc Phu and Po Hen, Ngai is spoken; in the townlets, in the plain, by the sea and on the islands generally, Pac Va. In Mong Cai they speak Pac Va. The pronunciation of Pac Va is said to vary considerably.

22. According to the article, San Diu are found in Bac Thai, Ha Bac, Tuyen Quang, and Quang Ninh provinces. This study was based on Vinh Thuc, a village on an island to the southwest of Mong Cai. At the time of the research the village had a population of 2,442 people. Ninety-five per cent were Kinh (Viet); there were three Hoa families and forty-five San Diu families. The San Diu language is classified as belonging to the Han-Tay group of the Han branch of the Sino-Tibetan family. Its pronunciation varies widely according to district, and it is also called Trai.

23. Edmondson (1992, p. 28) records Ngai as "a kind of Hakka spoken by a local peasant group" in Rongshui Miao and Luocheng Mulam Autonomous Counties in northern Guangxi province.

24. Dang Nghiem Van et al. (1984) give their number as 1,500; Dang Nghiem Van et

al. (1993) as 1,200.
25. On the Dan, see Nguyen Truc Binh (1972).
26. I suspect that this observation is based on a misunderstanding. The modern distinction between Hakka and Cantonese, found in Hong Kong for example, was traditionally expressed as a distinction between indigenous inhabitants (*bún deih yàhn*) and Hakka. This term was rendered as "Punti" by the British authorities in Hong Kong, and can still be seen in police wanted posters in Hong Kong ("wanted for armed robbery ... speaks Punti"). The term *bún deih yàhn* served therefore to distinguish the Cantonese from the Hakka. Whether it was understood by the Cantonese speakers of Quang Ninh province as a claim to indigenous status there is open to question.
27. Most of my conversations with people in Mong Cai were conducted in Cantonese, English, and French. I did also interview people using my limited Vietnamese, which was sufficient to ask them how long they had been in Mong Cai, where they came from, what family members they had there, what they thought of it, how business was, and so forth. Some of the Chinese traders from Shanghai spoke English, as did some of the Vietnamese businessmen.
28. In general, it seems that Vietnam is more anxious to delay full liberalization of the border than China; this reflects the relative vulnerability of Vietnam's economy in the face of consumer goods from China, and the fear that an open border will escalate the loss of further raw materials that are needed within Vietnam.
29. In 1995, Vietnam had a shortage of cement, and the Kobe earthquake had pushed up the price on the international market, making it difficult for Vietnam to obtain supplies from outside. The cement shortage has since eased. An article in the *Vietnam Economic Times* suggested that Vietnam was heading for a glut (1997).
30. This is not to say that the category has necessarily disappeared in its entirety in Vietnam.
31. Urciuoli concludes that border-marking language elements are locational markers: "They assign people a place, often opposing places between those who 'have' the language and those who do not. Borders are places where communality ends abruptly; border-marking language elements stand for and performatively bring into being such places." (1995, p. 539).
32. Of course, this is a simplification of the situation in Europe. For example, migration within and to Europe since World War II has complicated the picture, but these migrants are in general found in urban areas. They do not have regional centres, except in as much as they predominate in particular urban areas. The war in Yugoslavia is the latest stage in the modern process of ethnic levelling in Europe.
33. She and her family cannot be returned to Vietnam as Vietnam does not regard them as nationals. An asylum-seeker who likewise holds Taiwanese papers said in an interview with the *South China Morning Post*: "In Vietnam, my family and I were punished for being Chinese. In Hong Kong, for being Vietnamese." (Wan 1995).

REFERENCES

Anderson, Benedict. *Imagined Communities: Reflections on the Origin and Spread of Nationalism.* Rev. ed. London: Verso, 1991.
Batha, Emma. "UN Accepts Former Viet Soldiers as Refugees". *South China Morning Post*, 3 June 1997*a*.
Batha, Emma. "An Old Soldier Wins His Fight for Freedom". *South China Morning Post*, 15 June 1997*b*.
Batha, Emma. "Ethnic Chinese Lose Appeal". *South China Morning Post*, 6 January 1997*c*.
Buttinger, Joseph. *The Smaller Dragon: A Political History of Vietnam.* New York: Praeger, 1958.
Castillon du Perron, P. "Étude d'un peuplement Man Xanh-Y". *Bulletin de la Société des Études Indochinoises* 29, no. 1 (1954): 22–42.
Chen Min. *The Strategic Triangle: Lessons from the Indochina War.* Boulder and London: Lynne Rienner, 1992.
Chen Yongling, ed. *Minzu Cidian* [Dictionary of ethnology]. 2nd ed. Shanghai: Shangha Cishu Chubanshe, 1989.
Chuong Sau. "Dan Toc Hoa". In *Cac Dan Toc It Nguoi o Viet Nam*, pp. 388–95. Hanoi: Nha Xuat Ban Khoa Hoc Xa Hoi, 1978.
Cook, Beryl. "Illegal Immigrants Sail into Trouble". *South China Morning Post*, 23 April 1993.
Dang Nghiem Van, Chu Thai Son, and Luu Hung. *The Ethnic Minorities in Vietnam.* Hanoi: Foreign Languages Publishing House, 1984.
Dang Nghiem Van, Chu Thai Son, and Luu Hung. *Ethnic Minorities in Vietnam.* Vietnam: The Gioi Publishers, 1993.
[Dossier]. *The Hoa in Vietnam: Dossier.* Documents of Vietnam Courier. Hanoi: Foreign Languages Publishing House, 1978*a*.
[Dossier II]. *The Hoa in Vietnam: Dossier II.* Documents of Vietnam Courier. Hanoi: Foreign Languages Publishing House, 1978*b*.
Edmondson, Jerold. "Some Kadai Languages of Northern Guangxi, China". In *Pan-Asiatic Linguistics: Proceedings of the Third International Symposium on Language and Linguistics*, vol. 1, pp. 28–43. Thailand, Bangkok: Chulalongkorn University, 1992.
Fall, Bernard. *The Two Viet-Nams: A Political and Military Analysis.* 2nd rev. ed. Boulder and London: Westview Press, 1966.
Harris, George, et al. *U.S. Army Area Handbook for Vietnam.* Washington, D.C.: Foreign Areas Studies Division, U.S. Army, 1962.
Haudricourt, A. "Note sur les dialectes de la région de Moncay". *Bulletin de l'École Française d'extrême-Orient.* Tome L. Fasc. 1 (1960): 161–77.
Hu Qiaomu, ed. *Zhongguo Da Baike Quangshu (Minzu)* [Encyclopaedia Sinica: ethnology]. Beijing: Zhongguo Da Baike Quangshu, 1986.
Lewallen, John. *Ecology of Devastation: Indochina.* Maryland: Penguin, 1971.
Mackenzie, Annette. "Thousands of Vietnamese in China Set to Flee to Hong Kong". *South China Morning Post*, 13 July 1993.

MacMahon, F. and S. Furlong. "Fears for Repatriated Minority". *South China Morning Post*, 5 August 1992.
Maspero, Georges. *Un empire colonial franҫtais, L'indochine*, vol. 1. Paris: G. van Oest, 1929.
Ng Kang-Chung. "Unwanted Campers Plan Their Escape". *South China Morning Post*, 17 July 1993.
Nguyen Dinh Khoa. *Cac Dan Toc o Mien Bac Viet Nam* [The minorities of northern Vietnam]. Hanoi: Nha Xuat Ban Khoa Hoc Xa Hoi, 1976.
Nguyen Truc Binh. "Ve toc danh dan, sin trong nhom ngoui hoa o vung ven bien Quang Ninh". *Thong bao Dan toc hoc* 1 (1972): 90–96.
Nguyen Van Ai. "Vai net ve he thong ngu am tieng San Diu". Pages 125-138 In *Tim hieu ngon ngu cac dan toc thieu so o viet nam* [Investigations into the languages of the ethnic minorities of Vietnam], vol. 1. Hanoi: Uy Ban Khoa Hoc Xa Hoi Viet Nam, 1972.
Nguyen Van Canh. *Vietnam under Communism, 1975–1982*. Stanford, California: Hoover Institution Press, Stanford University, 1983.
[Nung]. "Request for Help from a Group of Minority People Who Migrated from the Highland of North Vietnam — the Nung", translated by Ka Fue. Mimeographed. Hong Kong, 1990.
Olson, James. *Dictionary of the Vietnam War*. New York: Greenwood Press, 1987.
Prados, John. *The Hidden History of the Vietnam War*. Chicago: Ivan R. Dee, 1995.
Savina, F.M. *Dictionnaire Etymologique. Français-Nung-Chinois*. Hong Kong: Imprimerie de la Société des Missions Étrangères, 1924.
Schrock, Joann et al. *Minority Groups in North Vietnam*. Washington: U.S. Government Printing Office, 1972.
Torode, Greg. "French Lobbied in Border Dispute". *South China Morning Post*, 7 May 1997.
Unger, E.S. "The Struggle over the Chinese Community in Vietnam". *Pacific Affairs* 60 (1987): 596–614.
Urciuoli, Bonnie. "Language and Borders". *Annual Review of Anthropology* 24 (1995): 525–46.
Vaillant, Louis. "L'Étude anthropologique des Chinois Hak-ka de la province de Mongcay (Tonkin)". *L'Anthropologie* 30 (1920): 83–109.
Vietnam Economic Times. "Too Much? After Years of Chronic Cement Shortages, Vietnam May Be Heading for a Market Glut". Supplement, June 1997.
[Vietnamese government]. "Nomenclature of Vietnamese Ethnic Groups. Report persuant to Directive No. 83-CD of the Government Council of Vietnam, in which 54 groups were identified (December 1978)". *Vietnamese Studies* 2, no. 72 (1978): 161–68.
Vu Ba Hung. "Buoc dau tim hieu he thong nhu am tieng hoa". In *Tim hieu ngon ngu cac dan toc thieu so o viet nam* [Investigations into the languages of the ethnic minorities of Vietnam], vol. 1, pp. 105–38. Hanoi: Uy Ban Khoa Hoc Xa Hoi Viet Nam, 1972.
Vy Thi Be, Janice E. Saul, and Nancy Freiberger Wilson. *Nung Fan Slihng-English dictionary*. Manila: Summer Institute of Linguistics, 1982.

Wan, Mariana. "We Don't Belong in Vietnam". *South China Morning Post*, 1 May 1995.

Western, Neil. "Hope for 250 as Court Frees Viet". *Hong Kong Standard*, 31 May 1997.

Weinrich, Uriel. *Languages in Contact: Findings and Problems.* Publications of the Linguistic Circle of New York, no. 1. New York: Linguistic Circle of New York, 1953.

Whitfield, Danny. *Historical and Cultural Dictionary of Vietnam*. Metuchen, New Jersey: Scarecrow Press, 1976.

Womack, Brantly. "Sino-Vietnamese Border Trade". *Asian Survey* 34 (1994): 495–512.

14

Regional Development and Cross-Border Cultural Linkage: The Case of a Vietnamese Community in Guangxi, China

Cheung Siu-woo

My first visit to the Vietnamese community in Guangxi province in the People's Republic of China (PRC) was made possible thanks to special arrangements made by Mr Li,[1] a retired middle-ranking government official of Fengcheng county. Mr Li is also a respected scholar of the Jing, an ethnic minority of Vietnamese descent. He brought me to his natal village Wanwei, where we joined a meeting with village elders to plan the celebration of the annual Hat^2 Festival which would be held a week later in late July 1996. Wanwei is situated along the Gulf of Tonkin (Beibuwan) less than 20 kilometres from the Vietnamese border.

In the morning, Mr Li and I were picked up at his home in Fengcheng by Mr Zhang and his chauffeur in his Toyota Crown, a status symbol in post-Mao China. Mr Zhang, who is also from Wanwei, has been one of the most successful businessmen in the local Vietnamese community since he started cross-border trading in 1989, when the Sino-Vietnamese border re-opened. He now runs a big trading firm in Fengcheng. His Han-Chinese business partner from Sichuan, who was visiting Fengcheng, shared another car with three of Mr Li's fellow villagers who also were middle-ranking local government officials. This car was provided by their work units. It was thus a very mixed group that embarked on a trip of very mixed purposes — academic research, local religious affairs, and business.

A newly constructed toll highway links Fengcheng with Dongxing, a market-town right on the Vietnamese border. Half way along this road we turned off onto a well-paved road leading towards Wanwei, and before noon we arrived at the temple in the middle of the village. While discussing the arrangements for the *Hat* Festival with the village elders, Mr Li and Mr Zhang explained to me that this festival in honour of a local deity was important because it demonstrated the unique ethnic culture of the people.

The people living in Wanwei speak Vietnamese and call themselves Kinh, a term which has the same pronunciation in local Cantonese. The Chinese character for this ethnonym is *jing* in Putonghua. The Kinh are officially designated as one of the fifty-five ethnic minorities in China. Their identity as a minority in the Chinese nation is quite complicated, as a comment made by Mr Zhang reveals. He said that the Kinh were "both the smallest and the biggest *minzu*". The Chinese term *minzu* has a double meaning, denoting both individual "nationalities" (ethnic groups) and the "nation", that is, the whole population of the country. He was referring, on the one hand, to the small number of Kinh compared with other ethnic groups in China and, on the other, to their majority status in Vietnam.[3]

Strolling round the village after the meeting, I found my first impression of the village somewhat puzzling. What I saw were clusters of ornately constructed and decorated private properties, many having five to six storeys, along the two sides of the 20-metre-wide paved concrete street. This did not match my idea of a small fishing village, the term Mr Li had used to characterize Wanwei. While the elders had a humble meal of rice porridge at the village temple, the visiting élite and I were treated by the Chinese businessman from Sichuan to an extravagant seafood lunch in a local restaurant, said to be one of several seafood restaurants doing big business by serving tourists on weekends. Sitting beside me, Mr Zhang boasted about his business clout, and privately expressed to me his contempt towards Mr Li for his failure, or lack of attempt, to get rich by exploiting the access he had to economic opportunities when serving in the county government. After the meal, the group made a tour around Wanwei in the two cars. Wanwei is a 13.4 square kilometre "island" that has been linked by dikes and reclamations to two smaller islands which two decades earlier were not attached to the mainland. Together, they are known as the "Three Islands of the Kinh".

We stopped at the sites of development projects and tourism facilities scattered along the nicely paved road traversing the whole "island". Mr Zhang tried his utmost to persuade his Chinese business partner to invest in one of the local development projects. He emphasized the prospects of developing the 8-kilometre-long beach into a popular tourist resort with a view across to Vietnam (less than 10 kilometres away), and also of expanding the existing wharf into a small port for cross-border trade with Vietnam.

The rest of the group left Wanwei in the late afternoon, but Mr Li and I decided to stay overnight to prepare for my fieldwork on the *Hat* Festival that would start the following week. I was lodged in a small guesthouse run by the family of Mr Li's nephew. The three-storey building, with poorly furnished rooms sharing common washing facilities, looked quite dilapidated compared with the nearby, more neatly constructed buildings with air-conditioning and private washrooms. Yet, the whole guesthouse was fully occupied by some long-term tenants. Except for one room that was rented by two businessmen from Guangdong province, all the other six guest-rooms were shared by groups of young women. After I had got to know Mr Li's nephew, I found out that this guesthouse was in fact a brothel. That evening, I had dinner with the family of Mr Li's nephew and two of their female Vietnamese tenants who had crossed the border to China illegally to work as prostitutes. I also saw some young female tenants, who were from various parts of inland China, being approached by men asking for service. Mr Li's nephew frankly explained to me that he gained commissions from the sex service by providing space for customers. They were mainly businessmen from Guangdong and Fujian provinces, who, with the help of local villagers acting as middlemen, bought seafood from Vietnamese fishermen across the sea. Other customers were weekend tourists.

Leaving the village the following afternoon, I found myself preoccupied with a complex feeling towards what I had encountered during this trip. The re-opening of the Sino-Vietnamese border has provided the local Vietnamese community with privileged economic opportunities and allowed them to develop economically. Some external influences, such as capital investment, have been largely welcomed, while others, such as prostitution, have probably been unwanted but perhaps inevitable. Under such circumstances of drastic socio-economic change, members of the local community have inevitably embarked on re-ordering social positions and also on reconstituting identities premised upon categories such as age, class, gender, ethnicity, and citizenship.

This chapter aims at investigating the articulation of the various identities of the local Kinh community through focusing in particular on their transnational cultural links with Vietnam across the border. I will attempt to show how the transnational identity of the Kinh has served as a significant medium for the articulation of their other identities.

In the following pages, the observations that I made during the *Hat* Festival on the transformation of the Kinh's cultural linkage with Vietnam, as revealed in their religious beliefs and practices associated with the festival, will first be highlighted. Religion as a "text" (Geertz 1973) or as a "social drama" (Turner 1957) is the vantage point for my observation of the restructuring of social positions and of the reformulating of identities. Yet, specific religious acts and meanings also need to be understood in their particular historical and spatial contexts of political and economic relationships. I then go on to explore the vicissitudes of international politics that has shaped the identities of the Kinh living in the region around the Gulf of Tonkin, especially after the national border between China and Vietnam was created. Finally, I investigate the flourishing regional economic development around the Gulf of Tonkin in the 1990s and its impact upon the Kinh community and the cultural premises of the people's identities in relation to the transformation of their cultural linkage with Vietnam across the border.

TRANSFORMATION OF CROSS-BORDER CULTURAL LINKAGE: THE HAT FESTIVAL

The Kinh community worship five main deities in the village temple, represented by the five wooden tablets arranged in a line on the main altar. The *Hat* Festival is held annually to commemorate the paramount deity, the Sea God, which stands in the middle. A series of ceremonies are held throughout the festival, which lasts for a ritually prescribed period of seven days, starting on the tenth day of the sixth lunar month.

On the morning of the first day, the festival begins with the transfer of the Sea God from its main shrine located at the tip of the nearby Bailong Peninsula to the village temple. This year, I followed a procession team of more than one hundred temple elders and associates who marched out from the village temple to receive the deity. The whole team had at its centre a sedan chair on which was placed an incense burner. This was carried on the shoulders of two persons. To inform the villagers about the initiation of the festival, members of the procession team were wearing colourful ritual clothes, hoisting flags and banners and were beating gongs and drums, while marching to the deafening noise of firecrackers. The team marched along the main road towards the beach, with more and more people joining the procession. After arriving on the beach, temple elders headed by religious specialists performed various rituals. These mainly consisted of prayers directed to the Sea God in its shrine far away across the sea on the Bailong Peninsula. The deity was symbolically received by means of divination and the igniting of incense in the burner on the sedan chair. Temple elders told me that in the past they used to get the burning incense directly from the deity's shrine across the sea by boat. The deity, as represented by the burning incense, was then carried back to the village temple, with many of the local villagers setting off firecrackers in front of their houses as the deity passed.

It is not hard to understand why Wanwei, a fishing community which has traditionally made its living from the sea, should have the Sea God as its patron deity. Yet, beyond its relevance for immediate economic subsistence, the beliefs associated with the Sea God also provide the community with a framework in which regional socio-cultural links with various communities in the Gulf of Tonkin can be conceptualized, as well as giving the community a sense of connection with the natural and the supernatural worlds. This socio-cultural linkage between communities in the region is reflected in a myth about the origin of the *Hat* Festival. This story, entitled "The Legend of the Three Islands", is indeed a myth about the origin of the Wanwei community in the historical context of the region. It first appeared in a volume of Kinh folktales edited by Mr Li, the man who brought me to the festival. The story reads:

> There was a mountain called Bailongling [Mt. White Dragon] along the northwestern coast of Beibuwan [the Gulf of Tonkin]. Ships going between Dongxing and Beihai had to pass around it. A huge Centipede Spirit lived inside a deep cave in the mountain. Whenever a ship passed in front of the cave, people on the ship had to offer a human sacrifice to the Centipede Spirit as food, or else the spirit would produce big waves and the ship would capsize. ... One morning, a beggar carrying a big pumpkin on his back approached a ship in Dongxing and asked for a free ride to Beihai. The captain was happy to agree, as he secretly planned to present the poor beggar as a sacrifice to the Centipede Spirit. He told the beggar to come the next morning. At dawn, the ship set off from Dongxing along the Beilun River, gradually began to cross the Beibuwan and finally neared the cave in which the Centipede Spirit lived. The beggar then asked the sailors to heat up the big pumpkin. When the Centipede Spirit came out of the cave and approached the ship in the sea, the captain tried to push the poor beggar down into the water as the human sacrifice. The beggar asked the sailors to wait a moment, then threw the red hot pump-

kin toward the Centipede Spirit. The Centipede Spirit immediately swallowed the pumpkin, only to find the heat burning its stomach. After a short struggle that caused huge waves, the Centipede Spirit died. ... The people on the ship finally realized that the beggar was an Immortal who had come to kill the malicious Centipede Spirit. After its death, the Centipede Spirit broke into three pieces — the head, the trunk, and the tail. The three pieces of the dead body later became three islands: Wutau island, Shanxin island, and Wanwei island — the three islands of the present day Kinh people. [In Chinese the second syllable in each of the three names means "the head", "the heart", and "the tail," respectively.] Who was that Immortal? He was said to be the Sea God who is now worshipped in the village temple on each of the three islands. Every year people on each island hold a festival to thank their Sea God and ask for good catches in fishing. (Su et al. 1984, pp. 1–3)

This story is depicted in murals painted above the entrance to a long pavilion outside the village temple in Wanwei, featuring the Centipede Spirit broken into three pieces, the ship in the sea, and the red pumpkin. Similar figures are also found embroidered on the blouses the temple personnel wear for the ceremonies. On the first day of the festival, display boards recounting this origin myth are put outside the temple for any interested visitors to read. Indeed, similar versions of this myth also appear in many publications on the Kinh nationality. However, when I talked to some village elders, including the former religious leader of the village, who had officiated the festival's ceremonies in the past, I got a slightly different version. According to this one, the Centipede Spirit broke into four pieces instead of three after its death. The extra piece was the mouth, including the two big teeth, of the Centipede Spirit. This part of the body later became Wanzhu island, with the second syllable in the name Wanzhu being a homophone for the word for teeth in local Cantonese. I was told that Wanzhu island was located on the Vietnamese side across the sea, known as Tra Co island in Vietnamese, and that local Kinh communities on the Chinese side throughout history had had close interactions with the people on this island.

I asked Mr Li, who is the author of the first version of the story found in some publications, what he knew about the different versions. He answered that the "four-piece" version was the more authentic one, but that he and other Kinh scholars had decided to change the story into the "three-piece" version for political reasons. He explained that since Wanzhu island did not belong to China, it was better to exclude it from the story in order to avoid confusing the official national boundary and the identity of the local Kinh people.

When I read the story again in *Jingzu Jianshi* ("Concise history of the Jing nationality"), I found that the story stops with the death of the Centipede Spirit and omits the part about how many parts it broke into and what these parts finally became (Jingzu Jianshi Bianxiezu 1984, p. 48). *Jingzu Jianshi* is the official version of the Kinh people's history, arising out of a state project for the production of an authoritative history for each nationality in China. Mr Li's explanation seems to make this editorial cut much more understandable.

However, when I read the story in its earlier form, published in a 1953 report written by a state research team (Yan et al. 1987), I found yet another version. Though also a "three-piece" version, it differs from those published in the 1980s. This version recounts that the tail piece became Wanwei, the trunk piece became Wanzhu, whereas the head piece became Tushan (ibid., p. 80). The author indicates that the former name of Tushan was Taushan, with the first syllable *tau* referring to the head in Chinese. Tushan was said to be an island near Haiphong in northern Vietnam, and the place of origin of the Kinh in Wanwei. Their earliest history of migration traces back to AD 1511, as recounted in a local document (Jingzu Jianshi Bianxiezu 1984, p. 6).

The development of the different versions of the origin myth seems to reveal a gradual detachment on the part of the local Kinh from their original community in Vietnam. The "four-piece" version, prevalent among local elders, cuts their connection with their home of origin in Tushan, yet clings to the island of Wanzhu across the sea on the Vietnamese side. The "three-piece" version, promoted by the Kinh élite in their publications, confines the mythical origin of the local Kinh communities totally within the boundaries of China.

The national border has not only preoccupied the local Kinh élite's religious belief of the *Hat* Festival's mythical origin, it has also shaped the festival's religious practices, as reflected in the role of some female ritual performers. In general, few women take part in the *Hat* Festival. All the members of the temple's organizing committee are male, and no women participated in the meetings held by the village elders to make arrangements for the festival. Only male household representatives are allowed to attend the temple feasts on the afternoons of the fifth and sixth day; however, this year there were two exceptions. One was a woman from the village who works as a doctor in the county hospital, and the other was a Chinese businesswoman who has come to Wanwei to run a jet-ski rental store on the beach. The whole team of ritual specialists for the festival are male, and all members are elected from the community by formal rules to hold formal positions in the series of elaborated ceremonies. Yet, five female performers, called *hat co* ("female singer") in Vietnamese, played a significant role throughout the whole festival, performing songs and dances as part of the ritual. These female ritual specialists were paid for their services. Four of them were hired from the nearby Wutau "island", and the fifth was Mr Li's wife.

These women, who are all from China, have served as ritual specialists only for the last two years, and in doing so seem to have broken a cultural tradition involving the local Kinh's cultural linkage with Vietnam. The practice of hiring a team of female ritual singers from Vietnam probably has a long history, as this was the practice before the communist take-over, as the 1953 report makes clear (Yan et al. 1987, p. 133). The *Hat* Festival was also popular in the coastal areas of northern Vietnam close to the border (ibid., p. 151). After 1949, these cultural links were interrupted, and the Kinh community in Wanwei started to train their own female singers. Mr Li's wife was one of ten women who were trained by a specialist from Vietnam who had married into the community. Soon after, religious activities nation-wide fell foul of political ideology and official hostility to religion. This eventually led to the demolition of the village temple at the end of the 1950s. Not until 1985 was the temple reconstructed and the festival resumed. In the years that followed, the Kinh community re-established their cultural links with Vietnam through hiring female ritual singers.

The tenth anniversary of the reinstating of the *Hat* Festival in Wanwei took place in 1995, and for this occasion the village elders planned a large-scale celebration. They sent invitations to provincial and local commercial, academic, and governmental institutions, to the public media, as well as to friends and organizations overseas — including Hong Kong and Taiwanese businessmen who had been doing business in Fengcheng. Interestingly, a Vietnamese delegation composed of various governmental organizations from the neighbouring province of Quang Ninh, and of officials from Hai Ninh district on the opposite side of Wanwei across the sea, was also on the invitation list.

A week before the festival, a team of representatives from Wanwei attended a *Hat* Festival held in a village in Hai Ninh district. This was the village from which they traditionally hired female ritual performers for their own *Hat* Festival. They went there as guests, crossing the sea on their bamboo rafts, and reciprocated by extending an invitation to the village leaders for the tenth anniversary celebration to be held in Wanwei a week later. When the day came, more than two thousand guests from outside flooded Wanwei, including a delegation team of about fifty people from Vietnam. In addition to officials from the provincial and district authorities, the Vietnamese delegation also included the village team who were making a reciprocal visit to Wanwei. Interestingly, the village team had chosen to join the official delegation by crossing the national land border through official formalities, rather than by crossing the sea on rafts as they used to do in the past. Thus, the distance of the informal sea route was tripled.

The most popular Vietnamese guests seem to have been the twenty members of the Quang Ninh Provincial Cultural Performance Team, who performed a series of singing and dancing programmes throughout the festival and became the centre of media attention, being featured in local newspaper coverage (Lu and Wu 1995). Interestingly, while the team from Vietnam offered modern-style cultural performances, the traditional duty of religious ritual singing and dancing was taken care of by several local women, including Mr Li's wife and his two daughters as well as an elderly woman from Vietnam who had married into the village.

In 1996 once again, no female ritual performers were hired from Vietnam for the festival. I was told that this was because the celebrations in the previous year had cost more than 180,000 renminbi; they needed to minimize expenses.[4] However I doubted whether the village elders will consider hiring singing teams from Vietnam in coming years, as they have already designated four local women to start singing and dancing lessons for ritual performances with Mr Li's wife once the festival this year is over. However, the modern-style cultural performances will probably continue. In 1996, a performance in this style was held in the open area outside the village school next to the temple during the first afternoon of the festival. It also included a song-and-dance performance by Mr Li's wife and his two daughters. The cultural performance programme attracted most spectators, with lines of chairs being arranged in front of the village school to serve honorary guests from outside, whereas local villagers crowded round the performing area in a circle. The traditional religious rituals which were being performed simultaneously inside the temple were, however, attracting very few people besides the team of religious specialists.

The above observations on the religious practices during the *Hat* Festival in Wanwei attest to the fact that the cultural linkage between the local Kinh community and Vietnam has somehow changed in nature. Wanwei's traditional cultural links with local villages in Vietnam, which took the form of the hiring of female ritual performers, have been terminated, while modern-style cultural performances have been introduced from Vietnam through the visit of a Vietnamese delegation. Wanwei and local communities in Vietnam were traditionally connected by the unregulated sea route, whereas the modern connecting link between Wanwei and the state authority of Vietnam is made through official custom formalities across the national land border. These changes correspond to the transformation of the myth about the origin of the *Hat* Festival and of the local Kinh communities, as illustrated above. It thus seems as if the local Kinh community, in becoming more and more aware of their relationship with the Chinese and the Vietnamese states, has altered their perception of their relationship to Vietnam, as reflected in their religious beliefs and the practices associated with the *Hat* Festival. Indeed, the national border seems to have become an increasingly significant reference point for the definition of the local Kinh community's identity. This official border did not exist until the deal made between France and China as late as 1887. Let us now turn to the making of this national border and the subsequent historical events that shaped the identity of the Kinh community in Wanwei.

THE MAKING OF THE BORDER AND TRANSNATIONAL IDENTITY

Besides the Sea God, the Kinh community in Wanwei also worships four other deities in the village temple. They are represented by four wooden tablets standing on either side of the Sea God. Heading the pantheon are the Sea God and the Mountain God. The main shrine of the Sea God is located at the tip of the nearby Bailong Peninsula, whereas the Mountain God has its own shrine on Wanwei island.[5] During the *Hat* Festival, both the Sea God and the Mountain God are symbolically received in the temple in the form of burning incense from their main shrines. No villager can remember the origin of the other three deities, whose names suggest they are figures from Vietnamese history. One of the gods has an official title related to the Chen dynasty in Vietnam. Some specialists in the studies of the Kinh nationality surmise that these three deities are the patron gods of individual localities in Vietnam from where the ancestors of the Kinh community migrated (Gupo et al. 1993, p. 122). This pantheon largely reflects the history of the migration and settlement of the Kinh. While migrating, they carried with them the supernatural patronage of the deities from their original communities. When they settled in this new place and interacted with its physical environment, they gradually developed additional local patron deities — the Sea God and the Mountain God.

Mr Li told me that his lineage, the biggest one in Wanwei, has lived there for more than ten generations. The 1953 report states that some villagers on Shanxin island traced their settlement back thirteen generations (Yan et al. 1987, p. 79). According to a village record of customary rules discovered in Wanwei by an official research team in 1953, the Kinh first settled on the three islands in AD 1511, the third year of the Hungshun Reign of the Vietnamese Li dynasty, after their ancestors accidentally discovered the place during fishing and decided to migrate from their original home in Tushan, a small island close to Haiphong in North Vietnam (ibid., pp. 78, 80). The interesting point of this document is not so much the exact year of the settlement, which is given by the Vietnamese dynastic year, but that the Vietnamese dynastic year is also referred to for the date when the document was written. This was 1856, which is written as the tenth year of the Side reign of the last Vietnamese dynasty, rather than the sixth year of the Xianfeng reign of the Qing dynasty in China (ibid., p. 78). In other local documents and in temple inscriptions found in the local Kinh communities, there are various references to dynastic reigns in Vietnam. In Chinese historical records the national boundary between China and Vietnam was very fuzzy. Not until 1887, when the boundary was formally drawn under the negotiations between France and China, were the Kinh settlements in Fengcheng designated as Chinese territories.[6] Local documents seem to attest that before 1887 the local Kinh communities had close connections and allegiance to the Vietnamese state. A land-deed in Wanwei was, for example, issued by a local official with a title in the Vietnamese local administration during the Mingmang reign of the last Vietnamese dynasty, sometime in the first half of the nineteenth century (ibid., pp. 77–78). Some village elders in Wanwei recounted that in the past the three islands were administered by the local government stationed on Wanzhu island on the Vietnamese side across the sea, and that their ancestors had to go there to attend administrative meetings for local affairs. However, once the national border was formally demarcated, the Kinh communities on the Chinese side developed a transnational identity in relation to the two states. This identity was at times ambivalent, and reflected the Kinh's complex position in the subsequent political vicissitudes in the region.

The confrontation between the French and the Chinese, and the subsequent making of the Sino-Vietnamese national border which formally incorporated the Kinh communities under China's sovereignty, was certainly a turning point for the development of the identity of the Kinh people. In the first half of the nineteenth century, the Kinh community in a village near the market town of Jiangping had been converted to Catholicism by French missionaries (Yan et al. 1987, p. 145). Before the formal demarcation of the national boundary, the intrusion of French troops to the region of Jiangping in 1883, and their occupation of the region in 1886, including that of Bailong Peninsula and the various Kinh communities, had exacerbated the ethnic tensions between the Kinh and the local Chinese (Yuan et al. 1987, p. 20; Yan et al. 1987, p. 152). The Chinese accused the French troops of killing only those who spoke Chinese and wore Chinese clothes, and not the Kinh, because they had assisted the French troops in killing Chinese during the occupation. After the French withdrew, some of the local Chinese plotted revenge, and the Kinh were generally despised. In order to avoid hostility and discrimination, many Kinh people tried to disguise themselves as Chinese by wearing Chinese clothes and speaking Chinese. To vindicate themselves and adjust themselves to their new identity as Chinese citizens, they glorified their hero, Du Guangfei, who was said to have fought side by side with the Chinese against the French colonial power (Yuan et al. 1987, p. 21).

The pantheon of the Kinh cosmology in Wanwei, as it appears in the sacred texts recited everyday by ritual specialists during the ceremonies of the *Hat* Festival, includes a series of minor deities. Many of them are the ancestors of local villagers. They have achieved this status through a combination of religious power, moral conduct, and financial contributions. The most prominent is Du Guanghui, the ancestor of the local Du lineage. A small altar dedicated to him, with his name on a tablet, was placed at the main entrance of the village temple throughout the festival to ward off evil spirits, as he was generally considered the guardian of the village. On the tablet the honorary title, "Official of the Eighth Grade", was written above his name, a title said to have been granted by the Vietnamese imperial court for his military efforts while fighting against the encroaching French colonial power in the second half of the nineteenth century. He was said to have led the Kinh community in the struggle against the French, side by side with Liu Yongfu. Liu Yongfu was a Chinese national hero who with his renowned "Black Banner Militia" fought against the French in northern Vietnam in the mid-nineteenth century (ibid., p. 21). The legend of Du's association with a Chinese national hero and the Vietnamese source of his honorary title is indicative of how the Kinh have had to manœuvre between their twin allegiances towards the Chinese and Vietnamese states.

Du's glorious deeds have been continued by his descendants. Before the temple feast started on the fourth afternoon of the *Hat* Festival, the great grandson of Du Guanghui's younger brother, Mr Du Guoqiang, was the villager honoured as a representative of all those working outside of the village. This took the form of a ceremony in which he received tea-offerings from the female ritual performers. Du Guoqiang was a veteran of the Indochina War in the 1960s; he had served in the Vietnamese army in their struggle against the United States. After graduating from the national army's language institute of China, he became a military interpreter, probably because of the advantage of his native tongue. In 1988, he retired from the army with the rank of vice-regiment commander, and currently serves in the government of the Dongxing Economic Development District as deputy director of the personnel department and director of the labour department.

No one from Wanwei had ever reached such a high rank in the army, and Du Guoqiang is one of the most respected men in Wanwei. When he received the tea-offering at the ceremony, he gave a short speech about moral behaviour directed at the young people. Unfortunately, some of them complained to me that they barely understood the authentic Vietnamese that Du spoke, which is somewhat different from the local Vietnamese dialect.[7] When I talked about this to Mr Li, he remarked that Du's authentic Vietnamese was in keeping with the festival, which represented authentic Kinh cultural tradition. He then went on to denounce the village Party-Secretary, who had also given a speech at the ceremony, but had used Cantonese instead of Vietnamese.

The linguistic divide between the local Kinh and people in Vietnam correlates with the gap between the respective cultures and identities which gradually developed after the demarcation of the national boundary. People in Vietnam categorize the Kinh in Guangxi as "Chinese" because of their adoption of Chinese-style clothing as well as of customs, while the Chinese in Guangxi call the local Kinh group "Vietnamese" because of their native language (Yan et al. 1987, p. 76). Although, the groups of Kinh people on either side of the border share the same self-appellation *nguoi Kinh* (the Kinh people), they call each other "Chinese" or "Vietnamese", depending on where they live. The Kinh in Guangxi call those who live across the sea in Vietnam "Vietnamese" (ibid., p. 149).

When I went with Du Guoqiang to visit the graves of Du Guanghui and his younger brother, and later to the home of Mr Du's brother nearby in Wanwei, he recounted for me the glorious past of his family. While Du Guanghui was fighting against French troops on land, his younger brother, who was Du Guoqiang's great grandfather, was fighting against French troops at sea. During the Republican period 1911–49, his grandfather was a "Jiazhang" (Neighbourhood Security Chief) and his father's sister's husband was a "Baozhang" (Village Security Chief) — the two lowest levels of government officials in local administration. His uncle (father's sister's husband) survived the fall of the Republican regime in 1949, yet was caught and imprisoned in the village temple. He finally escaped from the temple by digging a tunnel, and made his way to Vietnam on a bamboo raft. Under the communist regime, Du Guoqiang's father became the head of the village production team, and then the head of the fishery production team of the collective.

The participation of the members of the Du family in the Republican government's local administration indicates how the Kinh have been able to manœuvre in the modern Chinese nation. This was important for their survival during periods of ethnic conflict between themselves and the local Chinese.

In the Republican period, competition over natural resources and territories often led to village feuds (ibid., pp. 152–53). For example, the Kinh on Shanxin island settled there later than the Chinese and consequently found themselves deprived of most of the land resources. They were also often beaten up by the Chinese for collecting firewood on the hillsides. On the other hand, they fought hard against the Chinese to protect their own fishing resources and equipment from pillage by their Chinese neighbours. Serious village feuds occurred more than ten times during the Republican period. On the northeastern side of Wanwei island, the Chinese settlers were the latecomers, and they were eager to expand their territory by cutting the forest. This led to confrontations with the Kinh, who considered the forest a windshield for their village which faces the sea to the south. To stop frequent village feuds, the local authority erected stone tablets to mark the boundary between the two communities. Soon, however, the tablets disappeared and the two sides were accusing each other for the misdeed. The two villages refused to allow their children to study in the same school, and they thus operated their own schools in their respective village temples. A year before the communist take-over, the Chinese settlers raided the Kinh village during the Spring Festival, seized all property, and even extorted a ransom by kidnapping a few Kinh villagers.

In addition to these direct confrontations over territory and natural resources, the Kinh and the local Chinese had a very unbalanced economic relationship (ibid., pp. 162–63). Chinese fish merchants used to secure their fish supply from Kinh fishermen by offering loans. Being clients, the Kinh fishermen were forced to sell all their fish to the same Chinese merchants. They were not paid a fair price for their fish, and the scales used were also fixed. Many of the Kinh people who did not possess farmland suffered from high rents, because they were tenants of Chinese landlords.

Many local Chinese even threatened to drive the Kinh back to Vietnam. Because relations were so tense, many of the Kinh changed their clothes to pass as Chinese and did not dare to reveal their true identity, as in the period after the French occupation in 1887. This continued well after the communist take-over (ibid., p. 152). In fact, many of the Kinh people in Wanwei fled to Vietnam because of economic hardship. That hardship was compounded by the necessity of paying bribes to the local authorities in order to escape the draft into the Republican army during wartime (Yuan et al. 1987, p. 22; Yan et al. 1987, p. 111).

Ethnic conflicts were probably further aggravated by the tense political atmosphere in the early years of the communist regime. The various political struggles — such as the "Removing Bandits and Overlords" (*qingfei fanba*) campaign in 1950, which targeted local representatives of the collapsed Republican regime, and the Land Reform (*tudi gaige*) campaign against landlords and the upper class in 1952 — caused more than seventy Kinh to flee to Vietnam from the various Kinh communities (Yan et al. 1987, p. 152). One such example is Du Guoqiang's uncle (father's sister's husband) (ibid., p. 92 for individual cases). From the Catholic Kinh community next to the Jiangping market-town, another group of twenty-six fled to Vietnam after their priest was imprisoned and strangled to death. He had been charged with conducting subversive activities on behalf of foreign imperialists. There were also widespread rumours that the Communist Party's campaign against religion would lead to the killing of all believers (ibid., pp. 144–45). During these tumultuous years of political transition (1949–53) the Kinh were constantly threatened by rumours that all of them would be driven back to Vietnam. Therefore, the majority of them who did not consider leaving became circumspect about revealing their ethnic identity (ibid., p. 150). For instance, the official questionnaires issued by the local authority during the Land Reform in 1952 made the Kinh community very suspicious, because they inquired about their ethnic identity and personal histories. The visit of the state research team in 1953 to investigate the history of the Kinh triggered a similar suspicion.

In 1953, the fear of being driven away from their homeland finally ended with the establishment of the three "nationality autonomous townships" in Wutau, Shanxin, and Wanwei (Yuan et al. 1987, p. 54; Yan et al. 1987, p. 150). Through this administrative arrangement, the Chinese government conferred citizenship on the Kinh people and also recognized their special ethnic identity. At that time, the Kinh were officially addressed as *Yuezu* (the Yue nationality), an ethnonym which in Chinese historical documents refers to various indigenous groups in southern China and Vietnam. Their distinct identity in relation to *Yueqiao* (Overseas Vietnamese) was further emphasized in official documents, such as the 1953 report produced by a state research team on the ethnohistory and society of the Kinh (Yan et al. 1987, pp. 149–50). The *Yuezu* were said to have settled in China more than 400 years ago, while the *Yueqiao* had come as late as 1945, after the French colonial domination over Vietnam. Besides cultural differences between the two groups, their different political allegiances were highlighted through the pictures of national leaders that were hanging in their houses — the picture of Chairman Mao Zedong for the *Yuezu* and Chairman Ho Chi Minh for the *Yueqiao*.

The identity of the Kinh people in relation to Vietnam and China continued to be ambivalent, regardless of the efforts made by Chinese officials and scholars to reinforce the national boundary. Economic, cultural, and kinship linkages between the Kinh and Vietnam were still well in place (ibid., p. 151). Not until 1957, when the official ethnonym for the Kinh was changed from *Yuezu* to *Jingzu* (Yuan et al. 1987, p. 54), were the Kinh finally incorporated into the minority institution of the People's Republic of China. Even after the establishment of the nationality autonomous townships, the Kinh had not been formally recognized as a minority nationality, as the ethnonym *Yuezu* was not included in the list of the thirty-eight minority nationalities formally recognized in the 1953 national census (Huang 1995, p. 148). In 1964, the ethnonym *Jingzu* finally appeared in the list of fifty-three minority nationalities formally recognized in that year's national census (ibid., p. 150). The change of their official ethnonym, from *Yuezu* to *Jingzu*, symbolically severed their relations with Vietnam, as their new name differs so much from the term Yue, the name the Chinese have used throughout history for the Vietnamese and indigenous groups living in southern China.

The incorporation of the Kinh into the Chinese state, through their status as an ethnic minority, was in 1958 formally institutionalized by the establishment of the *Dongxing Gezu Zizhixian* ("Dongxing autonomous county of various nationalities") (Yuan et al. 1987, p. 54). To create the new county, the former *Bianzu Yaozu Zizhiqu* ("Autonomous district of the Bian and the Yao nationalities") and the three former *Yuezu Zizhixiang* ("Autonomous township of the Yue") were merged. Furthermore, the Zhuang, the Yao, and the Jing minorities together with the Han-Chinese majority in the territory of the former Fengcheng county were incorporated into it.[8] The border town of Dongxing became the county seat. Thus, with its new name, the Kinh minority was no longer a separate ethnic group with an ambivalent national identity; it was given a place within the categories and institutions of the Chinese state.[9]

The 1958 report stressed that changing the Kinh's official appellation from *Yuezu* to *Jingzu* was undertaken at the request of the Kinh people. The report, however, also reveals how the county government mobilized a sustained campaign in various Kinh communities in a drive for consensus (ibid., p. 54). Almost forty years later, my Kinh informants in Wanwei interpreted the change as "showing their heart toward Beijing", a reference to the fact that the character for their new name, *jing*, is also the character for "capital" found in the name Beijing ("northern capital"). Whether it was the Kinh/Jing themselves or the Chinese government who actually initiated the change in 1957 is still not possible to determine. However, the emergence at around that time of the legend of the Kinh hero Du Guanghui, who was said to have led the Kinh community in the battle alongside the Chinese against the French in northern Vietnam in the mid-nineteenth century, definitely reflects a strategy on the part of the Kinh to justify their position in China's consolidated system of national minorities. The heroic legend of Du Guanghui does not appear in Chinese historical documents, nor is his name mentioned in the 1953 report on the Kinh community, in which many other local oral stories are recorded (Yan et al. 1987). The story first appeared in a 1958 report (Yuan et al. 1987, p. 21) produced by a state research team on the Kinh (see Guangxi Zhuangzu Zizhiqu Bianxiezu 1987, p. 185). It was not until the mid-1980s, when indigenous Kinh scholars such as Mr Li participated in research on the Kinh nationality, that the legends of Du Guanghui flourished (see Gupo et al. 1993; Ta 1988). Mr Li told me that in his pursuit of local oral traditions he had made great efforts to recover the story of Du's heroic deeds from village elders, including his own father.

After its demolition during the Cultural Revolution, the Institute of Minorities was re-established in the late 1970s. In this context, there was an upsurge of publications on minority nationalities in the 1980s, largely as the result of efforts to reinstate the Chinese system of ethnic classification and its institutionalization. Understandably, indigenous scholars like Mr Li were keen to assert their own people's glorious past in their writings. However, it is interesting to see how Mr Li portrayed Du as a Kinh hero in the Chinese national context. Both of the tablets erected, one at Du's altar in the temple and the other one at his grave in the village, have an honorary title literally meaning "National Hero" (*minzu yingxiong*). Yet, the Chinese term *minzu* or "nation" can refer to either the Chinese nation as a whole, or to individual ethnic minorities like the Jing. In Wanwei, I never heard of any association between Du's militia and that of Liu Yongfu, the Chinese national hero who combated French troops in northern Vietnam. In order to fit the Kinh hero into the national context of China, Mr Li's works highlight the association between Du and Liu Yongfu. When Mr Li mentioned Du's merit to me, he praised Du's "patriotism" (*aiguo zhuyi*) and "internationalism" (*guoji zhuyi*). In effect, he was applying categories created by modern national boundaries to events that took place long before those boundaries were formed.

The Kinh's long struggle for a position in the Chinese state can help us understand why Mr Li and Du Guoqiang placed so much emphasis on the Kinh's "patriotism", as exemplified by the Du family's illustrious history. Du Guoqiang's views about the Kinh's political identity nevertheless are also related to his career fighting in Vietnam in the name of "internationalism" in the 1960s, and the subsequent glory and awards bestowed upon him. The family tradition was carried on by his nephew, Du Guoqiang's brother's son, who was a veteran in the Sino-Vietnamese War of 1979. He survived the war, unlike two of his village fellows, and is still serving in the army. His rank is now that of vice-regiment commander, which, like the title his uncles had, imparts a sense of pride. This time, when a family member was fighting against the Vietnamese instead of assisting them, it was more difficult to adjust their own ethnic identity to a Chinese national context than it had been during the period of his uncle. When I questioned Du Guoqiang about the seemingly ambivalent identity and awkward position of the Kinh in the bloody conflict between Vietnam and China, his answer, like all of those I got from other Kinh élite members, was emphatic. As a minority group in China, the Kinh considered themselves Chinese and therefore pledged their steadfast loyalty (*lichang jianding*) to the protection of Chinese territory. However, Kinh villagers in Wanwei were also happy to point out that Vietnamese troops did not attack the Kinh area just a few kilometres across the sea during the Sino-Vietnamese War, except for some mock shooting and espionage.

Mr Li had been full of praise for the Du family:

> Based on their ancestors' accumulated merits by virtue of their patriotic spirit and internationalism, this revolutionary family produced successive descendants who have achieved the honor of becoming Vice-Regiment Commanders.

Du Guoqiang told me that in the 1960s, when the Kinh first began to earn a living outside their home village, most of them started their careers by serving in the Indochina War during that time. He was very proud of his family, because during past decades about forty family members had obtained positions in various state institutions. A career as a state employee used to carry substantial prestige, particularly among those from the countryside. In the rapidly developing market economy in China this is no longer the case. Someone like Mr Zhang, the successful Kinh businessman from Wanwei, frequently expressed contempt for those of his fellow villagers who had failed to capitalize on their official position to advance their economic fortunes.

The villagers who hold high positions in various state institutions, nevertheless, have an important role in the lives of the Wanwei villagers, especially when they are facing the merciless encroachment of the forces of economic development and when they get into conflicts and disputes. On the final morning of the festival, I followed a group of people from the village temple to the nearby small shrines in the village. To conclude the ceremony, they performed rituals in honour of minor local deities. To access one particular shrine near the recently constructed post office, we had to pass through a gate in the brick wall which encircled the whole area. The shrine was located in the middle and was thus hidden from the view of the villagers. I was told that the land was the property of the post office, which, like many other public institutions, had invested in Wanwei's real-estate development projects. However, the group of people performing the ritual argued that when local villagers had sold their land to the developer, they had not included the area where the shrine was located. Some of them resented the fact that the deity, which they called "Grandpa", had been put "in jail". They cursed those who were responsible for this, and expressed the wish that they be punished by the supernatural power. There was an opening in the wall directly facing the shrine and they explained that this was an opening for "Grandpa" to breathe. This was the result of a long struggle among their fellow villagers who were state officials in the district or municipal government, the developer, and the property owner. They had high hopes that these men of honour from their village would be able to liberate their spiritual "Grandpa" by getting back the land where the shrine was located, though no one could foresee the final outcome.

Another dispute involved the elders associated with the village temple and the village authority headed by the party-secretary, who have been deeply involved with the real-estate developments in the area. The previous year, the village authority had taken it upon itself to construct a concrete driveway from the main road to the temple, as the village was expecting a huge number of guests for the tenth anniversary of the reinstating of the *Hat* Festival. The temple elders understood the work as a donation from the village government, but after the conclusion of the festival the village authorities attempted to claim expenses from the elders. The elders were infuriated and argued that the village authorities had benefited from the construction project. Again, they relied on their fellow villagers working as state officials in the district or municipal government to straighten out their grievance.

The interaction between the sacred realm and the secular domain during the *Hat* Festival in Wanwei was by no means limited to the level of the local community. According to my own observations in 1996, and from what I was told about the tenth anniversary in 1995, the festival should be seen in the context of much wider political and economic developments in the Tonkin Gulf during the past decade. The key players in the festival included local villagers and the village authority, Kinh élite members from outside the village at higher levels of state institutions, official delegations from across the national boundary, and investors from provincial, national, and international levels. In one way or another they have all been involved in the regional economic development — either as agents or as victims, or as both. Let us now turn our attention to this wider political economic context of regional development to further our understanding of the transformation of the Kinh's identity and their cultural linkage with Vietnam as reflected in the festival.

REGIONAL ECONOMIC DEVELOPMENT: A NEW CONTEXT OF CROSS-BORDER CULTURAL LINKAGE

In the afternoon of the fifth and the sixth day of the annual *Hat* Festival, a communal feast was arranged inside the temple. About thirty tables were set up. Six men were sitting around a round wooden board put on the floor, each of them representing the head of his family's household. The six household representatives were divided into two groups, and each took turns to provide food for the feast. Delicacies were supplied on an extravagant scale in a display of competitive ostentatiousness. Guests from outside, including Kinh élite returning to their natal village, representatives from other Kinh villages, and some non-Kinh honorary guests, were seated around the tables. Before the feast started on the fifth day, several individuals were invited up to the shrine to receive a ceremonial tea-offering from one of the four women who sang and danced in the ceremonies throughout the ritual period. These honoured individuals in return presented a small sum of money as a gift to these women. Besides myself and my research partner from the Guangxi Institute of Nationalities, the honoured group included the party-secretary of the village, a Chinese official from the authority of Dongxing district, a Kinh official representing all fellow villagers working elsewhere, the party-secretary of a neighbouring Kinh village, and a local dignitary representing the local residents. This local representative was said to be the most successful businessman in the village. As a middle-aged man, he praised the village elders' hard work in organizing the festival, and urged the youth to maintain a good standard of social morality, including filial piety towards the elders and business ethics.

According to Mr Li, this respected local businessman, who in the beginning of the 1990s became a multi-millionaire through trading coal from Vietnam, was a moral exemplar. He financially supported the collective activities of his lineage, answered the call from the local authority to assist the poor, and had the previous year donated the biggest sum of money for renovating the temple for the tenth anniversary of the reinstatement of the festival. In Mr Li's words, this local businessman had gained the hearts of fellow villagers, state officials, and the god. His merits were well represented by his huge six-storey mansion under construction on one side of the main road — the biggest private property in the village. This call for social morality on this ceremonial occasion was probably a collective effort to counter the declining moral standards of the village *nouveaux riches*. Some of those who had grown rich in the border trade have become the subject of village gossip. One had for example deserted his wife, children, and parents and was now living with his mistress in the nearby town of Jiangping; another man kept a concubine at home and paid no respect to his own wife.

Some of the young *nouveaux riches* had other concerns on this religious occasion. One young man who took part in the ceremonies told me that young people were eager to donate money for restoring the past grandeur of the temple, particularly for rebuilding the images of the deities to replace the existing humble-looking wooden tablets. The old images had been demolished during anti-religious movements in the late 1950s, and young people could thus only hear about the craftsmanship of the past from the elders. On the other hand, he complained that the seven-day ritual period of the festival was too long, especially for those young people who were chosen from a communal roster to serve in the ceremonies. It was a hindrance to their business activities. He suggested that the festival be shortened. This young man had made his fortune by dealing in sea products bought from local and Vietnamese fishermen across the water and sold them to seafood merchants from Guangdong and Fujian provinces.[10]

The Kinh in Wanwei play a privileged role as brokers in the cross-border trade with Vietnam, simply because of their language ability to communicate in Vietnamese, their kinship connections across the sea, and the proximity of Wanwei to Vietnam. Even during the period of tense Sino-Vietnamese relations in the early 1980s, shortly after the war, unregulated cross-border trade by sea is said to have taken place in the Wanwei area. A specialist in Vietnamese studies at the Guangxi Institute of Nationalities told me that in 1981, when he was on the seashore at Wanwei doing research, he was targeted as a prospective customer by some Vietnamese fishermen who had came across the sea to sell watches. The re-opening of the border in early 1989 and the boom in cross-border trade in the next few years offered the local Kinh communities special opportunities. Many villagers of Wanwei made their fortunes in this period. In the early 1990s, the gradual formalization of state control on trade on both sides of the border put a damper on business activities. During this period Wanwei became an important smuggling centre. Mr Li recalled that his nephew (his sister's eldest son), on patrol as a customs official, once confiscated a car submerged in the water close to the shore of Wanwei. The car appeared to have been smuggled in from Vietnam; as it turned out, the car was a business venture of his younger brother.

The change in the style of Wanwei's houses is a good indicator of the recent economic boom. I was told that after 1949 brick houses with tiled roofs had gradually replaced thatched cottages. Concrete houses with flat roofs, locally known as *pingdingfang* or "flat-roofed house", started to become popular in the 1980s after the implementation of economic reforms. At present, more than half of the total population of 3,800 are living in about 500 flat-roofed houses. Luxury mansions with more than three storeys did not appear until the 1990s, and were largely confined to the area of the Kinh community. This probably reflects the Kinh's privileged economic position during the boom in cross-border trade in the early 1990s.

Another indicator of change is the fact that many villagers have given up farming. About 2,000 acres of farm land out of the total of 2,745 acres have been leased to farmers from the rural areas of Guangdong province. Local villagers have thus been freed from the task of farming and are able to concentrate on fishing, aquaculture, dealing in fish products, and different kinds of trade. In 1996 the net income per capita in the village was 1,850 renminbi, close to the national goal of *xiaokang* or the "medium level" of development, which was locally set at 2,100 renminbi.

The impact of economic development was not only confined to local initiatives. As a result of the intense cross-border trade, capital flow from all over China into the border region of Guangxi arrived in Wanwei in the form of huge real-estate development projects aimed at developing the tourist potential of the region. Under the aegis of the Dongxing Economic Development District Government, a standing committee of the "Wanwei Golden Beach Tourism Development Project" was established in early 1993. According to the general manager of the project, seventy-five companies from all over China, as well as from Hong Kong, and Taiwan have invested in it. They have pledged to invest 1,200 million renminbi, with 160 million renminbi already in place. In 1993, the project accomplished its goal of buying 5,405 acres of land from local villagers. This accounts for more than one-fourth of the "island's" total land area. Since then, improvements in infrastructure have been carried out as part of this development project, including 15 kilometres of main road, a wharf, a fresh water supply, a power supply, a telephone network, and so on. Other projects in progress include a three-star hotel, a sanitarium, a number of guest-houses, restaurants, and resort centres, as well as various buildings owned by public organizations as training, convention, and resort centres. Due to the implementation of a nation-wide budgetary policy for controlling capital flow in mid-1993, many of these projects have been abruptly suspended.

For many of the Kinh élite, such as for Mr Zhang, tourism development in Wanwei is just at the beginning, relying as it does on the fifteen existing restaurants, the twelve guest-houses, the ten or so beach-facility stores, and the twenty or so evening amusement stands (providing drinks and karaoke facilities outdoors). In recent years, faced with the disintegration of their community, many villagers have vented their frustration over these development projects. They have lost farm land needed to grow their own produce, and the collective residential areas have also been broken up, due to the lack of firm policy guidelines for selling land. Furthermore, the periodic intrusion of arrogant tourists, the influx of rapacious businesspeople, and the presence of hundreds of prostitutes from Vietnam and inland China have disrupted village life. Yet, many members of the élite still have high hopes for future development. Mr Li, for example, had argued strongly for the holding of an economic fair during celebration for the tenth anniversary of the reinstatement of the festival in 1995. He believed that such a fair could attract external investment. He also proposed that the village train its young people to form a cultural performance team in ornate ethnic costumes for tourist receptions, and that these young people serve as shopkeepers during the idle time between receptions. Mr Li's failure to harness enough support from local leaders for his plan largely reflects the lack of local consensus over the issue of development.

Development in the Kinh community has by no means been confined to Wanwei. In Wutau, a smaller Kinh settlement to the north of Wanwei, the 1,200 Kinh villagers, who account for more than 90 per cent of the total population there, have been even more eager to take part in development. All of their farm land has been rented out to people from Wuhan, Hubei province, enabling most of the villagers to be involved in fishery, aquacultural production, and cross-border trade. In 1995, with the average per capita net income of 4,200 renminbi, Wutau headed development not only in Guangxi province but also in many areas nation-wide. Wutau was awarded the title of the "Top Model Minority Nationality Village" of Guangxi, and has been under consideration to become the "Top Model Minority Nationality Village" of the whole country. The village government has been undertaking a project of tourism development, building an "Ethnic Cultural Village" with the main attractions being the local Kinh cultural traditions and the proximity to Vietnam.

In Shanxin, another Kinh settlement northeast of Wanwei, I was told by the local authority that the pace of development has been slower because of the underdeveloped road system. Yet, I still found clusters of luxury private mansions in the vicinity of the village temple, and this temple is also the most ostentatiously renovated Kinh temple of the four in the nearby Kinh communities, including the one in Wanwei.

North of the three Kinh "islands" lies Jiangping, a market-town situated halfway along the highway linking the former county-seat of Fengcheng with the border town of Dongxing. The old name of one of the main streets in Jiangping — *Annanjie* (Annam Street, which local Chinese refer to as the area of the Vietnamese) — indicates the prominence of the Kinh settlement in the past. Today, the Kinh settlements are interspersed among the Chinese majority. The only exception is Hengwang, a Catholic community surrounding a church and an almost purely Kinh community. In the centre of the town, clusters of recently constructed real-estate properties stand side by side with old buildings, and the whole area is traversed by busy streets with many shops on both sides. Most of all, I was struck by the concentration of guest-houses on the main streets. There are supposedly more than one hundred guest-houses, including the one run by the family of Mr Li's sister, at which I lodged during my stay in the town. Mr Li's sister's husband, also a Kinh from Wanwei, was the former deputy head of the town government during the heyday of border trade between 1989 and 1993 (Womack 1994). He told me that in those days the town was flooded with business people who came from all over China for border trade opportunities, to the extent that those who could not find rooms in which to stay in guest houses had to rent the working desks in government offices as beds for overnight lodging.[11] The intensity of border trade subsided rapidly during the second half of 1993, but he managed to make a good fortune from it while it lasted. Since then his family has been running the guest house.

Though cross-border trade since mid-1993 has been curbed by state regulation on both sides of the border and by the nation-wide budgetary control of capital flow in China, its intensity demonstrated the possibilities for future development around the Gulf of Tonkin and southwest China (ibid.). In May 1993 the former Fengcheng county was upgraded to become Fengcheng Harbor City, at a similar administrative level as Nanning, the provincial capital 150 kilometres to the north (Zhou and Ling 1994, pp. 2–3). The goal of this strategic move was to create a deepwater harbour as an outlet for the landlocked southwest China. The harbour, which is located east of Wanwei, with the Bailong peninsular in-between, rivals its two nearby competitors — Qingzhou Harbor and Beihai Harbor — for its advantageous physical topography suitable for a sheltered deepwater harbour (Zhou and Ling 1994, p. 41). According to an officer from the Harbor Bureau that I interviewed, Fengcheng was designated one of the nineteen major national ports in 1995. With its twenty-four piers — nine of which could handle ships of up to 10,000 tons — the harbour was able to handle up to 8.5 million tons of goods in 1995. The harbour has a potential for 115 piers and is expected to handle 15 million tons of goods per year by the end of this century. A massive transportation system linking the five inland provinces/autonomous districts in southwest China (Tibet, Yunnan, Sichuan, Guizhou, and Guangxi) with this sea port is under construction. This includes the Nanning-Kunming Railway, the Nanning-Qingzhou Highway, and the Qingzhou-Fengcheng Highway.

The founding of the Fengcheng Harbor City has led to the reorganization of the former Fengcheng county administration. Fengcheng Harbor city is composed of the harbor district, the Fengcheng district, Shangshi county, and Dongxing city. With the new municipal government located in the newly established Harbor district, the former county-seat of Fengcheng has become the base of the Fengcheng district. Shangshi county, a remote inland mountainous area in the north, was incorporated into the Fengcheng Harbor City as the hinterland for development.

The border town of Dongxing has also experienced administrative changes. The town used to be part of the former Dongxing Economic Development District. In September 1996 the district was incorporated into the Jiangping district — where the "Three Islands of the Kinh" is located — and upgraded to become a county-level city due to its enormous potential for cross-border trade with Vietnam.

Given that one of the main emphases of China's "Ninth Five-Year Plan", promulgated in 1995, is the economic development of inland provinces, the founding of the Fengcheng Harbor City has special strategic meaning. The co-ordination of regional economic development among areas in southwest China had been on the agenda as early as the mid-1980s, as the founding in 1984 of the "Committee of Co-ordinated Economy for the Seven Areas in the Five Provinces" indicates. This agreement linked the provinces of Sichuan, Guizhou, and Yunnan; the autonomous districts of Tibet and Guangxi; and the Cities of Chengdu and Chongqing (Wu Shengqu Qifang "Zhongguo Daxinan Zai Guqi" Bianxuezu 1994). The development of Fengcheng Harbor as an outlet for the region is a strategic move targeting economic ties between southwest China and Southeast Asia in the next century. In the forthcoming years, the harbour will certainly have a significant impact upon the regional development in the Gulf of Tonkin, especially in the context of Sino-Vietnamese relations. The Kinh community in Fengcheng, as indicated by their economic success in recent years, might have privileged roles to play in this process. Indeed, Mr Zhang, the most successful Kinh businessman from Wanwei, has strongly advocated the expansion of the small wharf at Wanwei to facilitate the development of cross-border trade with Vietnam.

Interestingly, the history of Fengcheng Harbor can be traced further back in a different context of Sino-Vietnamese relationship. It was built in early 1968 as a secret military port for logistical support for North Vietnam in order to break the U.S. blockade of supplies along the land routes. It thus came to be called the "sea-route of the Ho Chi Minh Trail" (Zhou and Ling 1994, p. 41). To the Kinh, the military role Fengcheng Harbor once had, and its current role as a strategic stronghold for regional economic development, have quite different meanings in the context of Sino-Vietnamese relations. Many of the Kinh élite members from Wanwei told me about their personal involvement in the Indochina War during the 1960s. Someone like Mr Du Guoqiang, who in the name of internationalism joined the Chinese army to fight in Vietnam in the 1960s, probably found his national identity as a Chinese citizen in harmony with his ethnic identity based on Vietnamese decent. For his brother's son, who joined the army to fight against Vietnam in the late 1970s, the two identities were certainly in conflict. Yet, since the normalization of Sino-Vietnamese relations in the late 1980s, Kinh men have been going to Vietnam solely with the purpose of making their fortune. Their cultural affiliation with Vietnam with regard to language and kinship has definitely been an advantage. This advantage also served the Kinh men in the old days when they were seeking refuge in Vietnam from economic hardships and political or religious persecutions in China during the Republican period and the transition to the communist regime.

The flow of people between Vietnam and the Kinh communities in China has in recent history varied greatly depending on which gender is being discussed. In contrast to the direction of the flow of men discussed above, women have often moved from Vietnam to the Kinh communities in Fengcheng. According to the 1953 report, which mentions about thirty cases on the three Kinh "islands", local Kinh men have been taking wives from Vietnam across the sea for a long time (Yan et al. 1987, p. 151). When I attended the 1996 annual *Hat* Festival in Wanwei, I also met a few elderly women in Wanwei whose natal homes were said to be in Vietnam. The number of Vietnamese women marrying into the Kinh communities in China has drastically increased in recent years, as the more than twenty cases I found in Wanwei show. The women had come either as refugees seeking political asylum and had later decided to stay, or had come as illegal immigrants attracted by the prospects of a better living. These women have to maintain their official identity as *Yueqiao* (Overseas Vietnamese), and will never be granted membership in the Jing nationality.

In a ceremony on the final day of the festival, a team of villagers who had been serving in the rituals handed over their duties to those who would be serving next year. A young woman came inside the temple to watch her boyfriend assume his new duty. I was told that she had arrived from Vietnam after her mother, a widow, had married a local Kinh man. The young woman worked as a helper in her boyfriend's beauty parlour situated close to the village temple. They lived together in that small building without being formally married. It seems that he had asked her to come to the ceremony to gain communal recognition of their relationship. On the same occasion, four young women, who seemed to be the friends of the one inside the temple, were watching the ceremony from outside the main entrance. They were driven away by the temple elders when they attempted to join their friend inside the temple. The elders told me that these four women were prostitutes who stayed in the cottage behind the beauty parlour to run their business, and that they were considered to be spiritually "polluting". Nevertheless, sacred purity seems to be just a matter of degree. When the party secretary of the village entered the temple, the woman inside the temple looked uncomfortable and left. Unfortunately, women from Vietnam were classified in terms of their degree of purity according to the nature of their relationships with men in the community, who were either local villagers, tourists, or businessmen from elsewhere. Their relationships with local men had to be communally recognized as "proper" in order for them to be allowed access to the sacred world. In the course of regional economic development, this "proper" relationship has been largely based on the local reference to the national border. It is highly unlikely that the female ritual performers from Vietnam — who have already gained proximity to the sacred world — will return unless they are invited as modern cultural performers and can cross the national border at the official check-point.

In the past two decades of Vietnamese diaspora, many Vietnamese refugees have passed through the various Kinh communities in Fengcheng on their way to seek asylum in Western countries. I was told about a huge influx that hit Wanwei in 1990, when within a few months about six hundred Vietnamese refugees arrived in Wanwei by boat, one group after another. They stayed with individual families on the "island" for a few months. With the help of local people they were able to buy bigger and better-equipped boats to continue their voyage to Hong Kong. Many of them finally settled in North America or Europe as refugees. During their stay in Wanwei, they prayed to the deities in the local village temple for patronage. After safely arriving in Hong Kong and finally settling down in a Western country, they sent letters back to Wanwei to express their gratitude for the local people's help and for the patronage of the local deities. Some even sent money back for the annual festival of the temple. Some of them instructed their relatives back in Vietnam to come and pray to the deities in Wanwei regularly. In each of the four *Hat* temples located in the Kinh communities I visited, there were sacred objects said to be donated by people from Vietnam. In this way the local Kinh community has become a source of religious power and patronage for some Vietnamese who are dispersed overseas.

Throughout history, the religious traditions of Vietnam have provided the Kinh community with patron deities. At first it was in the form of local communal gods brought along during migration; lately it has been through the female ritual performers crossing the sea. Vietnamese traditions still have a powerful hold on the Kinh in Wanwei, as can be seen from the desire of young people to have the images of deities which they have never seen restored in the temple. The request was made after the conclusion of the temple's annual festival in 1996. The young *nouveaux riches* offered financial support for a project in which the new images would be made in Vietnam so as to secure authenticity. However, it could be argued that, rather than showing their respect to the power of these temple deities, and in turn to the power of the religious traditions in Vietnam, they were trying to show off their own economic power in order to gain communal recognition of their status.

CONCLUSION: TRANSNATIONAL IDENTITY AND ITS MULTIFARIOUS ARTICULATION

This chapter has examined the cross-border cultural links between the Kinh in Guangxi province, China, and in Vietnam. By focusing on the revival of the annual religious *Hat* Festival in Wanwei, a community of the Kinh ethnic minority of Vietnamese descent, I have illustrated the transformation of this relationship.

A change in the local religious belief and practice associated with the *Hat* Festival indicates a transformation of the Kinh's cultural linkage with Vietnam, as the following two examples will show. The first one is the myth of the Sea God, worshipped in the festival, which makes special geographical reference to the origin of the Kinh community. That reference has changed in the past decades from one that reflects the linkage of the community with its origin in Vietnam before migration to one that emphasizes the localization of the community's origin on the Chinese side of the border. The other transformation occurred in 1995, when villagers stopped the tradition of hiring female ritual performers from Vietnam to serve in the festival. Instead, they invited official delegations and modern-style cultural performance teams from Vietnam to attend. Rather than taking the unofficial short sea route from Vietnam to the village of Wanwei, as female ritual performers had done before, the official delegation and cultural performance team made a long journey by land and crossed the official national border which involved tedious formalities. Thus, in the old days, the linkage was largely based on the communal connection at the local level, while today, it is based more on institutional relations at the state level, with a significant reference to the national border.

To further understand the transformation of the Kinh's cultural linkage with Vietnam I have also explored two complementary perspectives. The first one is the historical perspective, starting with the creation of the Sino-Vietnamese border in 1887 by France and China. I then discussed the Kinh's identity in relation to China and Vietnam during the following vicissitudes of international politics. From the making of the national border that formally put the Kinh communities under the rule of China, we see that the identity of the Kinh has changed. From being members of Vietnamese society they have become an ethnic minority group in China. In the contemporary minority policies of socialist China, the Kinh have been able to consolidate their position in the Chinese state by taking up the political status of a *shaoshu minzu* (minority nationality).

The second perspective is socio-economic and focuses on the recent regional economic development around the Gulf of Tonkin, with particular reference to the booming border trade and the development of Fengcheng Harbor as an outlet for the landlocked southwest China. The privileged position of the Kinh in border trade and the development of Fengcheng has gained them the status of a model ethnic minority in China. While the Kinh in general have become more and more entrenched in the Chinese nation as a successful minority, their cultural links with Vietnam are increasingly constructed by reference to the national border and state policies. Thus, the geographical reference of the Kinh community's origin myth is now restricted to the Chinese side of the border. The Vietnamese state delegation which attended the festival in Wanwei by crossing the land border through official channels has supplanted the local Vietnamese female ritual performers who used to take the unofficial sea route.

Since the formal demarcation of the Sino-Vietnamese border in 1887, the Kinh in Guangxi have gradually developed their transnational identity premised upon their special relationships with Vietnam and China. This transnational identity has been at the mercy of the Kinh's position in the national politics of China and international relations as they have impacted on the region. It has also served to articulate different social identities, such as class, gender, ethnicity, and citizenship. Today, the Kinh's citizenship in China is mainly defined by its ethnic status that is predicated upon its unique cultural traditions.[12] Since the mid-1980s, the Kinh's ethnic identity and its links to Vietnam have been re-enforced through the reinstatement of the *Hat* Festival and the consequential revival of the Kinh traditions. Yet, since the re-opening of the border after the Sino-Vietnamese War and the subsequent development of cross-border trade, the Vietnamese source of the Kinh's ethnic identity has acquired a new meaning. In the old days, Vietnam to the Kinh mainly meant the source of folk cultural traditions and informal communal networks. Today, Vietnam has a state bureaucratic system with which the Kinh need to struggle, while at the same time maintaining their relationships for economic purposes. This exchange between the Kinh and the Vietnamese state administration has been facilitated by their improved stature as a successful minority in China, and also by the advantage of their social and cultural affiliation with Vietnam in terms of language, folk religion, and kinship.

Nevertheless, this new dimension of their transnational identity is perceived differently by the various social strata of the Kinh community. For successful Kinh businessmen like Mr Zhang, the cultural connection with the Vietnamese state administration — such as the Vietnamese state delegation attending the Kinh's festival — is meaningful and favourable to their business in border trade and regional economic development. Understandably, Mr Zhang was the paramount financial supporter for the *Hat* Festival's tenth anniversary held in Wanwei and a prime mover in the decision to invite the official Vietnamese delegation. The annual festival has become a battlefield for Kinh *nouveaux riches* to compete for communal recognition for their social status. For Kinh officials who hold positions in the Chinese state institutions, such as Mr Li, the formal visit of the Vietnamese state delegation greatly reinforced their identity as indigenous élite in the state minority institution. Although their status has been somewhat surpassed by successful businessmen in the new social hierarchy, they are still the guardians of social morality in the local community. This was especially so when the impersonal force of economic development concomitant to the new dimension of the cultural linkage with Vietnam impinged upon the community and created conflicts with the old cultural tradition of Vietnamese folk heritage. In a period of regional economic development, the old tradition of practising folk religion is probably the only cultural asset to which the deprived and disadvantaged sector of the Kinh community can still cling to for guidance in resisting the merciless forces of the rapidly changing socio-economic order.

The new form of cultural linkage with Vietnam is also predicated upon the differentiation of gender roles in the Kinh community. While the Kinh men groomed their relationship with the Vietnamese state administration by inviting the official Vietnamese delegation and cultural performance team, the local Kinh women on the contrary took the place of female ritual performers from Vietnam who traditionally had served in this function. Most of these local female performers were being granted proximity to the male-dominated religious world for the first time. The Vietnamese women who have come either as wives to local Kinh men or as prostitutes for tourists and businessmen, are always denied access to the sacred realm and remain outcasts of the Kinh community, both in terms of the political border of citizenship and of the religious border of purity.

14. A Vietnamese Community in Guangxi, China   309

NOTES

1. All personal names appearing in this chapter are pseudonyms, except for names of historical figures.
2. *Hat* is Vietnamese for "singing". In this essay, Vietnamese terms are put in the romanized form of Vietnamese writing and Chinese terms are put in the pinyin romanization of Chinese writing.
3. According to the 1990 census, the Jing nationality has a population of 18,749. They are the fourteenth smallest group among the fifty-five ethnic minorities in the Chinese system of ethnic classification.
4. Renminbi is the official currency in the People's Republic of China (PRC). In 1996 the exchange rate of renminbi to the U.S. dollar was about 10:1.
5. According to oral history, the Kinh ancestors migrated from northern Vietnam to the Kinh islands, and some of them first settled at Bailong peninsula before they finally moved on to Wanwei island (Yan et al. 1987, p. 79).
6. When negotiating the demarcation of the Sino-Vietnamese border, France and China had a long-standing deadlock dispute over the territories including the Kinh islands and the Bailong peninsula. China eventually got these territories by conceding some islands west of the Beilun River estuary to France and by opening up Longzhou, an inland border area including present-day Pingxiang, to be a free trade zone (Chen 1995, pp. 37–42; Xiao and Wang 1993; Yan et al. 1987, pp. 78–79).
7. Kinh villagers in Wanwei said that they did not have any problems communicating with people from Vietnam who spoke standard Vietnamese, when they talked about daily issues. But they did have problems understanding the language when they listened to the Vietnamese radio broadcasting, where a lot of political terminology as well as neologisms were used which they were unfamiliar with.
8. The Bian were classified as a sub-group of the Zhuang nationality (Fengcheng Gezu Zizhixian Gaikuang Bianxiezu 1986, p. 28). The population of the autonomous county was 202,926 in total, with the Han accounting for 83 per cent, the Zhuang 14 per cent, the Jing 1.6 per cent, and the Yao 1.4 per cent (Yuan et al. 1987, p. 54).
9. See Conner (1984, pp. 322–28) for a discussion of the PRC's practice of gerrymandering in drawing the geographical boundaries of the minority autonomous administrative system.
10. I visited him in his ornately decorated three-storey house and saw his three children. He told me that he did not mind paying a fine of several thousand renminbi for an extra child. The permitted quota for each couple in the minority area is two children.
11. By 1990 the Chinese border town of Dongxing hosted provincial trade representatives from twenty-eight of thirty Chinese provinces (Womack 1994, p. 499). Per-

sonnel of private enterprises and individual fortune-seekers also flooded the town. Just about twenty miles by highway away from it, Jiangping became a logistical hinterland to provide extra accommodation and other facilities for the overcrowded border town.

12. The re-establishment of the minority institution took place after the Cultural Revolution, in the late 1970s. The Kinh gained citizenship in China as an officially recognized ethnic minority in the 1964 census (see Huang 1995, p. 148).

REFERENCES

Chen Guchao. "Guangyu Zhongfa Kanjie Douzhengzhong de Beibuwan Haiyu Wenti" [On the issue of the Sino-French border demarcation dispute over the Beibuwan sea area]. *Zhongguo Bianjiang Shidi Yanjiu* [The study of Chinese border history and geography] 15, no. 1 (1995): 37–41.

Connor, Walker. *The National Question in Marxist-Leninist Theory and Strategy.* Princeton, N.J.: Princeton University Press, 1984.

Fengcheng Gezu Zizhixian Gaikuang Bianxiezu. *Fengcheng Gezu Zizhixian Gaikuang* [The general situation of the Fengcheng autonomous county of various nationalities]. Nanning: Guangxi Minzu Chubanshe, 1986.

Geertz, Clifford. *The Interpretation of Cultures.* London: Hutchinson, 1973.

Guangxi Zhuangzu Zizhiqu Bianxiezu, ed. *Guangxi Jingzu Shehui Lishi Diaocha* [A survey on the society and history of the Jing nationality in Guangxi]. Nanning: Guangxi Nationality Press, 1987.

Gupo Wei et al. *Jingzu Fengshuzhi* [A monograph on the customs of the Jing nationality]. Beijing: Central Institute of Nationality Press, 1993.

Huang Guangxue. *Zhongguo De Minzu Shibie* [China's ethnic identification]. Beijing: Minzu Chubanshe, 1995.

Jingzu Jianshi Bianxiezu. *Jingzu Jianshi* [Concise history on the Jing nationality]. Nanning: Guangxi Nationality Press, 1984.

Lu Jinju and Wu Fu. "Qian duodao Wuodaolai Youhuan" [Please come often to visit my island]. *Dongxing Press,* 24 July 1995.

Su Ruanguang et al., eds. *Jingzu Minjian Gushixuan* [A selected collection of the folktales of the Jing nationality]. Beijing: Chinese Folk Literature and Arts Press, 1984.

Ta Zhuhe et al., eds. *Fengchengxian Minjian Gushiji* [A collection of folktales of Fengcheng county]. Fengcheng: Fengcheng Gezu Zizhixian Santao Jicheng Lingdao Xiaozu, 1988.

Turner, Victor W. *Schism and Continuity in an African Society.* Manchester: Manchester University Press, 1957.

Womack, Brantly. "Sino-Vietnamese Border Trade: The Edge of Normalization". *Asian Survey* 34, no. 6 (1994): 495–512.

Wu Shengqu Qifang "Zhongguo Daxinan Zai Guqi" Bianxuezu. *Zhongguo Daxinan Zai Guqi* [The rising of southwest China]. Nanning: Guangxi Educational Press, 1994.

Xiao Dehao and Wang Sheng, eds. *Zhongyue Bianjie Lishi Ziliao Xuanbian* [Selected collection of historical data on the Sino-Vietnamese border], vols. 1–2. Beijing: Shehui Kexue Wenxian Chubanshe [Social Science Documents Press], 1993.

Yan Xueyun et al. "Fengcheng Yuezu Qiangkuan Diaocha" [A survey on the Yue nationality in Fengcheng]. In *Guangxi Jingzu Shehui Lishi Diaocha* [A survey on the society and history of the Jing nationality in Guangxi], edited by Guangxi Zhuangzu Zizhiqu Bianxiezu, pp. 66–184. First published 1953. Nanning: Guangxi Nationality Press, 1987.

Yuan Darong et al. "Guangxi Jingzu Shehui Lishi Diaocha" [A survey on the Jing nationality in Guangxi]. In *Guangxi Jingzu Shehui Lishi Diaocha* [A survey on the society and history of the Jing nationality in Guangxi], edited by Guangxi Zhuangzu Zizhiqu Bianxiezu, pp. 1–65. First published 1953. Nanning: Guangxi Nationality Press, 1987.

Zhou Bingqun and Ling Yunzhi. *Keai de Fengcheng Gangshi* [The lovable Fengcheng Harbor City]. Nanning: Guangxi Renmin Chubanshe, 1994.

Women and Social Change along the Vietnam-Guangxi Border

Xie Guangmao

The year 1989 saw the opening of Guangxi province in China to the outside world, and in particular to Vietnam via the townships along the southern border of the province. Since then there has been a growing number of people from the frontier regions participating in various trading activities. They have grasped this chance to flex their business muscles and intelligence, and although they have had to overcome all sorts of difficulties, they have profited considerably from the China-Vietnam trading business. This chapter focuses on the border township of Dongxing situated on the eastern seaboard.

Dongxing is a small town with a population of about 50,000. The following figures give us a rough idea of how many of its residents are actually involved in this type of frontier trade. There are eighty-five families living on Heping Road, one of the main roads in Dongxing, of which eighty-one — that is, over 90 per cent of the total number of families (25 per cent of Dongxing's population living on this road) — participate in some form of business or other. As for the other main road, Xinghua Road, there are altogether ninety-five families, of which ninety are in various types of businesses — that is, more than 90 per cent of the total number of families (also 25 per cent of Dongxing's population living on this road). The three Beijiao villages in the rural areas of Dongxing house more than 200 families, of which more than 160 families are involved in business activities — that is, some 80 to 85 per cent of the total number of families. These villages have more than 1,000 people, of which more than 300 are businesspeople, that is, over 30 per cent of the total number of the villagers. From these figures, we know that around 20 per cent of the population in Dongxing (including those in the rural areas) are involved in various business activities. This works out to be about 10,000 out of 50,000 businesspeople in Dongxing.

The business activities of the Dongxing population vary, but can be classified into two main categories: (a) frontier exports — the merchandise involved include garments, cloth, toys, diesel engines, daily necessities, metal electronic devices, glazed tiles, chinaware, man-made flowers, and so forth; (b) frontier imports — for example, rice, scrap steel and iron, copper, wood, coal, marine products, jute, and rubber. Significantly, a large number of those engaged in trading these goods are women.

WOMEN'S INVOLVEMENT IN THE CROSS-BORDER TRADE

From 1989, when Dongxing was opened up for cross-border trade with Vietnam, women of all strata in the town have seen great changes in terms of the trades in which they engage, the incomes they earn, and their position in the home and in society. No doubt it was this phenomenon along the whole of the border region which gave rise to the movie *Frontier Trade Woman* released in 1994.

Prior to the opening of cross-border trade, the border town of Dongxing had been greatly affected by the Sino-Vietnamese War and the subsequent tense relations between the two countries. There was no trade across the border and all of Dongxing's trade was carried out with other cities within China. The economy of the area was originally quite backward and there were very few factories. Those that did exist included a fireworks factory, a weaving factory, and a few small textile factories. In such an environment, for women in urban areas who were not fully occupied with domestic duties, the only jobs available to them were making fireworks and hand-weaving. The incomes from such jobs were paltry, a day's work bringing in at most a few yuan; there was no way the women could use their skills profitably, and those living on the rural outskirts had no opportunities of a sideline. Some of them planted small patches of vegetables and, because of the low prices these vegetables fetched, what was derived from one *mu* of land was only several hundred yuan. After deducting for costs, this was not much of an income.

With the opening of cross-border trade in 1989, and following the development of Dongxing, traders from all over China, as well as from Hong Kong and Macau, converged on the town. All kinds of companies, hotels, and restaurants have sprung up; there is a great increase in the immigrant population; the number of tourists has grown; and diverse service trades have emerged. These changes have created tremendous employment opportunities for women at all levels in Dongxing. While some have found jobs in companies, offices, hotels, and restaurants, an even greater number enthusiastically join the vibrant border trade. These women have proven themselves to be very capable and skilful, and a number have prospered and become quite prominent.

Because of the many tourists and traders going to Dongxing, a very large number of hotels and restaurants have sprung up. There are now eight large hotels, about ten large restaurants, and numerous medium-sized and small hotels and restaurants, which provide plenty of employment opportunities for the women of Dongxing. Previously, there was not much work for women outside the home, but now things have changed. If the women do not have the capital to start a business, they would work in a hotel or a restaurant and earn a monthly salary of about 300 yuan.

Those with sufficient capital would erect a stall in the street and this would enable them to derive quite a good income from the business. Because of the heavy human traffic in Dongxing, women who set up small stalls selling cigarettes, fruit, or other items can earn over 500 yuan a month. Those who set up "telephone stalls" can make in excess of 700 yuan. Dongxing previously had very few telephones for public use, but now they are available almost everywhere. Although there are only a few streets in Dongxing, the telephones installed for pubic use number about forty, and most of the telephone stalls are run by women. Quite a few other women have opened clothing shops and grocery shops, and business has been good.

A considerable number of changes have also occurred in the lives of the women who plant vegetables in the outlying areas. Before the days of cross-border trade, vegetables fetched very low prices, and most of them had to be sold to the state vegetable company. The poor returns for their efforts discouraged many, and only very few people opted to plant vegetables. Those who continued in the activity were generally farmers in the northern suburbs. Then with the opening of cross-border trade, more people have gone to work and live in Dongxing. The increased population requires more food, which also means a higher demand for vegetables. The price of vegetables has shot up — from a few *fen*, or at most a few *mao*, per catty to several yuan[1] per catty (500 grams). There is thus incentive for the farmers to increase their supply of vegetables. Not only has the number of vegetable farmers increased, but there is also a greater variety of vegetables planted. In addition to those in the northern suburbs, farmers in the eastern suburbs are also planting vegetables for sale. Because of the thriving cross-border trade, many of the men from the suburbs have also joined in the cross-border business, leaving the responsibility for planting the family fields to the women. As the profits from vegetables are high, many women plant vegetables on their land, thereby deriving a considerable income. For example, Mao Zhenqin, who lives in the northern suburbs and whose husband has gone away to make money, plant close to two *mu* of vegetables while looking after her children at home. The water spinach, cucumber, Chinese cabbage, and other vegetables she plants earn her about 15,000 yuan a year. Similar examples are common throughout the northern suburbs.

Apart from those planting vegetables, there have appeared many skilled animal-raisers among the women of Dongxing. Few women were involved in this activity prior to the opening of cross-border trade. With the development of the trade, the price of livestock has risen, and they can now be sold more widely. They are sold not only to Chinese but also to Vietnamese who come to Dongxing to purchase meat and vegetables. Of the many women skilled in pig-raising in Dongxing, Huang Yingheng is representative. She raises over twenty pigs a year, which earns her over 60,000 yuan. In addition, she raises chickens and ducks, and this brings her annual income to about 100,000 yuan.

Following the increase in the number of visitors, the demand for vegetables by the numerous hotels has increased. Locally produced vegetables were insufficient to satisfy the daily increasing demand. So Dongxing now sees the emergence of a group of women who deal in vegetables and poultry. While a few of these women hail from urban areas, the majority are from the rural outskirts. Most of them are young women, though some are middle-aged. Some bring in products from Nanning, Qingzhou, and Fengcheng, while others simply purchase vegetables from local farms to sell. The major venue for trading is the

Dongxing State Trading Market. Those who bring produce in from outside generally do so by the truckloads, with each load being valued at several hundred yuan. Those who purchase their vegetables from local farmers make a few dozen yuan a day. As this business is not too arduous and requires little capital, many young women are drawn into it.

With the opening of cross-border trade, there have also appeared a large number of private female tourist guides, some of whom are from the urban areas, while others come from the rural outskirts. In addition to the tips they get from their customers, they also receive commissions from the shops, hotels, and restaurants they take tourists to. The income is good and they can make at least 100 yuan a day. Feng Fang is a typical female private tourist guide from a four-person household on the eastern outskirts of Dongxing. Her husband stays at home and does the housework, and the livelihood of the family depends solely on the income Feng Fang earns from her work as tourist guide. It is understood that her monthly income from this is generally no less than 5,000 yuan. Clearly, the income of the women in this business is considerable. Of the approximately 150 tourist guides in Dongxing today, about 130, or almost 90 per cent, are women.

The economic activities of the women mentioned above are generally only indirectly linked with the border trade. These can be called second-line activities. However, there are also a number of women who are directly involved in the border trade — the front-liners — who earn the highest incomes. According to a sample survey by the Women's Federation in the town, such women account for about half of all women employed locally, while their incomes constitute over 70 per cent of the income earned by all women. Among these women are some who go to Vietnam to buy seafood and bring it back to sell in Dongxing. The majority of these women are middle-aged or older. They can be divided into the small operators and the bigger operators. The small operators purchase only a basket or two of seafood or even just a few catties of it on each trip, while the bigger operators return with several tons of seafood. The small-scale operators generally make their purchases in Vietnam and then sell the seafood to the people of Dongxing. The large-scale operators transport their purchases to other places in China or sell what they have purchased in Vietnam to other wholesalers in Dongxing. The small-scale traders earn a few tens of yuan a day, while the large-scale traders earn several hundred yuan a trip. Some even make as much as one thousand yuan. A women with the surname of Deng who lives on the northern outskirts and has been in the trade since 1991, brings fresh squids and other seafood products from Vietnam to sell in Dongxing. She has prospered, and the value of her assets is in excess of one million yuan. This has brought her prominence and she is now known far and wide. At the beginning of 1995, she sent her daughter to an "élite" school in Nanning, paying the school 150,000 yuan in a single payment. She intends to send her young son to study at this school as well.

Of the women who trade in fish, some sell salt-water fish brought in from Vietnam, while others assist their husbands in selling fresh-water fish purchased from other places in China. The annual income from this activity can at times amount to tens of thousands of yuan.

Of the women engaged in the cross-border trade, there is a group who deal in piece-goods trading. These women are mostly from Dongxing and their sales outlets are mainly located along Heping Road, Caishi Street, Zhongshan Road, and Xinmin Road. About 200 to 300 women are involved in this trade, and they form partnerships with friends and relatives, with the more experienced ones guiding the inexperienced. The goods are brought in from Guangdong and are sold in Dongxing. As there are many women in this business, and the profits are considerable, these female traders attract considerable attention in the cross-border trade. The peak period for this type of cross-border trade was from 1990 to 1994, when the small traders were making 10,000 to 20,000 yuan per year, the largest taking in hundreds of thousands of yuan annually. Women play a prominent role in this trade. Lin Zhenying is one such representative. She has been in the cross-border trade since it began and now has assets exceeding one million yuan. Her family is in the interior decorating business and they are prominent in Dongxing. Their home is entirely air-conditioned. Another prominent trader is Huang Cuiqin, whose assets also exceed one million yuan.

In addition, there are many women who trade in onions, melon seeds, fruit, and other foodstuffs, and some of these have also become wealthy. One such woman is Huang, who lives in the northern rural suburbs of Dongxing. When the cross-border trade first began, she only carried melon seeds and groceries and traded between Dongxing and Mong Cai. After two years in the trade, at the end of 1991 she began trading on a larger scale in onions, melon seeds, and apples, frequently travelling between Dongxing and other provinces in China and venturing into various places to source products for sale in Dongxing. Today, her assets also exceed one million yuan. She lives in a five-storey house furnished with a washing machine, a refrigerator, and even a new model Panasonic colour television set. Although her husband is also involved in the business, it is she who has the final say on the sourcing and sale of goods.

Another success story is that of Huang Houzhen. Her husband is a teacher in a primary school, and her family of four lives in Daxing Street. In the early period of the cross-border trade, she opened a small sundry stall and did a little wholesaling. Her business has grown with the border trade, and today she is a rich woman who owns two buildings, has two wholesaling centres, and has assets valued at several million yuan. The wholesaling centres she operates sell all kinds of everyday necessities and the daily turnover ranges from several thousand yuan to 10,000 yuan.

CHANGES BROUGHT TO THE STATUS AND ROLE OF WOMEN BY THE OPENING OF THE BORDER TRADE

Before the Sino-Vietnam border was opened, the incomes of the women of Dongxing were very low, limited by the employment opportunities available to women. Of the few that managed to find employment, many were in weaving or fire-cracker production. The majority stayed at home doing domestic chores and looking after children while the men occupied the dominant position in the household. By 1989, following the growth of trade across the Sino-Vietnam border, an increasing number of women went out of their homes and participated in the border trade, thereby contributing to the economic development and reform of Dongxing. Excited by the many new opportunities now available to them, they are eager to give of their best. By their involvement they are also creating a new identity for themselves. Thus, it can be said that the opening up and development of the cross-border trade has changed the position of women in the Dongxing economy.

Following the development of cross-border trade, the number of types of products imported and exported jumped from the former figure of ten-plus to over 200. This has increased opportunities for the women of Dongxing to participate in the cross-border trade.

The fine economic situation brought to Dongxing by the rise of cross-border trade has provided good opportunities for women to get out of the house and join the market competition. They have been able to capitalize on their ability to speak Vietnamese to obtain timely information. Also, capitalizing on their advantageous situation in terms of geography and connections, they have been able to participate in the cross-border trade network. From small-scale retailers of single commodities they have developed into large-scale wholesalers and traders of diverse varieties of commodities. Women who started off trading in small quantities of thermos bottles and flu medicine are today large-scale wholesalers of beer, medicinal goods, and so on.

In Dongxing today 2,000 women are engaged in border-trade activities, and this is a trend which cannot be ignored. Many of these women have established shops in Mong Cai in Vietnam and often make daily trips to Vietnam and back to China again. The majority of these women earn more than 50,000 yuan a year. Some of the more prominent ones (such as Ji Xianwen, Peng Lailian, Huang Houzhen, Wu Cuifang, Huang Aiping, and Huang Cuiqin) are regarded by the local community as "very wealthy", having incomes in excess of 50,000 yuan annually. They have used their extraordinary skills and nimble minds to improve their lot, transforming themselves from the pre-border trade days where "the husband took the lead and his wife followed" to becoming astute businesswomen. As cadres from the Third Street Residents Committee in the town noted: "Third Street is no longer a single street. There are now two streets — one is the street at ground level and the other is the street in the air" (referring to the multi-storey private houses). The street in the air has been built with the money earned by the women. The secretary of the residents' committee noted:

> We in Third Street have become wealthy mainly through the women. It seems that women not only hold up half the sky, but 70 per cent of it. Now we men are quite willing to do the household chores, look after the children and let our wives go out and earn money.

In Dongxing, because much of the border trade involves family businesses, each family is like a company. The woman (wife) is often the main figure in the family, and usually she is the one who runs the business. This has changed from the previous situation where males held the dominant position. At the same time, the taxes these women pay have made a great contribution to local development, and have thus played a very major role in local economic development. While making money from their cross-border trading, the women have the opportunity to hone their skills to capitalize on the demands of the market economy.

CROSS-BORDER TRADE AND IDEOLOGICAL CHANGE AMONG WOMEN

The border trade has not only brought to Dongxing prosperity and a great improvement in the people's livelihood, but it has also brought obvious changes to the women's outlook and thinking. The women understand that it is only through reform and opening up that they have been able to become prosperous, and they are full of confidence for the future. According to a survey by the Women's Federation of Dongxing, over 80 per cent of the women feel that making a great contribution to the state is a major indicator of an individual's success, and they all hope that border trade will continue to grow and thrive in order to facilitate the development of their own undertakings. "Information" has become a buzzword for the local women. They hope that through studying, they will be able to master and utilize information and thereby be better able to participate in cross-border trade and become more useful socially. Many of the women hope to give up work totally or only work part-time so that they can attend courses at night school. It is understood that every year several dozens of women participate in Vietnamese language classes at primary school level. From this we can see the value the women place on education, for themselves as well as for their children. They are even prepared to pay more to get their children into a good school.

With the development of the cross-border trade, women have gradually begun to seek a better quality of life. Now that their basic needs have been met, they look forward to pleasure, knowledge, and beauty. Throughout the town of Dongxing, about 90 per cent of families have karaoke machines at home, and close to 80 per cent regularly have family karaoke sessions. Prior to the opening of cross-border trade, Dongxing had no special dance halls, but since the opening of the trade, at least ten song-and-dance halls have opened in Dongxing. In after-work hours and during the holidays, many of the women of Dongxing go to dance halls to have a good time.

Cosmetics is being accepted by an increasing number of women in Dongxing. Prior to the opening of cross-border trade, there were very few hair salons catering solely for women, and no beauty parlours existed at all. However, today many of the women who are engaged in business go to hair salons to get their hair washed. They can afford it and consider the convenience and pampering they are treated to well worth the money spent. The business of the Dongxing Development Zone Hospital Beauty Parlour, which is located next to the Dongxing Movie Theatre, is flourishing. It is understood that of the large numbers of customers, many are women from rural areas. Today, there are also many fully fledged beauty parlours in Dongxing, and the women have begun to learn how to beautify themselves and dress fashionably. Besides the attention to their hair and face, they try to keep up-to-date in their clothing and accessories. It has been said that in the past women in Dongxing cared little for what they wore. Today, however, in every street and lane, one sees Dongxing women dressed up in fine clothing. While previously Dongxing had virtually no fashion shops, now such shops are found on every main street and in many lanes. On just two streets — Jiefang Road and Guizhou Road — there are twenty to thirty fashion shops, and all are enjoying good business. This is particularly so of shops dealing in women's clothing. In Guizhou Road, a fashion designer who hails from Liuzhou in Guangxi has opened a fashion design shop. Business is very good and it often stays open into the night. The designer says that the women of Dongxing understand and appreciate beautiful clothes and if they like a particular item they will buy it without considering the cost.

CHANGES IN THE POSITION OF WOMEN IN THE HOME AS A RESULT OF CROSS-BORDER TRADE ACTIVITIES

The continued rise in the economic position of women has meant that their position in the home has seen changes. They have moved away from their former reliance on their husbands, and this has promoted a sense of equality between men and women. In the past, women in Dongxing were not major bread-winners in the family, and their main duties involved looking after their husbands and children. They were docile and obedient before their husbands and did as they were told. They often had quite legitimate requests unreasonably refused by their husbands and they had no autonomy. Since the growth of the cross-border trade, many women, relying on their own intelligence and skills, as well as hard work, bravely thrown themselves into the large market made possible by the cross-border trade. They have come to realize and recognize their own value; their labour has not only promoted the prosperity of the cross-border trade, but their husbands and other family members are now unable to deny the value of their labour. Their income is greater than what they would earn in factories or in government organizations, and they often earn more than their husbands. Thus, many examples of "reverse subsidies" are now occurring. In wealthy families, the women bring even more prosperity to the household, while in poorer ones the women bring new wealth. Thus, men now look on women with a new respect. Ji Xianwen, who specializes in wholesaling biscuits, owns a five-storey house, decorated and equipped with top-grade furniture and facilities, quite a contrast from the old ramshackle wooden house and dilapidated furniture they previously had. All this has come about as a result of Ji Xianwen's intelligence, courage, and hard work in the cross-border trade.

A survey by the Dongxing Women's Federation shows that today over 70 per cent of important family matters are jointly decided by both the husband and the wife. The increase in women's income has meant that women have more power and autonomy in the family, and decisions are no longer taken solely by the male. They have begun to pursue an affluent lifestyle which in the past they did not dare imagine. At the same time, through their intelligence, skills, and hard work, they are promoting the development of the Dongxing economy and the progress of the whole society.

PROSTITUTION

Sino-Vietnamese frontier trade has undoubtedly brought considerable wealth to Dongxing people, but this has also given rise to social problems. Since the improvement in their material lives, many Dongxing people, particularly the young, have come to seek stimulation and pleasure. Furthermore, Dongxing's location in the special frontier region between China and Vietnam, where foreigners abound, inevitably promotes certain negative elements — for example, gambling, drug-taking and trafficking, prostitution, and the like. In recent years, gambling has become very popular in Dongxing, and many have lost family fortunes; many juveniles have also become addicted to drugs. These people will often band together to commit crimes such as theft and robbery. Many Dongxing people also frequent brothels, and this has brought about family quarrels and broken families.

Large-scale prostitution in Dongxing only appeared with the opening up of the region in 1989. Although prostitution existed before 1989, prostitutes were only a small minority, who kept a low profile and could be seen in only one or two restaurants. Once the region opened up, however, the main sources of Dongxing prostitutes have been the western mountain area of Guangxi (for example, counties like Mashen, Douan, Hechi), Sichuan, Hunan, Zhejiang, and Guangdong provinces, and from Vietnam. The bustling economy and numerous travelling traders have attracted prostitutes to Dongxing.

In addition, and for various reasons, many women who come to Dongxing to be workers sometimes end up being prostitutes. Since the region opened in 1989, the scale of the influx of foreigners has made it difficult for Dongxing people to provide accommodation for them, and the additional number of foreign women has intensified the problem of providing employment for the female work-force. As there are no industries in Dongxing, and guest-houses and restaurants have already employed many people, there is no capacity to provide employment for all foreign women, as a result of which it is very difficult for them to find employment. Some owners of salons and beauty parlours take the opportunity to employ these women and use all the skills of the trade, including temptation and force, to turn them into prostitutes. According to a salon owner in Jiefang Road, most Dongxing prostitutes have been forced into prostitution. They come mainly from villages of Sichuan and Hunan provinces, and are deceived by go-betweens about the availability of work in factories along the coastal areas. On arrival, their identity cards are confiscated, and they are forced to work in places like salons or beauty parlours; without their identity cards they are unable to return to where they come from. At the beginning, these shopowners do not force the women into prostitution. But the women need money to pay for their food and accommodation. Besides, everything they see and hear in salons is about prostitution, and in the course of time they adapt themselves to the new environment and very soon begin participating in it willingly. Once they are in the trade, they get used to the good life, and very few are inclined to return to their previous life of poverty.

Elsewhere, some women employees in many small restaurants along the streets also turn to prostitution for money. Undoubtedly many have been forced into it initially. According to someone running such a restaurant, in order to employ women who can work in restaurants as well as work as prostitutes, the restaurant owner has to go to Mashan and Hechi in western Guangxi to recruit them. They invite applicants ostensibly to work in Dongxing factories. Once the women are in their employ, they are tempted or forced to prostitute themselves; and if the women submit and do as expected of them, the boss could thereby derive income from both the catering business and the prostitution trade.

Since the opening of cross-border trade, large numbers of businessmen have come to Dongxing, and after a year or two many bosses have become rich. Among the local community are many land sellers, businessmen, land speculators, security service providers, and ferry owners in Dongxing who have also prospered from the bustling economy. With their increased wealth, they can afford to take life easy, and many pursue physical pleasure and and live luxuriously and lasciviously. This group of people virtually lay the foundation for the existence and development of widespread prostitution in Dongxing.

Dongxing prostitutes are found on all main streets, and they work in compartments in beauty parlours, salons, and karaoke bars. Nearly every street has several such shops, particularly in Yongjin Street, Laodong Street, Shati Street, and Jiefang Road. At present, there are around forty to fifty such pleasure spots in Dongxing, with the number of prostitutes totalling some 300 to 400, inclusive of those working in small restaurants.

Generally, Dongxing prostitutes fall into three categories. The first category is made up of those working in small restaurants run by gangsters. Besides working as prostitutes, they also take on other jobs such as dish-washing or work as waitresses. They come mainly from urban and rural areas of Mashan, Hechi, and Baise in Guangxi, and generally serve local people of the lower-middle income group such as ferry owners and foreign workers, although they may also cater to rich men of rural areas and rich old men, for instance. This category of prostitutes generally dress simply, sometimes even appearing rather shabby and untidy, and are far from beautiful. They serve both young and old, and are generally not picky about their customers so long as they get paid for their work.

The second category constitutes those working in compartments in salons, beauty parlours, and karaoke bars. This category forms the largest group of prostitutes in Dongxing, coming mainly from provinces like Sichuan, Hunan, and Zhejiang. Such women live solely on prostitution. They have bodies that look good as well as attractive faces, and dress fashionably and are beautifully made-up. Their customers are generally corrupt officials and all kinds of bosses. Their pimps generally provide special cars to take them to clients, or rent guest-houses or rooms for them to stay for extended periods. As their clients are mainly bosses from Guangdong, who are often afraid of infection, each often sticks with one sexual partner on a long-term basis.

In the third category are the Vietnamese women brought over by bosses from Dongxing and Vietnam to work as prostitutes in Dongxing. These women often do not have fixed place of abode, and their customers are generally the local "gangsters", the low-income groups, and those in Dongxing who wish to try a "foreign prostitute". As is to be expected, these Vietnamese prostitutes are often infected with various sexual diseases.

Dongxing's prostitution industry started in 1989 and reached its peak in 1991–93, during which time the number of salons was more than double the number in 1996. During those years when prostitution was a flourishing trade, prostitutes did not have to sit outside salons to wait for customers to come along. After 1993, following the cooling down of the frontier trade, many bosses went bankrupt or moved away, and many companies relocated from Dongxing to other places. Business for prostitutes then went into a serious decline, and now there are prostitutes hanging around every evening on the streets waiting for customers or trying to attract them.

INCOME

The income of prostitutes can be considered relatively good. Those working in small restaurants get paid 30 to 50 renminbi for each session of prostitution, and generally get a salary of about 200 to 300 renminbi per month (food and accommodation excluded). According to the owner of a small restaurant, these worker-prostitutes serve several customers, sometimes more than ten in a day. These women may earn around 5,000 renminbi a month. Usually the prostitutes return home after having worked two years in Dongxing and with the money they have earned, build themselves homes. Those who are still single may decide to settle down and get married, while those who are married may choose to stay at home to raise their children and not return to prostitution.

Prostitutes working in salons earn even more. During the flourishing days of the industry, they could earn close to 10,000 renminbi each month, but now, with fewer customers, they earn only a few thousand renminbi a month.

PERSONAL TREATMENT

Although Dongxing prostitutes earn good incomes, they are treated very poorly. If they do not perform as expected or if they refuse to serve the customers assigned to them, they are beaten up by their bosses. Also, part of their income from prostitution — generally half — must be submitted to their bosses. On top of that, they suffer all kinds of physical tortures and abuses, and are expected serve whenever there is a customer, with no freedom of choice at all. They also do not feel secure in their jobs. For example, a prostitute who once worked in a salon became pregnant as a result of a contraceptive failing to work. As she already had two children at home and could not afford another, she decided to go for an abortion, but this required the signature of a relative. The boss of the salon simply ignored her plight and refused to foot the bill for the operation. Fortunately for her, in the end it was the head of the hospital who signed and paid for the operation. There have also been cases of salon girls "taken to hilltops" and raped and murdered in Dongxing.

According to reports, many Dongxing prostitutes have husbands and children at home. Some husbands are aware of the occupation of their wives but accept it as they need their wives' earnings. Many salon girls have been sending money back home frequently to meet the upkeep of their families.

Prostitution has affected law and order in Dongxing, and has brought misfortune to many Dongxing families. Many social problems in Dongxing have involved "salon prostitutes". The existence of these prostitutes has drawn many male family members to frequent brothels, and this has brought about domestic conflicts.

Before 1989 the government would take strong measures against prostitution whenever it was discovered. Since then, however, the numbers of prostitutes and of people who frequent brothels has been on the increase, and almost every main street and every large hotel has seen prostitution activities. Nevertheless, only token arrests have been made, thanks to the connivance of the government, which is pleased that the prostitutes can draw rich businessmen to come and invest in Dongxing. Bosses of salons involved in such activities usually rely on their connections with influential power, gangs, or military forces to prevent the façade of their shops from being smashed.

CONCLUSION

The opening up of the border trade after 1989 has allowed the people of Dongxing to transform what was previously an economically backward township into a vigorous market-oriented society. Women in particular have been able to free themselves from outdated ideas of their place in the home and in society, and have become independent and self-reliant. They have changed their status at home and have won recognition in society. The mass media have covered extensively the story of the "strong women" emerging from the tide of border trade and praised their undertakings. Of course, the praises sung of these market-oriented developments are partially cancelled by the evils of prostitution, although this too has provided some women with new opportunities.

15. Women and Social Change along the Vietnam-Guangxi Border   327

ACKNOWLEDGEMENT

The Dongxing Women's Federation and the Dongxing Culture Bureau have both given the author much assistance during his fieldwork. The author would also like to thank Dr Grant Evans and Dr Kuah Khun Eng for their support. Dr Geoff Wade arranged for the article's translation into English, for which I am grateful. The data presented in this chapter is largely derived from the author's own fieldwork in Dongxing over 1995–96. Additional information has been provided by the Dongxing Telecommunications Bureau, the Dongxing Border Trade Bureau, the Dongxing Women's Federation, and the Dongxing Culture Bureau. Many of the reports about women who have been extremely successful in border trade appeared in local newspapers such as *Dongxing Journal* and *Fengcheng Port Journal.*

NOTE

1. 1 yuan (renminbi) = 10 *mao*; 1 *mao* = 10 *fen*.

Index

A

A Notice for Further Liberalizing the Border Towns and countries of Nanning, Kunming City, Pingxiang Town, Ruili, and Hekou Country by the State Council 77
acculturation 116
Achang 51
ADB 126
Admiral Zheng (Ma) He 223
aggression 115
agricultural development 197
agricultural products 132
agriculture 90, 204, 209
AIDS 170
aiguo zhuyi 294
airports 136
Akha 2, 3, 99
Akha caravan 206
Akha entrepreneurs 206, 212
Akha oral texts 206
Akha traders 207
Akha-Chinese 217
Alavi 147
alcohol abuse 190
America 116
Americans 104, 109

amphetamine 211
An Giang 237
Ananda Thera 147
Annam 42, 106
Annamites 261
Announcement of Several Problems Pertaining to Border Trade 91
anthropologists 254
anthropology 7
anti-communist 108
anti-government armed forces 63
anti-Manchu 32
Anti-Rightist Campaign 55
Arabic 228
Arakanese 227
Archibald Colquhoun 105
Argentina 114
arms trafficking 185
Asia Inc 11
Asia Times 12
Asia Watch 260
"Asian capitalism" 2
Asian Danube 234
Asian Development Bank 126
Asian economic crisis 1
"Asian Economic Miracle" 1
Asian Megatrends 13

Asian "tigers" 8
Asoka 147
assimilation 5, 32
Association of Overseas Chinese (*Hoi Kieu Lien*) 247
asylum 272
Australia 114
Austronesian 117
authoritarian 16
autonomous 38
Autonomous district of the Bian and the Yao nationalities 293
autonomous regions 112, 164
Autonomous township of the Yue 293
autonomy 32
Ayutthaya 103, 191

B
1979 border war 264
Ba 37
baahkwá (Vietnamese: *Pac Va*) 261
baht 198
Baker, Chris 8
Ban Gu 31
Ban Lau 239
Ban Me Thuot 257
Bandaai 156
Bandan 130
bandits 43, 208
Bangkok ix, 103
Bangkok Post 18
Bangladeshi 228
Bangsa 57, 155, 157
banking 91
Banna Mansion Hotel 167
Baoshan 207
bap 151
barter 5
baskets 209
Bau Ham 259
beauty parlours 320
Beihai 226
Beijing 9
Belgium 209
benevolence 40
Bengal 104
Berlie, Jean vii, 4, 6
Bernatzik 208
Bhutan 72

Bianzu Yaozu Zizhiqu 293
bilateral trade 237
Binh Tien Plastics Company 246
biodiversity 51
biological diversity 51
Black Banner Militia 288
black economy 23
Black Flag 107
Black Hmong 117
black market 67, 198
Black River 107
Black Tai 163
black tea 229
Blang 51
boat people 263
BOOT 20
border conflict 238
border crossings 131, 237
border peoples 32
border provinces 77
border regions 2, 6, 44, 75, 236
border studies 33
border trade 73, 133
Border Trade Policy 73
border traders 74
border trading 75
border zone 244
borderlands 6, 25, 123, 136
borders 2, 3, 5, 29
Boten 133, 154
boundaries 29
Boundaries in China 29
boundary between China and Vietnam 287
Bouyei 51
bribe 172
bribery 88, 172
bridges 250
Britain 186
British 23, 102
British empire 38
brothels 184, 185
Buddha 147
Buddhism 151
Buddhist 106, 145
Buddhist monks 150
Buddhist revival 146
budget deficits 249
buffaloes 209

buffer 111
Build, Own, Operate, and Transfer 20
Bukhara 224
Bulang 164
bun 151
Bunchum 155
Bunyalaekanthasiri 148
bureaucracies 88, 126
bureaucratic 88
Burmese 22, 74
Burmese king 208
businessmen 279
businesswomen 319

C
Cam Duong 238
Cam Pha 264
Cam Ranh 12
Cambodia ix
Cambodians 19
Can Tho 237
Canada 114
Cantonese 261
Canyuan 57
Cao Bang 109, 238
Cao Faa Sirinor 148, 153
Cao Khatiyawong 146
Cao Loc 239
Cao Mahaakanthawong 157
Cao Saengsii 146
capital 236, 316
capitalism 9, 177
capitalist 11
caravan 104
caravan routes 133, 207
cars 135
cash crops 55
Catholicism 288
Catholics 214
cattle 195
Central Government 76
Central Highlands 257
central planning 5
centralization 12
Chai-anan Samudavanija 11
Chaiyong Limthongkhul Foundation 11
Chakkri dynasty 111
Cham 223

Chao Fa 164
Chaozhou merchants 226
chaozhou 228
charisma 157
Chatichai, Prime Minister 126
Chau Thi Hai vii, 4, 6
Che Zhimin 166
Chengdu 64, 239
Cheung Siu-Woo vii, 4, 6
Chiang Kham 112
Chiang Khong 123
Chiang Khong–Houayxay 129
Chiang Mai ix, 11
Chiang Rai 18
Chiang Saen 135, 156, 212
Chiang Saen–Tonpheung 129, 131
Chiangkok 155
Chiangtung 146
Chin-Ho 233
China ix, 2, 3, 4, 5, 6
China Environmental Conservation
    Agency 62
China-Laos border 67, 154
Chinese 28
Chinese administration 38
Chinese administrative structure 39
Chinese army 303
Chinese borders 5, 34
Chinese Communist Party 9, 257
Chinese culture 28, 30
Chinese customs 237
Chinese emperor 40, 208
Chinese empire 164
Chinese hegemony 175
Chinese historiography 39, 43
Chinese Islamic Association 222, 227
Chinese language 214
Chinese literati 31
Chinese medicine 228
Chinese Muslim 230
Chinese Nung 256
Chinese overseas 82
Chinese Revolution 208
Chinese settlement 45
Chinese settlers 45
Chinese society 30
Chinese sphere 45
Chinese state 38

Index   331

Chinese women 176
Chinese world order 31
Chineseness 41
Chongqing 303
Christian 105
Christianity 214
Christianized 106
Chu 36
chunqiu 35
CIA 271
CIDG 271
CITES 64
civil society 10
Civilian Irregular Defence Groups 271
class 307
class oppression 33
classification of ethnic groups 270
coastal areas 323
coastal provinces 77
Cohen, Paul T. vii, 6
collective 54
collectives 54
collectivization 160
collectivized agriculture 9
colonial 24, 39, 104
colonialism 192
colonialist 24
command economy 10
commerce 204
commercial sex workers 187
commodification 190
communism 176
communist 3, 4
Communist Party of Burma 127
Communist Party of Thailand 112
comprador capitalists 258
Confucian 40
Constitution of the Democratic Republic of Vietnam 117
Contagious Disease Control Act of 1908 192
Convention on International Trade in Endangered Species of Wild Fauna and Flora 64
core and periphery 29
corrupt officials 324
corruption 1
corvée 38

cosmetics 320
cotton 209
counterfeit currency 244
counterfeiting 90
CPT 112
credit 248
credit organizations 248
crimes 322
cross-border 4, 5, 6
cross-border automobile "campaign" 242
cross-border caravan trade 224
Cross-Border Categories 254
cross-border trade 22, 66, 142
cross-border trade networks 211
cross-cultural ix
cross-ethnic relationships 205
CSWs 187
Culas, Christian vii, 5
cultural borders 30
cultural diversity 51
cultural exchange 250
cultural pollution 75
Cultural Revolution 4, 54, 153
currency exchange 243
currency traders 267
Custom Inspection and Preferential Tax Privileges Pertaining to Trading along the Sino-Myanmar Border of the People's Republic of China 77
customs 4, 22
customs officers 139

D

Dai 51
Dai Autonomous Prefecture 55, 226
Dai (Tai Lue) Autonomous Region of Xishuangbanna 163
Dai Viet 41
Dalat 257
Dali 35, 223
Dalou 59, 169, 170
Dalou Economic Zone 59
Damenglong Nature Reserve 56
dams 17, 19
Dan 263
dance halls 320
Dang Nghiem Van 263

Daweishan Nature Reserve 59
de-naturalization 7
Deal 32
Deang 51
debt 199
decentralization 76
decolonization 112
deforestation 52, 55, 113
Dehong County 85
demarcation of the national boundary 289
demerit 151
Democratic Republic of Vietnam 107
Deng Xiaoping 9, 73
Déo Van Long 107
Déo Van Tri 107
deregulation 139
Derung 51
detoxification 196
dhamma 151
di 41
Diem regime 257
Dien Bien Phu 108
Dikötter, Frank 30
Dinh Quan 259
direct sex workers 187
discrimination 258
division of labour 209
Do Muoi 239
Dodd, W.C. 164
Doi Chiangteum mountain 145
doi moi 10
domestic tourism 168
domestic tourists 169
domestic violence 190
domination 12
dong 243
Dong Dang 242
Dong Nai 237, 258
Dong-son 28
Dongxing ix, 6, 57, 246
Dongxing autonomous county of various nationalities 293
Dongxing Economic Development District 289
Dongxing Gezu Zizhixian 293
Dongxing–Mong Cai free trade zone 84

Dongxing–Mong Cai inter-market system 241
double identity 230
drug abuse 1
drug addiction 211
drug crops 198
drugs 4, 90
dry rice 145
DSWs 187
Du Guangfei 288
Du Guoqiang 289
Du Wenxiu 226
Duara 32

E
E-er-tai 39
East India Company 104
Eastern Han dynasty 35
Eastern Jin 35
"ecochange" 51
Ecole française d'Extrême Orient 108
ecological 51
ecology 51
economic activities of women 316
economic boom 299
economic co-operation districts 83
economic co-operation zones 83
economic development 21, 57, 74, 280
Economic Development Committee of Xishuangbanna 171
economic differentiation 205
economic liberalization 77, 94
economic networks 222
economic planning 3
economic position of women 321
Economic Quadrangle 122
Economic Quadrangle Joint Development Corporation 123
economic reforms 3
economic zones 83
economics 2, 7
ecosystems 4, 51
ECVIIs 256
education 10
EGAT 21
eighteenth century 104
Eighth Five-Year Period 75
electricity 130

Electricity Generating Authority of
 Thailand 21
emperor 40
Emperor Yongle 42
endangered animal 169
English 16
entrepreneurs 4, 127
environment 51
environmental 19
epidemics 102
ethnic 44
ethnic categories 215, 217
ethnic Chinese 162
ethnic conflicts 291
ethnic diversity 5
ethnic groups 34
ethnic identity 95
ethnic minorities 1, 6
ethnic nationalism 227
ethnic tensions 288
ethnic Vietnamese 236
ethnic-tourism 167
ethnicity 5, 24, 94, 307
ethnographers 255
ethnolinguistic categorization 255
Europe 57
European 100
Evans, Grant vii, 3, 5, 6
ex-China Vietnamese illegal immigrants
 256
exports 83, 87, 249
expulsions 261

F
factories 313
Fairbank, John 31
family businesses 319
famines 102
Fan Chengda 38
fan 41
Far Eastern Economic Review 23
farm land 300
farmers 175
Farmers' Union 53
farming 299
fashion 321
Feingold, David A. vii, 5
female ritual performers 284

female traders 317
Fengcheng ix, 246, 257, 302, 315
Fenshuiling 61
festivals 250
Fifth Special Forces in Nha Trang 260
fishing 299
food crops 198
foot-binding 208
foothills 115
forced labour 199
Foreign Investment Management
 Centre 80
foreign investors 179
foreign tourism 168
foreign tourists 169
Foreign Trade Corporations 16
foreign women 323
foreigners 323
forest products 132
forest resources 57
forestry 54
formal economy 22
Forney, Matt 166
Fourth Islamic tide 228
France 114
free market 10
French 16, 102
French Guyana 114
French missionaries 288
frontier regions 312
frontier trade 57, 67
Frontier Trade Woman 313
frontiers 3, 29
FTCs 16
Fujian 37
FULRO 259
Fuzhou 15

G
gaitu guiliu 39
gambling 250
gangsters 324
Gansu 28
GDP 22
gender 176
Geneva Accord of 1954 108
Geneva Agreement 257
geo-politics 19, 21

German Democratic Republic 265
Germany 186
Gladney 29
global economy 74
global market-place 3
global markets 8
GNP 23
Goh 162
Golden Quadrangle Economic Bloc 84
Golden Triangle 22
goods 74
Great Leap Forward 4, 54
Great Mekong Development Area 211
Great Peace 118
Great Wall 34
Greater Mekong region 136
green tea 229
gross domestic product 22
gross national product 23
growth circles 11
Guangdong 9, 37
Guangxi 6, 10
Guangxi Institute of Nationalities 297
Guangxi Zhuang Autonomous Region 239
Guangxi Zhuang Minorities Autonomous Region Preferential Tax Policies Pertaining to the Encouragement of Outside Investment 81
Guangxi Zhuang Minorities Autonomous Region Regulation Pertaining to the Encouragement of Investment of the Taiwanese 82
Guangxi Zhuang Minorities Autonomous Region Temporary Law for the Leasing and Management of Land for Development Purposes by Outside Investments 81
Guangzhou 225
Guanlu 58
guanxi 12
guerrilla 112
Guiyang 12
Guizhou 37
Gulf of Tonkin 280
guns 209
guoji zhuyi 294
Guomindang 32, 229

H

Ha Bac 245
Ha Giang 109
Ha Tuyen 260
Hac 256
Hac Ca 263
Hai Ninh 259
Hainan 223
Haiphong ix, 239
hair salons 320
haj 234
Haji Na Shunxing 229
Hakka 213
Han 53
Han Chinese 5, 56, 98
Han dynasty 28
Han ethnicity 168
Hani 117, 164
Hani (Akha) 51
Hanification 167
Hanoi ix
Hanshu 31
harbour 302
Hat Festival 278
Haw 103
Hay, John 29
health 10
Heaven 40
Heaven's mandate 40
Heilongjiang 72
Hekou ix, 57, 59, 65
Hekou–Lao Cai economic co-operation district 84
heroin 22
Hershatter 29
highlanders 100, 113, 196, 204
highlands 99, 100
hilltribe women 192
hilltribes 112, 162
Hindi 234
Hindustani 234
Hinton, Peter viii, 2, 7
HIV 187
Hmau 99
Hmong 2, 5, 250
Hmong diaspora 113
Hmu 99
Ho 223
Ho Chi Minh 292

Ho Chi Minh City 4, 237
Hoa Association 244
Hoa Binh 109
Hoa Kieu 237
Hoanh Mo 239
Hong Gai 264
Hong Kong 9
Hong Kong camps 265, 266
Hong Kong government 260
Hong Kong Vietnamese camps 265
Honghe 208
Hongsa 125
Hor 233
Hor Phra Kaew 156
horse caravan trade 206
horse caravan trading 206
horse caravans 207
Houayxay 123
Houei Sai 58
Houqiao 63
Household Responsibility System 9, 170
housing 10
Hsieh Shih-chung 165
H'tin 100
hua 30
Huaphan 110
Hubei 36, 163
Hue 35
Hui 32, 223
Hunan 36
Hutton, Christopher viii, 2, 6
hydro-electric 127
hydro-electric power 66
hydropower 18

I
identity 5
ideology 11
IDUs 194
IIs 256
illegal immigrants 256, 304
imam 227
Imam Na 230
IMF 8, 14
immigrant 115, 314
immigration 133
imperial 34
imperialism 44
imperialists 34

Import and Export Custom Tax Guidelines of the People's Republic of China 76
import and export taxes 141
import duties 249
imported cars 135
imports 78
India 38, 72
Indian 232
indigenous 36, 38, 59
indigenous peoples 204
indigenous ruler 38
indirect rule 38
indirect sex workers 187
Indochina Massif 113
Indochina War 24, 289
Indochina Wars 98
Indra 148
industrialization 88
infant mortality 189
informal economy 14
infrastructural 5, 19
infrastructure 4, 127
injection drug users 194
inland trade 207
Institute of Medicine State Farm 170
Institute of Minorities 294
Institute of Southeast Asian Studies (ISEAS) ii
insurrections 112, 115
integration 134
inter-ethnic marriages 205
inter-ethnic negotiations 212
intermarriage 272
International Monetary Fund 8
internationalism 294, 303
internment 260
investment 78
investors 89
Irrawaddy 207
irrigation 18
Islam 222
Islamic 222
Islamic revival 234
Islamic school 229
Islamization 224
ISWs 187
Italy 209

J

Jahariyya Sufism 225
Jan English-Lueck 29
Japan 57
Japanese 32
Jean Dupuis 105
Jiang Zemin 239
Jiangbian 55
Jiangping 288
Jiangxi 36
Jiaozhi 36
Jiegao trading district 86
Jilin 72
Jinghong 53, 57, 103, 162, 168
Jingpo (Kachin) 51, 188
Jingshuihe 57
Jingzu 292
Jino 164
joint ventures 15, 87

K

K. Surangkhanang 192
karaoke 320
Karen 106
karma 151
Kashmir 72
Kemu 52
Keng Tung 125, 208
Kesa Thancai 156
Keyes 151
Khampheng Thipmuntali 163
Khmer Rouge 112
Khmu 113
Kho Da 239
Khoen 155
Khruba Bunchum Yaansuamro 146, 155
Khruba Siwichai 160
Khun Sa 199
Kien Giang 237
King of the Sky 118
King of Xianyang 224
Kinh 109
Kinh businessmen 308
Kinh cosmology 288
kinship 95, 303
kinship networks 5
Kokang 197

Kontum 257
Koreans 189
Kuah Khun Eng viii, 6
Kublai Khan 224
Kunming ix, 15
Kunming City Encouraging Outside Investment Policies 86
Kunming-Hanoi Railway 226
Kuomintang 229
kyat 198

L

labour 5, 199
labour camps 260
Lahu 51, 113, 157
Lai Chau 61, 107, 109
Lampang 231
Lamphun 160
Lancang 171
Lancang Jiang 18
land mines 189
land reform 291
landlord 34
Lang Son ix, 57, 162, 238, 239
language 303
language policies 255
Lanten 167
Lao 16
Lao Airways 166
Lao Cai ix, 57, 109, 117
Lao government 3
Lao lum 110
Lao People's Democratic Republic (LPDR) 122, 154, 155
Lao State Fuel Company 131
Lao sung 110
Lao theung 110
Lao traders 131
Lao-Cambodian borders 242
Lao-Chinese 133
Lao-Chinese trade 133
Lao-Thai trade 133
Laos ix, 2, 3, 6
Laotian 66
large-scale traders 316
Lattimore 34
Lê Hao 41
Lee Kuan Yew 25

Li Jili 42
Li Peng 239
Li Renfu 229
Li Xinhua 246
liangshandaohu 55
Liaoning 72
liberalization 124
liberated zones 110
liberation 33
life expectancy 189
Lijiang 207
Lim Joo-Jock 100
liminality 29
lineages 103
Lingnan 36
linguistic categories 255, 269
linguists 254
Lintner, Bertil 163
linyesanding 55
Lisu 51, 100
literacy 116
Liu Hongxuan 33
Liu Yongfu 288
Lo clan 109
loans 83
local development 319
local governments 78
Loei-Phitsanulok 112
logging 21
logging rights 135
Lolo 117, 234
Lord of the Nagas 149
Lower Mekong 18
lowland 100
Lowland Lao 189
lowlands 5, 100
Lu 165
Lua 113
Luang Namtha ix, 3, 57, 110, 123, 162
Luang Namtha province 145
Luang Prabang 18, 58, 110, 131
Luchuan 37
Lue 133, 145
Lue script 155
Lue writing system 155
Lung Vai 239
luxury cars 135
Ly clan 109

M
Ma Huan 223
Ma Mingxing 225
Ma Yuan 36
Ma Yuting 229
Maalao 262
Macau 237
macro-categories 268
madrasah 229
Mae Sai 132, 156, 188, 223, 225
Mae Sai–Tachilek 128
Magouhe 65
Mahathir Mohamad 25
mainland Southeast Asia ix, 52, 223
malaria 53
Malay 223
Malaya 38
Malaysia 213
Mamushu 58
man 41
Man 261
Man Jinglan 53, 166, 170
Man Ting 166, 171
Manchus 31, 32, 102
Mandalay ix, 128
mandate of Heaven 42
Mang 52
Mangshi 224
mansions 301
manufactured goods 135
manufacturing 79
Manwan 26
Manzhang Dai village 59
Mao Zedong 9, 54
Maoist 15, 23
Mara 160
Marcus 7
marginal identities 254
maritime commerce 207
maritime trade 226
market economy 3, 5
market reforms 4
market socialism 74
market system 190
market values 190
market-town 301
markets 61
Marquez 25

Marshal Sarit 186
Marxist-Leninist 164
massage parlours 185
Massif 102
Mecca 231
media 16
medicinal 103
medicinal plants 67
medicines 64, 65, 169
mega-trends 8
Mekong 17
Mekong Basin 211
Mekong dam 127
Mekong River ix, 17
Mekong River Commission 17
Mekong River Economic Sub-Basin 84
Mengban 230
Menghai 164
Mengla ix, 15
Mengla Nature Reserve 56
Menglun Nature Reserve 56
Mengyan Nature Reserve 56
Menlar 57
mercantilism 44
merit 151
merit-making 151
Messiah 118
messianic 115
Meuangsing 57
Miao 99
Miao (Hmong) 51
Miao National Minority 99
Miao-Yao 99
Michaud, Jean viii, 5
micro-economy 4
Middle East 232
middlemen 251
migrant 5
migrant labourers 4, 5, 265
migrant workers 1
migrations 4, 5
migratory 106
Mike Forces 271
military conquest 37
Min 37
mines 136
Ming 28
Ming dynasty 207

Minh Hai 237
mining 130
Ministry of Foreign Economic Relations and Trade 16
Ministry of Forestry 62
Ministry of Public Health of Thailand 187
minorities 5
minority groups 77
minority nationality 307
minority regions 98, 164
minority women 170
missionaries 105
missionary 105
mixed marriages 206
mo 41
mobile phones 212
Mobile Strike Forces 271
mobile telephones 212
modernization 74
MOFERT 16
Mohan 61, 133
Mojiang 224
Mojiang county 55
money economy 172
money-changers 243
Mong Cai ix, 6, 57, 162
Mongolia 32, 72
Mongols 32
Mons 106
Montagnard 99, 111
moral communities 145, 158
Morita, Noritaka 190
mortality 190
mosques 224
Moulmein 103, 207
Mu-Se 87
Muang Cae 156
Muang Hai 157, 169
Muang La 153
Muang Long 155
Muang Mang 153
Muang Mom 137
Muang Phong 153, 156
Muang Sing district 145
Muang Sing reliquary 145
Muang Sing town 57, 131, 133, 145, 232

Index 339

Muang Wen 156
Muang Yong 156
Muang Yu 153, 156
Muang Yuan 153
mule caravan 206
mules 234
multi-ethnic 34
multi-ethnic social networks 214
multi-lingualism 215
multinational investors 211
multinationals 74
Muong Khuong 239, 242
Muse 57, 87
Muslim caravans 226
Muslim identity 227
Muslims 3, 103, 222, 232
Musur 157
Myanmar ix, 22, 199

N
Naang Khemmaa 146
Naang Thoranii 149
Naga 147
Naipaul 25
Naisbitt 8
nak bun 156
Nakai Plateau 20
Nam Ngum 20
Nam Phu 16
Nam Theun 20
Namhkam ix, 87
Nan 104
Nan Yue 17 36, 46
Nanjing 64
Nanning ix, 64
Nanning-Kunming Railway 302
Nanning-Qingzhou Highway 302
Nanpanjiang 54
Nanzhao 35, 37, 224
Naqshabandi 223
narcotics 22, 184
nation-states 12, 126, 208
national border 287
national identity 303
National League for Democracy 23
national security 260
national states 51
nationalisms 8, 33

nationalities 44
Nationalities Affairs Commission 33
nationality autonomous townships 292
Nationality Park 170
native office 38
natural resources 52, 67, 140, 250
naturalized categories 7
nature reserves 56
negotiations between France and China 287
Nei Ku Chau detention centre 256
NEM 128
Nemkan 57
Nepal 72, 156
Neua 145
New Economic Mechanism 128
New Economic Zones 259
New Religion 222
Ngai 256
Ngai-ization 264
Nghe An 109
NGOs 20, 21
nineteenth century 37
Ninth Five-Year Plan 302
nirvana 151
NLD 23
nomadic 108
nomadism 101
nomads 34
non-Chinese 30
non-governmental organizations 20
non-Han 99
non-Thai 111, 195
Nong Khai 58
normalization of Sino-Vietnamese relations 239
North Korea 4, 72
North Vietnam 23
northern Laos 134
Northern Song 223
Northern Thai 151
northern Thailand 134
northern Vietnam 109
nouveaux riches 298
Nu 51
Nung 250
Nung ethnicity 260
Nung Security Platoon 260

O

occupational identity 216
Office for Special Economic Zones 84
official corruption 1
Ohmae, Kenichi 2, 6, 8
Old Religion 222
open-door policy 94
opiate 184
opium 6, 23
opium trade 207
Opium Wars 104
oppression 34
oral history 309
Oudomxay 57, 66, 154
Outong 261
Overseas Chinese 12, 86, 168
Overseas Vietnamese 292
ox traders 209

P

1985 Period 75
Pachay revolt 105
Pacific Rim 251
pacification 42, 198
pacifying 43
Page, Tim 24
Pak Beng 58, 67, 125, 131
Pakistan 238
Pakistani influence 222
Pakse 163
Pamir Mountains 28
Panthay rebellion 226
Panyaa Naak 148
Panyaa Tanhai 146, 147
paper mills 58
Pasuk Phongpaichit 8
Pathet Lao 110
patriarchal societies 184
Pavie, Auguste 107
PDR 154
peasants 210
People's Bank of China 83
People's Communes 54
People's Liberation Army 110
People's Republic of China (PRC) 5, 6, 28
petty-traders 267
Pham Van Dong 239

Phami Akha 218
pharmaceuticals 67
Phong Tho 107
Phongsaly ix, 57, 110, 163, 208
Phra Chiangteum 146
Phra Uppakrut 149
Phrae 225
Phrao 156
Phu Hoa 259
Phu Noi 162
physical anthropology 270
Pianma 63
piece-goods trading 317
pilgrimage 145
Pilgrims 158
Pillar Point open camp 269
Pingxiang ix, 57, 237
Pingxiang–Lang Son economic cooperation district 84
Pingyuan 10
pirated goods 91
Pleiku 257
Po Hen 239
poaching 60
Pol Pot 11
Policies Pertaining to the Guangxi-Pingxiang Border Trading Open District 85
political boundaries 2, 31, 72, 211, 254
Popular Republic of China Constitution 117
population density 52
porters 209
ports 127
Portuguese 104
Post-Socialist 7, 9
poverty 323
Prasenjit Duara 34
PRC 6, 28
primary forests 56
privatization 20, 141
proletariat 33
prostitutes 4, 192
prostitution 1, 6
Protestants 214
proto-China 44
provincial governments 77, 79
Puer 225
Putonghua 265

Index 341

Q
Qin 34, 35
Qin dynasty 207
Qin Shi Huangdi 36
Qing 208, 31
qingfei fanba 291
Qingzhou 315, 302
Qoxiong 99
Quadrangle 123
Quang Ninh 239
Quang Ninh Provincial Cultural Performance Team 285
Que Do Bank 244
Qujing 65

R
1978 Reform 74
R&R 186
races 30, 32
Raglai 257
railroad 226
railways 136
rainforests 56, 66
rape 201
rare animals 241
raw materials 4
re-education 114
rebellion 101
Red Guards 155
Red River 36, 107
Red River Delta 36
Reform Era 73
refugee 115
refugee camp 265
refugee status 256
regional autonomy 33, 79
regional economic development 297
regional economies 138
Regulation Concerning Criminal Offences Regarding the Hybridization and Sale of Improper Goods 91
Regulations and Policies Governing Yunnan Jiegao Border Trading District 86
religion 10
Removing Bandits and Overlords 291
renminbi 252
rental income 172
repression 185
republic 32
Republic of China 6, 258
republican 33
Republican period 290
resettlement 189
responsibility system 55
restricted zones 260
reunification 258
revival of Islam 228
rice 22, 174
rice traders 261
river ports, 132
road system 301
roads 136
robbers 153
robbery 207
ROC 33
role of women 318
Rongshui Miao and Luocheng Mulam Autonomous Counties 272
royalists 110
rubber 56, 164
rubber plantations 56, 165
Ruili ix, 15, 57
Rules and Regulations Pertaining to Outside Investment by the State Council 76
rural areas 299
rural people 21
rural women 1
Rushdie 25
Russia 17

S
Sa Buakham 148
Sa Pa 117
Sacred Hills 56
sacred topography 152
Saengthong Photibupbaa 146
Sai 132
Saigon 257
salt 134, 219
Salween ix, 207
Same Big Pot 55
same-year organizations 248
San Diu 256
San Y 256
Sangha 160
Sankampaeng 156

Sariputra Thera 147
sawmills 63, 132
Sayaburi 110, 113
Scandinavia 186
school system 175
sea-borne trade 207
secessionist movements 255
secondary forest 61
secret societies 32
sedentarization 98
self-determination 33
semi-nomadic 111
service sector 244
sex industry 184
sex tourism 170
sex work 188
sex workers 186
sexual abuse 198
sexual services 184, 192
sexualization of Dai women 169
sexually transmitted diseases 187
Shan 106
Shan rebel groups 128
Shan rebels 142
Shanghai 4, 9, 218
Shanhai Jing 30
Shanxin 292
shaoshu minzu 307
shifting cultivation 52, 55
Shiji 31
shrines 151
Shu 37
Shujing 30
Shuncheng Jie 226
Siamese 107
Sichuan 28
Sichuanese rubber workers 165
Sikkim 72
Silver 219
Sima Qian 31
Simao ix, 127, 188
Singapore ii
sinicization 36, 264
sinicized Yao or Yao-ized Chinese 268
Sino-Tibetan 100
Sino-Burmese Street 84
Sino-Vietnamese relations 240
Sino-Vietnamese trade 236

Sino-Vietnamese War 81
Sip Song Chau Tai 107, 179
Sip Song Panna 163
Sipsawng Panna 165
Sirenfa 42
slash-and-burn 162
slaves 191
SLORC 22
small traders 23
small-scale traders 316
smuggle 66
smuggled goods 239
smugglers 197
smuggling 23
Soc Trang 237
social change 15
Social Darwinism 32
social pollution 72
social problems 322
socialism 9
socialist 9, 25
socialist market economy 227
soil erosion 113
Son La 107, 109
Son of Heaven 40
Sondhi Limthongkhul 11
Song 35
Songhuaba 224
South China 6, 95
South China Sea 35
Southeast Asia ii, 2, 6
Southeast Asian 7, 93
southern China ix
southwest China 6, 58, 303
sovereignty 4, 5, 139
Soviet 9
Soviet Union 4, 10
special economic zones 57, 74
Special Forces 271
sphere of influence 5
Spratly Islands 93
Sri Lanka 156
Ssu-mao 225
standard of living 249
State Bank of China 244
State Bank of Vietnam 244
State Council 76
State Council Revised Import and

Export Custom Tax Guidelines
 of the People's Republic of
 China 77
state enterprises 89
state farms 164
state intervention 138
State Law and Order Restoration
 Council 22
status stratification 209
STDs 187
Steles 224
sticky rice 174
stock market 17
Su Yongge viii
subsidy period 238
subsistence economy 205
subsistence farmers 204
subversive 17
Sufi 223
Sufism 222
Sui-Tang 34
Sultan Suleiman 226
Sun Yat-sen 32
Sunni 222
Sunnites 222
surplus 249
swidden 145
swiddeners 108, 110, 115
swiddening 101

T
Tachilek 139, 155, 225
Tai 37
Tai cattle caravan 206
Tai chuu 213
Tai Federation 107
Tai Lue 145
Tai Mao kingdom 37
Tai Neua 145
Tai Yai 205
Tai-Meo Autonomous Region 117
Taiwan 57
Taiwanese 67
Taiwanese Christian churches 214
Tak 103
Tambiah, S.J. 160
Tan Phu district 259
Tan Qixiang 35

Tan Thanh 239
Tang dynasty 206, 222
Tapp, Nicholas 100
tax 78
tax incentives 89
taxation 3, 78
Tay 250
Tay Bac (Northwest) Autonomous
 Region 117
TE 15
tea 208
teak 57
telecommunications 250
Temporary Policy for Small-Scale
 Trading along the Border
 Region 77
Temporary Regulations Governing
 Border Trade in Yunnan 79
Tengchong 63
Teochiu 228
Thaat Chiangteum 145
Thaat Chiangteum Festival 148
Thaat Luang 149
Thaat Muang Sing 145
Thah Hoa 109
Thai 11
Thai investments in Yunnan 232
Thai Muslim 230
Thai-Lao border 129
Thai-Myanmar border 128
Thailand ix
Thailand's Boom and Bust 8
Thailand's Boom 8
Thaization 231
*Tham Tamnaan Thaat Luang
 Chiengteum Muang Sing* 147
*The Chinese World Order: Traditional
 China's Foreign Relations* 31
The End of the Nation State 6
The Manager 11
Theewabut Luang 148
Theravada 151, 177
Third World 19
Tho 100, 261
Three Islands of the Kinh 302
Three Kingdoms 38
Three Objects of Forestry 55
Thuan Hai 257

Tianshun Emperor 41
Tibet 32
Tibetan Plateau 207
Tibetans 32
Tibeto-Burman 100, 217
Tien Yen 258
Tientsin treaty 107
Tiger Economies 2
timber industry 135
timber trade 62
tobacco 218
ton bun 156
tongbao 32
Tonghai 225, 229
Tonkin 103
Tonkin Gulf 296
Top Model Minority Nationality Village 300
totalitarian 17
Touby Ly Fong 109
tourism 4, 80
tourist guides 316
tourist industry 175
tourist trade 171
tourist-traders 91
tourists 3, 59
township enterprises 15, 238
Toyota, Mika viii, 4, 6
Tra Linh 242
trade 45, 204
trade in women 250
trade routes 36, 204
traders 3, 76
trading networks 4
trading-posts 127
traffic in girls and women 185
trafficking 60, 67
trafficking in women 185
Tran Ninh 104, 109
transit 136
transitional identities 264
transnational corporations 14
transnational identity 286
transportation 84
transvestite cabarets 170
travel agencies 233
Treaty of Nanking 104
trekking 189
Tribal Research Institute 113

Tropical Crop Institute 170
Tru'ng sisters 36
tudi gaige 291
Tungaraja 146
Turner, Frederick Jackson 29
tusi 38
Tuyen Quang 272
two breakthroughs 87
two linkages 87

U
U.S. Special Forces 260
Ubya Akha 215
Udomsai 110
Ulo Akha 215
uncivilized 38
Unexploded Ordnances 189
UNHCR 256, 113
UNICEF 189
United Nations High Commissioner for Refugees 113, 256
United Nations International Children's Emergency Fund 189
United States 11, 23, 114
upland minorities 193
uplands 5
Upper Mekong 123
Upper Yangtze 45
urban areas 313
Urdu 228
Uttaradit 225
UXOs 189

V
Vang Pao 110
VE 15
vehicle imports 135
venereal disease 192
verbal agreements 247
Viangphoukha 127, 136
Vientiane ix, 3, 12
Vientiane Times 16
Viet Minh 106
Viet Tri 245
Viet-Hoa Bank 244
Vietnam ix, 2, 3, 4, 6
Vietnam War 23, 109, 186
Vietnamese 2
Vietnamese army 289

Vietnamese ethnographers 263
Vietnamese ethnography 263
Vietnamese Kinh 5
Vietnamese nationalism 261
Vietnamization 108
village boundaries 217
village enterprises 15
Vinh 103
Vinh Phu 245
virginity 193
visas 3
Vo Van Kiet 239

W
Wa 51
Wa states 197
Wade, Geoff viii
Walker, Andrew viii, 5, 6
Wan Mohamad Nor Matha 234
Wanding 57, 63, 80, 82, 83, 87
Wang Feng 33
Wang Gungwu 30
Wang Jingwei 32
Wang Shao 45
Wanwei 292
Wanwei Golden Beach Tourism
 Development Project 299
Wanwei island 290
war 105
warfare 196
Wat Dornreuang 157
Wat Luang Paa Fang 146
Wei Zhengqing 246
Wei Zhenxing 246
Weishan 224
West 13
West River 36
Western Jin 35
Western medicine 234
Westerners 105
wet-rice 145
White Tai 107, 113
Whitehead 266
wildlife 59, 63
women 316
women and social change 312
women traders 4
work ethic 176
World Bank 20

World War II 230
written contracts 247
Wuhan 64
Wumeng 39
Wutau 292, 300

X
Xanh Y 256
Xiaguan 225
Xiangkok 133, 142
Xiaowan 26
Xicuan 35
Xie Guangmao viii, 6
Xieng Hong 164
Xieng Khouang 109, 208
Xieng Tung 146
Xinjiang 72
xiongnu (the Huns) 31
Xishuangbanna 3, 162
Xishuangbanna Autonomous
 Region 180
Xishuangbanna Tai Minority
 Autonomous County Government
 Encouragement of Outside
 Investment Guidelines 85
Xishuangbanna Tour Vacationland 177
Xuan Loc 259

Y
Yang Genhua 229
Yangon ix, 126, 128
Yangtze 35
Yangwu 54
Yao 51, 113, 250
Yao Lue 2
Yao rebellion 153
Yellow River 37
Yi (Lolo) 51, 117
yi 41
Ying khon chua 192
Yinjiang County 57
Yoshinobu, Shiba 44
Yuan dynasty 34
Yuan people 151
Yuan Xinchang 231
Yue 35
Yue-ization 37
Yueqiao 292
Yuezu 292

Yuezu Zizhixiang 293
Yugong 30
Yunjinghong ix
Yunnan 3, 6
Yunnan Airlines 166
Yunnan People's Government Policies Concerning the Encouragement of Outside Investment 80
Yunnan People's Government Supplementary Policies Pertaining to the Promotion of Border Trading 80
Yunnan Province Temporary Provisions on Border Trade 166

Yunnanese associations 234
Yunnanese Muslims 223
Yuxi 225

Z

Zhejiang 324
Zhou dynasty 30
Zhou Enlai 258
Zhu Yuanzhang 42, 43
Zhuang 51, 94
Zhuoxi 55
Zou Rong 32

GPSR Compliance
The European Union's (EU) General Product Safety Regulation (GPSR) is a set of rules that requires consumer products to be safe and our obligations to ensure this.

If you have any concerns about our products, you can contact us on

ProductSafety@springernature.com

In case Publisher is established outside the EU, the EU authorized representative is:

Springer Nature Customer Service Center GmbH
Europaplatz 3
69115 Heidelberg, Germany

www.ingramcontent.com/pod-product-compliance
Lightning Source LLC
LaVergne TN
LVHW041619060526
838200LV00040B/1345